the german mind

the german mind

by *William J. Bossenbrook*

PROFESSOR OF HISTORY, WAYNE STATE UNIVERSITY

DETROIT   WAYNE STATE UNIVERSITY PRESS   1961

Grateful acknowledgment is made to the Ford Foundation for
financial assistance in making possible the publication of this
volume.

to my wife

Preface

*W*hy the Germans have not been "integrated" into the Western community of values is the key question of the "German problem." This book attempts to set down some of the basic answers to the question. As the Introduction indicates, the book is based on the assumption that the Germans and the French have played the chief dialectical roles in the formation of the European community of values. These are conceived as a historical development and not as ideological residues variously labeled as "democracy," "rationalism," "humanitarianism," etc. Hence the German mind is regarded not as an eccentric national product but as a major strand of the unfolding self-consciousness of the West. The Introduction develops this notion.

Much of *The German Mind* was originally intended as part of a general history of the Germans proposed by Professor Allan Nevins. But a variety of circumstances made it expedient for me to confine the work to a consideration of the German mind as a reflection of the changing self-consciousness of the Germans with respect to their role in the world.

I have put emphasis, therefore, on mutations in mental structures rather than on the temper of each historical epoch or on an analysis of causal relationships. My concern with the process of historical development has naturally led me to rely upon a "secondary level of generalization," which is reflected in the bibliography at the end of the book.

I am especially indebted to Professor Milton Covensky and to Professor Harold A. Basilius for many ideas and much bibliographical information. Professors Hayden White and Orville Linck read the manuscript and gave me many suggestions for its improvement. I am also indebted to Dr. Richard Mönnig and to Mr. H. Geissler, of Inter Nationes, of Bonn, Germany, for reproductions of the illustrations.

W. B.

Contents

Illustrations

Introduction

The Interpretation of German History

The fundamental problem in any view of German history is that of explaining National Socialism. The most elementary explanations see in it an expression of momentary madness or a reflection of an indelible national quality. Both notions reflect the revulsion following the collapse of National Socialism and the revelations of its inhumanity, but actually they offer no rational interpretation.

An historical explanation involves the question of how National Socialism is to be reconciled with the achievements of the German mind not only in earlier centuries but particularly in our time. The Germans have laid the intellectual foundations of a new view of man and the universe, as is indicated by the names of Einstein and Planck, of Freud and Max Weber, of Nietzsche, Jaspers, and Heidegger. Consideration of the general problem of the cultural role of the Germans can provide a more satisfactory interpretation of National Socialism.

The historical interpretations of the last decade differ not only as to time-span envisaged but also with respect to the logic of history. A brief consideration of these interpretations may serve as an introduction to the plan of this book, which seeks to illumine German development by viewing it in the frame of the process of secularization which has characterized the West.*

THE GEOPOLITICAL ANALYSIS

National Socialism, it is argued, was a German expression of the crystallization of mass society in the twentieth century. The break-through assumed different forms in the three basic regions: western seaboard Europe, central Europe, and eastern Europe. In western Europe the dominance of the bourgeoisie in state and society made for uniformity of values within long established nation-state molds. In central Europe the persistence of the gradations of the traditional social hierarchy and the multi-national complexion of the area made the state an agency of a particular social or ethnic group. Hence nationalism became the vehicle of a supra-political and supra-social mass insurgence. In eastern Europe, comprising the area of the old Russian empire, the predominant agrarian-peasant society ruled by an alien monarchical-bureaucratic state and permeated with a strong sense of ecumenical mission was transformed by Communism into an industrial-workers' society ruled by a single-party state with a driving sense of world mission.

This explanation, stressing the fundamental regional differences of Europe rather than its cultural and ideological unity, views the history of the world not in terms of closed cultural entities but of a typology of socio-political structures. Thus links can be established between Europe and the non-European world of middle-class colonial areas, ancient peasant societies, and mixed social caste systems. Such relationships have become tremendously significant in the twentieth-century global situation.

In view of these regional differences the western European ideological yardstick embodying the assumption of the universal validity of bourgeois liberalism should not be applied to central and eastern Europe nor to the globe at large. Moreover, a distinction must be made between the mass democracy of the twentieth century,

---

* The bibliography at the end of the book lists most of the general works which have served as a basis for the consideration of these interpretations.

concerned with welfare and equality, and the bourgeois liberalism of the nineteenth century, concerned with liberty and legal order. The revolutions of the twentieth century, impelled by the breakthrough of the technological order and mass society, are quite different from the bourgeois revolutions of the early nineteenth century based on rationalistic and romantic ideologies.

One assumes that the technological breakthrough of our century will bring about greater changes than those of all previous centuries, since the time when man made the transition from hunting to agriculture. The twentieth century is not merely another period of transition but ushers in a wholly new order attended by vast social and political upheavals and convulsions such as the Communist Revolution and National Socialism.

Totalitarian nationalism seeks to dissolve the traditional political and social forms and create a mass society with a united national will under a charismatic leader. The Thousand-Year *Reich* presumed to transcend the continuity of historic, traditional, and constitutional development and achieve the mobility and flexibility necessary to the increasingly rapid tempo of technological change.

This emphasis on the impact of contemporary forces in a geopolitical area tends to ignore the feeling of individuality and the sense of mission which has motivated most modern nations. To understand the interplay of forces, one must look from the inside as well as at the outside, and this requires a much longer historical perspective.

THE IDEOLOGICAL JUDGMENT

The liberal ideological approach is more concerned with the historical continuity of ideas in relation to institutions than with the analysis of forces in their contemporaneous and regional setting. National Socialism is regarded as the consequence of a moral failure. The Germans failed to achieve a real liberal-democratic regime within a nation-state such as was realized by the western countries. The Germans took the wrong turn about the end of the eighteenth and the beginning of the nineteenth century. Up to the Enlightenment, German development followed the general pattern. But from then on a basic divergence developed, especially in the reactions of

German intellectual leaders of the Idealist movement and Romanticism to the rationalism of the Enlightenment and the Revolution, which constituted the chief formative influences of European liberalism.

The German distinction between nation and state was a basic divergence from western liberalism. The state developed a power-state character in Prussia under Frederick the Great and his immediate predecessors, whereas the term *nation* assumed a cultural and even racial connotation in Romanticism. German national thinking and feeling flowed into philosophic and ideological channels and was not taken for granted as it was in the western countries, where it had long since become associated with a concrete political mold. German nationalistic ideologies came to focus on such elements as *Volk* and state, race and soil, which harbor dangerous values in themselves from a liberal-democratic point of view. In the crucible of the liberal nation-state, they lose their "demonic" potentialities. But in the German situation they contributed to the drive of the power-state for hegemony, to the authoritarianism of a military-bureaucratic organization, and to totalitarian irrationalism.

The failure of the Germans to follow the Western political pattern was manifested in various abortive liberal movements, such as the revolutions of 1848, the attempt of Prussian liberals to establish a parliamentary regime, and the Weimar Republic. The failure of these attempts is traced principally to the fact that German liberals were divided in mind and sentiment. They wanted liberty but also a strong state. They wanted national unity but also German dominance over neighboring Slavs.

Because the German distinguished between state and nation as opposed to the Western primary distinction between state and society, he regarded the nation as the embodiment of unique cultural values which assumed primacy over the nation as the embodiment of the democratic ethos of the people and even over the nation subordinated to a power-state.

The power-state nationalism engendered during the second half of the nineteenth century with the establishment of German unity under Prussian hegemony came to be regarded, especially during World War I and its aftermath, as the formative force in the creation of the German national tradition. But the sense of the inadequacy of this power-state unification under Bismarck kept alive other nationalist ideological expression, especially among intellectuals.

The late nineteenth century also saw the appearance of a nationalistic idea in France which sought to revive the tradition of Catholic-monarchical-regional France as a reaction against the "decadent" revolutionary tradition of the Third Republic. By contrast, the Germans obviously lacked a national event such as the French Revolution to mark a great divide in their national history and thus create a conflict of traditions. They could only look backward to the attrition of the power of the Holy Roman Empire. But even for National Socialism this empire represented not a national tradition but only a mythical symbol.

ECUMENICAL SELF-CONSCIOUSNESS

The ideological judgment of modern German development is obviously almost wholly determined by the pattern of history of the western nations. It gives little or no consideration to the German's consciousness of his own ecumenical role—the consequence of lying between the western nations and the ecumenical world of Russian-Greek Orthodox messianism and imperialism. Like the Russian, the German was preoccupied with the philosophy of history as the vehicle for arriving at the expression of cultural individuality. In the case of both peoples, this concern was the product of the persistence of the tradition of a *sacrum imperium*, definitely to be distinguished from the French conception of themselves as the chief national exponents of advancing civilization.

The German was always conscious of his polar relationship to the "superior" Western civilization under French leadership. But he was also always mindful of his Christianizing and Germanizing mission to the east among the "inferior" Slavs whose guardians the Russians assumed themselves to be. Westward, looking toward the French, the German's orientation was nationalistic, while eastward, toward the Slavic world, it remained largely ecumenical. *Nationalism* had a secular connotation; *ecumenical*, a religious one. The German's dual role produced a heightened degree of self-consciousness not to be found among other Western peoples.

The medieval *sacrum imperium* or Holy Roman Empire represented in its early phase the ecumenical union of western Europe under German leadership. The breakdown of this German hegemony began with the assertion of papal leadership over Western Christendom from the eleventh to the fourteenth centuries. When the national monarchs of the western seaboard countries asserted their independence of papal hegemony, Europe emerged. The Germans, deprived of their leadership role, became just one of the peoples of the European community of nations.

The Germans retained a sense of their ecumenical role, however, by virtue of their continued eastward expansion and "civilizing" mission there. Juxtaposition to the Slavic world with its predominantly Greek Orthodox religious and Byzantine cultural ethos was a powerful factor in keeping alive the German feeling of being a bastion of the Western world. Indeed, the Russian claim to being the unique link between European and Asian culture was fostered by this German feeling. The thinking of the German philosophers Herder, Hegel, and Marx permeated the long controversy between Westerners and Slavophiles during the nineteenth century and the conflict between the advocates of "world revolution" as opposed to "socialism in one land" which took place within Communism.

The French lay across Europe, linking the peoples of the Mediterranean with those of the north. While the Germans had a similar north-south axis, their east-west orientation was much the stronger. The French and the Germans were thus the chief pivots on which European culture hinged. England, Spain, Italy, Scandinavia, Poland, and Russia were after all peripheral. The dialectic between the French and German cultural temperaments has served as the principal intellectual focus of the West in modern times.

Since the twelfth century, France assumed the cultural leadership of Europe, and in modern times she also became the clearing house of ideologies and the headquarters of the revolutionary movement. The French played a positive role in the quest for an objective rational point of view with regard to man and the universe, as is evident in the two chief European movements of intellectual synthesis, Scholasticism, and the Enlightenment.

France brought to fruition the two basic cultural syntheses—the medieval aristocratic-chivalrous social ideal and its counterpart, the scholastic dialectic of reason and faith, as well as the modern bourgeois-conventional society and its counterpart, the revolutionary role of the intellectual. Perhaps the self-contained geographical form of France, her centralized national mold, and the lucid character of the French mind account for her role as a clearing house of intellectual and cultural movements whose original inception may have been elsewhere.

The Germans, occupying a land open on all sides and with a highly amorphous regional differentiation, turned away from the objective rational order to a concern with the subjective dynamism of faith and spirit within the traditional social and political framework. Rather than project a new order, they sought to recapture the theonomous essence of the *sacrum imperium* with its characteristically German fusion of body and spirit. They were basically concerned with self-realization expressed in highly speculative philosophies of nature and history formulated by solitary great thinkers.

Hence the German reaction against the heteronomy of the sacerdotal *ordo* and of the cosmic order of reason. The reaction culminated respectively in the freedom of faith of the Reformation and in the pure creativity of the spirit of Romanticism. These characteristic German movements, Reformation and Romanticism, were the supreme European expressions of the dynamism of individual faith and of creativity of spirit and were not concerned with creating an objective order of either a sacerdotal or secular character. German development should therefore not be judged in terms of a rational intellectual synthesis nor of the creation of political and social institutions. It must instead be viewed as the polarization of inner subjective dynamism with outer objective order. The same polarity marks the coming to self-consciousness of the technological breakthrough of our day.

Since roughly 1850 French-German polarity has, however, assumed a different form as a consequence of the decline of French creative leadership in the European community. The French have been concerned principally with the problem of national decadence; the Germans, from Nietzsche to Heidegger, with the broader question of nihilism arising out of the general process of secularization. Having no definite national mold to preserve like the French, and especially conscious of their ecumenical role, the Germans naturally were primarily concerned with the attrition of religious and spiritual values.

THE PROCESS OF SECULARIZATION

The secularization of values has occasioned the most profound changes in modern culture. Its most immediate consequences, decadence and nihilism, present the underside of the appearance of a technological order in which all the old substantival values of sacred *ordo,* cosmic order, social hierarchy, humanistic culture, urban and country life are being dissolved. This underside of technological society is far more important than the surface panoply of apparatus and explosive energy. The technological breakthrough involves not only the conquest of space and the mechanization of the mode of life but a basic mutation in cultural values such as mankind has not witnessed since the neolithic revolution.

The basic assumption underlying the conception of nihilism is the irreversible process of attrition of religious or spiritual substance in Western culture since the high Middle Ages, or as Nietzsche argued, since the high noon of Greek culture. This process may be likened to the dissipation of free energy (entropy) in the universe according to the second law of thermodynamics.[1]

It is argued that with the Germans this process of attrition became definitely self-conscious by the nineteenth century. The emphasis on the polarity of immanent divine and demonic forces in nature and history distinguished early German intellectual development from Eckhart to Böhme. During the eighteenth and nineteenth centuries the religious polarity of divine and demonic became transformed into an immanent dialectic of reason culminating in Hegel, for whom his own philosophy was the fulfillment of history and who suggested that the philosopher was therefore no longer necessary, only the functionary or technician.

Thus the process of secularization should become completely self-conscious in the technological breakthrough. But secularization has limits just as Christianization has. If total Christianization is possible only by an "eschatological act" then total secularization will be realized only in the complete technological breakthrough. For example, science and Marxism are not the end-products of secularization. Science still embodies a reassuring *Weltanschauung* although it is on the road to becoming pure technics. Likewise Marxism still embodies a plan of salvation for millions even though it is on the way to providing merely the tactics of economic and social progress.

The ambivalence of the secularizing process originated in the Christian emphasis on the polarity of God and the world and of the city of God and the earthly city. The spiritualizing drive of Christianity was in itself a secularization of the ancient magical world in that it separated the world of nature from the world of history and regarded the latter as primarily the area in which divine purpose with regard to human destiny was being unfolded.[2] The Reformation reflected the same ambivalence in bringing about the rationalization of the state and of culture and the spiritualization of faith and of cult.

Modern German thinkers have viewed secularization not as the displacement of a sacred and magical *ordo* by a secular and rational order but as an immanent historical process presenting two concomitant aspects, the attrition of primordial values and the fulfillment of a new age. The German looks backward to the dissolution of the sacred *ordo* of the *sacrum imperium* while at the same time he anticipates the breakthrough of a new age. But he is more concerned with the inner dynamic of the process than with the resultant shape or form of the new order. He perceives secularization as a time-process, as the coming to complete historical self-consciousness by mankind of human possibilities and limitations. The principal concern of his philosophers and historians has been with the role of the German in this development.

Another aspect of the process of secularization is its apparent irreversibility; like entropy, it has only a one-way direction. The ideological conception of history assumed the possibility of free movement both backward and forward as the prevalence of the words *renaissance* and *revolution* in liberal and socialist interpretations indicates. History as event signifies the ability to transcend the cycle of nature by setting goals, but as process it implies an objective and irreversible movement toward a functional perfection.

The German historian is particularly aware of this polarity of history as process and history as event because he has been most sensitive to the process of secularization and the consequent threat of nihilism. He always made a sharp distinction between change at large, exemplified in the regularities and uniformities of natural phenomena, and change as uniquely individual development exemplified in history. In the ideological age historians paid little attention to the process side of history because of the fear of doing violence to the freedom of creative individuality. Today we are beginning to realize that history as process and history as event are not mutually exclusive no more than process and event are in the world of nature where they are being reconciled by scientists.

This book is concerned mainly with the impact of the process of secularization on the German mind. The logic of this process, in its German form, derives particularly from the inherent drive of Christianity to attain to freedom and purity of faith and spirit as the fulfillment of history. During the five centuries or more which followed Charlemagne, three ideal types of religious aspiration emerged, represented by the Holy Roman Empire (*sacrum imperium*), the sacramental-hierarchical church (*sacerdotium*), and heretical groups (sectarianism). With Charlemagne begins the real *sacrum imperium*. The reactions to it, *sacerdotium* and sectarianism, were the secularizing consequences of the spiritualizing drive of Christianity. The *sacerdotium* was concerned with distinguishing between a priestly-sacramental *ordo* and the exercise of earthly power. Sectarianism went beyond the *sacerdotium* in emphasizing the distinction between the existing sacramental *ordo*, in compromise with the world, and the impending pure spiritual community. This fundamental constellation of religious forms went through a further phase of secularization when the forms were abstracted from their original sacred molds in the course of modern German development.

The whole process was conditioned by three patterns of change peculiar to the German scene, which may be summarized as follows:

(1) The lack of a German national mold channels new and changing intellectual and spiritual forces, which elsewhere achieve incarnation in political and social forms, into inconclusive, confessional, ideological, and technological conflicts.

(2) The German tends to assimilate the classic expression of a foreign movement of thought or art and develop it to an extreme in which the classical and rational order is transposed into the

irrationalism of sheer subjective dynamism. Witness the Reformation and Romanticism.

(3) The process of secularization involves a cumulative development of historical self-consciousness which rejects fulfillment in an objective order and seeks a breakthrough in what Nietzsche called a "transvaluation of all values."

The dynamic of these German patterns of change is derived by most interpreters from the spiritualizing drive of Christianity. Hence, the German mind is most often viewed as presenting a curve of development attaining its zenith in Idealism and Romanticism and then rapidly descending into power politics and materialistic values. It may also be viewed in terms of a steady dissipation and depletion of the religious and spiritual values embodied in *sacrum imperium*, *sacerdotium*, and sectarianism leading to the complete leveling of contemporary technological and mass society. An ascending line of development may also be projected in which the spiritualizing drive is a transitional phase from the archaic magical world of the *sacrum imperium* to the coming breakthrough of a scientific-technological *ordo* as a global phenomenon. This book leans in the direction of this interpretation as a backdrop against which the mutations of the German mind are considered.

1

From a Sacred Ordo to the Freedom of Faith

800-1600

I

Forms: Sacrum Imperium, Sacerdotium, and Sectarianism

For a thousand years after the great invasions of the fifth century the strongest unifying force in the West was embodied in the conception of universal rule. The disorders of the centuries of movements of peoples naturally led to the idealization of the Roman imperial and religious tradition. Rome became the symbol both of civilized order and of the true faith. On the one hand, she represented the ancient Caesars, the embodiment of the *imperium*, the universal and supreme rulership. But she also became the residence of the popes—the successors of Peter, the greatest apostle and the embodiment of the universal priesthood of the church.

The conjunction of these two ideals raised a problem which was to trouble Europe and particularly the Germanies for centuries. How could *imperium*, implying power and domination, be yoked with *sacerdotium*, implying renunciation of the world and self-sacrifice? This opposition was very old in Christian thought. It formed the central theme of St. Augustine's *The City of God*. From the eighth to the eleventh centuries the two ideals were fused in the *sacrum imperium*, the sacred or holy empire. Then for the following three centuries the *sacerdotium* of the popes may be said to have held the two principles in an unstable union. Sectarianism represented a radical repudiation of power and authority embodied in empire and state in the interest of achieving absolute and immediate obedience to the one supreme ruler, namely, God.

Both for Charlemagne and Otto the Great the ruler was a priest-king. As the counterpart of the heavenly ruler, the earthly king had not only to maintain the peace but to see that the earthly kingdom reflected the glory of the heavenly kingdom. The word *Reich* stood thus not for the notion of a state with frontiers and a definite area, but for a sacred, authoritative order which had descended from heaven and had become embodied in a ruler and his loyal followers. This was the early medieval version of the very ancient notion of the sacred monarchy.

RESTORATION OF THE EMPIRE IN THE WEST UNDER CHARLEMAGNE

Much has been made of Charles's coronation as emperor *by the pope* on Christmas Day, 800. In our time, we tend to place more emphasis on the "substance of power," on material resources and military strength, than on symbols and ideas. The imperial title meant no increase in the realities of power. The manner of its assumption apparently made a greater impression on his successors than it did on Charles himself. He might have assumed the title on his own initiative, but the fact that it was conferred upon him by the pope established a precedent which was to have far-reaching influences on the relations between popes and emperors in succeeding centuries.

Charles was the first Germanic king to assume the imperial title by which he claimed a sovereignty over and above that of a chieftain or of a representative of the Eastern emperor. By assuming the imperial dignity he sought to raise his realm from that of a mere barbaric conquest to a universal sovereignty like that of the Roman Caesars.

Naturally, he was driven into opposing the Eastern Roman Empire, not merely in defense of particular interests in Italy but on behalf of his own imperial claims which, according to the Byzantine attitude, constituted a usurpation by a barbarian chieftain. On the other hand, Westerners were beginning to regard the Byzantine rulers as schismatics and heretics because of their iconoclastic religious policy. In spite of these fundamental cleavages, however, Charles established a *rapprochement* with Constantinople largely on the basis of the mutual recognition that neither Empire could conquer the other. In fact, the great Moslem caliph, Harun al-Rashid, recognized Charles as the leader of Christendom.

The idea of empire also embodied a conception of government under which many peoples might find peace and justice. The equating of empire with peace and order was also expressed in the Roman conception of law as having a universal character, transcending local tribal custom. This conception was reinforced by the philosophic notion of a natural law of which positive, that is, particular, laws are a reflection.

Contrasted with these conceptions, the Germanic idea persisted throughout the Middle Ages that law arises out of the consciousness of a community expressing itself first in local practice and custom. This Germanic idea was a powerful antidote to the universal and hierarchical conceptions derived from the Mediterranean environment and embodied in church and empire.

The vitality of local forces is also apparent in the rising power of a great landed aristocracy. But it was not until after the death of Charles that this aristocracy really came into its own.

Charles maintained an equilibrium of forces and values, universal and local, Roman and Germanic. While he might suppress the independence or autonomy of Saxons and Bavarians, he did not destroy local custom or language. His appreciation of Germanic culture is evident in the collection of ballads and songs which he promoted. It is also evident in his tastes, dress, and habits, in his love of combat and the chase. Along with these inclinations and habits of a barbarian chieftain, he combined an avid interest in theological discussion and ancient literature. On occasions he and his intellectual cronies apparently got together in the manner of the ancient banquet. Clad in togas and assuming Latin names, they engaged in disputations on profound philosophic themes, such the nature of virtue and justice.

THE CAROLINGIAN RELIGIOUS AND CULTURAL REVIVAL

Charles sought especially to purify popular religious life of the persistent vestiges of heathen practices and forms. It must be recognized that the Christianity of the recently conquered and converted peoples of the Frankish realm was little more than skin deep. As a rule Christianity was first accepted by the chieftains, and then the general populace conformed more or less outwardly. In the process of conversion, the Christian faith was, of course, adapted to native customs. The worship of sacred groves and pools was now associated with the miraculous achievements of saints.

It was difficult for these conquered peoples to accept Christ as the Savior whose salvation of man was achieved by an ignominious death on a cross. In an Old Saxon poetic version of the life of Christ called *Heiland,* He is presented in the guise of a heroic warrior who even descends into hell to defeat Satan and his demons. Baptism was likened to initiation into a band of Christ's followers, and, like the leader of a war band, Christ demanded unswerving loyalty and trust from His followers. Saints were also presented as popular heroes who overcame their demonic adversaries through martyrdom.

To Charles and his advisors the raising of the general spiritual level of the population depended upon improving the education of the clergy, which in turn depended upon immersing the clergy in ancient religious and cultural tradition. During the seventh and eighth centuries, the Frankish church had dropped to a new low in cultural level and superstitious practices. The stimulus to reform came originally from such Anglo-Saxon missionaries and scholars as St. Boniface and Alcuin. The latter became Charles's chief adviser in these matters.

Christianity and Latin culture in England had been wiped out almost completely by the barbarian invasions but had made a new start as the result of missionary enterprises emanating from Ireland and Rome. In the British Isles, Latin, the language of worship and learning, bore little resemblance to English, the popular tongue. In Gaul, the popular spoken tongue bore obvious kinship to literary Latin and undoubtedly contributed greatly to the barbarization of the latter. In the British Isles, however, emphasis was placed on the use, both in worship and learning, of pure Latin. This accent on classical Latin led scholars back to ancient literary forms. St. Boniface, in fact, asserted that the Bible was not comprehensible except through an understanding of antique culture. This idea was carried to the continent, especially to the areas east of the Rhine where cultural conditions were similar to those in England. One must know the language used by the Christian fathers, Jerome and St. Augustine, in order to drink of the springs of Christian faith.

It was this yearning to return to the sources which characterizes this Carolingian renaissance and, later, similar cultural renewals down to the seventeenth century. This phenomenon of return to antiquity which distinguished the West was to constitute probably the most revolutionary cultural and religious force in its development down to the appearance of modern science.

Alcuin was interested in grammar and rhetoric as a basis of education because these constituted an introduction to Latin language and literature. He was the leader in the so-called "palace" school, and later, as abbot of the famous monastery at Tours, made the monastery an intellectual center in which the copying of ancient manuscripts was the chief concern.

Perhaps at no other time were books so completely the objects of veneration, even of worship. Since books were hand-lettered, they were naturally difficult to obtain and were thus more highly prized than in our age of mass production. Christianity, along with Islam, made a book the central focus of its worship. Book and altar competed among Christians, whereas in Islam the Scripture (the Koran) exercised complete dominance.

Perhaps the most important cultural reform of the Carolingian age was in handwriting, which was brought about by the introduction of the use of capital letters derived from Roman monuments. These replaced the free-flowing script which had become almost illegible with the disappearance of an educated lay class of merchants and officials who used it in everyday affairs. Writing had virtually become an artistic accomplishment, especially the writing of monks concerned with the copying of manuscripts and their illumination or decoration and illustration. Generally, as in the case of the initial letters of the books of the Bible, the decorative interest predominated. But in the Utrecht Psalter the drawings illustrating incident and story were intended for popular edification.

The style of ornamentation often reflected influences of barbarian background. This is especially evident in the accent placed on the dynamic interweaving or interlacing lines of organic and geometric forms. In some Irish and Anglo-Saxon manuscripts, the human figure either disappears almost completely or is subordinated to the over-all pattern. In Carolingian manuscripts one sees a return to the classical emphasis on the human figure. However, the figure is not presented in a three-dimensional plastic form but seems to float on the surface plane of the page and thus becomes like the letters of the script. One "reads" the illustrations like a script. The concern with telling a story leads to a time-surface presentation of movement rather than to the space-depth representation of static being, as in ancient classical art.

Such great abbeys as Tours to the west and Fulda to the east of the Rhine played a more important role in the religious and cultural life of the time than any of the bishoprics. The abbeys held vast landed possessions and engaged in the draining of swampland and the clearing of forests. They revived ancient agricultural practices and preserved the ancient crafts and skills. Each monastery was associated with a founding saint whose relics were preserved in the crypt of its church. In fact, to popular fancy these relics were the visible means through which the power of the founding saint continued to be exercised.

Relics played a role in the West comparable to images in Eastern Christianity. Charles published a book, *Liber Carolina* (791), in which he followed the iconoclastic view in attacking the idea that images have an inherent divine quality. He also attacked the cult of emperors and the conception of holy places. But in this "rationalistic attitude" he was far beyond his subjects.

It should be noted that he dissociated the veneration of relics from the worship of images. The image was a mere work of art or artifice presenting some kind of likeness, while the relic was directly associated with the miracles performed by a saint.

The Carolingian renaissance laid the basis for the fusion of the classical tradition with empire and church in the West. The fusion, in spite of the breakup of Charles's empire under his successors, was

to serve as a model for later architects of European unity. In succeeding centuries, Charles's fame became legendary. No ruler rose
to an equal stature. To both Germans and French, he was the great
founder of European unity.

THE OTTONIAN FUSION OF AGRARIAN SOCIETY AND
MONASTIC CULTURE

The more than one hundred years during which the Carolingian
empire dissolved into fragments marked the definite fusion of agrarian society and the religious ethos of the sacred monarchy. From
Otto the Great (962–973) to Henry II (1002–1024) the sacred
monarchy assumed its most characteristic form. The mode of life of
the royal household under the Saxon kings particularly reflects the
agrarian basis of society. Like Charlemagne, the Saxon kings went
from one royal domain to the other, there being no fixed residence
of government, although kings were crowned and buried in Aachen.
Among the many royal residences the one at Ingelheim may be regarded as typical. Within a walled enclosure were the living quar-
ters of the king and his entourage, a chapel, and the barns and pens
to house horses, cattle, and grain. The table at which the king sat
with his chief officials and retainers, each according to his station,
was the chief focus of political deliberation. The counterpart of this
household form of government was to be found on a smaller scale
among all the great aristocratic landowners.

Even more than in Carolingian times, the chief centers of learning and art were in the great monastic abbeys. Their economic base
was the great landed domain. Each establishment was self-sufficient,
comprising, in addition to the monks, the peasants, who did much of
the heavy work on the land, and, in time, an increasing number of
artisans, who assisted the monks in the various crafts, such as the
weaving of fabrics and metal working. The monks exercised a kind
of general supervision, under the supreme authority of the abbot,
over the work in field and workshop.

In the monastery we encounter a much more rationally organized
community than in the aristocratic domain. In observing regular
hours of worship, the monks naturally divided the day into definite

periods. To them is ascribed the invention, around 1000, of the clock. They also organized the work of the monastery into the various specialized activities of book illustration, ivory carving, goldsmith and enamel work, silk weaving, bell founding, and bookbinding. Such new processes were discovered as the mixing of oil colors and the production of glass. The monks also were the chief architects and builders until the twelfth century when the towns produced a class of lay artisans and architects.

As in Carolingian times, the greatest artistic achievement was in the realm of manuscript or book illustration, which surpassed sculpture and architecture down to the eleventh century. Most of the churches built during the Saxon period were destroyed or so remodeled as to lose their original form. But many manuscripts have survived, undoubtedly because vellum had replaced papyrus.

Under the Saxon dynasty (919–1024), book illustration reached its zenith, especially in such great abbeys as Reichenau, St. Maximin–Trier and St. Emmeram–Regensburg. Reichenau was especially important as the seat of the royal chancellory where royal documents were prepared. It was also at Reichenau that the art of medieval miniature painting reached its peak around 1000.

The scriptoria of the monasteries were really large workshops in which a division of function also appears. Mere copyists were distinct from illuminators or decorators, and those skilled in the production of elaborate initial letters were distinct from the printers of illustrations. The artistic forms and motifs were mainly those inherited from the Carolingian age. But the closer contacts of the Ottonian rulers with Italy and Constantinople brought in Byzantine influences.

A book was not only a means of communicating knowledge, nor merely a work of art, but the receptacle of sacred truth like the precious vessels used in the sacrament. Each book by virtue of ornamentation and decoration had a highly individual character. Later, books obviously lost this quality largely because of mass production. The most highly decorated books were the gospels and liturgical works, the gospels affording the chief themes for illustration and decoration.

Gospel of Otto III (Bamberg), end of 10th century

Gospel of Henry II (Bamberg), early 11th century

ARCHAIC RELIGIOSITY

The Ottonian manuscript illuminators, even more than the Carolingian, sought to make visible the divine in picture and symbol; hence, the latter are in some sense the embodiment of the divine and not just didactic illustrations or sermons in paint.[1] The Carolingian representation of the evangelists is a lifelike portrayal of them engaged in writing and enveloped in the contemplative atmosphere of philosophers. But in a gospel of the time of Otto III, the evangelist Luke is presented as seated on a rainbow and bearing in uplifted hands Christ and his symbol in a circle of prophets and angels. The language, or rather scripture, of religious symbolism here has obviously triumphed completely over any consideration of lifelike representation. A complex iconographical scheme determined by theological conceptions takes the place of the earlier rather idealistic representation of Luke at work. Even more significant is the whole bearing of the figure: the staring eyes and tautness of arms reflect the almost terrible urgency with which the symbols of salvation are presented to mankind.

This intense emotional religiosity of the time is reflected also in a Reichenau miniature showing an angel announcing the birth of Christ to the shepherds. Here the action is reduced to a highly schematic arrangement, centering on the angel standing on a rocky hummock. The puppet-like gestures which transmit the tidings of the birth of Christ are not the product, one feels, of the articulated movement of the members of the body but are superimposed to convey the urgency of the message, not just to give pictorial form to the meaning of the scriptural passage. The gestures are like the symbols of a written language. There is no three-dimensional character. There is no environment. The rocks are but symbolic props which accentuate the startling appearance of the monumental figure of the angel. The figures seem to lie on the surface of the page like the letters of a script. They are not tied together by an environment but only by the symbolic meaning of the gestures. Moreover, each individual figure seems to be an agglomeration of autonomous parts, as in a puppet. Each part seems to be a physically isolated unit;

spiritually, however, the figures are unified, transfixed in awe and wonder by the vision which confronts them.

That the Ottonian age was capable of a very realistic rendering of the human form is evident from the carved representation of Christ hanging on the cross in the Cologne cathedral. Few crucifixions capture with such realism the stretch of muscle and tendon across arms and breast produced by the lifeless weight of the drooping figure. This realism, however, is accompanied by archaic symmetry, especially in the precise and schematic modeling of the hair and the folds of the loincloth; such modeling is likewise characteristic of the features, limbs, and distended abdomen which provide a kind of rigid formal quality upon which the fluidity of muscular strain is imposed.

In architecture this same archaic autonomy, this lack of rational articulation of individual forms, is evident in two of the few remaining churches of the period, the monastic church in Genrode and St. Michael in Hildesheim. The rhythm of arches, with their alternate columns and piers, gives no sense of movement of the whole in the direction of the altar. The nave looks through a great arch upon the altar, which is shrouded in mysterious gloom. The arcades almost close off the side aisles into individual rooms. This lack of total articulation is also evident in the exterior, especially in the accent laid on the individual towers, from which one can, as from the watchtowers of a fortress, look out upon the countryside.

The chief unifying factor in the arts lay in the religious mood of the time. In books and buildings one senses the awe and fear that enveloped all in the face of divine and demonic powers struggling for the possession of man's body and soul. Against the omnipresent demonic powers, the miracles of sacrament and of saint embodied in relic served as fortress and weapon. In addition to its sacramental purpose, the altar also served as a repository of relics as did the crypt underneath, where the bones of the saints rested side by side with those of the noble lords of the domain. The sacrificial miracle of the altar on which bread and wine were transformed into blood and flesh was thus joined here with the sepulchre of saintly and ancestral relics to transmit to the living the full magical and mystical power which the dead had achieved in their struggle with the Evil One.

Religious worship found expression in the concrete visible symbols of the liturgy, in the celebration of the sacrament accompanied by song and prayer. The sermon played a very minor role. In monastic churches, day and night were divided into seven periods of prayer and song. This division, the work of the Lord, *opus Dei*, consisting of prayer and song, was but the reflection of the heavenly chorus of praise and reverence accorded to the Most High.

The heavenly and the earthly were completely intermingled in the religious attitudes of the time. The conception of the supranatural did not really emerge until the thirteenth century. The distinction between spiritual and temporal was blurred, and even obscured, with the earthly ruler being regarded as a projection of the heavenly king. He was the priest-king in whose charge was placed men's souls as well as their bodies. He was the protector and guardian of the church and derived his temporal, earthly authority and sovereignty principally from this source. As God had his apostles and saints upon earth, so the king had his priests and monks who carried out the work of the Lord of heaven and earth. Loyalty and allegiance were required from all. Sin was regarded as treason for which God would seek vengeance. In this religiosity there was no sense of faith as an inner conviction based on a belief or doctrine.

From the time of Otto the Great to that of Henry II the Saxon kings took their rule as priest-kings most seriously. Otto did not place the royal crown on his head until he had prepared himself by fasting and prayer. His belief in dreams as revelations of divine guidance and his zeal in the collection of relics are evidences of how completely he was enveloped in the religiosity of the sacred monarchy. Under the circumstances, it was no mere matter of political expediency that led him to lean so heavily on the bishops as the chief agents of government.

The chief seats of royal ecclesiastical power were the great archbishoprics of Mainz, Cologne, and Trier located along the Rhine. But scattered over the whole of the realm were similar centers of support for the monarchy. The raising of the bishops to the position of princes within the realm demanded of them the performance of military and court service to the king, and princely prestige led them to enhance the splendor of religious ceremonial and ritual. They were the builders of magnificent churches. Most of the bishops were drawn from the aristocracy and, especially under Otto, from the royal family. Most of them had, therefore, a sense of superiority and the prestige of rank.

OTTO III AND RENOVATIO IMPERII

The crumbling of the *sacrum imperium* began with the last Saxon emperors, especially with Otto III (983–1002), whose main concern was not with the *sacrum imperium* as a mystical embodiment but with reviving Rome as a center of religious and political authority. The death of his father when Otto III was but three years of age left the rule of the kingdom and the education of the young prince largely in the hands of his very able mother, the former Byzantine princess Theophano, who educated him in the Byzantine tradition. Theophano chose as a tutor Gerbert of Rheims, regarded in the West as the most learned man of his time. Both mother and tutor instilled in Otto that extremely high regard for the dignity and mission of the imperial office which was to be the guiding star of his reign.

The significance of Otto III's reign lay in the projection of an idea and not in what was actually accomplished. During his reign of only six years, he sought to raise Rome again to the head of the world. Rome was to combine the universal rule of the Caesars with the religious mission of the apostles Peter and Paul, whose holy relics reposed there. Rome was to be restored to pre-eminence as the center of world sovereignty and of the true faith.

As might be expected from his education, Otto clothed these grandiose ideas in Byzantine dress. He introduced the court ceremonial and aped the titles and forms of Byzantine imperialism. He was also imbued with an absorbing interest in the more austere forms of asceticism. In Italy the growing religious revival of the times turned to the exaltation of the hermit type of monk so characteristic of the Byzantine religious world. Otto and a confidant of his, the Bishop of Worms, retired to a cave and there in the robes of penitents spent fourteen days in fasting and prayer. In moments of religious despair, Otto, it is said, thought seriously of laying aside his imperial robes and going as a humble pilgrim to Jerusalem.

In his imperial proclamations, he called himself "the servant of the apostles of Christ." It is in the theocratic conception of his role that his importance lies. To the Slavic peoples of the eastern borderlands, he appeared as the apostolic ruler who sought to bring them within the fold of a universal church and empire and not just to bind them to the German kingdom and church.

In allowing Poles, Czechs, and Magyars to establish independent bishoprics instead of tying them in with the German church, Otto III departed from his predecessors and followed Byzantine practice. He visited the Czech lands on the occasion of a pilgrimage to the grave of St. Adalbert at Prague, a former friend who had suffered martyrdom as a missionary. He accorded to Duke Bolislav of Poland the ancient title of patrician and ally of the Roman people, a title customarily conferred by the popes. Thus Otto took under his imperial wing these border peoples formerly regarded by the popes as their peculiar wards.

The combination of his extreme youth, his notion of *renovatio imperii*, and his ascetic piety all contributed to his being called by a later generation the "Wonder of the World." Historians have generally regarded him as an impractical dreamer. But men live by visions and ideas as much as by economics and politics. We now realize more fully the potent influence of the medieval dream of universal empire as it later culminated in Frederick II and in the writings of the greatest Christian poet, Dante.

THE MOVEMENT FOR THE FREEDOM OF THE CHURCH

In the eleventh century a profound change took place in the position of the *sacrum imperium*, later generally known as the Holy Roman Empire. It found itself confronted by a revolutionary movement in which the claims of the Roman bishops to universal rule were combined with the call to free the church from lay control. Through the four or five centuries following the eleventh, the movement assumed a variety of guises but two were dominant, the sacerdotal and the sectarian.

Sacerdotalism gained its greatest momentum in the eleventh and twelfth centuries, and, under papal leadership, aimed at freeing the church from feudal and imperial trammels. The popes would also take the place of the emperors as the lords of Christendom in the war against the infidel and as the final authority in a community of European peoples, all equal before their tribunal. In the eyes of the popes only a church which had cleansed itself of ulterior political and social interests could rise to the spiritual leadership of Christendom.

Much less definite was the sectarianism revolving around the conception of evangelical poverty. It sought to free the church from the corrosion of great wealth and power by a return to that fusion of preaching and poverty which Christ had enjoined on His disciples. This notion provoked a number of heresies which sought to set up their own purified version of the church after the model of the earliest Christian communities. Within the church the mendicant movement of the Franciscans and Dominicans manifested the influence of this idea. Potent also was the expectation among such individuals as Dante of the coming of a new age of the spirit ushered in by a messianic pope or emperor.

Among the immediate successors to Otto III, Henry II and Henry III (1039–1056) especially possessed a sense of their own theocratic mission of freeing the church of abuses. Henry III was frequently seen at the head of troops clad in the hair shirt of a penitent. He did not deem himself worthy to assume the royal crown on holy days without first doing penance by baring his back to the blows of the whip. Although he did not give up the appointment of bishops and abbots, he did forego the gifts which it had been customary for newly elected bishops and abbots to pay to the king. Henry thus recognized the point of view of the papal reform party: that simony, the buying and selling of ecclesiastical office, was a sin. He unseated those who were unworthy in their private lives. He set up new popes. The most important of his appointments was Leo IX (1048–1054), former bishop of Toul in Lorraine and one of the few German popes of the Middle Ages. With Leo, sacerdotal reform definitely took over in Rome.

The reform movement was in the first instance directed against such abuses as the marriage of the clergy and simony. In the Roman church of the time, as well as in the Eastern church, the lower clergy were generally married. But the movement did not stop with the removal of such practices. The next step was the call to free the church from all entanglements with the world, especially those growing out of the feudal requirement that all land contribute public service.

The movement came to acquire a vision of a new order of things as the powerful ascetic current of withdrawal from the world of the eleventh century took on a positive character. Only by purging the church of its worldly trammels could the church conquer the world. Here is exemplified a characteristic of Western asceticism: that withdrawal from the world supplies the dynamic force for domination of the world. The "freedom of the church" was one of those catchwords, which had a double-barreled appeal. It might mean to some that the church should be independent of lay control to the extent that it could perform its proper religious functions. But to others, it might also mean the establishment of papal absolutism in the church and an ecclesiastical theocracy over lay rulers and powers.

Put in still another way, the cry of "freedom of the church," apparently embodying the removal of external trammels, actually derived its inner dynamic from the positive aim of establishing a "right order" in the world, by the ascendancy of the priest, who, as the dispenser of the means of salvation, would be the molder and shaper of both the temporal and spiritual orders. A priestly hierarchy with its apex in the papacy would therefore take the place of the sacred monarchy culminating in the emperor. Christ should reign over Caesar, *sacerdotium* over *imperium*.

THE GREGORIAN PROGRAM OF REFORM

The ambivalent character of the movement became apparent as it came under papal direction, particularly with Gregory VII (1073–1085). No pope, either before or after, so impressed his ideals and personality upon his time as Gregory VII. It was not the novelty of his ideas that distinguished Gregory but rather his terrific drive toward carrying them to their utmost consequences. This made him a revolutionary to his contemporaries, who referred to him as that "holy Satan" in Rome. Gregory once wrote: "The Lord did not say I am tradition, but I am the truth," and this may be regarded as the guiding motif of his career. Christ had founded the church as the means of salvation and had placed Peter and his successors at its head. Consequently, the church and pope stood above the kingdoms and rulers of the world, who existed only to maintain the conditions of civil order within which the church could realize the supreme aim of mankind, salvation. This truth cut through all considerations of customary practices and law embodied in feudal investiture and proprietary church. Obviously, the church could not realize its supreme aim fully if it were tied up in the affairs of a *sacrum imperium* in which temporal and spiritual matters were so mixed up as to be indistinguishable.

Gregory laid great emphasis on the implications of these premises for the power of the papacy. First, the pope as the head of the church had the unlimited power to appoint and depose bishops, he had the sole right to call synods, and his legates or ambassadors ranked above all bishops. Second, and as a consequence, the pope was the supreme sovereign of the world and might set up and depose the rulers of kingdoms, who owed him homage and fealty and were obligated to kiss the toe of his boot. It follows also that the pope might relieve subjects of their loyalty and allegiance to their rulers. These unrestricted powers were necessary to free the church from lay control and to maintain the primacy of the priestly office.

Gregory also sought to create a series of papal fiefs among the kingdoms and peoples along the periphery of Latin Christendom. Hungary, Spain, Corsica, and Sardinia recognized papal suzerainty. The reforming papacy thus began to take over the leadership of the defense of the true faith. Gregory was the first pope to project a crusade against the Moslems. Here also the papacy took the lead away from the empire.

The controversy over investiture marked the coming-to-grips of the two powers, *sacrum imperium* and *sacerdotium.* The controversy could have been compromised, as it was shortly thereafter in France and England, if it had not widened into a conflict of principle involving the relative authority of each in both temporal and spiritual matters. However, in England and France the royal authority was not pivoted on the church but on feudal domain and conquest. The claims of the German priest-king to suzerainty over the church had a long tradition going back to Charlemagne. It also ran counter to all the thinking of the time to assume, as we do today, that the affairs of church and state can be separated. Perhaps if Emperor Henry IV (1056–1106) had been as devout a reformer as his father and had not viewed the church as a political instrument, the lines between the two powers might not have become so sharply drawn. Many saw that the church certainly needed reform, for it threatened to be swallowed up in the existing feudal and imperial order to the obvious detriment of its spiritual functions. But did the freedom of the church necessarily mean the subordination of rulers to a papal theocracy, as the reform party at Rome envisaged it?

POLARITY IN THOUGHT, ART, AND ACTION

The conflict had a great effect on the presuppositions on which the sacred order of things had been based. People became aware of the line of demarcation between the spiritual and temporal in human affairs. These two realms were, as we have seen, indistinguishable in the sacred *Reich* of Otto the Great and his immediate successors. The Concordat of Worms (1122), which brought to an end the first phase of the struggle, manifested this awareness in giving to the king the right of investiture of bishops and abbots with lands and sovereign rights and giving to the church election and confirmation with spiritual insignia.

The greatly heightened awareness of the polarity of spiritual and temporal values was also reflected in the controversy over the relationship of faith and reason. In the past the argument had been based largely on the appeal to authorities by the traditional method of stringing together statements culled from the Church Fathers. Now, however, young scholars of the cathedral schools at Paris, Rheims, and Chartres were inspired by the "discovery" of reason as the means of unraveling the mysteries of the relationship of faith and knowledge. For some of them, such as Abelard, the authority neither of church father, of council, nor of pope was acceptable, since contradictory statements of the fundamental dogmas of the Christian faith were the inevitable result of determination by authority.

These scholars turned to the logic of Aristotle as the rational instrument for overcoming the contradictions. Obviously, the scholars were not rationalistic in the modern sense of being skeptical with regard to the faith itself. They stayed within the frame of the "true Christian faith" but were not satisfied with mere authoritative statements of the truth; they wished to make the truth binding by showing its rationale. But in seeking to find rational grounds for the faith, they obviously deprived it of much of its sacramental mystery.

Nowhere is the religious ferment of the time more apparent than in the great wave of church building which began in the eleventh century. A description of the building of the cathedral at Chartres indicates that the whole community participated with a fervor resembling a crusade. Men, women, and children dragged the carts on which the stone and lumber for the building was placed. Led by the priest, they accompanied this work with the singing of hymns and with prayer.

A new monumental style of architecture called Romanesque now appeared, and architecture again took precedence over book illustration and illumination. The new Romanesque forms are especially evident in the bishops' churches of the old Roman towns along the Rhine, at Trier, Mainz, Speyer, and Worms, and in the monastic churches founded by the Hirsau congregation.

One feels that the part of the edifice provided for the audience is a mere appendage to the altar and the choir. The great towers and spires over the latter are monuments of the tomb of the Lord, embodied in the sacrament on the altar and in the relics in the crypt beneath. Here reside the spiritual powers which can overcome the forces of evil. Christ and His apostles are presented in the tympanum of the portals as sitting in perpetual judgment, thus separating the saved from the damned. In the sculptured figures and mural paintings, the same theme breaks through the old hieratic forms as a dynamic expression of religious fervor and even frenzy. This crusading era retained in a much more intensified form the notion of Christ and His saints engaged in eternal warfare against Satan and his legions.

That the Romanesque was the peculiar expression of the crusading spirit is evident not only in its mood of militant religiosity but also in the fact that a number of the most important Romanesque churches were built on the pilgrim routes, especially those leading from France into Spain. France was the chief source of the Peace of God and of the early crusading movements.

In the first crusade no kings or emperors participated. The popes were the main promoters, and most of the rulers were at odds with the papacy over the reform program. It was the French nobility who took the lead in the First Crusade (1096–1099). Not until the first half of the twelfth century, with the preaching of St. Bernard of Clairvaux, the chief promoter of the Second Crusade (1147–1149), did the movement begin to exert an influence in the Germanies. Successive waves of crusading enthusiasm thereafter swept over the whole of Europe until the middle of the thirteenth century.

The reform movement contributed to the definite separation of the Eastern and Western churches as well as to the heightened antagonism between Moslem and Christian. With the widening of the schism since the middle of the eleventh century, the *Reich* was drawn away from affiliations with the Byzantine world. Although still the defender of the eastern borders of Christendom against schismatic and heathen peoples, the *Reich* was no longer really the embodiment of Christendom. The real leader was now the pope, presiding over many rulers and kingdoms and chief promoter of the warfare against infidel and heretic.

ST. BERNARD VERSUS ARNOLD OF BRESCIA

There was no one among the popes of the twelfth century to carry the reform program to a conclusion. It took a monk, St. Bernard of Clairvaux (1091–1153), to serve as the scourge of his time in pointing out the evils in church and society. Indeed, after the great exaltation of the Investiture Conflict and the First Crusade, the church rapidly dropped into the slough of spiritual apathy and material luxury.

St. Bernard embodied the drive to free the church from the vices of luxury and pomp, to guard it against the temptations offered not only by vast power and influence but also by the presumption of human reason in attempting to unfold the mysteries of the faith. He was essentially a conservative whose thinking still moved in the orbit of the *sacrum imperium*. He did not envisage the establishment of a priestly "right order" nor the creation of a purely spiritual community in the manner of the sectarians. He thought the best antidote to the spread of heresy was for the clergy to live in accordance with the example set by Christ and His apostles, and for the laity to take up the cross against the infidel. Above all, he aimed at giving an inner spiritual dynamic to a faith which had begun to emphasize outward forms.

His sermons to the monks of Clairvaux revealed the mystic's outer abasement but inner yearning to ascend to union with the Most High. Bernard departed, however, from that metaphysical strain of mysticism which came from the East, whereby the soul ascends on the rungs of the ladder of contemplation to final ecstatic union with the divine. In this context, the historical figure of Jesus, His ministry, and even His very death on the cross seem to be almost completely pushed out of the picture. Bernard focused his whole attention upon the suffering Jesus, from the helpless infant in the crib to the wounds on the cross. Christ descends, so to speak, from the heavenly ethereal realm and from the judgment seat to the earth as a ministering and suffering servant of man.

Thus a much more realistic image of the Savior came to the fore. Pilgrimages and crusades to the Holy Land had already turned men's thoughts to the places Christ had visited, the paths He had trod, and to the exemplary character of His life and the lives of His disciples. Not only the sacrifice on the cross but the whole life of Christ served as an object of devotion and of example especially to those who, like priests and monks, professed to serve Him exclusively.

Christ's command to His disciples to preach without recompense was now to be applied to all the shepherds of men's souls. The earlier Gregorian reform movement had sought to free the clergy from lay control. The next and more important step was to free their lives from the corrosive influence of wealth and worldly pomp and power which had completely taken over in the church itself as a consequence of the church's quest for universal dominance.

The chief exponent of evangelical poverty in the days of St. Bernard was a pupil of Abelard, Arnold of Brescia. A most eloquent representative of a class of popular preachers, he advocated the life of evangelical poverty for all the clergy and the complete separation of church and state.

Had the idea of evangelical poverty been applied rigorously to the clergy, it would have had a revolutionary effect, for it meant not merely relinquishing wealth but that the legitimacy of priest and bishop and the efficacy of the sacraments they performed would be judged by the worthiness of their lives. It would have broken down the whole conception of the apostolic continuity of spiritual authority descending from Christ to His disciples through the sacrament of ordination. The underlying conception of the church as a spiritual community rather than as a sacramental-hierarchical organism was to be revived again and again throughout medieval and modern times.

In 1141 both Abelard and Arnold were condemned by a church synod, largely under the influence of St. Bernard. A few years later Arnold was in Rome as a leader of the populace against the pope. For a short time, he became the virtual ruler of the city, and he then attempted to restore the ancient republican institutions on a democratic basis. Finally forced out of Rome, he fell into the hands of Emperor Frederick I who had him hanged and his body burned. Neither emperors nor popes condoned rebellion against divinely constituted authority and were equally zealous in bringing about its suppression.

Arnold was a leading representative of the fusion of the popular movement in cities with a new religious drive arising from the notion of apostolic poverty. The church had failed to accommodate itself to the rise of cities, especially in northern and central Italy, southern France, and along the Rhine. The religious needs of the lower population of the new urban centers were not taken care of by a church organization which had adjusted itself to an agrarian society. Popular preachers, naturally critical of the lives of the upper clergy, filled the gap. This opposition to clerical authority reached its culmination in the great sectarian movements of the Catharists and Waldensians. However, it must not be assumed that these heretical movements were recruited only from the urban centers. They also included many peasants and nobles, notably in France.

SACERDOTALISM VERSUS SECTARIANISM

Under Innocent III (1198–1216) the Gregorian dream of universal sovereignty was given its greatest substance. He was the first on the throne of St. Peter for whom it was claimed that he was "less than God but more than man." In this view, the pope was the divinely established intermediary between God and man.

A definite distinction between the natural basis of all earthly power and divinely instituted ecclesiastical authority followed. The supreme spiritual and sacramental power was regarded as the source of all power on earth; the sanctions of temporal authority were derived from this sacred power. These vast claims to papal central authority were implemented through papal envoys and the extension of papal judicial authority and of papal appointment to ecclesiastical office. The priesthood was distinguished from the laity, both high and low, because the sacramental power necessary to confer salvation on mankind resided exclusively in the priests. In the course of the twelfth century the seven sacraments came to be separated from other ceremonies of religious significance and became a virtual monopoly of the priest.

This demarcation of supranatural from natural and of priest from layman did not, of course, mean an irreconcilable clash of opposing principles in the thought of the time. No absolute cleavage existed between the realms of nature and of grace. The distinction was emphasized only to make men aware of the superiority of grace. Grace was really the fulfillment of nature.

St. Thomas Aquinas, the great scholastic philosopher and theologian of the thirteenth century, presented a hierarchical ladder of gradations extending from heaven to earth. On it all the spheres of human activity from the lowest instinctive level to the highest vision of the divine had their proper function and place. All men's actions were, of course, to point toward the supreme goal, union with the divine.

This philosophy of gradualism enabled the church to keep its feet on the ground of earthly temporal activities while at the same time turning men's vision toward the celestial realm. In seeking to maintain this reconcilability of the two realms, the church was often led to stoop to conquer—to make all manner of compromises with the natural appetite for power, wealth, and prestige.

Renewed opposition to this great hierarchical sacramental order came from the two old sources: the sectarian movement and the imperial claims to world supremacy. Each assumed a new guise.

Heresy ceased to be a matter of sporadic individual acceptance of apostolic poverty; it became an organized movement of independent communities with their own religious leaders. Sectarianism also developed a full-fledged religious philosophy. It looked back to the early Christian congregation before the rise of the episcopal-sacramental church for its model community. All were to live in daily expectation of the coming of the Lord. Consequently, separation of the whole community from the ways of the "pagan" world surrounding it was to be maintained. The clergy were to live strictly in accordance with the precepts of evangelical poverty enjoined upon His disciples by Jesus.

The religious ethos of sectarianism was based on a very old heretical tradition in Christendom and differed among individual sects. Basic to it was the assumption that the religious community should consist of the saved or elect who in this world already constituted the kingdom of God. The community was not to be regarded as an instrument of salvation set up as the church by Christ and his disciples. Obviously the sectarian stood absolutely opposed, at least in principle, to any compromise with the world and regarded all manifestations of authority and culture as essentially evil.

Innocent II combated the two principal heresies, those of the Catharists and the Waldensians, by preaching crusades against them, by establishing the Inquisition, and by calling upon the secular arm to punish them. But at the same time the church acquired in the Franciscan and Dominican friars the means of dealing more positively with the menace of heresy. These mendicants, unlike the older orders, did not isolate themselves from the world in secluded monasteries but devoted themselves to popular preaching and missionary work. Both by their devotion to individual poverty and by ministering to the spiritual needs of the populace they embodied the ideal of evangelical poverty. Particularly, St. Francis of Assisi (1182–1226) expressed the ideal of Christian discipleship which threatened to disappear with the rise of the great hierarchical-sacramental edifice.

THE SECULAR MESSIANIC IMPERIALISM OF FREDERICK II

Another great menace to the popes in the first half of the thirteenth century came from the assertion of a new kind of political and cultural ethos by a sprout of the great Hohenstaufen family, Frederick II (1215–1250), one of the most puzzling personalities in history. Reared in the semi-oriental atmosphere of southern Italy among German officials, Norman barons, Saracens, and Greeks, he was really non-German. Early in life he acquired a strong sense of political calculation and an amazing virtuosity of aptitudes and interests.

He based his power not on German dynastic holdings but on the south Italian kingdom where he carried forward what was in that time a radical policy of centralization. Frederick destroyed noble castles, prohibited private warfare, and banned the carrying of weapons. The king was regarded as the fount of all justice before whose courts all cases must appear. The jurisdiction of ecclesiastical courts was limited. Frederick operated his government through a hierarchy of salaried officials. He promoted commerce, and an elaborate system of indirect taxes provided the royal treasury with considerable revenues. These characteristics of his rule anticipated those of the absolute monarchies of northern Europe some two centuries later.

Frederick's style of life may be compared with the Moslem and Byzantine princes of the Mediterranean area. His harem and menagerie, his interest in science and in troubadour poetry, make him a typical product of the fusion of cultures and peoples. He employed not only Latins but also Byzantines and Moslems. A Greek admiral commanded his navy; his army contained a large contingent of Moslems.

The struggle with the papacy no longer involved control of the church as a main issue. The conflict of power was for the control of Italy. Increasingly, the papacy had become conscious of the threat to its independence, for Frederick, somewhat like Otto III, seemed bent on making Rome the center of imperial power and authority and thus reducing the popes to a position of subservience.

In its culminating phase, with Frederick confronted by Popes Gregory IX (1227–1241) and Innocent IV (1243–1254), the conflict became more and more a propaganda war. In this kind of war the popes commanded the greater resources. They leveled excommunication and interdict at Frederick, but their repeated use had blunted the edge of these instruments. They preached crusades against him as they did against heretics and infidels. Most important were the new agents for the dissemination of papal propaganda, the Franciscans and the Dominicans.

The popular preachers drawn from these orders spread far and wide the stories that Frederick was the anti-Christ, the beast of the Apocalypse, and that he believed that mankind had been deceived by three great impostors, Moses, Jesus, and Mohammed, who had aroused conflict and dissension among peoples. Even though the story cannot be traced to Frederick, its currency at the time reveals a new spirit of criticism and skepticism. At the same time, the prevalence of heresy and the emergence of the mendicant orders reveal a new current of emotional religious piety, especially among the lower orders of the towns. The existence side by side of such opposing currents is, of course, not unusual in a time of great intellectual and religious ferment as characterized the first half of the thirteenth century.

Frederick retaliated in the war of words. He accused Pope Gregory of being a promoter of heresy and rebellion in his support of the Lombard towns. Yet Frederick also followed the line of the religious radicals in calling upon the church to return to apostolic poverty and relinquish its pursuit of earthly wealth and power. He sought to induce the other kings of Europe to collaborate in the defense of monarchical principles against the papal claim to supremacy. Frederick claimed that he, as the successor to the ancient Caesars, was the incarnation of universal rule and law. His thinking was very close to the conception of the self-sufficient autonomy of the political community which the revival of Aristotle was bringing to the fore.

Frederick clothed his ideas as well as his political actions in religious symbols and phrases. Thus he represented himself as the divinely chosen ruler whose role it was to bring peace and justice and to end the dissension and rebellion fomented by heresy.

These overtones of messianic imperialism coupled with political hardheadedness and an almost scientific skepticism have made Frederick a controversial figure to historians. He shared with Otto III a conception of a universal imperial mission detached from German hegemony. Both became legendary figures in the popular imagination.

39

What had now become of the Holy Roman Empire as a universal and ecumenical idea? We must always bear in mind that it was not the power exercised over peoples and territories that lent the Empire prestige and pre-eminence, but its claim to embody a universal idea or principle. It began in the days of Charlemagne as the community of true Christians arrayed against the heathen and the infidel. Under the Saxon emperors and their immediate successors, it became the *sacrum imperium*, the projection of the heavenly kingdom upon earth. Most of this aura of holiness was lost with the reform movement and papal revolution.

While the phrase "Holy Roman Empire" was probably first used by Frederick Barbarossa, he and his successors, especially his grandson Frederick II, were forced in the face of papal claims to resort increasingly to temporal justifications and means. They appealed to the authority of the ancient Caesars and Roman law and sought thus to build a power basis in Italy. The collapse of their power after the death of Frederick II in 1250 left the papacy dominant in Italy.

THE SECULAR STATE AND THE THIRD AGE

In the following centuries the popes came face to face with the emerging nation-states whose rise they had promoted, both as a counterpoise to the Empire and in the ideal interest of forming a Christian community of free peoples united in one faith under themselves as the guardians of the faith. In undermining first the religious basis and then the political power of the Empire, the popes prepared the way for the emergence of modern Europe. But this Europe, which did not crystallize until the seventeenth century, was really an alien secular departure from the organic Christian community. It was a community of states based on the dynamic equilibrium of the thrust and counterthrust of power interests and on the progessive advance of human control over nature.

France became the chief dynamic force of this new community. As early as the twelfth and thirteenth centuries its rulers were making claims to leadership. Unlike the German rulers, the French kings actually succeeded in building a strong state power around the original Capetian domain with Paris at its center. From this central core the royal power extended outward. As the Capetian kings acquired lands by one feudal expedient or the other, they extended royal institutions of control to them. Thus the French royal power, unlike the German, rose from medieval grass roots to the creation of the institutional frame of the state. The German *Reich* had its sources in an ecumenical heritage and role, and not in a parochial feudal domain. Not until the nineteenth century did parochialism become the source of unity of the German *Reich* under Prussian leadership. It is curious that while France proceeded from parochialism to ecumenical universalism, Germany took the opposite road.

Although the Empire, as a political entity, became after 1250 virtually a dynastic football among German ducal families (the most successful being the Hapsburgs), it assumed even more grandiose significance as an ideal. The great Italian poet Dante castigated both emperors and popes for sacrificing Italy and the Empire to dynastic or power interests. The establishment of peace and order could come only from an emperor who, standing above party and faction, would defend justice and restore the church to its ancient holiness, to poverty and service.

The papacy had waged a war of relentless annihilation not only against the Hohenstaufen emperors but also against the heretical sects. It had not, in fact, succeeded in completely suppressing heresy, which persisted in small groups and in inconspicuous corners. More important, there appeared within the ranks of sectarianism a new historical perspective whose significance has been realized only recently. This new orientation revolved around the idea of a coming "Third Age" and has been a guiding thread in revolutionary movements, both sacred and secular, of modern times.

In his very influential *The City of God*, St. Augustine (354–430) had argued that earthly rule, embodied in empire, must forever be distinguished from the spiritual community of the church, whose destiny is the eternal heavenly city. Both empire and church would exist side by side until the end of time—when a new earth and a new heaven would supercede the old. The Roman Empire was but one of many historical forms of power; the church, however, was the one institution divinely established for the salvation of mankind and would persist until the end of time. Thus there really were but two ages of mankind, set off by the great divide of Christ's redemptive role, which was perpetuated by the church.

The idea of a Third Age received its first impetus from a group of Franciscans who insisted upon strict evangelical poverty for their order. There was to be no possession of lands, chapter houses, or churches. These Spirituals, in the face of papal condemnation, took over the eschatological ideas of the Cistercian abbot Joachim of Flora, who had presented a new interpretation of history of great significance. His ideas were published in 1254 as *Introduction to the Eternal Gospel*.

Joachim projected three ages: first, the age of the Father, that is, of the Old Testament and the rule of the law; second, the age of the Son and the rule of the church; and third, the age of the Holy Ghost, marking the pre-eminence of the monk. This last age would be the fulfillment of the two previous ages. Therefore the hierarchical priestly church would not usher in the end of time but would make way for a new age of the perfection of the Spirit, in which a rebirth of Christianity would be brought about by a return to its origins. This idea of a third age of the Spirit was to haunt many of the foremost European minds, especially in Germany, down to Hegel and his followers.

The Spirituals became increasingly more radical in their criticisms of the existing church as they were driven underground by papal denunciation. In Joachimite circles the pope displaced the Hohenstaufen emperors as the anti-Christ. Joachimite ideas merged with those of the Ghibelline imperialist opponents of the papacy to project the notion of the coming of a great savior-emperor who would usher in the new age. In Rome, during the papal residence at Avignon, there again appeared a popular demagog like Arnold of Brescia, called Cola di Rienzi, who preached the revival of the ancient greatness of Rome and the restoration of her leadership over the peoples of Christendom. His ideas had a pervasive influence over the pioneers of the Italian Renaissance, which extended to the supporters of Emperor Ludwig the Bavarian (1314–1347) in his controversy with the Avignon Pope, John XXII. However, these ideas were supplemented by a different approach, one which produced the modern idea of the separation of church and state. Pope John, who made high-flown claims to supremacy similar to those of Boniface VIII, declared Ludwig deposed because he had not received papal confirmation.

Ludwig was supported by the important work of two Parisian professors, *Defender of the Peace* (1326). This work might be called the first real defense of the lay or secular state. It argued for the complete autonomy and self-sufficiency of the political community as based on popular sovereignty. The church should confine itself strictly to spiritual matters. The community of believers rather than the hierarchy should constitute the sovereign body of the church.

Similar ideas were propounded by some of the Franciscan dissenters who came to Ludwig's support. Chief among them was the English philosopher William of Occam, whose pluralist philosophy constituted an attack upon the gradualism of St. Thomas Aquinas. Pope and church were subordinated by Occam to the sovereignty of emperor and the sanction of Scripture. The latter were regarded as independent of each other and as lying outside of the organic order of a *sacrum imperium* or of a sacerdotal hierarchy.

TRANSFORMATIONS WITHIN THE BASIC COMMUNITIES

The dissolution of the medieval order really began with this basic assumption of the existence of two independent realms, the secular and the spiritual. The *sacrum imperium*, the papal *sacerdotium*, and sectarianism—all three accepted the fundamental unity of things; there was no sharp division between heavenly and earthly matters, only a difference in the realization of spiritual goals. The contest between divine and demonic forces took place in both the earthly and heavenly spheres. The divine triumphed in heaven, while on earth its ultimate victory was postponed in accordance with a divine plan of salvation for mankind.

Although these presuppositions of the Christian faith were basic to all three forms of religious community, there were fundamental differences in accent between them which were to have a profound influence in succeeding centuries. The process of secularization already evident in the later Middle Ages tended to abstract fundamental principles from what were once concrete living forms. These principles acquired a new dynamic during successive incarnations down to the present.

The *sacrum imperium* permeated the whole of existence with a spiritual magic. Spirituality was embodied in emperor, bishop, church, sacrament, book, statue—actually in all things. Nicholas of Cues, Jakob Böhme, and Leibniz projected dynamic universal orders in which spirit and matter are indistinguishable in the creative process of self-realization. A somewhat different accent is expressed in the line of thinkers from Paracelsus to Herder and Goethe; from Liebig to Carl Jung and Ernst Jünger, for whom the universe is not dead soulless matter which man may manipulate for his own uses but a living organism with which man must seek rapport by an understanding of and reverence for its living forms and processes.

The *sacerdotium* stressed distinctions between the spiritual and temporal by singling out the mediating role of sacrament and priesthood in man's salvation. It achieved its most characteristic expression in scholastic philosophy in the distinction between faith and reason, although recognizing their fundamental unity within the frame of a hierarchical-sacramental *ordo*. This is the line of thinking into which we may place Luther, Kant, Frederick the Great, and Bismarck, and all those, especially numerous in France, who emphasized the polarity of reason and faith, of subject and object, of man and world.

The third form of religious community presents a less definite community structure, except with regard to historical orientation. Sectarianism in the Middle Ages was espoused by such leaders of movements as Arnold of Brescia and Rienzi, who sought a return to an earlier golden age, or by communities which sought to isolate themselves from the surrounding world, living in constant expectation of a coming new order of things. The whole period between the original golden age and the future millenium has an interim character during which one awaits either rebirth in terms of ancient and primordial values or projection into a millenium or utopia. Its most characteristic form of expression was the charismatic leader. In this line of thought we find the most diverse personalities from Thomas Müntzer to Zinzendorf, from Fichte to Richard Wagner, from Marx to Hitler.

Forms: Sacrum Imperium, Sacerdotium, and Sectarianism

In the German development these types of religious community appear more clearly differentiated than elsewhere because they exist in a state of suspension, often assuming an individual, radical expression. Sometimes they become allies, as *sacrum imperium* and sectarianism frequently did in opposition to *sacerdotium*. In any case, the persistence of the notions of the community as a dynamic totality and of a coming Third Age could produce either great philosophic systems or the most ruthless imperial conquests.

II

The Unification and Differentiation of Western Christendom

THE SIGNIFICANCE OF EASTERN AND WESTERN
ORIENTATIONS

A people has two axes in its cultural development: one vertical, representing the relation between the ideal and the actual; the other horizontal, involving its resistance and receptivity to influences coming from its neighbors. In the previous chapter we dealt with the first axis. The second was of equal importance to the Germans since they were peculiarly influenced by their situation in the middle of Europe between the Slavic-Byzantine cultural area to the east and the French-Romance sphere to the west.

The *sacrum imperium* of the tenth century had been peculiarly conscious of its mission eastward into the lands of Slavic heathendom. In the thirteenth and fourteenth centuries the Germans made new thrusts eastward leading to colonial establishments. These were to have profound effects on both Germanic and Slavic culture. Almost simultaneously, the Germans were on the receiving end of new cultural influences generated in the West, especially in France, and stemming there from the fusion of the new religious consciousness arising out of the reform movement with the recovery of ancient learning.

In both of these movements the Empire played a minor role. German settlement eastward was a grass roots movement of peasants, burghers, and nobles. The cultural reception of the new "Western rationalism" was the work principally of isolated individuals and was not promoted by monasticism, the chief cultural carrier in the *sacrum imperium.*

During the last half-century German historians have debated the relative influence on German cultural development of the impact of the new colonial areas to the east as compared with that of the western lands bordering on France. The controversy had an obvious nationalistic bias in that some historians assumed that eastward expansion was the chief formative influence in German history, like the westward movement in American history, and that the colonial areas became the basis of the distinctively German cultural achievements, while the western borderlands looked to France as the source of rational enlightenment. That there developed a difference in cultural accent between the two areas cannot be altogether denied, but certainly the difference never was as decisive an influence as alleged by the exponents of what among American historians has been called the "frontier thesis." The individual character of German culture was as much a product, furthermore, of the vertical or ideal axis as of the horizontal or frontier orientation.

The eastward movement in itself was no more the expression of a particular national drive than were the various crusading ventures in the Mediterranean from Spain to the Holy Land. It was one aspect of the tremendous release of creative forces as a consequence of which Western Christendom achieved final crystallization. It might be said that this unification was realized outwardly by the general extension of frontier and inwardly by the spread of philosophical and artistic forms and values emanating chiefly from France.

FACTORS PROMOTING EASTERN COLONIZATION

The German advance eastward from a line extending roughly from the mouth of the Elbe to the head of the Adriatic was uneven.

It followed three thrusts. The major one was to the northeast along the Baltic where the movement by land and sea supplemented each other. In the middle, looking out on Bohemia, the mountainous terrain and also the strong Slavic states of Bohemia and Poland held up the advance. A deeper thrust was made down the Danube. By the twelfth and thirteenth centuries the peoples of these areas had long since come into the fold of the church; there was obviously, therefore, no motive for crusade or missionary activity. The appearance of strong rulers in Bohemia, Poland, and Hungary served most to retard the German advance. However, to the northeast along the Baltic shores and over the great plain area eastward, no such obstacles existed. In the twelfth century, when the great German eastward movement in this area really began to make progress, the Slavs and Letts of this area were still predominantly heathen and lived in tribes. It was an area which lay open to the German with his superior political organization, economic technics, and religious and cultural forms.

The population of northern Europe increased greatly during the eleventh and twelfth centuries. This increase had found an outlet primarily in inner colonization, the founding of new towns and villages and, to some extent, in the eastward movement. Inner colonization simply meant extending the area of cultivation by draining swamps and clearing forest areas. Little clearing of forests took place in France in this period. The Germans and English excelled here and so may be said to have formed the distinctive "pioneer-type." [1] By the last half of the twelfth century, inner colonization had reached a saturation point, and the new excess of population turned to the regions beyond the Elbe. One must bear in mind always that the natural increase of those already on the frontier was as potent an expansive force as that of the population pressure in the interior.

The German nobility equaled the peasants in land-hunger. By participating in crusades against heathen Slavs or in the numerous wars among the native princes, they acquired lands which they naturally desired to populate with peasant farmers from back home. On the frontiers, large areas appear to have been sparsely populated, either because of devastating raids or because of the primitive agricultural technics of the native Slavs.

In time the process of settlement assumed a systematic character. An agent of the landlord known as a "locator" went among the peasants back home and presented enticing offers of virgin soil, plentiful fish and game, and easy rents and dues. He then led the emigrants to the new lands and received compensation in the form of land grants or the collection of certain dues and fees.

North German peasants, who were accustomed to the continual struggle with flood waters of the sea and river and therefore knew how to build dikes and drain lowlands, were in great demand. Moreover, the German peasantry were accustomed to the use of the efficient heavy-wheeled plough with its iron share. They could therefore cultivate the less favorable land which the Slav, with his more primitive methods, could not utilize.

Undoubtedly the chief innovation the Germans introduced in their settlement was the town. There were, of course, trading centers and depots among the Slavs, but no organized urban communities with laws of their own, distinguished from the manorial regime of the countryside.

Along the Baltic coast, the thirteenth century saw the emergence of such cities as Danzig, Riga, Dorpat, and Reval. Several of these coastal cities were founded by merchants from Lübeck, and the laws of that city became the model for these new foundations. The cities of the interior derived their law principally from Magdeburg, the ancient missionary and ecclesiastical center on the Elbe. Of the newly founded cities in the interior, Prague, Breslau, Krakow, Posen, Frankfort-on-the-Oder, and Thorn became chief centers of trade. In all these cities the ruling class was made up of German burghers who controlled the trade and manufacture of the colonial area and shaped the pattern of town life.

The genius of the Middle Ages for the formation of associations is well illustrated in the achievements of the Teutonic Knights and the Hanseatic League. The years from approximately the middle of the thirteenth to the middle of the fourteenth century marked the formation of these associations and their growth to a peak of power and influence.

ESTABLISHMENT OF THE TEUTONIC ORDER IN PRUSSIA

The Teutonic Order (founded 1197), like the Templars and Hospitalers, was established originally to protect pilgrims visiting the Holy Land and to wage war against the Moslems. It was comprised of noble warriors who took the monkish vows of chastity, poverty, and obedience. One farsighted grand master of the Order, Hermann of Salza (1209-1239), saw that, with the prospect of the Christian loss of the Holy Land, it was necessary to find a new field of activity. The Knights first settled in Transylvania at the invitation of the King of Hungary but were virtually forced out when they threatened to become a strong power there. Hermann then secured from his friend, Emperor Frederick II, not only a new charter providing a more close-knit organization but concessions to lands on the south shore of the Baltic.

The original invitation (1229) to Christianize and subject the heathen Prussians of the area to the east of the Vistula came from Count Conrad of Mazovia in Poland. During most of the thirteenth century, Poland, lapsing into feudal anarchy, was confronted by the devastating raids of the Mongols. Denmark, another interested party in the Baltic area, had been defeated in 1227 by an alliance of north German princes and retained only Esthonia far to the north. The political situation was thus favorable for the Order's entrance upon the scene.

The popes were also interested in establishing missions in the Baltic area, especially along the eastern shores. In 1202 under Innocent III, a crusading outpost, comprised of many German knights, was founded in Livonia by a military order known as the Brothers of the Sword. The city of Riga had been founded the previous year by German merchants encouraged by the papal missionary bishops of the area.

The Teutonic Knights managed, however, to avoid tying themselves closely to either emperor or pope; they became practically independent of all outside control. Under the astute leadership of Hermann of Salza, they secured imperial confirmation of all conquests, since all lordless land was subject to the emperor; but they held the conquered lands also as fiefs from the papacy. Both pope and emperor were so distant as to offer little interference. Even more important, episcopal authority over the area was incorporated within the Order.

THE ORDER AS A COLONIZER

During the middle decades of the thirteenth century, the Knights proceeded to bring the Slavic Prussians into subjection. As they conquered an area, they established forts and castles to hold it. A constant stream of nobles from the west provided badly needed new recruits for military expeditions and for the manning of forts and castles. There was also the serious problem of defending the territories of the Order against Lithuanians and Russians. In 1242 and especially in 1260, having suffered defeat by the Lithuanians, the Knights were faced with a widespread revolt which threatened their very existence as a territorial power in this eastern land. A crusade called by the pope plus the assistance of the eastern German princes enabled the Knights to recover their lost castles and holdings. By 1280 all Prussian resistance had been definitely suppressed and the devastated areas were colonized with German peasants. In time, Prussians and Germans, living under the same landlords, became indistinguishable.

The Teutonic Order was also compelled to come to the assistance of the Knights of the Sword in Livonia. Too far removed from the main body of Germans to receive many recruits and hemmed in by the Danes in Esthonia and by the Russians and Lithuanians, these Knights were always in a precarious position. They were taken over in 1237 by the Teutonic Order, which thereafter assumed the defense of Livonia and Courland. An attempt to move eastward and take Novgorod from the Russians was defeated by Alexander Nevsky in 1242. But the Order did expand westward across the Vistula into Pomerania, where it merged with German expansion from the west.

These last acquisitions placed the Teutonic Knights squarely across the Polish path to the Baltic. The resurgence of Poland and its union with Lithuania under the dynasty of the Jagellons in the fourteenth century paved the way for a series of wars which, in the fifteenth century, put the Knights in vassalage to the Polish king and resulted in the loss of all but the original conquests.

The great achievement of the Teutonic Knights was not only the promotion of German influence eastward along the Baltic but also the establishment of a strong state. Under the central authority of the grand master, acting through the commanders of the various districts, the Order achieved a unified and centralized administration comparable to that in the Kingdom of Sicily under Frederick II. It was not confronted by the usual independent feudality nor by autonomous jurisdictions of bishops and abbots. The church was absorbed in the Order, and feudal holdings were strictly limited.

The Order pursued a policy of planned colonization, particularly after 1280 when it had established supremacy in the Prussian lands. It has been calculated that the Order founded ninety-three cities and about fourteen hundred villages.[2] Many of these cities became members of the Hanseatic League with which the Order maintained friendly relations and collaborated in dealing with common foes. The peasants were treated with great leniency; most of them were under the direct supervision of the Order and not under a noble landlord. It is not surprising that peasants from the adjacent principalities flocked into the lands of the Order by the thousands.

These policies could not be pursued in the Livonian lands of the Knights of the Sword. Here the Order was confronted by established ecclesiastical authorities, feudal lords, and independent towns which it had to recognize. More important from the point of view of the future of the Germans there, the Order constituted only a thin veneer of the clergy, burghers, and knights ruling over native peasant peoples who were different in language and in culture. Very few German peasants migrated to these far-off regions.

The great, somber castles erected by the Order, such as the seat of the grand master at Marienburg, testify not only to the power of the Knights but to their ascetic military spirit. It has been argued that this ascetic-military spirit achieved a secular reincarnation in the later Prussian state, especially in the Junkers, who were its mainstay in army and administration. Nevertheless, the Order also promoted trade and commerce; and such cities as Danzig, Königsberg, and Riga became great centers of German commercial expansion in the Baltic, which during the thirteenth and fourteenth centuries virtually became a German lake.

THE HANSEATIC LEAGUE AND THE TRADE OF THE NORTH

German commercial expansion culminated in the development of that famous association of cities known as the Hanseatic League. At the peak of its development, between 1250 and 1350, more than seventy cities were included in the League.

Like other leagues of cities, the Hanseatic League had a grass roots origin. The merchants of the north German cities traveled far afield to trade at the great Champagne Fairs in France; and when these declined, they went to Bruges in the Low Countries. At both trading centers they encountered Italian traders, who brought products of the Mediterranean. They also went in great numbers to England, which was then an important source of raw wool. The woolen cloth produced by the Flemish cities was the chief article of foreign trade in the northern area.

For mutual protection these merchants formed an association which later became a league of cities and included cities from the Rhine to the eastern shores of the Baltic. Through Regensburg, Nuremburg, and Augsburg in southern Germany, the trade of the Baltic towns came to be linked with that of the Mediterranean. The great Italian commercial city of Venice became the principal outlet for German trade in that area.

Leadership in the League centered especially in the northern cities, Hamburg, Lübeck, and Danzig. Lübeck was the chief promoter of German trade in the Baltic and the principal link between the cities of the west and the new Baltic cities and trading posts. The chief trading posts in the north Baltic were at Wisby on the island of Gothland, and at Novgorod, which tapped the interior of the Russian hinterland. The trade of the Baltic cities was based principally upon the herring fisheries, on hides and furs, and on the forest products of these frontier areas; these were exchanged for the raw wool, textile cloth, and luxury products from the west and south. As the growing cities of Flanders and the Rhineland were

Gero Cross (Cologne Cathedral), end of 10th century

Der Reiter (Bamberg), circa 1230-40

Ekkehard and Uta (Naumburg), circa 1250-60

*Matthias Grünewald, Mary and Child, Isenheimer Altar,
circa 1510 (Kolmar Museum)*

forced to import foodstuffs, the Baltic cities, which tapped the colonial agrarian hinterland, found a new source of trade.

The League had a very loose-jointed organization. Only in crises, presented by the threat of outside powers to the movement of trade, did its members coalesce to form a real united front. The most decided menace was Denmark, which occupied a strategic position on the straits leading from the north to the Baltic Seas and threatened the herring fisheries off the south coast of Sweden. By the Peace of Stralsund (1370), the League finally forced Denmark to give it control of the Sound and such political guarantees as the right to a voice in the election of the king. The League then attained its peak in the Baltic trade and in political power. It had succeeded in linking together in one great network of trade the wool of England, the cloth of the Low Countries, and the sea and forest products of the Baltic area.

The whole movement of eastward expansion lost much of its momentum after the middle of the fourteenth century. This may be ascribed in part to the catastrophic disaster of the Black Death of 1348–49, which led to a leveling off of population and contributed to great social and religious disturbances during the latter half of the century. The entrance of new powers into the Baltic theater, the English, Dutch, Russians, and Poles, had a more direct impact during the fifteenth century.

The distinguishing feature of this German colonial movement was that its field of operation, unlike the foundations in the Holy Land, was not separated by vast seas from the motherland but was really an extension of it. However, as in all colonial areas, the transplanting of social forms tended to simplify and functionalize them by cutting them loose from their traditional matrix in the homeland. States that are founded in this manner are not only larger but have a tighter rational organization. Likewise, in the field of architecture, castles and churches are larger and more severe in style than in the homeland.

However, the chief impetus to cultural change came from France. It made itself felt particularly in the new movements of chivalrous literature, of Gothic art, and of scholastic philosophy. In them the revived religious idealism and subjectivism were confronted by a growing rationalism and naturalism.

FRENCH CHIVALRY AND COURTLY LOVE

The social group which most clearly expressed its values and interests in distinctive cultural forms was the nobility. The institution of chivalry grew up especially among the adventurous and wayfaring lower nobility. Knights were recruited from younger sons, or they rose through the ranks of the *ministeriales*. They sought employment with a great noble or king; they went on crusades or took part in the Italian expeditions. Along with the clergy, this service nobility now became an important cultural force.

The code of manners and morals called "chivalry" emerged in the circle the knights formed around lord and lady. They also formed an order of knighthood which required not merely evidence of courage in battle and loyalty to the lord, but the taking of an oath to protect the widow and orphan and to defend the church and faith. Around the lady of the castle there emerged a court society which prescribed definite forms of behavior in relation to women, summed up in the word "gallantry." It was the function of the lady to educate the sons of her lord's vassals in the spirit and forms of this society to prepare them for formal entrance into it.

The mode of life of the nobility also changed with the influx of such luxury products as carpets, mirrors, silks, and brocades; it was further modified as the result of contact with other peoples on various expeditions to Italy, Spain, and the Holy Land. All these factors contributed to a new refinement of manners and tastes and to a greater sensitivity to nuances of attitude and feeling.

The most important result of such transformations was the ideal projection in poetry, both lyric and epic, of a new conception of man, represented as transcending natural appetites and desires not only by divine grace but by the love of the lady. Love was presented as a yearning for one who was unattainable. The sense of distance between the lover and the loved one, who was presented as remaining cold and aloof, produced the inner tension out of which lyrical fervor and passion grew. The sense of unending longing found supreme happiness "independent of any consummation." [3]

THE GERMAN VERSION: WALTHER VON DER VOGELWEIDE

In the greatest of the German Minnesingers, Walther von der Vogelweide, we find an individualizing tendency which seeks to go beyond the courtly cult of the lady. Coming from the lower nobility, Walther became a wandering troubadour. We first encounter him in Austria, but he served many princes and three emperors. From Frederick II he received, toward the end of his life, a small fief which enabled him to end his wanderings. His poetry reveals his highly individual reaction to the interests of his time, from love to imperial politics.

Love for Walther became more than courtly convention and less than an exalted metaphysical idea. In both, love had no direct relationship with marriage or with erotic passion, either of which would have detracted from the exalted purity of love. One married for feudal political reasons, and one sought gratification of one's sensual desires with a woman outside one's class. Walther sought to bring the natural passion between man and woman in association with the spiritual exaltation of courtly love. In so doing, however, he prepared the way for the descent of the courtly lady who had been the only one among women to whom love could be accorded. He marks the beginning of the end of the golden age of the courtly lyric.

Walther was also a critic of the political abuses of the time. His most important experience in this area was the chaotic period in imperial politics between the death of Henry VI and the accession of Frederick II, the period of the supremacy of the papacy under Innocent III. Walther was a Hohenstaufen partisan and ascribed most of the ills of Germany to the ambition and greed of the popes. But he was also concerned with the moral degeneration of his time, the lack of discipline, moderation, and stability.

The courtly epic was a story of a great love, or of a quest for spiritual purification, or merely a tale of adventure. The materials were drawn from ancient sources, such as the deeds of Alexander the Great, the German migrations as in the *Nibelungenlied*, or the achievements of Charlemagne and his warriors. The most popular and most fanciful stories were of Celtic origin, dealing with King Arthur and the quests of his Knights of the Round Table. Many of the epics involved merely fantastic adventures of the knights rescuing maidens from the clutches of giants, ogres, witches, and sorcerers, who used all the weapons in the arsenal of magic. Their contemporary counterpart is science fiction.

In the *Parzival* of Wolfram von Eschenbach, the quest becomes much more than a search for adventure. Parzival seeks the Holy Grail, the symbol of spiritual knighthood. He seeks it with knightly valor, but he learns that only through penitence and humility can he become worthy. Wolfram thus places general Christian virtues above those of a particular social caste.

The whole movement of courtly culture in Germany reached its culmination virtually in one generation of poets who came to fruition around 1200. After that, the creative spirit ebbed, and only the conventional forms and aspirations of courtly society were given expression in poetry.

FRENCH GOTHIC: LOGIC OF STRUCTURE AND DYNAMIC OF SPACE

What is called Gothic art originated in the general neighborhood of Paris and attained its classic form there roughly in the period from the middle of the twelfth to the middle of the thirteenth century. In Germany, its influence was not decisive until after the middle decades of the thirteenth century. In the Gothic church, pointed arch, ribbed vaulting, flying buttresses, and clustered columns, already used in the Romanesque as isolated structural elements, are brought together in one great functional and dynamic totality. They serve to break up and disperse weight and thrust, thus dematerializing the wall and making way for enormous glass windows. While each architectural member plays its individual functional role, together they create a logical structure. Thus a dynamic equilibrium is created unlike the static massiveness of the Romanesque.

The Romanesque is mainly an expression of the *sacrum imperium*; in fact, some of the greatest monuments in Germany were associated with the names of the emperors. The very block-like massiveness of the Romanesque expressed the majesty and power of the Empire. The Gothic is a fusion of the rational outlook of the towns with the religious fervor of reform and crusade in which the attempt is made to discover in the edifice of faith its own inner dynamic of logic and spirit.

In the Gothic, space is so consciously molded and shaped as to assume an almost palpable character. In the Romanesque, the walls still dominate, closing one in. In the Gothic, the walls have disappeared, and the light streaming through the windows seems to unite inner and outer space. Space is no longer broken up as in the Romanesque, but is unified so that the eye is carried both upward to the soaring crown of the vault, and, following the movement of the arches, forward toward the altar.

Nature is no longer regarded as the locale of demonic forces. The Franciscan reverence for all natural forms as God's creation and as therefore good is manifest in the depiction of a profusion of plant and animal life. Grotesque fantasy and naive playfulness exist side by side with the representation of the learning of the great encyclopedias. What is presented is a mirror of the whole range of human existence from God on his heavenly throne down to the meanest creature that crawls on the surface of the earth.

HALLENKIRCHEN AND LATE GOTHIC SCULPTURE

German masters and artisans worked on the French cathedrals, at Amiens and Rheims, for example. The two outstanding German Gothic churches are those at Cologne and Strassburg. The former was directly influenced by Amiens. But while the French cathedral shows a classic restraint, its German counterpart reveals an over-ripeness, an over-accentuation of verticality on the outside.

The Gothic was a process of growth, an organic development of functional and spiritual possibilities, of new religious values and social needs. These possibilities reached their full medieval expression in the *Hallenkirchen* (hall churches), which began to appear toward the end of the thirteenth century but did not reach fruition until the fifteenth century. They were specifically parish churches built in cities and adapted to the new emphasis on preaching. They appeared first in northwest Germany; then they spread eastward into the colonial area, where they assumed their grandest form.

The *Hallenkirchen* mark a dissolution of the classic Gothic space composition, in fact, a decomposition of the traditional basilican form. The definite vertical and horizontal axes disappear. The side aisles are now integrated with the nave to constitute one great hall. Their ceilings are raised to the level of the central nave, and the central piers and columns no longer mark off dividing lines between nave and side aisles. Transepts and choir are also merged with the general area which now looks in all directions. Here we see the culmination of the Gothic drive toward the unification of space. But there is no longer the heavenward leaping and soaring spirit of the classic Gothic. The eye follows the horizontal unfolding of space in every direction and not just toward the altar. In the *Hallenkirchen* there is, therefore, the feeling of the community mystically bound together in worship.

We note a similar trend toward turning the eye inward when we examine the development of Gothic sculpture. The figures on the Romanesque façade gaze out into the empyrean in a kind of rapt wonder and awe as if a miracle had just taken place before their eyes. But the Gothic figures turn toward each other as if they were members of a festive company witnessing the coronation of the Virgin, or as if they were engaged in a serious disputation over the problems of faith. They acquire an inner life; they are no longer merely outward signs and symbols pointing to the divine and the demonic.

In the late Gothic, the figures also stand out from the building as if occupying a space of their own. They no longer merely accentuate the vertical lines of the skeletal structure. This growing independence of sculpture from architecture was not fully realized until the Renaissance.

In German sculpture of the first half of the thirteenth century, this tendency is also marked, especially in certain of the figures at Bamberg and Naumburg. The equestrian statue at Bamberg is not only an ideal representation of a knightly figure but the whole posture reveals that dynamic tension which characterizes the Gothic generally. He seems to have just leaped into the saddle and to be intent upon what is happening in the distance. Such presentation of a physical and psychological moment approaches the naturalism of the later Renaissance without sacrificing the spiritual idealism which characterizes the Gothic. The same polarity of naturalism and idealism is reflected in the figures of the founders in the choir at Naumburg. Each stands out almost like an individual portrait and expresses in his or her characteristic way the common concern with the tragic death in battle of one of their number. The massive monumentality of the group suggests, however, the Romanesque rather than the elegance of the Gothic.

ARISTOTLE AND THE INTELLECTUAL CRISIS AT PARIS

In the realm of thought the two centuries between 1150 and 1350 also reveal a fundamental transformation. Just as the Christian basilica was given a new dynamic form by the functional and spiritual logic of the Gothic, so Christian doctrine was revitalized by the infusion of Aristotelian metaphysics in scholasticism. Abelard and others in the early twelfth century had already turned from static dogma to the application of the logic of definition, thus sharpening the distinction between reason and faith. The great body of scientific and philosophic materials derived from ancient sources, which came into the West initially by way of Moslem intermediaries through Spain and southern Italy, provided a new stimulus. The most important core of this new knowledge was provided in the works of Aristotle, who had sought to bring all knowledge into one vast systematic whole.

It was not the new knowledge that disturbed the minds of men at the time so much as the totally inclusive and rationally consistent approach presented by the Aristotelian synthesis. Aristotle was interpreted through the Moslem philosopher, Averroës (d. 1198), who underscored the conception of a closed rational universe. In it man becomes a particle of the universal mind which is God, who is but the active principle revealed in the eternal cyclical round of nature. Averroës pointed out that certain conceptions derived from sacred writings—the divine personality, the personal immortality of man, and the concomitant notions of heaven and hell—must be discarded by the philosopher, however expedient it might be for *hoi polloi* to continue to believe in them.

Philosophy thus presented as synonymous with Aristotle divested itself completely of its earlier close relationship with theology. The ecclesiastical authorities naturally proceeded to condemn this philosophy taught by members of the liberal arts faculty at the newly organized University of Paris. The condemnation aroused a bitter controversy both over the question of the relationship of philosophy to theology and over the autonomy of the university. The intervention of the papacy brought a settlement. The popes succeeded eventually in introducing members of the Dominican and Franciscan orders into the theological faculty, who effected a reconcilation between Aristotelian philosophy and Christian theology.

The two Dominican scholars, the German Albertus Magnus and the Italian Thomas Aquinas, contributed most to this reconciliation. Both came from the lower nobility. Both taught at Paris: Albertus from 1245 to 1257, and Thomas from 1252 to 1259. Both then returned to their native lands. Thomas, Albert's pupil, surpassed his master in logical acumen but not in breadth of knowledge.

The whole question of Aristotelian philosophy raised the problem of the relative spheres of reason and faith. Thomas sought to show that they did not contradict each other, that each had a validity in its own particular realm, but that obviously faith had the higher function. In his great encyclopedic work, the *Summa Theologiae*, he sought to bring all knowledge into one harmonious hierarchical order. One is led by stages upward from the sensual-animal to the rational-human and beyond to the intuitive-mystical vision of the divine. Each stage flows into the next higher, but retains, at the same time, its own individual character. The significant feature of Thomism was not only the hierarchical structure it projected, but the mediating position it accorded to man between the worlds of nature and of grace or the supranatural. Thomas revealed, especially by way of the dynamic of dialectics or logic, the tension between these realms.

This great architectonic work, never completed, was really an elaborate Christian apologetic which meant to show that Christianity was the universal religion, the fulfillment of all ancient thought.

Albertus Magnus (d. 1280) had a synthesizing mind of a different quality; it was less logical—more intuitive and mystical. He is best known for his wide scientific learning, which included botany, chemistry, and physics. In his own day this knowledge rendered him somewhat suspect of being a magician. In Albertus' thinking, Aristotle was less important than the Neo-Platonic frame of thought, which was so influential throughout the medieval period.

Albertus was more inclined to look at the universe and man from above than from the middle position. The universe presented a vast and variegated pattern permeated by a creative divine spirit. This spirit could not really be known by the senses but only by a kind of intuitive perception of the creative forms which continually flowed from the spirit. The sense world had really, therefore, only a negative character. Here Albertus departs from Thomas, for whom the senses are, so to speak, the windows through which reason gets its materials for a knowledge of the universe.

GERMAN MYSTICISM: ECKHART

These ideas, with a different accent, assumed a much more definite form in the speculative mysticism of that other great German Dominican, Meister Eckhart (1260–1327). Eckhart was of noble descent; he became a teacher at Paris and then a provincial head of his order. Finally, he became a preacher and teacher at the Dominican school at Cologne. His speculative works in Latin present a frame of scholastic thought like that of Thomas and Albertus. But his sermons in German are suffused with the glowing vision of the mystic.

As a mystic Eckhart was not concerned with logical distinctions nor with an inclusive synthesis of all knowledge but with the quest for the divine within the soul. He has been called "the discoverer of the human soul." For him, the soul was not a substance but an activity whereby God is born within. The birth of God comes when the soul is completely emptied of any concern or attachment to external things, when it ceases to have any will of its own, and when a state of complete passivity and solitude is attained. Then the divine spark in the soul becomes a consuming flame and completely envelops it. He believed that the mystic should not merely retire into the inner solitude of the soul nor seek only obliteration of the self in ecstatic union. Both of these as ends in themselves may become forms of self-indulgence. The mystic must maintain the consciousness of tension between the soul looking outward and looking inward. The spark should also become the radiating center which casts its light all about the world and manifests there the creative divine principle now come to consciousness in the soul.

Eckhart thus moved the center of gravity of religion from the external institution of church and sacrament to the interior of the soul. The implication of all mysticism is that each individual can directly approach God. Institutions and dogmas have but a negative function: to lead one away from them to immediate union with God. The mystic is, of course, not a deliberate critic of ecclesiasticism and sacramentalism, but his emphasis on sheer inner spirituality leads him to a far more radical position than those who criticize the unworthiness of the lives of the clergy. It is not surprising that a number of passages from Eckhart's writings were declared heretical. He died the year before his official condemnation was issued.

This German mysticism led to a spiritualization of religion and often to an emphasis upon emotional experience, upon vision and ecstasy. This is especially evident in the writings of Eckhart's two followers, Seuss and Tauler, distinguished preachers both, especially Tauler. They made no important additions to Eckhart's thought but clothed his speculative mysticism in popular forms. Like Eckhart, they preached in the vernacular, thereby reaching many more people than the official clergy.

A great body of mystic poetry expressing the yearning of the human soul for union with the divine made its appearance in the fourteenth century. Since many of its creators were nuns of noble birth, it is not surprising that their mystic poetry reflected the romantic and chivalric motif of love for the unattainable one. The metaphors, expressing the longing for union with the divine, were often drawn from troubadour love poetry.

INNER AMBIGUITY OF GERMAN EASTERN AND WESTERN ORIENTATION

We discern in all these cultural movements centrifugal tendencies within the frame of Western Christendom. Once the papacy freed itself from the *sacrum imperium* and undermined its religious vitality, it was confronted by cultural forces which were also released from bondage and which, in their drive toward individual autonomy, could only with great difficulty be fitted into the sacramental-hier-archical frame.

These centrifugal tendencies were accentuated in the German situation. Even the eastward expansion, while originally undertaken as the German counterpart of the crusading movements in the Medi-terranean, created a different situation. The newly acquired areas were not far removed, as were the Latin states in the Holy Land, nor did they constitute a rounding out, as in the case of Spain, of na-tional religious frontiers.

While the German colonial acquisitions were, on the one hand, an extension of the homeland, they were also a possible springboard for further conquests. This ambiguous situation of the eastern border-lands has particularly plagued the Germans during the last century. The American westward movement finally rounded out the frontiers and became a historic matter, but to the German, eastward expansion remained an ever-present challenge. Two solutions recently pro-jected indicate the intensity of the challenge: one, that of Hitler, proposed total conquest of the whole area to the east; the other, currently suggested, would give up the entire colonial area and with it the German mission to the east.

To the west the German encountered the French classic and rational embodiment of the Latin tradition. The German took over courtly culture, Gothic art, and scholasticism after these had already passed their zenith in France, which may explain the German re-action in principle against "rigid form and pure style" and the tendency to accentuate individuality and subjectivity in the French derivations, not only in this instance but in succeeding centuries.[4]

While the French classic expressions sought an architectonic synthesis, the German stressed the tension of polarities by shifting them to the realm of the subjective. For the German the center of gravity was no longer society as a body of conventions whose mo-tive power is courtly love, nor the church edifice as a spatial arrange-ment directed toward the most exalted devotion, nor philosophy as a dialectic whereby one rises to the contemplation of the highest truth. The German looked inward from these objective frames upon the experience of love rising to spiritual exaltation, upon the feeling of communal mystical fellowship in the House of the Lord and upon the eye turning inward to the soul to discover the divine spark.

Such German orientations eastward and westward—the former directed toward expansion and conquest, the latter toward reception and subjective experience—explain the great emphasis laid upon polarity in German thinking. Unlike the Frenchman, the German had no fixed inner center from which to view man and the world. Therefore his development did not take place within a traditionally accepted mold but in terms of a continuous tension growing out of a middle position facing two cultural fronts.

III

The Quest for Religious Immediacy and Cultural Autonomy

*W*estern Christendom from 1350 to 1450 submitted to a series of internal shocks and disturbances whose collective effects are difficult to assess. These major catastrophes included a great plague, the Black Death (1347–1350); the great schism in the church (1378–1415); such devastating wars as the Hundred Years' War between France and England; the Hussite Wars in central Europe; and, finally, a whole series of social revolts in town and country, especially during the last half of the fourteenth century. The impact of these events brought about fundamental changes, apparently less so in political and social forms—at least in the Germanies—than in religious mood and intellectual orientation.

THE BLACK DEATH AND THE DISLOCATION OF SOCIETY

The Black Death, a bubonic plague carried by rats and lice, spread from Asia by way of the Mediterranean seaports through Italy northward and westward along the trade routes. Approximately one-third to one-half of the population of northern and western Europe was wiped out. Two-thirds of the students at Oxford were casualties. The plague's impact was sporadic: some areas were completely depopulated, others suffered hardly at all. But both high and low seem to have suffered equally.

As with most major catastrophes, historians have been inclined to minimize the direct effects of the Black Death in arguing that most of the dislocations attributed to it were but evidences of fundamental transformations long in process of development. At most the catastrophe accelerated such transformations as the cessation of rapid population growth, the drift from country to town, the turning to extra-sacramental forms of religiosity, and the general mood of pessimism and resignation. These, it is argued, are symptoms characteristic of a society and culture which has passed its zenith and is entering a decadent phase.

Here the Black Death will be regarded as both a cause and a symptom of basic changes during a period of transition. In any case, its impact was apparently more virulent in the coastal areas than in the central European interior. But again we are dealing with that area as part of Western Christendom and not as an isolated national unit of Europe. Europe as a family of self-sufficient nations was coming into being in the period dealt with here from 1350 to about 1600 but didn't really crystallize until later.

Famines were endemic during the Middle Ages, when grain production was the basis of subsistence agriculture and the main source of food supply. Bad harvests proved particularly disastrous; there were few garden vegetables to supplement the cereal diet, and the transportation of grain from areas of abundance to those of scarcity was difficult. The series of bad harvests and consequent famines during the 1340's probably accelerated the catastrophic sweep of the plague by reducing physical resistance to its ravages.

The population increase had led to congestion within the restricting ring of the town walls, leading to the elimination of open spaces and, of course, creating the crowded conditions in which the plague flourished. It should be noted that most towns throughout the fourteenth and fifteenth centuries were compelled to extend their control over the neighboring countryside, both to ensure an adequate food supply and to include those suburbs which had been formed beyond the old walls.

The immediate effect of the population loss was more goods for fewer people. Prices, which had been rising previously with the growing population, declined precipitously. The drop was marked especially in agricultural products. In time, low prices caused a shrinkage of the area of tilled land. Land formerly brought under cultivation in the movement of inner colonization returned to wilderness while the greatly increased wealth of the surviving population promoted more extravagant living. Then, too, the plague had demonstrated that life might be short, and this prospect stimulated the consumption of luxury goods, which thus increased the members of the artisan class who produced these goods. A drift to the towns was also encouraged by the greater freedom and better living conditions prevailing in the urban centers.[1]

During the next three or more centuries, the rural classes—the peasantry and the nobility—showed a decided economic decline relative to the towns. The nobility were especially hit by the operations of the economic process. Rents were generally fixed by custom, agricultural prices declined, and manufactured goods rose steeply in price. The nobility naturally sought to increase the dues and exactions from the peasants, who retaliated by flight to the towns, or, in desperation, by periodic revolts.

This general economic and social dislocation was accompanied by a degradation of morals and manners. Both in ecclesiastical and political life offices suddenly vacated by wholesale deaths had to be filled by the often inadequate human material that remained. As a result a class of parvenus emerged. Adventurers and speculators came to the fore with the rapid fluctuations in social and economic life. The consequent lowering of the tone of social life was evident in the highly ornate and often bizarre costume of the upper classes, in exaggerated pose and gesture, in brutality and cruelty combined with effeminacy of manner, and in the profession of high-flown chivalrous ideals.[2]

The increasing congestion of population within the town walls naturally made townsmen not only easy victims of plague and epidemic but rendered them susceptible to anti-Semitic sentiment and the hysterical preaching of religious visionaries and quacks who predicted the end of the world and the coming of the anti-Christ. Waves of religious hysteria comparable to those of the eleventh century—only now not directed toward reform and crusade—swept over the mass of the population. Processions of flagellants, beating each other's backs to the raw, moved from city to city. Both brutish indulgence and the most ecstatic asceticism were characteristic of the period. Fear of death and of the catastrophic end of the world seemed to lie like a miasmic blanket over the minds of men.

THE GREAT SCHISM AND THE DEMORALIZATION OF RELIGIOUS LIFE

This overwrought state of mind was further perturbed by the great schism in the church which began in 1378. This schism arose out of a conflict between the Italian Pope Urban VI (1378–1389) and the large French faction in the College of Cardinals. Because the French resented the transfer of the papal residence from Avignon back to Rome and Urban's proposal to introduce reforms and Italianize the College, they proceeded to elect another pope, Clement VII (1378–1394), who continued to reside at Avignon. As each pope sought to build up as wide an obedience as he could, the schism at the top reached down to the parish church.

The emergence of national monarchies in which rulers tended to appeal to popular sentiment and which, moreover, exercised some control over ecclesiastical affairs, prevented outright anarchy in the church. Yet political rivalries also prevented rulers from getting together to end the division. The French king supported the Avignon pope and carried with him most of the clergy and people within his realm. The reaction in the Germanies was mixed: the emperor and many of the princes supported the Roman pope; but there were in each area, particularly in the borderlands, both regional and factional conflicts over the question of allegiance. The papacy ceased, at least for the time, to be a unifying axis of Western Christendom.

Religious life was thoroughly demoralized. The popes resorted to mutual excommunication and interdict against rival obediences. As a result the sacraments performed were called in question. The disturbance in the minds of believers undoubtedly contributed to an increasing interest in extra-sacramental means of securing divine favor, from mystic union to veneration of miracle-working relics.

The schism also made it impossible to unite Christendom in a crusade in the Balkans against the menace of the Ottoman Turks. It is surprising how popes and emperors and many learned men, in this age of waning medieval enthusiasms, clung to the idea of uniting Christendom again—not so much, it is true, to recover the Holy Land as to safeguard bastions of Christendom to the east. The threat that the Turks would conquer the last fragments of the Byzantine Empire, including Constantinople, brought forth constant cries of alarm in the west and served to allay greatly the old hostility toward the Eastern Christians.

An even more important consideration was the Hussite movement in Bohemia. Here a national religious movement, spearheaded by John Hus, a professor at the University of Prague, threatened not only the unity of the church but also the German position in the borderlands, where Slav and German had come to live under the same political and religious roof.

THE CONCILIAR MOVEMENT AND THE FAILURE OF REFORM

Since neither of the two popes would give up his office, and the two Colleges of Cardinals continued to elect popes, there seemed no way out but to return to the ancient idea of the general church council as the means of healing the schism. The chief promoters of this idea were professors at the University of Paris, which numbered among its faculty and students representatives of all the peoples of Christendom. The University thus came to occupy an ecumenical position capable of voicing the opinion of Christendom, in view of the virtual abdication of emperor and pope.

After the abortive Council of Pisa (1409), which merely added a third pope, the Council of Constance (1414–1418) succeeded in ending the schism. However, the Council of Constance disappointed those who aimed at pervasive reforms which would bring about a rebirth and regeneration of Christendom. After much debate and even more backstairs politics, the Council put the problem of ending the papal schism before the problem of reform. The existing triad of popes were either deposed, induced to resign, or isolated and ignored. A new pope, Martin V (1417–1431), was elected by the College of Cardinals. He immediately proceeded to sabotage reform efforts and dissolved the Council.

In the course of its proceedings, the Council adopted two resolutions: one asserting the superiority of Council over pope; the other providing for the meeting of general councils at regular intervals. These actions seemed to imply the setting up of what in modern times might be called a parliamentary organization in the church as against the centuries-long development of papal absolutism. But, had these resolutions succeeded, they might have come closer to setting up the rule of an oligarchy of great bishops, not unlike the princely oligarchy in the *Reich*.

No pope could accept what would, from the point of view of the tradition of the Roman Catholic Church, introduce an even worse source of division than the schism. Acceptance would have meant a return to the theological quarrels and struggles for power which had characterized an early phase of church history. To overcome such quarrels, Catholicism had, in the course of centuries, moved toward the unification of faith and discipline in the spiritual authority of the papacy. It is not surprising, therefore, that Martin V, in dissolving the Council, declared it to be contrary to the faith to appeal to a council over the head of the pope.

Perhaps the most important obstacle to reform was the rising distrust between the "nations" whose representatives had gathered at Constance. The Council was organized into "nations" on the plan of the University of Paris, principally to avoid dominance by the Italians. These "nations" did not as yet conform to their modern successors. The German nation, for example, included the Scandinavian peoples. But the fact that the Council voted according to such groupings of peoples is indicative of an emerging national sentiment. Italian and German merchants were encountering an increasing anti-foreign sentiment during the fifteenth century in their commercial operations in England and France. There was also widespread complaint in the *Reich* over the influx of Italians into church positions, particularly on the upper levels of the German ecclesiastical hierarchy.

The most obvious national trend in religious affairs was the increasing practice of rulers, especially in the seaboard countries, to restrict papal appointments and taxation within the country.

THE HUSSITE REVOLT AND CHRISTIAN COMMUNISM

The Council of Constance had taken up the problem of heresy in a manner hardly calculated to deal with its fundamental causes. It proceeded to a policy of forcible suppression. It condemned the ideas of Wycliffe; it burned Hus and his associate, Jerome of Prague, at the stake in 1415. Hus had come to the Council of his own volition, filled with burning zeal to convert the learned fathers to his way of thinking. He also came under a safe-conduct, granted from the emperor. His execution let loose in Bohemia a storm of rebellion, which threatened not only to drive Bohemia out of the *Reich,* but, in its more radical phase, to arouse the whole of central Europe into one vast peasant revolt.

The Hussite movement went through several phases. Hus criticized the conception of the indelible sacramental character of the ecclesiastical hierarchy; he placed emphasis on the preaching of the Scripture as the chief task of the clergy, who were to be distinguished by moral and religious zeal. These notions were not particularly new; in fact, most of Hus's ideas were taken over bodily from Wycliffe. In Bohemia, they had an explosive effect because they were directed against the upper clergy, most of whom were German. Hus himself was filled with the "conscious pride" of being a Slav and of belonging to a "holy people." The religious regeneration of Slavdom as opposed to the corruption and degeneration of the German imperial church was to become in a secularized form the basis of the Pan-Slavism of the nineteenth century, of which the Czechs were initially the chief promoters.

The burning of Hus drove the movement to extremes. The radicals came mainly from the lower orders of the population, especially from the peasantry. They founded a new city on a high mount in south Bohemia, which they called Tabor. Here they gathered by the thousands to establish that kingdom, foretold in Revelations, which would inaugurate the thousand-year period of preparation for the second coming of Christ. During this period, it was the divinely appointed mission of the Taborites to purify the world with fire and sword. Once this was accomplished, Christ would come and establish His empire, in which there would be neither rulers nor subjects, neither dues nor taxes, neither priests nor sacraments. Even the Scriptures would be superfluous since the Gospel ethic of love would be written in each heart.

The elimination of all social distinctions, an idea based upon the "freedom of the gospel," was perhaps the chief ideological force among the Taborites. Peasant and burgher sold their goods; on Mount Tabor they "held all things in common."

This Christian communism drove the Taborite masses like a storm over Bohemia, leaving behind them ravaged castles, churches, and monasteries. Pope Martin V called Christendom to a crusade, but every army led against the Taborites suffered ignominious defeat. Great military leaders, first the blind Ziska and then the priest Procop, developed new military tactics, as had the Swiss. Their armored wagons, carrying goods and warriors, gave them mobility and protected them against the onslaughts of horsemen.

The momentum of the Hussite movement carried it beyond the borders of Bohemia into the central and northern regions of the *Reich*. Hussite raids, extending as far north as the Baltic, left destruction in their wake and threatened to raise the whole countryside against lord and bishop.

But the very social radicalism which gave the movement its chief *élan* turned noble and burgher against it, split the movement, and, ultimately, defeated it. The Council of Basel (1431–1449) arranged an agreement with the conservative wing, comprised mainly of the upper classes, in the Compact of Prague (1433), whereby certain concessions were made to the Hussites in such matters as the cup for the laity, in return for which Bohemia would return to the bosom of the church.

The radical Taborites suffered a catastrophic defeat the following year at the hands of the conservatives and then disintegrated. Among the fragments, a pacifist trend developed which culminated in the small sectarian group known as the Bohemian Brethren, whose members turned inward toward the development of a mystical piety.

By being linked with social revolution, the idea of evangelical poverty came to signify heretical subversiveness against both church and state. Henceforth the expectation of the heavenly kingdom was definitely associated in the minds of the ruling powers with the forcible establishment of a new economic and social order. So, these hopes of reform were driven underground, but they were kept alive, to break through violently in the sixteenth century.

POPULAR RELIGIOSITY AND MYSTICAL DEVOTION

The prevailing religious mood of the later Middle Ages was one of the fear of death and judgment. In its more gruesome and morbid aspects, the fear is evident in the representation of diverse forms of death, from agonized suffering and putrefaction to decomposition. The numerous wars, plagues, and other natural catastrophies were regarded as signs of the approaching end. The world had grown old and was approaching its apocalytic consummation.

The preoccupation with death and judgment has been explained by some historians as deriving from the discipline of the church, which, in the interest of promoting its sacramental means of salvation, had increasingly minimized the joyous coming of the "Kingdom." As faith in salvation declined in the crises of schism and heresy, fear of death and judgment was naturally enhanced. Consequently, people turned to such extra-sacramental means as relics, pilgrimages, and strange religious nostrums. The crisis in religious mood which emerged went hand in hand with the crisis in religious and political organization, and was reflected first of all in mass emotionalism and hysteria.

At Nikolashausen in 1476, the preaching of a simple swineherd brought thousands to worship at the shrine of the Virgin because, as he contended, only there could they secure absolution from their sins. He preached that all things were to be held in common and that the world would soon come to an end. Priests were to be killed since they no longer held power from God. He exhorted the people to do away with luxuries and ornaments in dress and return to an early simplicity and sobriety. Bits of his clothing were snatched by those who regarded him as an inspired prophet. He was finally taken into custody by the Bishop of Würzburg, and thousands marched on the castle demanding his freedom. This multitude was dispersed, many were killed, and the Piper of Nikolashausen, as the swineherd came to be called, was burned at the stake.

This incident embodies the chief features of late medieval religious emotionalism on the popular level. In it and in similar episodes we find expressed the resentment against priests, the prophecy of the imminent end of this order of things, and the yearning for a return to the simplicity of the early Christian community, when it was assumed that all things were held in common. These same elements existed in the Taborite movement, and they appear again in the great revolt of 1525. It took such vast social upheavals to bring them to the fore.

In contrast to this popular religiosity is the movement of *devotio moderna,* which had its beginning in the latter part of the fourteenth century in the small community of Deventer in the Netherlands. Here a lay preacher, of which there were many at the time, gathered about him a number of friends and disciples who took no vows but lived in accordance with the spirit of the Sermon on the Mount. Other communities of the Brethren of the Common Life, as these disciples were called, appeared in the Netherlands and spread down the Rhine. The Brothers maintained themselves by various kinds of labor, principally by the ancient monastic practice of copying manuscripts. In time they came to be best known for the schools they established on the level of what we would call secondary education. Nicholas of Cues, Erasmus, and Luther, among many other leaders, received their early education in the schools of the Brethren of the Common Life.

The piety of the Brethren was distinguished by its sober common-sense character; its practical moderation was eminently suited to the burghers of the towns. Lacking both the visionary flight of Eckhart and the hysteria of popular religiosity, it brought mysticism down from the clouds of ecstatic tension and union to a kind of simple and quiet inner devotion. This devotion was best expressed in the famous work, *The Imitation of Christ,* ascribed to one of the Brethren, Thomas à Kempis, a work which, in the centuries that followed, became second only to the Bible as a source of religious piety. This form of piety appealed to both Protestant and Catholic because of its non-dogmatic and non-institutional character. It desired only to return to the original simplicity of the gospel message as a norm for individual conduct. There were no social revolutionary implications in this piety.

Characteristic in general of later medieval piety was the pictorial and dramatic presentation of episodes and incidents in the life of Christ. He now came down to earth to share the ordinary joys and sufferings of men. We even see Him as a boy playing pranks on his rather stupid father, Joseph. The consequence was a certain trivialization of sacred matters.

Both in this kind of realistic presentation and in the mystic sentimentalization of the Christ-image by the *devotio moderna*, the tendency was to lose sight of the distinction between the sacred and the profane. Late medieval religiosity sought to feel concretely in the here and now both the bliss of heaven and the agony of hell. Consequently, the religious atmosphere became surcharged with an explosive emotionalism. It was the spark of a great religious personality, Luther, which eventually ignited this combustible mass.

CUES AND THE COINCIDENCE OF OPPOSITES

Nicholas of Cues (1401–1464) illustrates yet a third and related religious tendency of the time. The son of a poor fisherman, through the aid of a patron he was able to attend the school of the Brethren of the Common Life at Deventer and the Universities of Padua and Heidelberg. Padua was a chief center of mathematical and scientific interests; Heidelberg was preoccupied with theological studies. At the Council of Basel, Cues at first sided with the conciliar party; then he became a papal partisan as the Council proceeded to attack the very foundations of the Roman Catholic edifice. The confidant and friend of a number of popes, Cues was made a cardinal, and he died as Bishop of Brixen.

The guiding motif in his life was his concern for the unity of Christian society. Christendom included for him not only the West but all of humanity, which was to be brought into the Christian fold.

Unity, he thought, demanded a single head and not a plurality, as the extremist group at Basel advocated. But in neither the church nor the empire was he an advocate of absolutism in the sense of a dictatorial one-man rule. Pope and emperor were the coordinate heads of an organic body comprising many parts, each of which had its own peculiar role and function in that body. What Cues actually wanted was a return to the *sacrum imperium* of the time of the Saxon emperors. Then pope and emperor were united in the headship of a unified Christendom in which the secular (temporal) could not be distinguished from the spiritual (eternal).

Both as papal legate in Germany and Bishop of Brixen in the Tyrol, Cues was an indefatigable worker for the reform of abuses in the church. He held that all its moribund or diseased organs must be restored to activity and health in order that they might assume their proper role, along with the head, as vehicles of the unifying sacred force.

Cues sought to return to the *sacrum imperium* by a way of thinking which was radical and yet was an extension of that mode of thought we have encountered in Albertus Magnus and Meister Eckhart. He did not appeal to authority but to the creative, synthetic role of the mind.

Cues tells us that it was on a sea voyage returning from Constantinople to Rome that he arrived at his basic idea of how the one and the many were to be brought into harmony through the coincidence of opposites. He went to Constantinople as a papal envoy to invite Greek Orthodox attendance at a church council in order to bring an end to the great schism between East and West in Christendom.

In his temper of mind he resembled Leibniz, whose ecumenical universalism and unitary philosophy were anticipated by Cues. The main concern of these uniquely German thinkers was not with a method by which to arrive at objective truth but with the quest for a dynamic inwardness as the basis of a unitary conception of man and the world. This search had its starting point in the mystical speculation of Eckhart, to whom Cues was greatly indebted.

The philosophy of the fifteenth century manifested the same turmoil that we have encountered in the religious, political, and social life of the time. Since the middle of the fourteenth century a number of universities, most of them founded by princes, had been established in Germany. In these, the full fury of the conflicts of philosophical schools and sects so characteristic of late medieval intellectual life broke forth. Each of the factions, the Thomists, the Occamists, the Averroists, and the Scotists, claimed to possess the one invaluable method of arriving at the truth.

Cues, like all medieval philosophers, was indebted in some measure to the schools of ancient thought. These philosophers were concerned with drawing on the whole arsenal of that thought to demonstrate that Christianity was the truly universal religion. They were convinced that the thought of the Greeks and Romans had been moving steadily toward a fulfillment, which in its late phases—for example, in Stoicism and Neo-Platonism—might serve the true faith. The great scholastic philosophers, and Cues too, thought of themselves as bringing this mission to fruition.

But Cues transcended the medieval schools. He sought a new synthesis in the idea that God is the completely *other than*, not to be understood either by logical definition or by an accumulation of empirical knowledge of his creation, the universe. Cues questioned the way of knowing as well as the adequacy of the knowledge which could be provided.

Knowledge in general, according to Cues, rests upon three bases, each of which presents an ascending competence. First and lowest, there is observation; but this merely gives approximations, never completeness. Second, logic merely makes distinctions between truth and nontruth and thus emphasizes contradiction rather than harmony. There is finally the method of the union of opposites, which Cues owed to Eckhart.

Most of the medieval philosophers, particularly St. Thomas, had been mainly concerned with how far reason could go in making God's ways comprehensible to man. This view assumed that reason is only a logical instrument which makes distinctions, such as the basic one between God and the universe. God is the one and the universe the many. How can the many proceed from the one? How can the variety and individuality of form in the universe be reconciled with the oneness of the absolute?

Cues began with the proposition that God as the absolute must contain the greatest as well as the smallest. He is the union, therefore, of opposites. Mathematics reveals how this is possible. The segment of a circle indefinitely extended becomes one with the radius; similarly, a point extended becomes a line. The triangle, when completely flattened or closed, becomes a straight line. All things therefore are merely gradations between extremes, which in turn are mere gradations. There is no absolute position. The earth cannot be the absolute center, as the Ptolemaic conception assumed; there must be many centers. Cues thus anticipates Copernicus.

Cues's relativism marks the breakdown of the hierarchical conception of earlier scholastic thinking. He recognized the individuality of each thing by virtue of the fact that it has its own independent position and is not merely an approximation to one absolute center or point. God created everything at once, or, what is equally true, has never ceased creating. Creation, therefore, did not take place in a series of stages whereby degrees of dependence are implied.

One is struck by the suggestive character and profound implications of the thought of this ecclesiastical statesman, who spent a lifetime trying to uphold the unity of the church with its apex in the papacy. He sought to give a new intellectual validity to old values and institutions, but in doing so, he threatened to burst the limits of the sacerdotal order, which made all kinds of sharp distinctions, such as that between reason and revelation and between grace and nature (in spite of the Thomist sacerdotal ladder). Thus, a definite line of demarcation had been maintained between the realms of the supranatural and the natural. For Cues, however, reason and revelation were not opposites but became one at their extremes and not by any mystical ecstatic leap when reason had reached the end of its tether. In his philosophy the universe is a continual process of creation. Man, in becoming conscious of creation, comes to participate in it. The role of reason is not, therefore, to provide a method for buttressing dogma but to become conscious of itself as revelation. On the highest speculative, intuitive level a fusion of reason and revelation is attained.

In all three manifestations of late medieval religiosity, there was a common tendency to seek support outside of, or at least on the very periphery of, the hierarchical-sacramental order. Revelation was either interpreted to mean the vision of a new kingdom of the community of goods and the end of authority; or as the turning inward to find the image of Jesus in one's soul; or again as the awareness that the unity and diversity of the cosmos as a whole are reproduced in the smallest particle. The same tendency was reflected in the increasing prominence of the secondary order of religious worship represented by, for example, the veneration of saints and relics and the going on pilgrimages. Both the emphasis on subjective piety and on the externals of devotion revealed centrifugal tendencies away from the hierarchical-sacramental order but not away from the church.[3]

CORPORATIVE AND CLASS CONSCIOUSNESS

As the vitality of the universal powers of church and empire declined, men increasingly sought security within corporate and local groups. The later Middle Ages were especially prolific in the creation of associations, leagues, and corporations, which reflected not only class and occupational interests but also political and religious purposes. The church came to be regarded as the community of believers divided into various nations; the *Reich* was regarded as the organic totality of corporate entities, extending from the top of the social scale to the bottom. A most significant consequence was the juxtaposition, in the minds of many people, of papacy against church and emperor against *Reich*.

While the theory of a functionally organized society in the various estates, clergy, nobility, and burghers was maintained, actually the drift toward corporate organization contributed to the demarcation of class lines. There was an increasing tension not only *between* social groups, that is, between clergy, nobles, and burghers, but also *within* each of these—between upper and lower clergy, between princes and nobles, and between masters and journeymen.

The peasant was becoming self-conscious for the first time in Western history. In the literature of the period peasants were shown as overcoming their burgher and noble competitors by shrewdness and wit. Even the upper classes idealized the simplicity and naturalness of the life of the peasant; yet, at the same time, they also regarded him as a dumb brute who often broke out in terrible rages and went berserk in violent uprisings.

In spite of the cleavages between noble, burgher, and peasant, toward the end of the fifteenth century the lines of demarcation as to mode of life were becoming somewhat blurred. This tendency was evident in the uniformity of dress and in the burgher's enthusiastic interest in jousts and tournaments. Much of the lower population of the towns was recruited from the countryside. Because of poverty many knights lived much like peasants, yet the sons of peasants were "making good" in the wars and rising to noble rank. Such changes may be attributed in part to divisions which developed within each social group, leading to the crumbling of the outer class boundaries.

Since the decline of royal power and the victory of a princely oligarchy had brought with it the virtual exclusion of knights, peasantry, and townsmen from a role in imperial affairs, it is not surprising that these groups looked in varying ways to the restoration of the imperial power in the person of a great messianic emperor.

In the peasant mind there had long existed the image of a messianic emperor who would shortly come riding out of the Black Forest on a white horse and make all things right. Originally associated with Frederick II, in the fifteenth century the legend was transferred to Frederick Barbarossa, who then also came to be represented as sitting in the Kyffhäuser Mountains, awaiting the call of his people for deliverance. These messianic hopes must be viewed in the context of the prevailing prophecies of the approaching end of the world and the coming of the anti-Christ. A messianic emperor and a papal anti-Christ became increasingly sharply defined in the folk mind. Astrology, very popular among the educated and ruling classes, also contributed to such forebodings. Especially influential were the prognostications of Johann Lichtenberger, the astrologer of Emperor Frederick III, whose prophecies Luther later republished.

MAXIMILIAN AND THE NEW "EUROPE"

Under Maximilian (1493–1519), the power and prestige of the imperial crown were revived. Maximilian reflected the sharp contrasts of his age. He combined an interest in humanism and power politics with a pious devotion to miracle-working images and relics.

He surrounded himself with scholars and artists who were imbued with the current enthusiasm for the culture of the ancient Greeks and Romans; at the same time, he collected German folk poetry and song and initiated a great project for a German literary museum. In politics he mixed romantic imperial ideas with realistic dynastic interests. Many of his projects bordered on the fantastic: for example, the proposal to have himself made pope and thus combine the imperial and papal offices. One such plan had hardly been inaugurated when another was pushed forward; hence very few were carried to completion. This restless pursuit of often divergent aims and purposes may be ascribed in part to his temperament and the exuberant vitality of his times, in part to the multiplicity of problems presented by the mere dynastic union of the various territories he held—a situation which always plagued the Hapsburgs.

While Maximilian may have thought of himself as standing in the shoes of the Hohenstaufens in his intervention in Italy, actually the *Reich* was now but one political rival among a number of others. It might be argued that the *Reich* was not involved, that Maximilian represented only the imperial ambitions of the house of Hapsburg. Even the war against the Turks was in general regarded as a local struggle over Hungary, involving only the dynastic interests of the Hapsburgs, in spite of their attempt, combined with the Venetians and the papacy, to make out of it a crusade in behalf of Christendom. The French kings, who called themselves "the most Christian kings," entered into alliances with the Sultan against the Hapsburgs. The conception of a universal Christendom arrayed against the infidel world was definitely on the wane.

A new ecumene which the humanists called "Europe" was now arising on the basis of a complex of power entities; its gaze increasingly turned toward the great Western seas. The word "Europe" was, of course, not new; it was used by the ancients and revived in the time of Charlemagne. But it had passed out of use with the Western crusade against the East. Now again it came into use to designate a secular community characterized by a sense of the autonomy of political, economic, religious, and cultural spheres and the boundless creativity of man.

The new geographical orientation and the feeling of individual autonomy are also apparent in the economic life at the turn into the sixteenth century. The opening of overseas routes to the Far East, the discovery of new continents to the west, and the appearance of the great capitalist entreprenuer, in time, brought about a basic change in Western society. The chief centers of commerce shifted from the Mediterranean, where the Italian cities had played a pivotal role, to the western seaboard countries, Portugal, Spain, the Netherlands, France, and England. The economic individualist broke the medieval order. He was no longer concerned primarily with maintaining a traditional way of life nor even with mere money-making; rather he was interested in the same "adventure of risk, success, and power" which also excited the contemporary explorer and scientist.

Although the Italian trade centers suffered from the shift in trade routes in the early sixteenth century, the German cities then reached a peak of economic prosperity not to be duplicated again until the end of the nineteenth century. Both periods were of brief duration, having a boom-like character.

JAKOB FUGGER AND THE NEW TECHNOLOGY

The prosperity of the sixteenth century rose out of the circumstance that the German cities had become the centers of a European network of trade routes. No longer a peripheral area looking out upon backward colonial regions, the central and eastern portions of the *Reich* had become a transit region between the Mediterranean and the north, and between the Baltic and North Sea centers. The Hansa cities may have largely lost their political importance as a league, but the economic prosperity of such cities as Hamburg, Lübeck, and Danzig continued to the middle of the sixteenth century. Cologne on the Rhine and Frankfort-on-the-Main were also chief centers of exchange. But it was the south German cities, facing the passes of the Alps into Italy and connecting links with the north, which played the chief role. In these appeared the great merchant dynasties of the Fuggers, Welsers, and Höchstetters. The territorial states had not as yet established princely control over commerce and industry, so there was, except for the hazards of banditry, comparative freedom of trade.

In these south German cities the pure type of capitalist also emerged. Jakob Fugger (1459–1525), the real founder of the family wealth and power, upon being asked when he expected to settle down and enjoy his wealth, replied that he hoped to engage in business and accumulate wealth as long as he lived. He took no interest in political affairs except where they affected the price of commodities or the security of loans. He developed no real roots in his native Augsburg. When the city was threatened with siege, he was ready to pack up and move out for good, demonstrating the international character and mobility of wealth. The Fuggers had branches in the main European cities, any of which might serve as headquarters. Jakob promoted a model housing project for workers, which may still be seen in Augsburg, but he showed little interest in the patronage of the arts. He acquired an estate and a title of nobility, but again largely to augment his business prestige.

The great merchant now rarely accompanied his goods on its way to the distant market. He conducted his affairs from his office, hired conductors to guide transports, and employed factors to supervise trading posts. By the fifteenth century such specialization led to the keeping of accounts in writing. Double-entry bookkeeping, and, of course, the use of arabic numbers proved indispensable to this increasing emphasis on rational calculation in matters of trade. Thus the south German merchant's business was becoming an independent entity like the state; it was beginning to be regarded as independent of the person of the merchant entrepreneur.

The wealth of the Fugger family partnership had been originally accumulated in trade, but the real gains came from mining and banking, which supplemented each other. In the fifteenth century, mining was stimulated by the increased demand for iron to provide guns and cannon and by the demand of kings and princes for gold and silver to meet the increasing expenses of war, court, and administration. The mining boom was made possible by the new technics developed for sinking shafts and pumping water, the availability of large amounts of capital, and the new business methods.

Except for printing, the most important technical advances of the fifteenth and sixteenth centuries were probably made in mining and metallurgy. In both the Germanies played a leading role. Mining was peculiarly susceptible to capitalistic enterprise. Its hazards and uncertainties, the risks entailed in having the mine run out, all placed a premium on having considerable capital reserve.

The technological revolution of this period is usually associated with developments in printing, navigation, and warfare. The development of movable type, paper, and printer's ink, the improvement of compass and astrolabe, and the use of gunpowder in small arms and cannon played an important role in the development of what today would be called industrial capitalism. None of these was subject to gild regulations. Printing became a capitalistic industry after Gutenberg of Mainz developed the use of movable type in the 1440's. By 1500 there were already about a thousand presses in operation in western Europe. In Nuremburg individual printing establishments employed as many as a hundred workers.

Another important technological advance lay in the expansion and utilization of power, in the more adequate use of wind and water power, or, for that matter, animal and human power, for such purposes as beating hides, sawing wood, spinning yarn, and crushing ore. The use of the bucket line, revolving on an endless chain for lifting water out of mines, anticipated many later developments.

More important than inventions in themselves was the writing down of descriptions of technical processes. In the past this type of knowledge had been passed on from master to apprentice in workshops; innovations were carefully guarded secrets which were sometimes lost to posterity with the death of an individual master. Some of the first technical treatises published dealt with building. Mining and metallurgy also received great attention, culminating in the comprehensive work of *De re mettalica libri XII* by Georg Agricola (d. 1555).

Most of the early works were merely descriptive of the rule-of-thumb methods employed. Essentially, they were recipe books which incorporated very little theory. The beginning of a theoretical approach may be found in the drawings of Leonardo da Vinci and in the work of his German contemporary and counterpart, Albrecht Dürer. Technology, science, and art had a mutual fructifying influence for these artist-scientist technicians. In his drawings Leonardo anticipated the modern blueprint. The pictorial and graphic repre-

Albrecht Dürer, St. Ambrose in Study, 1514

Albrecht Dürer, Melancholia, 1514

sentation of the phenomena of nature and of man's fabrications now underwent an extraordinary development.

ALBRECHT DÜRER AND THE NEW ARTISTIC EXPRESSION

Seen also in the art of the period is the tendency toward autonomy. Painting and sculpture became independent of architecture, and art was no longer regarded as exclusively concerned with communicating religious values. As the building of churches declined after the middle of the fourteenth century, painting and sculpture developed their own peculiar technics. Of course, the decoration of the walls and the altars of churches continued to be a main staple of artistic production. But the new development of easel painting provided a more flexible medium of artistic expression suited to middle class interests and needs in the decoration of the home. The artist moved out of the mason's hut attached to the church building and into the workshop and studio, where he worked on commission from wealthy burghers.

Painting became concerned with expressing the interests and moods of a particular individual, with portraying man in a particular space-time situation. Man's environment was presented not symbolically but as a landscape enveloped in an atmosphere. Although religious subjects continued to predominate, the personages portrayed were frequently contemporaries.

A most important distinction between form and content appeared. The technical expression became wholly independent of the subject matter; it could be used to portray equally well the family of a prominent burgher or the holy family. This independence of art from religion marked one of the most important transitions to modern culture.

The artists of the Low Countries, beginning with Hubert and Jan van Eyck, had, in the early part of the fifteenth century, painted man and his environment with great realism. They presented, by the piling up of microscopic details, all the multifarious features of physiognomy, dress, and surroundings. The Italian artists from Masaccio to Leonardo da Vinci were concerned with a naturalistic presentation, which, proceeding on the basis of anatomy and perspective, focused attention upon the movement of man in a three-dimensional space. Space for them was not, as in the late Gothic, an "aggregate" of individual elements brought together in one composition, but a "homogeneous, continuous and centrally focused space." [4]

To make this important distinction clear, a comparison with contemporary map-making, then also beginning to assume a modern form, may be helpful. The maps, called *portolani*, used by sailors in the Mediterranean, were built up by a series of dead reckonings from one point of departure to a specific destination. By bringing all these detailed lines of direction and distances together, one could build up the shoreline of the Mediterranean. This was only feasible for small areas. For the representation of a global situation, the Mercator projection, with its cross-hatching lines called latitudes and longitudes, was imposed upon continents and seas, providing a homogeneous and continuous space pattern. As in the central perspective picture, this handling distorted things at the edges.

The Italian artist, by his theoretical and scientific approach, succeeded in most completely freeing himself from the rule-of-thumb methods of the artisan. In fact, as the greatest of German painters, Albrecht Dürer (1471–1528), recognized when he came to Italy, the artist had most completely liberated himself there from the gild.

German painting in the fifteenth and sixteenth centuries was influenced by these two artistic expressions. In the German artists there is evident the conflict of the two approaches, especially so in Dürer, who spent some time both in the Low Countries and in Italy. In him are combined in unusual fashion the minute and microscopic rendering of detail along with a deep-felt concern for the fundamental structure of nature in terms of anatomy and perspective.

During much of the fifteenth century, both Italian and northern artists turned mainly to problems of technics and the presentation of both religious and secular subjects with an exuberance of colorful pomp and circumstance. But at the end of the century, Savonarola in Florence, burning luxuries and preaching a return to sobriety and simplicity in preparation for the coming day of judgment, reflected a change in mood. In the art of Michelangelo and Dürer, religion became a soul struggle.

Quest for Religious Immediacy and Cultural Autonomy

It is well to consider briefly a contemporary of Dürer's. For Mathias Grünewald (1470–1528) the realistic technics of the late Gothic were the means of expressing both the contrasts and trivialization referred to above as characteristic of late medieval religiosity. In his famous *Isenheimer Altar,* we see against the background of the heavenly light shining through the clouds over land and sea Mary and the Child, presented with the homely articles used for bathing the child, along with a celestial chorus of angels in ecstatic glorification of the Saviour. This combination of plebeian realism and ecstatic piety point the way from the late Gothic to the Baroque. In Dürer we also encounter contrasts; but in his scientific naturalism and in his subjective individualism he combined the spirit of both the Renaissance and the Reformation.

Dürer was a native of Nuremburg, where his father was a goldsmith. This city was the center of the gold and silver metal-working industry and of the production of precise scientific instruments. It was the chief city in the Germanies devoted to mathematical and astronomical interests, and it had one of the most important printing establishments. This environment might not, on the face of it, be regarded as very congenial to the spirit of art. Yet it was characteristic of the time that science and art were closely allied.

Dürer's thorough training in the painstaking work of the goldsmiths greatly influenced his interest in the new graphic arts, the woodcut and engraving, which flourished in the Germanies in the sixteenth century. The woodcut presented a raised design, and it therefore tended toward a broad, rather coarse delineation, ideal for popular broadsides. The engraving, on the other hand, with its incised lines, tended toward refinement and attention to precision of detail. These crafts gained an ascendancy even over painting because of their importance in connection with bookmaking. The new printing press became the disseminator not only of literary materials of a wide variety but also of the work of artists. Rich burghers were the chief customers, but there was a wide dissemination of pamphlets and single sheets among the lower classes. Woodcuts and engravings played the same role then that cartoons and comic strips do today.

Thus new means of expression for the highly emotional religiosity of the time were available. Dürer's great woodcuts illustrating the Book of Revelations, with their broad contrasts of black and white, reveal with graphic naturalism the destructive forces let loose upon mankind. In contrast with early presentations, the main accent is placed first on the imminence of the catastrophe rather than on its actual consequences. The violent forces of doom hang suspended in the sky over the peaceful landscape on the earth beneath. Then there follows the realistic presentation of the havoc which attends the destructive ride of the Three Horsemen. Earlier medieval presentations relied largely on symbolic suggestion; in Dürer the effect is tremendously heightened by his use of naturalistic forms and settings.

The inner dynamic of religion also achieved expression in Dürer's many portrayals of the passion of Christ on Mount Olivet and in the Garden of Gethsemane. In these scenes, the merely troubled spirit which pervades the disciples stands in contrast with the terrible feeling of aloneness which envelops the Son of Man confronted with the dreadful choice. Again we see naturalism of setting and mood along with great intensity of subjective feeling.

Two famous engravings of Dürer's reflect the widening horizons of the age with respect to the study of man and nature. In one, the great church father Jerome is presented at work in his study. He provided the official Vulgate translation of the Bible from Greek into Latin, and he was, for the humanists, a kind of ideal symbol of the fusion of divine inspiration with ancient cultural values. He had been troubled, as many others were, by what effect an absorbing interest in the ancient pagan classics would have upon the welfare of the soul. The whole scene as depicted by Dürer is enveloped in the atmosphere of the contemplative life of study and meditation. The sleeping dog and lion at the entrance to the room seem to lie on guard against intrusions from the outside world. The perspectival lines which focus on the saint absorbed in study and the light cast on him from the windows seem to turn the whole scene inward. Homely objects of everyday life stand out in realistic detail combined with the paraphernalia of learning. Altogether the impression conveyed is that of retirement within oneself from the world of turmoil.

The other engraving, the *Melancholia*, exhibits a different spirit. The gigantic brooding female figure turns away from the vista of the declining sun. She is surrounded by the tools of science and of the crafts, especially those that weigh and measure. A playing child and a sleeping dog lend a touch of naive intimacy to the scene. In contrast with this is the depression pervading the main figure, who seems to brood over man's failure to fathom the secrets of nature.

Dürer was preoccupied, like many of the contemporary Italian artists, with the study of perspective and proportion in the human body and other organic forms. His studies are indicative of the boundless interest of the age in the study of nature, although in the northern artists the depiction of nature always seems to be accompanied by the feeling that all is vanity.

MEDIEVAL AND MODERN ORIENTATIONS

In the three personalities of the turn of the century—the emperor Maximilian, the merchant Jakob Fugger, and the artist Albrecht Dürer—the new currents of the age became manifest. These currents did not, however, break through decisively to master the political, the economic, or the artistic scene, as they did in Italy. The consequent state of suspension of the new with respect to the old characterized the German scene down to the twentieth century and contributed to a lack of political, sociological, and even cultural creativeness. The German might carry ideas to radical extremes, but he failed to achieve an embodiment of them in institutional molds.

Historians have found it difficult to distinguish modern from medieval traits in the fourteenth and fifteenth centuries. These transitional centuries exhibited great ferment, but generally speaking, no definite trends of development. The spiritual movements dealt with in this chapter—religious communism, mystical devotion, and metaphysical idealism—were not peculiarly modern. They were in fact variations on the themes of sectarianism, *sacerdotium*, and *sacrum imperium*, but in their late medieval form they exhibited new aspects. Hussitism embodied not only the old sectarian motif of a return to early Christian communism but a national social-revolutionary *élan* coming from the German borderlands, not to be encountered again until the nineteenth and twentieth centuries. *Devotio moderna* sought a simplification and spiritualization of Christian life centering in the Gospels supplemented by the ancients, which was later reflected more explicitly in Erasmian humanism. The metaphysical idealism of Cues, while it embodied the philosophic image of the *sacrum imperium* also pointed in the direction of Leibniz and the Romantic philosophers.

The same confusion of medieval and modern elements are to be found in the political, economic, and cultural realms. Emperor Maximilian combined an interest in orders of knighthood with the promotion of mercenary bands of *Landsknechte*. While capitalistic enterprises, such as the Fuggers', employed double-entry bookkeeping, they continued to be family enterprises rather than stock companies. Likewise, the artisan, while developing many new technics, such as printing with movable type, retained the craft point of view of the gild, unlike many Italians who developed a universal technological point of view. In Dürer is manifest the conflict of his own age between the Faustian drive for limitless knowledge and the yearning for the contemplative serenity of saint and sage which the ancients and medieval men had extolled.

Most of these tendencies, it should be noted, had their inception on the periphery of the *Reich*, in Italy, in the Low Countries, and in Bohemia. The borderlands along the Rhine, Elbe, and Danube rivers were always the areas of greatest ferment, both culturally and religiously. This may be attributed in part to the middle position occupied by the Germans but also to the fact that the chief arteries of communication, the rivers, lay along the boundaries of German settlement and thus were carriers of influences from the outside.

The turbulence of intellectual currents and attitudes may be ascribed basically to the pessimistic mood engendered by catastrophic events and by the sense of breakdown of the ecclesiastical means of salvation. The world was overwhelmed again by the dark, demonic forces which had been exorcised in the past by a confidence in divine providence, but divine providence now seemed unavailing to help man directly. Involved in a war between the divine and the demonic, man leaned more than ever on relic and wonder-working image, upon astrology and alchemy, and even upon witchcraft and demonology.

There also appeared, however, signs of a rebirth of confidence in man's cultural achievements, in the creative forces of the universe, and in salvation. On the German scene these trends assumed a much greater impact by being embodied in the early sixteenth century in three great personalities, Erasmus, Paracelsus, and especially Luther. They particularly illustrate the German tendency to express new movements through great personalities rather than through fundamental changes in political and social structure.

IV

Proposed Roads to Reformation

THE NEW HISTORICAL PERSPECTIVE

*W*e have already encountered the notion that only by restoring an earlier condition of simplicity and harmony
could men overcome the growing complexity and corrup-
tion in human affairs. This might mean recovery of the sinless state of
man in Paradise, or of the early Christian community without priest,
law, or property, or even of the ideal commonwealth of contemplative serenity and repose of the ancient philosopher. These "utopias
of the past" were already embedded in the consciousness of medieval
man. By the sixteenth century the conceptions of "rebirth" and "reform" projected a much more definite historical frame.

The notion of the regeneration of society and culture by return
to the ancient springs of national greatness was first put forward
during the fourteenth and fifteenth centuries in Italy by a class of
intellectuals known as the "humanists." They did not seek a restoration of the ancient Roman Empire, as did many emperors, nor of
institutional forms, as did Arnold of Brescia and Rienzi, who seemed
to feel, like most medieval men, that they still lived under the same

time-roof with the Greeks and Romans. The humanists had become conscious that a gulf of time and change—which they called the Middle Ages—separated them from the ancient world. They could return to the ancient world only via its literature and art to recover those norms of conduct and that style of artistic expression which they assumed reflected the truly human in man. These had been almost lost sight of, as they saw it, in the complexities and artificialities of scholastic philosophy, Gothic art, and the chivalrous cult of love.

This notion of a return to the ancient sources naturally affected religion as well as culture. Various heretical movements in the course of the Middle Ages had urged a restoration of the early Christian community. Now a rebirth and reform was to be achieved by drinking at the pure springs of Christianity as represented in the Church Fathers and the Gospels. Here the true gospel of man's regeneration could be found, no longer obscured by the intricacies of Aristotelian logic and scholastic dogma.

The desire for rebirth and reform was, moreover, animated by the idea that man is not bound by the authoritative tradition within which he lives, nor by fixed past models which he can only restore. He is free to mold his own past and future. Consequently, man now felt himself to be standing on the threshold of a new age of infinite possibilities.

The Spiritual Franciscans had projected a sectarian version of the new age idea since it meant the momentary expectation of the third Age of the Spirit, the repudiation of the church, and the institution of a new order of justice and peace. We encounter another variant of the new age idea among the alchemical scientists, both medieval and modern, who look to man's establishment of rapport with the creative processes of nature to usher in the technocratic age of long life and abundance.

The catchwords "rebirth" and "reform," embodying the consciousness that man is free both from the prescriptions of the past, either as tradition or as restoration, and from the future, either as a blueprinted utopia or as an inevitable "Third Age," were projected consciously first by the humanists who in this sense may be regarded as the fathers of the modern attitude of mind.

Rebirth and reform exerted a greater if more ambiguous influence among the Italians and Germans than among other peoples. Both lacked a state tradition fostered by a strong national monarchy. Both had been dependent upon the Roman imperial tradition, and, with the decline of the medieval Empire, both had sought increasingly a restoration either of the ancient republican institutions or of imperial forms of sovereignty. Here on the threshold of the modern age they entered still another phase of the idea of "return"; classical form and gospel truth became ideals to which man must continually return to recover the original promise and prophetic quality the ancient world possessed.

The three outstanding intellectual figures of the German scene in the first half of the sixteenth century, Paracelsus, Erasmus, and Luther, presented not merely highly individual interpretations respectively of nature, culture, and the Scriptures; they also had in common the general urge of the time to reform and rebirth. They did not look at nature, culture, and the Scriptures as purely autonomous spheres—in the modern secular sense—toward which they merely took an intellectual position. Nor did they view these spheres in the medieval sense as strata in the ascending series of a hierarchical pyramid where each derives its significance from the other. Rather, the spheres presented individual roads by which men had sought God since ancient times.

Paracelsus, Erasmus, and Luther thought, moreover, that by their own time these roads had become obscured by the accumulated debris of professional verbiage, ecclesiastical prescription, and subtle learning. It was necessary to sweep these aside and to proceed directly to the study of nature, culture, and the Scriptures in the light of their original simplicity, both historical and experiential.

THE ASTROLOGICAL AND ALCHEMICAL QUEST

The world of nature around 1500 was still seen mainly through the eyes of alchemy and astrology, the ancient sciences which attained their golden age in the Western world during the fifteenth and sixteenth centuries. The Italian humanist Marsilio Ficino (1433–1499) had translated the *Corpus Hermeticum* from Greek into Latin and thus made more generally available the chief work on alchemy of the ancient world, a work that went back to Chaldean and Persian sources.

Two characteristics distinguished alchemy and astrology from the modern sciences. First, scientific knowledge was assumed to have been passed on through inspired individuals (the *adepta*) who had an insight into the secret processes of nature. Only a few were initiated into its mysteries. To them only was communicated the secret word, number, or formula by which one tunes in with nature. Their mysteries were as jealously guarded from *hoi polloi* as the secret skills of a craft gild. Conversely, the distinguishing characteristic of modern science has been its public character.

Second, alchemy and astrology were inclined to promise much more than they could fulfill in the way of producing the immediate benefits of wealth, health, and wisdom. For instance, alchemy sought pragmatic short cuts to the attainment of these common desires of mankind by way of the transmutation of base metals into gold, through the elixir of life, and through the philosopher's stone. It did not distinguish between theoretical knowledge and its practical utility as does modern science, which has been concerned primarily with the former and has left the latter largely to technology, at least until recently.

The great popularity of alchemy and astrology in this age also may be ascribed to an apprehensive concern with the problem of purposeless chance in human affairs, manifesting itself in the morbid dread of death and of apocalyptic catastrophe. Scholastic philosophy had sought to show how the divine purpose is demonstrated by an ordered universe in which all things appear as a reflection of God's purpose with regard to man's salvation. Now fear of the imminence of death and of impending doom were evidences of the loss of confidence in this divine providence.

In the fifteenth and sixteenth centuries, as man gained confidence in his own powers, he dispensed to a considerable extent with reliance on a benevolent divine providence. But he had not yet developed in place of the divine a conception of the cosmos as an autonomous order of universal and invariable law. The loss of the assured sense of a providential order led to a revival of that fear of dark forces which had also pervaded late ancient and early medieval times. This explains the eruption of demonology and witchcraft, which flourished side by side with astrology and alchemy and which sought to propitiate these dark forces and even use them for personal ends. The charge of being in league with the devil and his minions, through the use of black magic or by the casting of spells, was directed not only against women but also against astrologers and alchemists.

The great minds of the period approached the problem of the fortuitous in human affairs on a higher level. Machiavelli pointed out that, even though one followed rational calculation in politics, the best plans were frequently upset by the turn of the wheel of fortune. Therefore, one must preserve an ever-present flexibility and vigilance to counter the slings and arrows of misfortune. Astrology sought a "scientific" solution by assuming that for each event in an individual's life there was an appropriate constellation of heavenly bodies which determined its evil or good fortune. It assumed that the infinitely large determined the infinitesimally small. The universe was viewed in qualitative rather than quantitative terms. Particular qualities were attributed to individual stars and planets with which individual men stood in sympathetic relationship by virtue of a mutual sharing of these qualities. Each individual is born and lives under the compelling influence of a conjunction or constellation of stars which are the guardians of human destiny, since they are the embodiment of divine intelligence.

The influence of the heavenly bodies was felt not only in the grand design of human destiny but in all the events and happenings of everyday life. Their power was as pervasive as that of saint or demon. According to Paracelsus, half the calamities of mankind may be attributed to the firmament.[1] Scarcely a decision could be made, a journey undertaken, without consulting the stars. The calendar with its prognostications and astrological advice was for many people the most useful work, second only, perhaps, to the Bible.

While astrology sought to eliminate the fortuitous by making all happenings predictable, it thereby imprisoned man in a vast web of forces from which he was not extricated until modern science rescued him by emphasizing the distinction between matter and spirit. Matter is assumed to be causally determined, but spirit belongs to the realm of individual self-determination.

Humanist philosophy sought to break through the astrological net by insisting on the peculiar dignity and value of man. In the famous *Oration on the Dignity of Man,* Pico della Mirandola (1463–1494) argued that man is distinguished not by belonging to a species of being which occupies a particular niche in the order of things but by being endowed by the Creator with the capacity to rise and descend the ladder of creation. He can ascend as high as the angels and sink as low as the beasts. He is distinguished, therefore, by the aspiration to rise and not by any static quality or position. His destiny is not bounded by the stars. Created in the image of God, he has the freedom to determine his own destiny. This idea we have already encountered, at least by implication, in the mystical philosophies of Eckhart and particularly of Nicholas of Cues.

In alchemy, the individual was assumed to have a much wider range of freedom. Alchemy was based on the conception of universal unity or totality, but as an organic creative process rather than as a network of causal determinants. The different forms that the elements—air, water, fire, and earth—assume reveal the transmutations that are basic to the creative process.

The alchemist was concerned with the transformation of base metals into precious ones, with the quest for the elixir of life and for the philosopher's stone. The alchemist attempted to find keys to the creative process in order that man might acquire what he seemed to want most: gold, health, and wisdom, and in that order. This quest now took the place of the search for the Holy Grail. The interest of later scientists in the study of perpetual motion and Goethe's interest in the discovery of the primordial plant form were similarly motivated.

Underlying the science of alchemy was the magical approach which sought to release the creative spirit imprisoned in material existence and render it available to man. So Michelangelo sought to release the form embedded in the raw block of wood or stone and render it visible.

The magical quest was illuminated with the vision of man's limitless possibilities in the attainment of knowledge and power. It is called "Faustian," after Goethe's great work, which was named after Dr. Johannes Faustus (ca. 1480–1540), a scientist-magician of legendary reputation. Some would argue that this magical view has survived in our modern notion of power exercised over the forces of nature.

Among the magician-scientists of the early sixteenth century,

Agrippa of Nettesheim occupies an important place because of his *De occulta philosophia*. Composed about 1510, it was not published until twenty years later, when he added a repudiation of the efficacy of all knowledge. His work was an encyclopedic summary of the occult knowledge of ancient and medieval times. It was a curious syncretistic conglomerate of Neo-Pythagorean number theory, Chaldean astrological notions, letter and word symbolism of the Jewish Kabbala, Florentine Neo-Platonism, and ancient and medieval mysticism. In the original encyclopedic work he sought to provide a philosophical basis for magic as the supreme key to the knowledge of the universe and its creator. Later, he repudiated magical knowledge, not because of its inability to fulfill its aspirations but in a mood of satiety and of yearning for the simplicity of the gospel message.[2] The tension between the new optimistic attitude toward man's capacity for knowledge and power and the pessimistic and resigned temper of mind of the later Middle Ages is manifest in Agrippa.

PARACELSUS' ATTACK ON CONTEMPORARY MEDICINE

Much more definitely than Agrippa, Paracelsus (1493–1541) crossed the threshold into modern times. Although his basic point of view was alchemical and astrological, his main concern was not with occult knowledge and practices but with nature. He sought to free man of occult intermediaries in order that he might be brought in direct union with the great creative work of nature, which is God's workshop or laboratory.

Paracelsus was born in Einsiedeln, Switzerland. He was given the rather extraordinary name of Theophrastus Bombastus von Hohenheim, but, following the custom of the time, he adopted what might be called a professional name, Paracelsus. It meant "greater than Celsus," an ancient Roman physician whose encyclopedic work on medicine had attained a great vogue in the course of the centuries.

Paracelsus' father was a physician who moved to Carinthia, one of the chief mining areas in the eastern Hapsburg lands. Mineralogy and alchemy were of course closely connected. The alchemist sought to achieve in his workshop what nature had already produced in the crucible of the earth. From his father Paracelsus not only learned the art of healing but also gained a great knowledge of mineralogy and metallurgy.

The most important formative factor in his career was his extensive travels during the years 1512 to 1524, when he roamed over the whole of Europe. At various universities and from the folk in all paths of life, he gathered wide knowledge of the properties of herbs, plants, and minerals and of the peculiarities of human illness and psychology. The experiential basis of much of his knowledge explains his opposition to the humanists, who relied on texts. He carried on a lifelong polemic against the ancient authorities in medicine, such as the Moslem Avicenna (d. 1037) whose principal work, *Canon of Medicine*, was the chief textbook of the time. Because Paracelsus also attacked the pretensions to knowledge of his fellow physicians, he came into continual conflict with what was already a very close-knit professional group.

During the years 1525 to 1528 he set up shop as a physician and teacher in Salzburg, Strassburg, and Basel. In Basel he cured the famous printer, Johannes Froben, who introduced him to the artist, Holbein, and to the great humanist, Erasmus of Rotterdam. Paracelsus was appointed city physician and professor at the university. But, as in other places, his sojourn there was brief; he lasted less than a year (1527–1528). He lectured in German because Latin, he argued, was too burdened with a traditional technical terminology. His arrogant assertion of his own views and his wholesale attack upon both ancient authorities and contemporary practitioners naturally provoked counterattacks. He was accused of being a charlatan and a quack, and even of having aided in instigating the Peasant Revolt of 1525. About to be jailed, he left Basel in the night. From then until his death in 1541 he became a wanderer. Most of his numerous writings, often hastily thrown together in the course of his journeys, found their way into print much later.[3]

Paracelsus insisted that the healing of the sick, the enhancement of the knowledge of the art of healing, and a sense of divine calling or mission must go hand in hand. A man who held such pronounced views, who could affect apparently miraculous cures, who virtually converted medicine into a priestly vocation, necessarily had both enemies and disciples. Legends came to be attached to his name which persisted in the popular memory long after his death. They ranged from his being on intimate terms with the devil to his being immortal.

THE UNITARY LIFE PROCESS

Perhaps his most important general idea was the oneness of man with nature. Man is a little world, a microcosm in the great all, the macrocosm. Therefore everything that is in the world is also in man. The interrelatedness of all nature makes for its self-sufficiency in the sense that it contains both creative and degenerative forces. In fact, it contains all the means of overcoming its own imbalances or sicknesses.

The universe as the great all is animated by forces which have a pre-eminently qualitative character and not merely the quantitative form of matter and motion. The stars are such forces and are not free bodies which respond merely to matter and motion. In place of the rather static elements of Aristotle's earth, fire, water, and air, Paracelsus projects three chemical forces whose names are mercury, sulphur, and salt. Each has a peculiar role or function: sulphur, that of growth and reproduction; mercury, that of regeneration; and salt, that of maintaining equilibrium. They are therefore not substances but fundamental forms of the life process, the separation of which leads to death.

In conformity with this conception of a unitary life process, Paracelsus assumes that nature contains an all-pervading vital force or spirit which, rising to consciousness in man, is an expression of the immanent creative activity of God. There is no duality of soul and body nor of matter and spirit; they constitute but aspects of a total creative process. Nature is the all-inclusive process of continued creation; nothing has been brought to completion in it. It is man's distinctive role to bring nature to perfection; he has been placed in the universe for that purpose. The world is, so to speak, a gigantic workshop in which materials and potencies are provided for the carrying out of this creative task. When the alchemist transmutes base metals into precious metals, he is tuning in with the creative process. And creation involves not merely material change but also spiritual transformation. It aims at the release of that *spiritus mundi*, that "light of nature" which is the supreme revelation.

To Paracelsus, the physician is a priest, the intermediary between man, nature, and God. In sickness man's oneness with nature is revealed. Sickness is a disturbance of the divine harmony. Since each of the forces of nature has its good and bad effects, one must be used as a counterpoise to the other. There is a specific remedy for each ailment. Moreover, each man requires a distinct remedy because each is a unique little world in a big world, which is also unique. The physician must discover the appropriate time as well as the appropriate remedy, since each individual life as one unique facet of the total creative process appears on the universal stage at a definite time, that is, under a definite astrological constellation. Paracelsus thus fused astrology and alchemy and thereby spiritualized and individualized both.

He created a philosophy, or, if one wishes, a religion of nature, which made it a category of knowledge or revelation. He contributed to some extent toward that disenchantment of the world which has characterized modern scientific development by depriving it of the dramatic contest of good and evil forces in constant competition for men's bodies and souls. The book of nature reveals not only all that man is, but God's purpose with regard to man. All men can in some measure read this book, and they do. Each man may and should become his own physician. One must, however, read not only with the physical eye but also with the eye of the spirit, for all our knowledge is but a self-revelation of the creative spirit of nature.

This highly speculative and rather mystical nature philosophy exerted an enormous influence on German thought down to the second half of the nineteenth century and even beyond. Its basic notion of nature as a creative process is to be found especially in Goethe and the Romantics.

The magical view of the universe pervaded the whole Renaissance. It embodied the optimistic view of the universe as a creative process with man as the technician-artist—and not its exploiter—who brings this process to completion. He will eventually achieve utopia. Paracelsus also adopted the Joachimite conception of a coming new age, not, however, as an apocalyptic event but as the creative spirit coming to complete consciousness in man. The utopias of the Renaissance were, in a sense, but the application to the whole of society of the notion of a total transmutation.

ITALIAN AND GERMAN HUMANISM

Humanism is generally associated with a revival of interest in the culture of the ancient Greeks and Romans. The whole Middle Ages for a thousand years had fed on the ancient sources of literature and philosophy. Medieval man felt himself to be living in the same age with Alexander and Aristotle, with Caesar and Cicero. In using the term "ancients," we imply that we are separated from these worthies by a chasm called the Middle Ages. But medieval men, without any such sense of historical distance, quarried from the writings of the ancients as they did from what remained of the monuments of antiquity. They used these materials for the training of clerics in the use of the tools of expression—grammar, rhetoric, and logic. Without being aware of the historical incongruity they used ancient pagan writings to buttress their own basic religious ideas.

In the fourteenth century in Italy a new attitude toward the ancient world became apparent. Italians began to regard the ancient Roman world as their own peculiar national past from which they could derive forms and values for the regeneration of their own culture, long submerged under French influences. Shaking off the shackles of this alien cultural predominance, Italians began to acquire a feeling of the distinctive character of their own culture, with its roots in the world of ancient Rome. The republican forms of government which emerged in the Italian city-states offered opportunities for the emergence of the orator and poet as the voices of civic and patriotic sentiment. Florence, the chief cultural center, was a prime example. Many humanists of the fourteenth century also found employment in the chancelleries of city governments; and, in public documents of all kinds, they sought to follow the form and style of the ancients, especially of Cicero. They felt themselves, as descendants of the ancient Romans, to be far above their northern contemporaries. Italy would again, as in ancient times, bring true culture to these northern barbarians after centuries of the Gothic night.

In the fifteenth century, at Rome, which had become the chief center of humanism after 1450, it assumed more universal interests under papal patronage. Its chief concern was with culture as an expression of individual personality and style in literature, painting, and sculpture. In this period, the humanists generally came to stand outside the schools, gilds, monastic orders, and civic life; they became free-lance scholars and literati. The arts were to be freed from the rigid rules and forms of grammar and logic, as taught in the schools. Style was to be the reflection of a man's own original creative force, or of what we now call genius, then regarded as an expression of the divine spirit in man. As man molds and shapes the universe, the divine purpose becomes conscious in him. We have already encountered this idea in Paracelsus. In Italy it was also manifest in such great artists as Leonardo da Vinci and Michelangelo, but it was pre-eminent in that Renaissance exaltation of man's superlative powers, Pico della Mirandola's celebrated *Oration on the Dignity of Man* (1486).

Pico and his older contemporary, Marsilio Ficino, were leading spirits in an intellectual circle in Florence, called by them the Platonic Academy, which sought to reconcile Platonic thought with Christianity in the following fashion: In the universe at large and in man, we find reflected the divine ideal forms; the divine image in man will shine forth if purified of its material dross, that is, if man will but realize his unique freedom of being suspended, so to speak, between heaven and earth. The accent was here placed on man's aspiration to rise rather than on God's grace flowing down to rescue him from sin. All religions present symbols of the one true God whom they seek to find, but, of course, Christianity has attained to the highest knowledge of the divine. This last idea was to have tremendous significance later for the development of the notion of a natural religion.

Italian humanism cast a spell over the minds of German students and scholars when they came in contact with it, as they did, for instance, on the occasion of the great church councils at Constance and Basel, which brought many of the leading Italian humanists north. Italy, rather than France, became the intellectual and literary mecca.

The second half of the fifteenth century marked the culmination of the pilgrimage of German students to Italy and the height of the *Wanderjahre*. In the sixteenth century, humanists, poets, and scholars began to settle down as professors at universities, in ecclesiastical offices, and in the service of princes and city government.

But how could this Italian humanism, with its sense of national cultural predominance based on the appeal to the pre-eminence of the Roman forebears and with its exaltation of an individualism above craft, social group, and ecclesiastical institution, be translated into terms suitable to the political, social, and cultural conditions north of the Alps?

The Germans could hardly appeal to the Romans as their national forebears. Moreover, the extinguishing of the lights of ancient culture and the ushering in of medieval darkness were attributed to the conquests of the German barbarians. Even more difficult was the promotion of a universal type of individualism in the frame of German city life.

The Italian cities were really independent city-states, which dominated the surrounding country and which, to a large degree, assimilated the nobility into the life of the city. In the *Reich* the isolation of town from country remained marked. The cities were but islands in a sea of princes, knights, and peasants. Consequently, in the German cities the peculiar craft spirit of the artisan, manifest in the tendency to think in terms of vocation (*Beruf*), predominated. Technical skills were emphasized rather than the aristocratic ideal of universal man. The latter was the product, in the Italian cities, of the fusion of the aristocratic amateur spirit with the narrower middle-class artisan point of view.

Few universal types such as Leonardo da Vinci and Michelangelo were found to the north of the Alps. Among the Germans, Nicholas of Cues and Albrecht Dürer approached them. But, in general, there was little of that union of art and science among the Germans which proved so productive of universality in Italy. The Germans seemed more inclined to retain the peculiar union of science or art with religion that was characteristic of the Middle Ages. They were to be really drawn out of the isolation of craft and class for a time only by the call of religious reform, linked in the minds of most humanists with educational reform, and, in the case of a very few, with a national rebirth. German humanism played an important role in the universities but not in the political life nor as an ideal of cultural personality.

The medieval university was organized around the idea that the liberal arts should provide a cultural preparation for the pursuit of theology, medicine, and law. Of the seven liberal arts, the three comprising grammar, rhetoric, and logic (the *trivium*) were regarded as the most important arts of expression. Again during the fourteenth and fifteenth centuries, the old lament was heard that corruption and heresy were due to an inadequately educated clergy. The humanists took up the cry with a different accent. They argued that the arts were being neglected in behalf of the professions and were inadequately taught.

THE CONFLICTS OF HUMANISTS AND SCHOLASTICS

The interest in logic, promoted by scholastic philosophy and by the popularity of disputation or debate, had pushed the literary forms of expression—rhetoric and grammar—to the background. The humanists turned their attack upon hairsplitting argumentation and upon the barbarous Latin, which they called "kitchen Latin," employed by the theologians and philosophers of the time.

The controversy reached its peak with the publication of *The Letters of Obscure Men* (1515–1517), the work of two leading humanists, Crotus Rubianus and Ulrich von Hutten. This work grew out of an attack by the scholastics at Cologne, directed against the very learned older humanist, Johann Reuchlin (1455–1522). Reuchlin's linguistic studies were not confined to Latin and Greek; they included the Hebrew writings, for which he compiled a grammar. The scholastics of Cologne led by one Johannes Pfefferkorn, a converted Jew, urged the burning of all Hebrew writings, except of course, the Bible, as a way of bringing the Jews into the Christian fold.

The humanists assumed a solid front against the scholastic obscurantists and barbarians, whom they rather promiscuously accused of ignorance, bigotry, and moral turpitude, and of a greater crime

—that of writing Latin in a most abominable style. The humanists wished to return to the pure Latinity of their great model, Cicero. For them, form and style became more important than content and substance. Style, they argued, reflects the whole man, not just a sharp intellect. Nowhere had man attained to fuller expression of all his emotional, intellectual and imaginative capacities than in ancient literature.

The humanist felt that he had to leap over the gulf of the Dark Ages which separated him from the ancient world to return to a religion and culture which could truly bring the human and divine into a living unity. He acquired a sense of distance between himself and the ancient world, a perspective like that which the painters developed as the consciously felt distance between the object and the observer. As the artist recognized that the person or object perceived had its own peculiar intimate space, so the humanist sought to view the ancients in the spirit of their own age. Their philosophy and literature must be interpreted in the context of the circumstances and values in which they arose. Only a return to the modes of expression and style of writing of the ancients would permit the re-creation of the spirit and values of ancient Christianity and culture.

The humanists argued that in the hands of the scholastics both religion and culture had lost their original promise and meaning. The Greeks and Romans had projected ideally human forms and values unsurpassed in former or later centuries. It was no accident, therefore, that the most universal of religions, Christianity, emerged in this cultural environment. Man must return to these pure springs of culture and religion to discover their common sources and their original harmony and simplicity, now distorted by barbarous forms of expression and complex theological argument.

In culture, the humanist maintained, man attains to his peculiar human stature. Neither the pure intellectual tool of logic of the philosopher nor the instrument of measurement of the scientist can truly reflect man's inner spirit. Only literature can adequately express the aspirations of religion and the inspiration of art, both of which distinguish man. Greek and Roman writings must therefore be restored to their ancient purity and significance. They must be freed from the interpolations of medieval scholars. They should be read not in the form of excerpts in anthologies but in their original, complete form.

The reproduction of the pure texts led, of course, to the development of critical techniques by means of which the spurious could be separated from the authentic. Thus the basis of modern philological-historical study was laid, a discipline in which the German universities were to excel.

THE NATIONALIST TREND IN GERMAN HUMANISM

The Germans had no such intimate sense of national continuity with the ancient Romans as the Latin nations had. They became conscious that a chasm separated them from the ancient world. As the general development of Christendom was broken by a new epochal consciousness arising out of the desire for rebirth and reform of religion and culture, the phrase "return to the sources" came to have an ambiguous meaning to them. It might mean drinking at the Greek and Latin springs of Western religion and culture, but it might also mean national rebirth by return to the Germanic folk sources. Consciousness of a conflict between these two returns became evident in the sixteenth century and was to be revived again and again down to the twentieth century.

Concern with the qualities of the early Teutons is particularly evident in Conrad Celtis (1459–1508) and Ulrich von Hutten (1488–1523). Celtis was the son of a peasant; Hutten sprang from the class of imperial knights. Celtis was one of the first German humanists to go to Italy (1486–1487). He returned with the fixed determination to rescue his countrymen from medieval barbarism. In his wanderings along the eastern borderlands he sought to promote the foundation of literary societies among the humanists as a means of combating the scholastics and of creating a truly German culture. His poetic descriptions of mountain and stream are suffused with the spirit of a nature pantheism which sought inspiration in the religion of forest and field of the ancient Germans and in the teachings of the Druidic priestly fraternity.

The ancient Germans were, of course, no longer regarded by these nationalistic humanists as merely the destroyers of ancient civilization who ushered in the Gothic night of the Dark Ages. The discovery of Tacitus' important work *Germania* had a decisive influence here. Celtis provided the first German translation, and he gave lectures in Vienna on the *Germania* and on Frederick Barbarossa. Tacitus had presented an idyllic picture of the simple virtues of the Germans as contrasted with the effete and decadent Romans of his day. The German romantic nationalists looked to him for arguments to counter the claims of the Latins to cultural hegemony.

The chief nationalistic firebrand among the humanists was Ulrich von Hutten. He possessed a bitter hatred of the papacy, which was, he believed, the financial exploiter of the Germans, the cause of the decline of imperial power, and the chief symbol of an alien Latin domination.

He wrote a dialogue in which the Roman Scipio, the Carthaginian Hannibal, and the German Arminius confront each other over the issue as to who was the greater leader. Arminius was the German prince who effected a union of German tribes which defeated the legions of Augustus in the Teutoburger Forest. Hutten has Arminius appear as the defender of the national soil and, as such, superior to the others who seem to be merely bent on conquest. This marks the beginning of that Arminius legend which played such an important role in German national aspirations far into the nineteenth century.

The national motif in the call for a return to sources was subordinate in the *Reich*, however, to the predominant question of the time, reform in the church. Hutten, in his fierce hatred of the papacy as a foreign exploiter, apparently would have created a national church along with a national culture. But to the greatest of the northern humanists, Desiderius Erasmus (1465–1536), the most important problem was the regeneration of religion and culture by a return to the common sources of Christendom—ancient Graeco-Roman culture and the Christianity of the Gospels.

THE SOURCES OF ERASMIAN HUMANISM

Erasmus was born in the Low Countries. He was a product of and spent most of his life in the western zone of the *Reich*, the area of the greatest ferment of ideas. The Low Countries and Switzerland comprised the terminal points of that most-traveled route of trade and ideas, the Rhine and its branches which connected the North Sea with the Mediterranean. Along it were strung like beads on a string such important cities as Cologne, Strassburg, Basel, and Zürich. Along it also were to be found the chief centers of religious and social disturbance and turmoil.

Eramus was the illegitimate son of a priest and a burgher's daughter, both of whom died of the plague while he was still very young. Throughout his life he felt the stigma of his obscure origin, which perhaps explains in part his avid search for recognition among people of prominent station in church and society. Placed in a school of the Brethren of the Common Life, he owed to them that combination of practical and mystical piety, along with an interest in letters, which later influences served to deepen and widen. His guardians saw no better place for the bright student of dubious parentage than the monastery at Steyn.

His monastic career produced an ambivalent attitude. On the one hand, it engendered a contemplative and meditative turn of mind and an inclination toward the secluded life of the scholar; yet throughout life he found the monastic bonds irksome. While he shied away from the crude and brutal contacts of "life," he yet longed for influence and fame in the world of ideas and letters, where he felt most at home. This realm was then emerging in the society of towns along the Rhine and at the courts of princes, both lay and ecclesiastical.

Employment as secretary with the Bishop of Cambray opened the way out of the monastery into the arena of human affairs. He was sent to Paris (1495–1499), where he combined the study of theology with the sowing of wild oats, interspersed with bouts of penitence in periodic returns to Steyn. The theology of none of the prevailing schools seems to have captured his interest.

His most decisive intellectual and spiritual influence came from a trip to England in 1505, where he came under the influence of the circle of humanists around John Colet and Thomas More. In Colet, he found a kindred spirit who elected neither the logical complexities of scholasticism nor the magical obscurities of Neo-Pythagoreanism and the Kabbalah, but rather a direct return to the Gospels as the way to the imitation of Christ. Erasmus thus found a spiritual center for his life, though not one calcuated to bring any lasting serenity to his restless soul.

Not a wandering scholar nor yet desirous of permanent tenure, he was always in search of security, both spiritual and economic, which he could never quite attain. The quest for economic security led him to seek favors from the well-to-do and influential and to continually angle for ecclesiastical sinecures. Only relatively late in life did the popularity of his writings bring him fame and fortune and a sense of security. The printing press was, in a sense, the chief basis of his success, as it was for Luther. Most of the last two decades of Erasmus' life were spent in Basel in the home of Froben, the great publisher of his works.

The fluidity of mind which we find so characteristic of Erasmus is but the reflection of the temper of his times. There was an almost universal syncretism, a borrowing and blending of ideas and attitudes. Humanism, mysticism, pietism, and scholasticism all contributed ideas and attitudes which, detached from their original molds, assumed an almost free-wheeling character. The most characteristic philosophic tendency was the rather vague, mystical, and speculative Platonism of the Florentine Academy with which Erasmus came in direct contact on the occasion of a long visit to Italy, from 1506 to 1509. The chief compelling interest of most of the humanist reformers was for a return to the simplicity of the ancient faith. Amid the flux of ideas and attitudes, security was not to be sought in a return to fixity of dogma and rite, but in a return to the simple tenets of the teachings of Jesus as presented in the Gospels. This was the guiding thread running through the truly colossal literary and scholarly labors of Erasmus.

In the best known of his writings, *Praise of Folly*, he not only directs his shafts of wit and satire in the usual humanist fashion against the ignorance of clergy and monks, but he also portrays the common foibles of mankind:

> "Without me," says Folly, "the world cannot exist for a moment. For is not all that is done at all among mortals, full of folly; is it not performed by fools and for fools? No society, no cohabitation can be pleasant or lasting without folly; so much so, that a people could not stand its prince, nor the master his man, nor

the maid her mistress, nor the tutor his pupil, nor the friend his friend, nor the wife her husband for a moment longer, if they did not now and then err together, now flatter each other; now sensibly conniving at things, now smearing themselves with some honey of folly."

Folly is thus often presented as the highest wisdom. It is a wisdom that has a higher value in the relations of men to each other than mere technical mastery, or philosophic profundity, or religious enthusiasm. Erasmus' main concern was not man's relationship to the universe, as with Paracelsus, nor his direct relationship to God, as with Luther. His interest was primarily in the particular individual man, his likes and dislikes, his prejudices and ideals. Thus man is viewed not as the isolated individual confronted by an arbitrary divine judge, nor as the center of a web of occult forces, but as sharing the foibles and sufferings of his fellowman.

This truly natural man appears no longer disguised by the theological conception of original sin nor by the astrological notion of sidereal fate. He does not really need relic and saint nor horoscope and crucible to give him assurance of salvation; he needs only the example of the Son of Man, who in His ministry and teachings revealed how the truly human and divine are fused. How can this image of the Christ-like life be recovered after centuries of encrustations of dogma, sacramentalism, and superstition have almost completely obscured it? To Erasmus, the way back was open only to the enlightened few who could slough off accumulated dogma and superstitions, and return to that universal conception of man which, foreshadowed by Socrates and the great Greek philosophers, was given complete form in Christ and in the teachings of the apostles and Church Fathers.

THE FUSION OF CLASSICAL CULTURE AND CHRISTIAN RELIGION

Basic to Erasmian humanism was the union of classical culture and Christian religion. This fusion was consciously achieved, particularly by the Church Fathers, and most of all by St. Jerome, who translated the Vulgate and deliberately cultivated a Ciceronian style.

It is not surprising that Erasmus devoted a good part of his scholarly labors to the publication of critical editions and commentaries on the works of these great founders.

He did not stop with the writings of the Church Fathers; he went beyond them to the incomparable source of Scripture itself. In this field he achieved his greatest monuments to religion: the first edition of the Greek New Testament in 1516 and a Latin translation in 1519 to replace the Vulgate version. The inadequacies of the Vulgate had been pointed out earlier by the great Italian humanist Lorenzo Valla. The importance of the Greek text lay in the reproduction of the "actual words" of Christ and his apostles so as to recapture their literal and plain meaning without looking for symbolical or allegorical hidden significance.[4]

The universal humanity embodied in the ministry and teaching of Christ made it possible, Erasmus felt, for all men to follow in His footsteps. One had but to compare the simple teachings of Jesus with those of Socrates and others to realize their similarity and consequent universality. Both Jesus and Socrates were mainly concerned with man's relationship to man as the way to peace, toleration, and enlightenment. To that end, such evils as war, greed, and class hatreds should be done away with.

Obviously, what Christianity had in common with Greek philosophy lay in the realm of morality and ethics and not in the field of religion, where it prescribed faith and sacrament as the means of overcoming human inadequacy. It was on this distinction that Erasmus broke with Luther, although he sympathized with Luther's attack on mechanical piety and external religiosity. The difference in their fundamental points of departure soon became evident, however, in their radically different answers to the question: Can man knowing the good do it? In general, Erasmus' answer was in the affirmative and Luther's in the negative. Erasmus was actively concerned with reform within the church, but primarily through the education of its leaders; as for the masses, they apparently, in his thinking, required a lower grade of religion involving assurances of salvation through sacrament, saint, and relic.

Erasmus soon came to see in Luther a factor of discord which hindered the slow reform based on culture and education, possible only in an atmosphere of peace and tolerance. Erasmus had experienced no soul struggle, and he was not a man of action. By temperament, he avoided taking a positive dogmatic stand because, under all circumstances, he wished to retain mobility of mind. This was no longer possible, however, in the bitter and heated controversy which opened with Luther's attack on the practice of indulgences in 1517.

In the last decade of his life Erasmus found himself in the position of opposing Luther while not sharing in the defense of the existing sacrosanct ecclesiastical institution with its abuses. He thus came to be charged with cowardice by both sides, although many of the greatest minds and personalities of his age continued to admire him and to claim his friendship.

THE SACRAMENTAL-HIERARCHICAL LADDER AND POPULAR PIETY

In the Middle Ages religion was so intertwined with politics, society, and culture as to be virtually indistinguishable from them, a condition which was most evident in the early *sacrum imperium*. The reform movements from the eleventh century on had all sought to emphasize the distinction between the spiritual and the temporal. But just as persistent was the drive to permeate the temporal with spiritual values. Hence, the dominant tendency of medieval thought and practice was to bridge the gulf between these polarities by institutions, practices, and ideas whereby a ladder was extended upward from the most earthly to the most high. Thus there was created a hierarchy of forms extending upward to its apex in God in which spiritual and temporal, faith and reason, and sacred and profane were intermingled on each stage upward.

In recognizing this gradualism the church could not, of course, accept the radical dualism of sundry heretical groups who argued that the Christian community must separate itself completely from the world, which was wholly evil. The church was dedicated to the principle that it was the priestly-sacramental ladder between God and man. As such, it rested upon the earth and had to make "compromises" with human weaknesses. Only specially endowed individuals could lead the truly religious life of complete isolation from the world; for them monasteries were provided. For the rank and file of humanity, there existed various less exacting requirements. By presenting many gradations of the Christian life, the church accommodated not only individual differences but distinctions between cultural and social groups.

In the fourteenth and fifteenth centuries, when there was a mounting concern with human guilt and divine judgment, the church responded by multiplying the means whereby man could make himself right in the eyes of a God sitting in perpetual judgment over man's sins. It must be emphasized that the vast multiplication of saints, relics, and wonder-working images came in response to the demands of popular piety. Through the sacrament of penance, the church provided an elaborate system of graded penalties whereby one could achieve satisfaction for sins committed here and now. The indulgence issued by bishop or pope was a means by which penalties were commuted, so to speak, into payment of a sum of money. It was this that provoked Luther's criticism and led him finally to break with the whole priestly-sacramental order of the church.

However, the enormous enhancement of the external aspects of devotion was accompanied by the intensification of the other pole of religious life, inward piety. This was evident in the appearance of many individuals and groups concerned with transcending the world of externals, both lay and ecclesiastical. Within the circle of the Brethren of the Common Life were those who saw the true source of salvation in Holy Writ rather than in the priestly-sacramental order.

Neither the religious emotionalism manifest in the veneration of miracle-working relics, bleeding Hosts, and weeping images of the Virgin, nor the quietistic forms of inward piety, which sought the divine image within the solitude of the soul, harbored within them the impulse to religious revolution. But they did provide the combustible materials which were to be ignited by the spark of Martin Luther.

LUTHER'S SOUL STRUGGLE

There was nothing extraordinary in the youth of Luther to indicate his later development. He was born in 1483, in Thuringia, of peasant parents who moved to Mansfeld in Saxony, a booming mining area. As a miner, the father achieved comfortable circumstances, at least sufficiently so to send his son to a university. He had the natural middle-class aspiration to have his son, who was an excellent student, follow a professional career in law and marry the daughter of a well-to-do burgher. In 1505 Martin received the degree of Master of Arts at the renowned University of Erfurt. But in that same year, when he had already entered upon the study of law, he suddenly decided to enter a monastery.

This in itself was not an unusual step. Many a young man had abandoned promising prospects in a worldly career to follow a life of renunciation. Certain aspects of his background may have gradually inclined him toward the religious life. He had been reared in the peasant atmosphere of fear of hell, devil, demons, and witches. He attended one of the schools of the Brethren of the Common Life. He had led the semi-monastic life of a university student at Erfurt. There he also came under the influence of the Occamist philosophy, with its emphasis upon God as an exacting and arbitrary judge.

The "trigger action" leading to his decision to enter a monastery came apparently from a vow he took during a severe thunderstorm as he was returning to Erfurt from Mansfeld. He vowed that he would become a monk if his life were spared. We may assume that, underneath a rather happy-go-lucky outward demeanor, he harbored a sensitive conscience and a serious disposition. Once his mind was made up, he was not to be deflected from his purpose by the persuasion of either parents or friends. Among the five monastic orders represented in Erfurt, he chose the Augustinian Hermits. It was a reformed monastery which had a high reputation for rigorous pursuit of the ascetic ideal.[5]

It might be assumed that, having made this supreme renunciation of the world, he would attain peace of mind in the routine of prayer, worship, and study prescribed by the monastic life. But the relative serenity of the novitiate was followed by an agonizing quest for peace of soul during the next five years. The same fear of death and judgment which had driven him into the monastery now came to plague him again. These fears were accentuated by the first requirement of the monastic life, that one concentrate all one's activities and attitudes upon devotion to God.

In Luther's monastery, emphasis was placed upon self-analysis and the frequent reading of the Scriptures to avoid the mere passive following of the monastic groove. Such self-analysis led many monks to excessive scruples since the degree of their devotion to the service of God was to some extent measured by the avoidance of worldly or carnal thoughts.

Luther, however, was not mainly concerned with the extent of his devotion in this sense. How could he satisfy a God who is holy and just and who would therefore require nothing less from man? God, being completely holy and just, cannot be approached by gradations; he must demand total fulfillment. Even if man does his utmost, how can he be assured that God will not just turn his face away? Neither the extent nor the intensity of man's devotion can compel God to acceptance.

It was this conception of God that produced that terrible sense of isolation which Luther came to feel in the face of the Great Judge, before whom he would stand all alone. Death always stood at the door; hence at any moment he might find himself before this just and holy Judge. As we have seen, the church sought to provide, through sacramental and other means, a kind of collective security. Weak and sinful man, in confronting the Great Judge, could lean for support on the great intermediary, the church, established by Christ Himself and imputing to man through the sacraments the divine grace which Christ's sacrificial death for the sins of mankind had gained for man. But, granted that this sufficed for all the sins of mankind if they but believed, how could he, Martin Luther, be assured that divine grace could be imputed to him?

JUSTIFICATION BY FAITH

Luther's intense concern with the problem of bridging the gulf between a righteous God and himself did not grow merely out of a hyper-sensitivity toward his own guilt; it also had an intellectual basis. Throughout the years of soul struggle he pursued an intense study of the Scriptures and the writings of the theologians.

Luther's prior had directed him to the study of theology at Erfurt. Later, in 1508, he joined the monastery at Wittenberg. There, in this small Saxon town on the Elbe, the Elector, Frederick the Wise, had established a university in 1502. Luther entered the university to continue his theological studies and to teach in the faculty of arts. After a brief return to Erfurt and a journey to Rome in 1510 in behalf of the affairs of this order, he was finally established at Wittenberg. In 1512 he was made a doctor of theology, and he assumed the duties of professor of theology at the university. He took over the teaching activities previously performed by the vicar of the order, Johannes von Staupitz, who had, in the course of a year or more of close contact with Luther, directed him to the study of the mystics as a way of bridging the gulf between God and man.

Luther tells us that he was of the school of Occam. The scholastic philosophy of William of Occam and his followers virtually deprived God of all rational attributes and made Him the abstract embodiment of will and power. God as an absolute sovereign will was bound by no considerations of obligation to the human creature who had sinned against Him. This conception rendered acute the soul struggle that cast Luther into deepest despair. The intensity of his feeling may be surmised from the fact that he confesses that sometimes he was led to almost hate and blaspheme God. But rather suddenly, in the course of 1511 and 1512, a light broke in his mind.

The reading of the mystics from St. Bernard of Clairvaux to Tauler (d. 1361) and an anonymous work, *Theologia Germania*, prepared the way. To these mystics God was not the raging storm but the still small voice. He was not to be pursued, but He entered the soul of man when one least expected it. From them Luther was led back to St. Augustine and finally to St. Paul, both of whom also came to a sense of both the remoteness and the immediacy of God through an intense soul struggle followed by vivid illumination.

From St. Paul Luther learned that the warfare between the flesh and the spirit goes on without ceasing and that the spirit has no power of itself to overcome the flesh. For the spirit to seek to conquer the appetites of the flesh served merely to make the recollection of the latter all the more keen. Spirit and flesh are so intermingled in man as to make it impossible to separate one from the other. Hence the monk's endeavor to purge the spirit of carnal desire was fruitless. Luther himself gave up his agonizing prayer and fasting. In fact, he became quite lax with respect to monastic devotional and ascetic requirements. It seemed not only futile but positively a sinful arrogance to assume that a majestic and holy God could be won that way.

Luther had come a long way when he arrived at the paradoxical conclusion that when God seems most remote from us, God is actually nearest to us. He saw that when God is referred to as just, this did not mean a legal justice requiring an equivalence of merit. Justice meant mercy, a recognition of the total inadequacy of man to satisfy God's standards of righteousness and perfection. Man must achieve a complete sense of his inadequacy and impotence before God will recognize him. He must have complete faith that God will then grant him grace. This is the meaning of the phrase "the righteous shall live by faith" (Romans I, 17). This assurance is a completely free gift, not to be earned. Man is endowed with a moral conscience, not to enable him mainly to lead a better life in order to earn merit before God, but to make him aware of his complete impotence in order that he may realize that salvation is a completely free gift. There is no compelling God. God freely bestows grace in conformity with His own sovereign will. Man must have faith in this assurance.

The Gospel as the word of God carries this assurance by its own inner power to the believer. Faith and assurance therefore go hand in hand. There is a mutual interaction of one upon the other; and available to all who read with the eyes of faith is the realization that it is not merit but the free gift that makes man's salvation possible.

Put in other words, the more God is abstracted from all human qualities, the more remote He becomes, the more man feels his own insignificance and impotence. Man realizes that he must strip himself of all dependence on intermediaries such as metaphysical concepts, ecclesiastical institutions, and priestly rites, down to where he has only the *will to believe*. This will to believe finds its center in Christ, in whom the divine and human are united in paradoxical fashion. Without Christ there would be no reconciliation between God and man. There would actually be no religion. Without Him, man could and would not know God. In Him the divine becomes embodied in a particular human personality of a specific time and place. In Him a holy and perfect deity assumes the form of a helpless babe and dies an ignominious death. But these depths of humiliation also reveal the immeasurable heights of divine mercy. We thus encounter in Christ both the judging God and the guilty man.

FROM CRITICISM OF ABUSES TO REPUDIATION OF AUTHORITY

To Luther religious inwardness meant only a return to the ancient purity of the faith of St. Augustine and St. Paul, and the repudiation of scholasticism and Aristotle. But some of his associates at Wittenberg were much more concerned with the consequences to be drawn from it for the external forms of worship and ecclesiastic organization. Only slowly did Luther come to make the "rediscovered faith" the basis for a criticism of ecclesiastical abuses and finally of authority in the church.

His position as a doctor of theology at Wittenberg gradually caused him to develop a critical point of view. It was the function of doctors of the church, in their role as teachers, to safeguard and maintain the purity of religious truth. The students soon came to sense, in the lectures he gave between 1513 and 1516 on the Psalms and on Romans, that a new breath of life was moving through the musty halls of theology. Luther's point of departure from the orthodox was neither that of evangelical poverty nor, as in the case of Wycliffe and Hus, that of ecclesiastical organization and dogma. Yet he did not adopt the purely ascetic inwardness of mysticism which regarded ecclesiastical organization and practice as the mere symbolical shells of religion. For him the center of religious gravity moved to the inward purity of a faith of conviction and assurance, away from the outward observance of rite and cult. The latter derived their spiritual values from the former and not from an independent sacrosanct source of ecclesiastical authority.

On October 31, 1517 Luther posted ninety-five propositions or theses for discussion on the door of the church at Wittenberg. Their main purport was that the payment of a sum of money for an indulgence as satisfaction for sins in no sense took the place of the inner feeling of penitence. This implied a criticism not so much of the institution as such, as of the way in which the distribution of indulgences was being commercialized by such hawkers as the Dominican monk Tetzel, who apparently gave the impression that the mere purchase of an indulgence was sufficient to cover both penitence and penalties. It covered the dead as well as the living, Tetzel indicated in the catchy couplet attributed to him: "When the coin in the chest clings, the soul from purgatory springs."

Three factors drove Luther to the abandonment of a life of religious meditation and scholarly study and teaching. First and foremost, his whole soul struggle had produced a new religious consciousness and conviction from which he increasingly judged the adequacy of institutions and rites. Second, his criticism of indulgences and other practices produced such widespread acclaim that he became the center of a great popular and national movement. And third, the opposition of ecclesiastical authorities impelled him step by step to the abandonment of traditional institutions and practices in the interest of remaining consistent with his fundamental convictions.

The widespread interest aroused by the theses was most amazing to Luther. He had intended them only for debate among his learned colleagues. But they were spread widely by the printing press. Their appearance coincided with the growing discontent and criticism of the papacy, fomented by the many itinerant preachers and by humanists such as Ulrich von Hutten. The papacy was felt to be a foreign power exploiting the Germans. The proceeds from the indulgence of 1517 were to go in part to Albert of Hohenzollern, archbishop of Mainz, to defray the cost of a papal dispensation for holding more than one ecclesiastical office; the remainder was to go to the building of St. Peter's in Rome. The German Diets also criticized the operations of Italian bankers and merchants in drawing money out of the country. The strong feeling of some of these Diets is evident in the reference to the pope as that "hell-hound in Rome."

Naturally, various ecclesiastical authorities sought to put pressure on Luther to avoid further controversy and disturbance of the public order. But, in the beginning, considerations of political and social expediency exerted little influence upon him. He was moved by the belief that the freedom of the Christian man was expressed through his disclosure of his fundamental convictions. This was all the more true for him as a professor of theology. In a debate with his leading intellectual opponent, Dr. Eck of Ingolstadt, in 1519 at Leipzig, Luther was driven by Eck's prodding to a repudiation not only of papal authority, but even that of a church council, when it was pointed out that the Council of Constance had condemned Hus.

Luther eventually came to admit that only the individual conscience can be the final interpreter of Scripture. He was thus led to a progressive insight as to how the fundamental principle of justification by faith alone ran counter to the whole ecclesiastical edifice of the time.

In three great pamphlets published in 1520 and widely distributed, he presented his fundamental ideas of Christian liberty. They were entitled *An Address to the Christian Nobility of the German Nation, The Babylonian Captivity of the Church, The Liberty of a Christian Man.* Luther attacked what he called the walls that constrained the Christian. Fundamentally, they were comprised in the authority claimed by the papacy to call councils and to interpret the Scriptures. In opposition to this universal claim Luther presented his conception of the universal priesthood of believers. Each man is his own priest in approaching God. Only believers, not men in general, are their own priests. Faith is necessary to bring one directly into contact with God—faith only. The church is not the authoritative interpreter of the Scriptures since each believer must derive his own assurance of salvation from them. The infallibility of the papacy is therefore a usurpation. Not even the church council can stand between the believer and God. The sacraments are viewed as symbols of inward change; they have no magical power in themselves.

For Luther these propositions constituted the declaration of the freedom of the Christian man. They meant in substance that there was no real reform possible through the external prescription of church or state. The real change could come only by way of an inward transformation which would bear fruit in external behaviour.

THE FREEDOM OF MODERN MAN

Neither Paracelsus, Erasmus, nor Luther contemplated the completely secular universe which seemed to be opening up to modern man. But each in his way contributed toward that prospect. While for them their quests followed roads which led directly to God, modern man has been increasingly more concerned with the road rather than with its direction. The approach by way of nature led to mechanistic science, and by way of culture to historical studies. The assurance of the Gospel was transformed into the acceptance of confessional creed. The Lutheran quest for a direct way to God continued the process of secularization initiated by the *sacerdotium* in depriving the *sacrum imperium* of its sacrosanct character. In the long run, it deprived the temporal spheres of all direct religious significance and eventually led to the completely secularized realms of politics, society, and culture. Man today seems to be going even a step farther by taking his eyes off the road and confining himself to the sheer experience of travel.

V

The Conflict of Confessions

*T*he religious position of Luther exerted a much greater immediate impact upon church and state than that of Erasmus and Paracelsus. Neither overtly criticized the church as such but only certain conditions within Christendom as a whole. Paracelsus, the exponent of a new role for the physician and of a new view of nature, did not become the protagonist of a reform program although some of his ideas and associations indicate affinity with sectarian circles and crisis groups. Erasmus, much as he shied away from the rough and tumble of public affairs, became perforce by the action of those who espoused his views the symbol if not the proponent of a reform program. Even Luther, in view of his insistence on the necessity of the inner transfiguring force of faith, was very reluctant to propose positive reform.

REFORM ATTITUDES AND POLITICAL AND SOCIAL GROUPS

In application to current problems, the religious positions of Luther and Erasmus became the basis of statements of faith on which programs of reform were based. These statements of faith assumed a confessional character as they became the test of allegiance to rival religious groups. In the first half of the sixteenth century the lines between religious groups were still fluctuating and the possibility of compromises and reconciliations still existed. But in the second half of the century, Catholics, Lutherans, and Calvinists hardened into definite molds, especially as rulers took up the cudgels in behalf of one or the other confessions. Thus the center of gravity shifted from the general problem of reform of the church to the organization of separate churches, each with its own confessional statement.

The initial impact of the new ideas was influenced by the existence of three major political and social groupings within the *Reich*. Each of these took over ideas appropriate to its interests as determined by its traditional orientation, and each showed marked inner divisions.

First, the circle around the emperor was strongly influenced by Erasmian ideas of reform, but the emperor himself was by temperament a traditionalist who, moreover, was so widely involved in political conflicts by virtue of the ramifications of his territorial possessions that he could devote relatively little attention to the religious problems of the *Reich*.

Second, the crisis groups—knights, peasants, and lower orders in the towns—sought either to give Luther's position a nationalist and class orientation or to take over ideas and aspirations from the sectarian heritage.

Finally, the most influential local ruling group, the princes along with the oligarchies in the towns, employed the Lutheran attack on the church to achieve liberation from ecclesiastical laws and prescriptions, and set up their own form of church organization and government.

ERASMIAN AND LUTHERAN REFORM

The Erasmian ideal naturally appealed to many of the humanists connected with political circles, for it sought enlightenment combined with tolerance and piety. The existing church, they felt, either catered to the superstition, bigotry, and ignorance of the masses or to the senseless jargon of scholastic philosophy. The humanists believed that Christianity must return to the basic, simple truths of the philosophy of Christ, which were in spirit and in substance like those of the great pagan ancients.

Furthermore, they held that reform should come from the top, beginning particularly with the education and enlightenment of the clergy on the principle that, where the humanities flourish, piety is nourished. It was the function of the prince to maintain peace and tolerance in order that culture and piety might mutually fructify each other. To this end, there should be the collaboration of the enlightened ruler with the humanist scholar. The new absolute princes were gathering about them circles of humanists, artists, and scientists, and apparently laying the basis for the promotion of reform from above. The Spanish King Charles, who was crowned Emperor Charles V in 1519, surrounded himself with men like the Burgundian Gattinara (d. 1530), the friend of Erasmus who was himself in direct correspondence with members of the imperial circle.

To the Germans, Charles was a Hapsburg, the grandson of Maximilian, who had sought to combine the greatness of the *Reich* with the promotion of a German national culture. Maximilian had been the idol of the humanists and the symbol of the rising national sentiment prevalent among some of them. Ulrich von Hutten, the most vocal of the humanists, had tried to link this nascent nationalism and Luther's religious opposition to the papacy with the revival of the Empire. But he failed in both of these projects principally because the new emperor had no sympathy for heretics and furthermore thought of the Empire in medieval universal terms, not in national German ones.

Luther always opposed using his religious position as a springboard for political and social reform. His reaction to an acute inner experience led him to regard any kind of meritorious works or institutional reform with the fear that the divine might again be enshrined in an institution, form, or thing. Here he was returning to the prophetic and early Christian attack on the imprisonment of the spirit either in priestly ritual or in the letter of the law. His prophetic attack upon the priestly sacramental role of the church did not rule out the priestly function altogether; he transferred it to what he called the preaching of "the Word."

Luther was, therefore, not greatly concerned with the organization of a church. He left this to the princes. He regarded the translation of the Bible, which he had begun in 1521, as his most important achievement. Since every believer was his own priest and could find the Word directly without the intermediary of ecclesiastical authority, it was obviously necessary to make the Bible available to him in a form which he could read. To Luther, the Bible spoke unequivocally, but he did not realize fully that it did not do so to other men who had not his intense personal experience.

There were varying reactions to Luther's basic position. The papal legate, Aleander, a prominent humanist, argued that this position was based upon sheer subjectivism and would lead to individual license in moral and religious affairs, since there existed no objective ecclesiastical authority for determining for the common people either goodness or religious truth.

An opposite reaction was that of the religious radicals. They contended that nothing should be allowed which was not specifically presented in the Bible, whose literal meaning must be accepted even to the extent of determining political and social conditions. This ran counter to Luther's point of view that the Bible is not the Word of God but that the Word is in the Bible.

A third reaction was implicit in the policy of the princes, who were concerned with filling the ecclesiastical vacuum created by Luther's repudiation of papal authority by putting in its place their own sovereignty. Luther's emphasis on the inwardness of the religious experience and the expanding power of the princes contributed toward making religion a matter of spirit or *Geist* whose other pole was that of authority or *Macht*. Authority should not determine man's inner religious experience, but it should insist on conformity of doctrine and worship in the interest of public order.

In his attack upon the papacy Luther became increasingly dependent upon the princes. They became for him the chief defenders of the laity against various forms of ecclesiastical exploitation. And against imperial prohibitions they became the chief defenders of the liberty to preach and teach. Here was the beginning of that fateful relationship between prince and professor which was to be a determining factor in German development down to the twentieth century.

It is conceivable that Lutheranism might have become the national religion of the Germans embodied in a completely independent national church. It is also conceivable that an independent autonomous church within a reformed Catholicism might have been achieved along the lines suggested by the Hussite church in Bohemia. In the first case, a series of national churches, independent of the papacy and conforming to the general political organization of Europe, would have been established in which the papacy would be reduced to a local Italian position. Or a series of autonomous national ecclesiastical organizations could have been created within the ancient Roman Catholic church which would retain the pope as its nominal head. Neither one of these projects, which occupied the minds of men at the time, was totally realized; both were in part achieved.

The inconclusive character of the whole movement must be borne in mind in considering the crisis period from 1521 to 1555. Neither the hope of Luther for a national church nor that of the Erasmians for a reformed church with local autonomy materialized. Nor did the dream of the crisis groups that the freedom of the Christian man would bring a new social and political order come true.

RADICALISM: SCRIPTURAL NORM AND INNER LIGHT

The fate of this dream was largely determined in the decade from 1520 to 1530. The Germans then stood on the brink of what looked like a social revolution. Luther's notion of the freedom of the Christian man opened up to many the vision of a new religious and social order. Not only were specific oppressions of landlord and clergy to be done away with, but all men were to be united in a truly spiritual church.

Again, both the Erasmians and radicals thought of the Bible as having a prescriptive character, as presenting explicitly the norms of moral conduct and of social and political justice. They differed fundamentally on how these norms were to be applied. The Erasmians stood for application by "enlightened" constituted authorities, such as the wise prince and cultured clergy, who could transcend the "natural" barbarism of men. For the radicals, the application flowed from the inner illumination of the spirit in each man's soul, the expression of which is thwarted by the coercion of ecclesiastical and political authority.

For Luther the Bible presented in the first instance an assurance of salvation, an assurance which had to be transformed in the believer into an inward conviction. The norms of conduct and of social order had, then, to flow from this transformation. Moreover, Luther's fear that a special sacrosanct quality might be attributed to outward forms of any kind made him reluctant to favor new forms or advocate the discarding of old ones. For Luther religion should be kept free from entanglement in the external matters of the world, otherwise it would lose its inwardness.

Many itinerant preachers and fugitive pamphlets, however, inveighing against the "corrupt clergy" and the "anti-Christ" at Rome, called for a total purge of all the old sacramental forms of worship. An outbreak of iconoclastic fury hit Wittenberg and other places while Luther was in the Wartburg in 1521. Among the professors at the University, moderates such as Melancthon sought to curb the outbreaks, but others, like Karlstadt, preached the sovereignty of the congregation and projected an ideal spiritual community. In this ticklish situation, which might have turned the "authorities" against all "reform" as subversive, Luther was recalled, and he then expressed his opposition to both the congregational principle and to the extreme purging of ancient practices and forms. He stood for a church in which officials would exercise authority against the community. He also stood for inner freedom against a legalistic and puritanical approach to the problem of outward conduct, both in religious and moral matters.

Among the disturbers of Christian order in Wittenberg and elsewhere were a number of enthusiasts called the "Zwickau prophets." Zwickau was a small mining town on the Bohemian border where Taborite and Lutheran influences had mingled. The mining towns—for example, Luther's home town of Mansfeld—were turbulent, but in Zwickau the weavers were probably the most active group. In the Middle Ages the words "weaver" and "heretic" were practically synonymous in certain areas.

Among the Zwickau radicals, Thomas Müntzer (1490–1525) was undoubtedly the most original and redoubtable. He was one of the most learned theological and humanist scholars of the time. Influenced by Luther's ideas he had already attained renown as a preacher in Zwickau, from which he was driven in 1521 to scatter the seeds of religious radicalism through the central part of the *Reich*.

Müntzer was by far the ablest opponent of Luther among the radicals. He accepted along with others the Joachimite idea of a third Age of the Spirit which would manifest itself in a Thousand-Year *Reich*. This was to be the actual fulfillment of the prophecy of Christ, that His spirit would eventually descend among men and reign over them. A second and related notion of Müntzer's was that of the return of prophecy, particularly among the poor and uneducated who have dreams and visions. The "inner world" was to manifest itself in this form as against Luther's emphasis upon the Scriptures as the Word of God, which, in this view, created a new tyranny in place of the old papacy. A third idea was that the elect, the real prophets, would eventually take over and destroy all the ungodly who sit in high places in both church and state.

Müntzer was driven from place to place, finally ending up in 1524 in Mühlhausen, in Thuringia, an important center of agitation among the lower populace of town and country. He became the chief ideological leader of the Peasant Revolt in 1525, and he shared its catastrophic demise.

A different type of radical was Sebastian Frank (1499–1545). In him we see an individualism which eschewed both sectarian utopianism and ecclesiastical authoritarianism and sacramentalism. He was influenced especially by the speculative mystical tendency of later medieval thought and became an admirer of Erasmus.

Probably the chief basic idea he propounded was that of the invisible church, not a new idea but made by Frank into a positive force. Christ is in every man in the form of an "inner light" which illumines his soul. Every man should therefore be allowed to maintain his own individual contact with the divine source of light. Here was expressed Frank's opposition to all forms of sacramentalism and bibliolatry.

Also distinctive was Frank's interpretation of history. The inner light must carry on a continual struggle against the forces of authority presented by popes and priests. In this dialectical conflict it is the peculiar role of the heretic to keep alive the inner illumination of the spirit in man's soul, always in danger of being extinguished by all manner of coercions. Here we have for the first time a conception of the heretic as playing a positive role in history.

Frank had served as a priest in Augsburg. He then became a Lutheran preacher in Nuremburg, but gave this up in 1528 to become a free-lance writer. He made a living by the humble and onerous occupation of soap-making. Persecution finally drove him to Basel, where he disappeared from sight. He himself had argued that it was also the peculiar role of the heretic to dwell in obscurity.

Müntzer and Frank exemplify the two extremes of religious radicalism of the sixteenth century. Communal radicalism appeared in great waves in the early sixteenth century and again in the twentieth century. Individualistic radicalism was a general pervasive force, encountered again and again in succeeding centuries.

THE THREAT OF SOCIAL REVOLUTION

We have already seen that the crisis groups were to be found especially among the knights, the peasants, and the burghers. Confronted by new economic, social, and political forces, these classes were in a state of ferment. It is difficult, however, to say whether they were more concerned with demanding recovery of ancient rights or with the coming of a new order of things. Ambiguity grew out of the suspension of these groups between an idealized old *Reich*, to which many looked back with a nostalgic yearning, and the "new order" of princely absolutism, proprietary landlordism, and commercial capitalism, which was actually coming into being and which in general presaged the depression and degradation of these groups.

The chief center of unrest was in the southwest, especially in the ancient duchies of Swabia and Franconia. Here had occurred, with the break-up of these duchies, the greatest degree of splitting up of principalities and peasant holdings. It is the area also which was influenced most by the example of the Swiss revolt, in which both peasant and burgher had attained freedom from princely and ecclesiastical domination. In the Swiss cantons, with their high degree of individual autonomy and self-government, radicals and sectarian groups found havens and even centers from which to disseminate their ideas.

The knights had sought to improve their condition principally by mercenary service and brigandage. They would probably have lapsed gradually into desuetude and oblivion if they had not found a leader and an ideology. Their leader was the famous *condottiere*, Franz von Sickingen (1481–1523). Educated under Reuchlin, he served in various capacities in the imperial service. He fortified the lands he held on the middle Rhine with many strong castles. From these he engaged in perpetual feuds with the princes and towns along the Rhine. He had also come under the influence of the ideas of Luther as interpreted by Ulrich von Hutten, who for a time found refuge with Sickingen at Landstuhl. Sickingen apparently aimed to restore the Empire and the ancient Germanic law against the princes and the "new" Roman law. He aimed to destroy the great ecclesiastical principalities and create a national church.

Sickingen led the knights against their old enemy, the Archbishop of Trier, but the Archbishop, aided by a coalition of princes, defeated Sickingen, who died from wounds on the day Landstuhl was taken by his enemies. Thus ended the dream of a common crusade spearheaded by the knights against the great enemies of the *Reich*, the princes and the priests.

From 1443 to 1517, the peasants were in sporadic revolt, known as the "*Bundschuh* rebellions." Peasant unrest was the product in part of the old grievances arising out of the encroachment of the landlord on the peasant's use of common field, forest, and stream. The Roman law, increasingly practiced in the courts, supported the landlord in these usurpations, so that the peasant always had to appeal to the old custom as against the landlord's rational law. It seems also that the peasant sensed a growing loss of role or function in the scheme of things. The old Germanic community consciousness was disappearing in the face of the new princely absolutism and proprietary landlordism. Luther, with his emphasis upon the Scriptures, provided a new basis of justice.

The great Peasant Revolt of 1525, like most peasant outbursts, had a very amorphous character. Gatherings of peasants occurred in various parts of southwest and central Germany. There was no concerted effort there. The only common proposals were presented in the Twelve Articles, which called for the free utilization of field, forest, and stream; the election of their own pastors; and the general easement of dues and labor services. In time the radicals took over, especially in Franconia, where the peasants were joined by town populations. Nowhere were there political leaders of vision among them who could view the role of the peasant in relationship to the structure of the *Reich* as a whole. A renegade noble, Florian Geyer, a former captain of *Landsknechte*, came the closest. He preached the brotherhood of noble and peasant, but he was, apparently, always regarded with suspicion by the noble-hating peasants. Attempts to unite the various regional forces failed.

When the peasants indulged in excesses, burning castles and murdering nobles, they incurred the wrath of Luther, who had initially urged upon landlords a more humane treatment of their peasants. He now resorted to the most drastic language, calling upon the princes to smite and slay the "murderous and robbing peasants." Luther's violent reaction may be ascribed to his feeling that the peasants had perverted the Word of God to justify their rebellion and ravaging. They had also raised their hands against divinely ordained authorities which had been established for the purpose of holding man in restraint. Authority, according to Luther, existed primarily to maintain the ordered conditions of society which would allow the preaching of the Word.

The peasant armies were defeated one by one and the movement brutally suppressed. Müntzer suffered torture and was beheaded. Peasant unrest still flared up on occasion but ceased to have political significance. In fact, not until the nineteenth century did revolution again raise its head among the lower orders of the population. There is no doubt that Luther's turning against the peasants and their allies, the townsmen, contributed toward the alienation of the lower orders of the population from the Lutheran movement, which tended henceforth to become increasingly a middle- and upper-class movement.

The common man of the gild had also been engaged in a long struggle with the ruling class of the towns, the oligarchy of gild masters. In retaliation against exclusion from the mastership and suppression of their own organizations, the journeymen and apprentices often joined forces with the peasants.

The most celebrated instance of the ferment in the towns was that which culminated in Münster, in northwest Germany, in 1534–35. Here again the religious ideas derived from Luther and Müntzer were combined with social and economic aspirations. Reform began with the expulsion of the bishop. In the course of the conflict with the patrician element, the reform party, under its radical leader, Bernard Rothman, invited the communist Anabaptists into the city.

The Anabaptists were in the main continuations of medieval sectarians like the Taborites, but they received a new stimulus from the Lutheran movement. They first appeared as a distinct group in Zürich, Switzerland from where they were driven by Zwingli. They then began to spread northward down the Rhine into Frisia and eastward into Moravia. The movement found its greatest response among the artisan class of the towns.

Their ideas had much in common with those of the Zwickau radicals such as Müntzer. They, too, subscribed to the notion of the inner light of prophecy as against the external tyranny of scripture and sacrament. But they also followed the religious communalism of sectarianism. Only those who were regenerated and saved could, by baptism, become members of the community. The ethic of the Gospel as expressed in the Sermon on the Mount was to be observed in every detail extending to the community of goods. All service to the state was forbidden as an expression of idolatry. The community of the regenerate awaited the coming of the Lord, who might appear at any moment and bring about the triumph of this community over the world, which now persecuted it.

Some of the Anabaptists were inclined toward a quietistic withdrawal from the world, but others were stirred by the call to destroy the ungodly. It was the latter element which took over in Münster during the long siege against the city by a coalition of princes, both Catholic and Lutheran. Jan Mathys and John of Leyden, both from Holland, took over the direction of the movement. They established community of goods and wives, and, while guilty of excesses against those who opposed them, showed the most amazing fortitude and faith. The city was finally taken, and, as in the case of the Peasant Revolt, the Anabaptists and their fellow travelers were hunted down and liquidated.

The Anabaptists were completely dispersed by the wave of persecution which set in. They found a haven in out-of-the-way corners, in Switzerland, in Bohemia, and mostly in Holland, where they came to be called Mennonites, after their leader, Menno Simons. These small groups, which also spread into the New World, have abandoned revolutionary social action and have turned inward to a purely quietistic communal existence.

Princely victory over the social revolution was decisive, and Lutheranism lost any stigma that might have attached to it of being subversive. The crucial problems became those of the reconciliation of religious beliefs and of the relations between emperor and princes.

THE FAILURE OF RECONCILIATION

The idea still persisted that all Christians would eventually be brought together again in a purified church to be achieved through a universal council. In the Lutheran territories—even in Electoral Saxony, where Luther lived—monasteries, the confessional, and the mass were not prohibited. This is indicative of the very fluid character of the situation.

An important influence in the attempt to effect a reconciliation of the diverse Protestant groups was Ulrich Zwingli (1484–1531). Under his influence, reform, the doing away with relics, images, and the mass was gradually inaugurated in Zürich after 1522. His primary concern was with moral reform as suggested by Erasmus, who influenced Zwingli as definitely as Luther did. Luther and Zwingli engaged in a disputation in 1529 over the nature of the Lord's Supper, but no agreement was reached. Luther again showed extreme reluctance to accept a basic change either in religious forms or in the political and social order.

At the Diet of Augsburg in 1530, the middle-of-the-roaders among both Protestants (as they were now called) and Catholics seemed to be in a position to effect a compromise. Melancthon appeared as Luther's representative. Like Zwingli, strongly influenced by Erasmian humanism, he was inclined to effect a reconciliation. Erasmus himself, while not present, was still in close touch with those within Charles V's circle who were bent upon reform as a means of bringing the Protestants back into the fold.

Melancthon presented the famous Confession of Augsburg as a basis for compromise. Long negotiations and arguments among the theologians ensued, finally resulting in failure. The Catholics presented a refutation, and the Zwinglians refused to accept the interpretation of the Lord's Supper. Reconciliation between Protestants and Catholics was not likely to succeed when the Protestants could not agree among themselves, nor when differences of dogma had to be reconciled among theological professors.

The Peace of Augsburg (1555) brought to a close, for the time being, the long struggle for the religious and political unity of the *Reich*. Victory went to the local ruling authorities: the princes in the territories and the ruling classes in the cities. *Obrigkeit*—authority combined with obedience—had definitely won out. The disintegration of the *Reich* into component territorial units, each with its absolute ruler, who was permitted to determine the religion of his subjects, was definitely inaugurated.

Charles, disillusioned, weary of spirit, and sick of body, abdicated and retired to Spain to lead the life of a recluse until his death in 1558. Here was a man who had won many battles and tactical victories but had lost a war. His own astuteness and command of great territorial resources had won him isolated triumphs, but the trends of the time pointed in other directions than that of unity of religious faith, the primacy of one church, and the union of Christendom under one ruler.

THE EXPANSIVE FORCE OF LUTHERANISM AND CALVINISM

At the middle of the sixteenth century it still looked as if Protestantism would make a complete sweep not only of the *Reich* but of the whole of Europe. Its onward march seemed to be carrying everything before it. A Venetian envoy made the somewhat exaggerated statement in 1557 that nine-tenths of the Germans had gone over to Protestantism. The old faith seemed to lack all power of resistance. Only the Hapsburgs, the Wittelsbachs, and a few of the rulers of the small states clung to the ancient church. Even Among the local nobility, Protestantism made great inroads, especially in the Hapsburg domains. The great ecclesiastical principalities along the Rhine—in particular the archbishoprics of Mainz, Trier, and Cologne —also appeared on the brink of going over. A preponderance of their population was Protestant. If these electoral principalities shifted over, the Protestants would definitely control the Electoral College of the Empire. Most of the imperial cities and the universities had gone into the Protestant camp.

"An original impulse weakens as it spreads; the living passion petrifies in codes and creeds; the revelation becomes a commonplace; and so the religion that began in vision ends in orthodoxy." [1] This analysis applies especially to Lutheranism, which in its inception was a great vision of Christian liberty; by the middle decades of the century it was already solidifying in dogmatic molds of orthodoxy.

After that, Lutheranism was carried forward largely by sheer momentum. Within the *Reich*, doctrinal controversy and confessional particularism increasingly sapped its strength. Elsewhere Lutheranism found a permanent lodging place only in the Scandinavian countries, where the initiative of the rulers overcame considerable general opposition. It spread into France, England, and especially into the Low Countries, but it succumbed to the pressure of hostile governments, to the march of a new variety of Protestantism, Calvinism, or to the Catholic Counter Reformation.

The second phase of the Reformation was inaugurated by two Latins, the Frenchman John Calvin (1509–1564) and the Spaniard Ignatius Loyola (1491–1566). They gave a new activism and militancy to the religious movements of the second half of the sixteenth century. The Lutheran movement originally had a spontaneous, popular character while Calvinism and Jesuitism were from their inception propagandistic and missionary in character.

Driven out of his own land by persecution, Calvin came to Geneva, Switzerland (first in 1536—permanently after 1541), which he made the headquarters of a missionary propaganda of tremendous sweep. He, like Zwingli, was indebted to Luther for the basic conception of justification by faith alone, but he gave it a new accent. Calvin emphasized not the inner experience of acquiring assurance of salvation but the sovereign act of God whereby some are predestined to be saved and others will consequently suffer damnation. Calvinists had a feeling of belonging to an elect group, of being an instrument in God's hands for the achievement of His glory. God was conceived as an active force; man was no mere passive receptacle of divine grace but a divinely appointed agent for the realization of God's purposes. Calvinism therefore manifested a more activistic spirit than Lutheranism, which tended, after the original insurgency, toward a passivity sometimes almost quietistic in character.

The Calvinists' insistence upon a "holy community" in which everyone toed the mark was regarded by Lutherans as a return to a religion of works. But to the Calvinist, works were but a projection of faith; he had no such lively sense of cleavage between faith and works as the Lutheran had. To the Calvinist works manifested themselves in the frame of a vocation or calling within which man *works* to the glory of God. The Lutheran's conception of *Beruf* had a much more static character. It implied being content with the station in life where God had placed one.

Calvinism also showed a much more vital political spirit than German Lutheranism. Through its close-knit organization based on the congregation, it could engage in an active resistance against a government which persecuted the faith. German Lutheranism only reluctantly took up arms even against those who persecuted it. This reluctance may be attributed to the particularistic policy of the princes in control of the church organization, who were always disinclined to collaboration and cooperation, even among themselves. In the Scandinavian countries Lutheranism manifested a quite different spirit.

Rigorous moralism together with democratic forms of church organization contributed to the continued splitting off of splinter groups from the Calvinistic churches. These groups were an expression not so much of dogmatic differences as of their conviction that the old religious community had become morally and spiritually lax. Their formation bears certain resemblances to the tendency in the medieval church for new monastic orders to separate from the old ones in response to the call for return to the rigor of the rule.

Sectarianism was of the greatest significance in sixteenth- and seventeenth-century England, resulting in the mingling of Calvinistic and Anabaptist currents in Congregationalists, Baptists, and Quakers who opposed both the state-church and absolutism in government. The consequent fusion of religious and political ideas produced radical democratic notions, which contributed greatly to the dynamic of the Puritan revolution.

In Lutheranism, however, as it became wedded to the princely absolutistic state, religious dissent came to be regarded as outright rebellion. There was no congregation taking the place of the bishop because the prince regarded himself as having stepped into the bishop's shoes. There could thus be no church juxtaposed to the state since the prince also organized the church. The capacity for religious dissent through the congregational organization gave Calvinism its power of resistance to hostile government and explains why, in the face of the latter, it easily supplanted Lutheranism.

Calvinism found lodging places in Germany in those areas along the Rhine and the eastern frontiers where Catholicism persisted among bishops, princes, and magnates. Large numbers of Calvinist refugees fled into the Rhineland principalities from either France or the Low Countries to avoid persecution and warfare, which began in the 1560's and continued with mounting intensity until the end of the century. These refugees formed scattered congregations, which here and there were accorded toleration, as in Cleve, Jülich, Berg, and Mark, where the rulers were Catholics but inclined toward an Erasmian reform program. Some princes along the Rhine went over to Calvinism and introduced it in their domains. The outstanding champion of Calvinism among them was the Elector of the Palatinate, Frederick III (d. 1576). Heidelberg University, in his domain, became the chief center of "reformed" —that is, Calvinistic—theology. The Heidelberg Catechism (1563) became the most widely accepted Calvinist doctrinal formulation.

PROTESTANT ORTHODOXY

The impact of Calvinism contributed greatly toward heightening theological controversy and toward the drawing of rigid lines of demarcation between religious groups. At the time of Luther's death (1546) it still was frequently difficult to distinguish Catholic from

Protestant except that the radical "left," the Anabaptists, were practically outlawed. The degrees of difference depended largely on how much of the forms of worship and organization of the old church had been discarded. Sometimes a priest held services first for his Catholic parishioners, then for the Protestants, dispensing with the mass for the latter. Obviously, this practice was likely to be characteristic of the highly mixed areas. But the influx of Calvinism, plus the heightened atmosphere of tension as religious conflicts broke out during the 1560's in the Netherlands and France, contributed to demarcation along confessional lines and to persecution.

In the face of Calvinism, which many associated with the radical sectarian Anabaptists, Lutheranism began to purify itself. Departures from the teachings of the "Master" were claimed to be oriented in the direction of heresy. Melancthon, who had stepped into Luther's shoes at Wittenberg, unwittingly contributed to the doctrinal turmoil by modifying the provisions of the Augsburg Confession with respect to the Lord's Supper in a direction suited to the Calvinists. Two factions developed among the Lutheran theologians: one group, following Melancthon along the path of reconciliation, was known as the crypto-Calvinists; the other comprised staunch advocates of an unalterable orthodoxy.

Each prince sought to issue statements of faith for the people of his territories. These were consequently complete statements of the articles of faith referred to generally as "confessions" rather than mere definitions of particular dogmas, as in the Middle Ages. Emphasis on the acceptance of these doctrinal molds took the place of inward experience, which was looked at askance as smacking of sectarianism. To Luther faith in God's assurance of salvation had meant a commitment whereby one took the gamble of not relying upon the collective means of salvation provided by the church. But now in the turmoil of religious and political conflict one sought absolute assurance and security in the correct doctrinal formulation.

Today we are inclined to regard the differences between these contending religious groups as trivial, but in our time we have encountered a furor of ideological strife and dogmatic formulation which future generations may regard in a similar light. Moreover, a difference in accent between Lutheran, Calvinist, and Catholic in the interpretation, for example, of the Lord's Supper was then related to the whole position of a particular faith by virtue of the theological interrelatedness of all parts of a confessional statement. Furthermore, the fundamental difference in ethos became more and more apparent in the succeeding two or three centuries as the process of secularization brought into relief differences with respect to authority and freedom, vocation and society, *Weltanschauung* and science.

The division between Lutherans and Calvinists was to render Protestantism weak in the face of a resurgent Catholicism, whose increasing aggressive power became clear in the 1580's—most of all in the south and west of the Germanies, where the various religious parties stood poised, waiting for the signal to begin action.

THE CATHOLIC REVIVAL

The revival of Catholicism during the middle decades was an event whose significance has been generally lost sight of in the depreciatory designation, *Counter Reformation*. It marked the crest of a wave of reform which began, as we have seen, in the fifteenth century—a reform of which Lutheranism and its allies were really a part.

In the middle decades of the sixteenth century the church became animated by a new sense of mission under strong papal leadership. It relied again on its medieval sources of strength, reform council and new religious orders. It developed the conviction that not only internal reform and regeneration were possible; it was possible even to root out heresy and restore the church throughout the Germanies and elsewhere. The recovery of religious unity was not to be achieved by an Erasmian program of compromise and reconciliation but by a definite demarcation of the lines of division so as to make fully clear what was heretical. This policy decision marked the appearance of what is generally called the Counter Reformation.

The Catholic revival derived its greatest impulse, as did militant Protestantism, from outside Germany. Spain and Italy were its main sources. Recovery of the ground lost was to be achieved by strict enforcement once again of the canonical rules and by return to the Roman tradition of a unitary authority. There was to be no scrapping of the medieval achievement by a return to the early Christian community, as the Protestants proposed.

A series of reforming popes appeared in these middle decades who, with the aid of the Jesuits, "cleaned house" in Rome and assumed direction of the Council of Trent (1545–1563). The lines of organization were tightened rather than relaxed. Above all, there was no compromise with the cardinal Protestant doctrine of justification by faith alone. There was no salvation outside of the church. The Thomist philosophy was virtually declared to be the official philosophy of the church. This came about largely through the prompting of the Jesuit doctors, who dominated the last session of the Council (1562–1563). Thomism, the classic expression of the medieval aspiration to achieve a synthesis of ancient thought and Christian belief, became, during the following centuries, a flexible instrument for keeping the church rooted in its ancient traditions and yet receptive to new currents of thought.

Of tremendous importance in the recovery of the church was the Society of Jesus, the new monastic order founded in 1534 by the Spaniard, Ignatius Loyola. It was originally intended by Loyola and his early companions to engage in missionary activity among the Moslems. But the church was confronted by the menace of Protestantism. Moreover, overseas expansion opened up new fields of activity in the new world of America and in the old world of Asia. In both areas, the Jesuits acquired great fame as explorers and missionaries.

The spirit and form of the new order came to be shaped increasingly by these prospects. It turned outward to combat heresy and heathendom rather than inward to the renewal of the contemplative religious life. Loyola, who had been a soldier, established a highly centralized organization culminating in the general of the order; it was based on careful recruitment of members and on vigilant mutual supervision. Founded on his own intense religious conversion and the writings of mystics, his *Spiritual Exercises* provided a psychological drill book which would serve to discipline the imagination and the will. The Jesuit went through a long period of probation that there might be no question about his competence or willingness to subordinate himself to the general will of the order. Once this basic decision was made, it was periodically re-enforced by his going through the *Exercises*.

Discipline of mind and will was carried over into the schools which the Jesuits established—schools which exerted their greatest influence from 1550 to 1650. Thomism was made the basis of university education. Since it was originally fashioned to combat Moslem rationalism, it would serve to defend Catholicism against heresy. Its very architectonic order provided intellectual discipline and assurance in debate. In the lower schools humanistic influence was apparent in the emphasis on ancient languages and literatures. Throughout, stress was laid on the grasp and retention of fundamentals by periodic drill and on the power and skill of persuasive argument. The Jesuit schools were so excellent and gained such reputation that many Protestants sent their children to them.

But in the early seventeenth century the Jesuits also became notorious in both Protestant and Catholic circles for their alleged political machinations. While they declined in general to assume ecclesiastical offices, they played an influential role as educators of the upper classes and as father-confessors to the influential and great among the nobility, princes, and kings of Catholic Europe. In these positions, the development of a princely absolutism, which was sloughing off feudal restraint but which had not yet been subjected to the "rule of law" or *raison d'état,* provided them with the opportunity of becoming the conscience of the prince. They thus assumed, in a sense, the role formerly played by the court astrologer. By virtue of their grasp of human motivation and temperament, they undoubtedly exerted a great, if indirect, influence on political affairs.

Nowhere were the opportunities for serving the church in both educational and political capacities more abundant and needed than in the *Reich.* There the church seemed to be losing out steadily; the Protestants had captured almost all of the universities, and they threatened, by the process of the secularization of lands and property, to take over ecclesiastical and monastic foundations. Even more important than the loss of these outer bastions was the spiritual decay and demoralization within the church. This might be attributed in part to the general apathy and resignation in the face of what looked like the irresistible onward march of Protestantism. But the Jesuit reformers ascribed it to the lack of adequate educational facilities for the training of priests. Thus, priests were ignorant, neglected their duties, and lived in concubinage, while monasteries were practically deserted.

By almost superhuman effort, a marked improvement was brought about at the end of the seventeenth century. The career of Peter Canisius, the first German to be admitted (1543) to the Society of Jesus, is indicative of how the recovery began. After a long period of education at Cologne, he was ordained priest in 1546; in 1548 he acquired his doctorate at the age of twenty-seven. He began missionary activities first as an eloquent preacher in Bavaria, Austria, and Bohemia, where Catholicism still retained its strongest footholds. He saw that what was required was a well-trained and devout priesthood. He devoted himself, therefore, to founding Jesuit colleges at Ingolstadt, Prague, Munich, and Innsbruck, and he encouraged those already in existence at Cologne, Augsburg, and Würzburg. He served as advisor to numerous princes and bishops, urging them to take a determined stand against Protestants in imperial diets and church councils. In addition, Canisius composed what became the standard book of religious instruction for the youth. All these activities extended over half a century, during which a new life began to course through the old church.

The Jesuits made much of impressive ritual and popular sermons, and they encouraged regular communion and confession. But the Counter Reformation would hardly have made the advances it did without the help of political rulers, and it was in this field that the Jesuits achieved their greatest successes. But like Protestantism, the new Catholicism also came under the domination of the emerging absolute state, and, subverted to political ends, it lost its original *élan*.

RELIGIOUS DIVISION AND TOLERATION

More than one-third of the Germanies had been brought back into Roman Catholicism by the opening of the Thirty Years' War in 1618. But the important consideration was that the Germanies did not achieve religious unity in spite of the crusading drives of Calvinism and of Catholicism. Germans continued to be divided between Catholics, Calvinists, and Lutherans, with the latter predominating in numbers. As a consequence, they came to be drawn culturally in three different directions: toward the Catholic south, the Calvinist northwest, and the Lutheran northeast. This regional differentiation was to have a continuing and decisive influence on national cultural development.

Religious and cultural diversity permitted considerable freedom of learning and opinion among the hundreds of German states. Many princes ruled over populations of mixed faiths, and therefore were constrained to practice toleration; a relatively small but significant number were tolerant in principle. In the communities where the contending religious parties were fairly evenly balanced, middle-of-the-road points of view naturally appeared. The Calvinist Hohenzollerns, while they could not win over their Lutheran subjects to their faith, established toleration for it.

The King of Poland, confronted with a seething mixture of religious faiths and groups in his kingdom, called a conference in 1645 at Thorn of Catholics, Lutherans, and Reformed to affect a reconciliation. Nothing immediate came of it, nor of a number of other such colloquies, but it was indicative of a mounting desire to overcome the religious conflicts on the part of a number of enlightened rulers and men of learning of whom the most influential was Georg Calixtus (1586–1656), of the University of Helmstedt. The following quotation indicates the limited tolerance of even this most enlightened humanist scholar, who at Thorn sought to point out that Lutherans, Calvinists, and Catholics were all indebted to and should return to the basic principles of Christianity laid down during its first five centuries:

> We do not fanatically reject everything which the Pope has; for if so, we would reject Christianity. But this we complain of, that the Pope will not abide by what he has inherited from the Apostles. . . . Antichrist indeed sits in the temple of God, and yet it remains the temple of God, by the sustaining power of Christ. Luther did not intend to introduce innovations: he held to the Creeds of the first centuries. If there was no Luther before the sixteenth century, neither was there a Council of Trent to make new dogmas. . . .[2]

The inner dimension of religious experience opened up by Luther and Loyola threatened to be lost sight of in the intellectualized frame of dogmatic formula, intended to insure orthodoxy. To provide the conceptual terms for describing justification by faith, even Aristotle was resorted to. But the very dogmatic externalization, which now took the place of image and relic in the old church, again produced a reaction in an emotional inwardness expressed in religious songs and hymns and in a literature of devotion like that of the *Imitation of Christ*. This tendency attained its culmination in Pietism, which will be discussed in a later chapter.

CULTURAL EFFECTS: THE IMPORTANCE OF UNIVERSITIES

The oscillation of both Protestantism and Catholicism between the poles of an intellectualized dogmatic orthodoxy and a heartfelt and glowing devotion resulted in different cultural effects. Lutheranism expressed its peculiar devotional ethos especially in music—in congregational singing, out of which grew its marvelous collection of hymns and songs. Catholicism, on the other hand, experienced a revival of church building in which the influence of the Jesuits was especially significant. The Catholics aimed at producing, by means of space composition and decoration, definitely calculated effects upon the feelings of the worshiper. Most typical of this tendency was the combination of ecstatic emotionalism with naturalistic rendering in the representation of saints and madonnas in the Baroque style, a style that did not reach its peak in the Germanies until the second half of the seventeenth and early eighteenth centuries in both religious and secular edifices.

The other pole, that of dogmatic interest, is evident in the importance of the universities, especially so in the Protestant communities. Reference has been made to the alliance of prince and professor in this age. Each prince sought to found a university in his own territory at which his brand of theology would be taught. The university became essential in supplying jurists and pastors, for whom the demand had greatly increased by virtue of the expansion of the practice of Roman law and the new theological interests.

In Germany's intellectual and public life, the university was of particular significance. Comparison has been suggested with the role of the salon in France, which also began the significant phase of its career in the seventeenth century. In it, people of many interests talked about many things in an informal give-and-take, interlarded by sparkling wit and the *bon mot*. Such conversation, enveloped in an atmosphere of good manners and taste, was promoted by the creative force of *esprit*.

The German university was something quite different. In the sixteenth and seventeenth centuries it assumed its role not as the arbiter of taste but as the authority in matters theological and legal. Princes called upon professors to give learned opinions on doctrinal matters and legal principles. The university thus came to assume the role of what may be called appellate jurisdiction in matters pertaining to the sphere of *Geist*, which stands over against *Macht*, embodied in the state. It was thus that *sacerdotium* and *imperium* came to be distinguished in the Reformation.

While Protestant and Catholic theology received a new inoculation of scholasticism, humanistic studies involving the ancient languages and literature, stimulated by Protestant emphasis on the Scriptures and their exegesis, continued to play a major educational role from the lower schools to the universities. In order to secure adequately trained recruits for the ministry Melancthon had promoted the study of Greek in the secondary schools, thus establishing the humanistic *Gymnasium*. It came to provide the educational background of generations of pastors, many of whose sons became men of great learning for which Germany was distinguished in the nineteenth century.

The basis of the great edifice of German humanistic learning and scholarship of that century was actually laid in the seventeenth-century universities. The main foundation was the philological-historical approach to the study of religion and culture. It was motivated on the Protestant side mainly by the desire to demonstrate by the appeal to historical evidence that the characteristic Catholic institutions and practices such as the papacy, monasticism, and sacramentalism had not existed in the first five or six centuries of Christianity, but were later medieval fabrications. There were those who, like Calixtus, inferred from this proposition that both Protestants and Catholics had peculiarities that were not to be found in those early centuries; that common beliefs and practices were, however, certainly to be found there and then; and that these common elements were, therefore, genuine Christianity. Thus there was the persistence of the humanistic aspiration to return to the pure springs and sources of the Christian faith in its ancient cultural matrix.

Emphasis on the development of institutions as the embodiment of truth and grace turned Catholics to the production of books on saints' lives and monastic histories, to which textual criticism was also applied. The search for criteria to determine the authenticity of texts, charters, and histories contributed to the foundation of a great array of sciences dealing with writing, seals, coins, and charters. They were concerned mainly with determining the authenticity of a particular document by fixing time and place of composition. This strong sense of historical timeliness served eventually to undermine men's attachment to particular beliefs and institutions, as it was recognized that they arose in response to the needs and aspirations of a particular age long since gone.

THE SPIRIT OF ERASMUS VERSUS THE SPIRIT OF LUTHER

There were two trends in seventeenth-century religious thought which were coming to the fore and which served to mitigate the bitterness of religious controversy—trends which, in the long run, contributed toward laying the basis of religious toleration.

There was the urge of some princes and a number of men of learning to bring about a reconciliation of the contending confessions by insisting that the common denominators of belief and practice were basic to the Christian faith and that the differences were of minor concern. One might, of course, proceed to the further assumption, as the Englishman Herbert of Cherbury did, that the common denominators of all religions composed the basic elements of natural religion.

There was also an emphasis on religious experience as purely inward and mystical. Dogma and ritual were but the outward shells. In the seventeenth century this conception of religion was directed against the assumption that any one confession in its theological formulas embodied the true faith. It was naturally the view of the "still in the land" and limited to individuals and small groups. Its pervasive influence nevertheless pointed to the new discovery of religion as a private affair of the individual conscience. These ideas contributed toward breaking down the walls of dogma and tradition and were the bases of modern liberalism. In them is reflected preeminently the critical spirit of Erasmus.

The greatest exponent of the "freedom of faith" was Luther. A distinction must be made, however. On the one hand, there is the freedom to hold to whatever belief one's conscience dictates. This is the modern view. On the other, Luther's conception was that of freedom arising out of the Gospel assurance of salvation. This kind of freedom is a free gift whose necessary accompaniment is faith. For Luther, this was the only kind of real freedom available to man since it involved his fundamental welfare, that is, eternal salvation.

The confessions were thus in a sense constitutional guarantees setting up the conditions of belief necessary to the latter kind of freedom. They were intended to guard one's approach to the Word so that one would not be hindered or hampered by false ideas and deception.

It is obvious that the Erasmian conception of freedom of belief—as against freedom of faith—also assumed guarantees, however, of the enlightened few as against the ignorant masses. The guarantees would be provided either by the wise ruler and enlightened clergy or later, by actual constitutional guarantees. Only much later, in the nineteenth century, was it assumed by many that all could become enlightened. Today the distinction no longer exists or has been reduced to the question of the degree of credulity or gullibility.

Looking back toward the *sacrum imperium* we are struck by two other decisive and complementary changes. First, the religious unity on which the *Reich* had been based from its inception was decisively broken. Neither Protestantism nor Catholicism achieved a decisive preponderance, as they did in most Western countries. In the long run the religious schism served to hinder an effective national union of Germans. It made them, in general, eschew political solutions for the more profound but irreconcilable considerations of *Weltanschauung*. In the united Germany of the late nineteenth century the parties even reflected "fundamental" differences of *Weltan-*

schauung, which stemmed from the conflict of religious ideologies of the second half of the sixteenth century.

A second decisive change, long in process of development, was the victory of the princes in the *Reich.* From a complex of feudal claims there now definitely emerged the territorial state ruled by an absolute sovereign. Since the Augsburg Peace accorded to this sovereign control over the religious persuasion of his subjects, the church as an *outside* power exercising decisive influence through the exaction of fees and taxes or the determination of dogma and rites or the exercise of discipline over the clergy had virtually ceased to exist. This came to be true in the main for both Catholics and Protestants. Thus religion and government came to be indissolubly linked. It was in a sense a complete reversal of the reform movement of the eleventh century, which had sought to free the church from political trammels. It meant obviously no return to the *sacrum imperium;* it fastened upon the Germanies a state particularism reinforced by religion which was not to be sloughed off until far into the nineteenth century.

2

From a Cosmic Order to the Creativity of the Spirit 1600-1850

VI

Forces: Utopia, Science, and State

To many historians, the first half of the seventeenth century marks the appearance of the modern world and life view. The chief figures of that period, Descartes and Hobbes, Pascal and Böhme, Bacon and Comenius, Galileo and Kepler, Althusius and Grotius, Milton and Rembrandt, were the great founders of modern culture. That Germany shared in this development is evident from the names of Kepler, Althusius, Jakob Böhme, and Comenius. But these names, except perhaps for Kepler's, have an unfamiliar sound when compared with those of the Italian Galileo, the Frenchman Descartes, the Englishman Bacon, and the Dutchman Grotius. The German names suggest a mystical, magical, and occult atmosphere more akin to the medieval climate of ideas than to the modern. It may be argued, therefore, that although the Germanies also experienced the springtime burgeoning of a new age, they did not reflect the rationalistic spirit characteristic of the Western communities.

Solitary, mystically profound, but unorthodox thinkers seem peculiar to the German scene. The dialectical radicalism—the tendency of thinkers to carry ideas to polar extremes—of German thought manifests itself in these singular individuals more characteristically than in dissident groups, whether sectarian or revolutionary. Nor were the characteristically German thinkers really creators of systems or promoters of a key idea; they reflect with individual variations and increasing secular coloration the basic theme of dynamic totality which had its genesis in the *sacrum imperium*. The line of these German thinkers proceeds from Eckhart and Nicholas of Cues to Paracelsus and Jakob Böhme, and then to Leibniz, Schelling, and Hegel.

By the seventeenth century the basic ideas underlying this mystical and speculative line of thought had acquired the following content: (1) There is a divine spirit or force manifest in both man and nature which is realizing itself in a great creative process in history. (2) The mode of this realization is by the differentiation and union of opposites which are both creative and destructive. (3) The divine creative process is moving toward a great consummation in the reign of the Spirit which now already illumines the minds of the chosen ones who prepare the way. This is, of course, a highly generalized picture of the ideas and aspirations which formed the background of the thinking of a number of relatively isolated thinkers, of whom in the first half of the seventeenth century Jakob Böhme and Johann Amos Comenius were the most characteristic and influential.

JAKOB BÖHME AND THE SELF-REALIZATION OF THE DIVINE IN NATURE AND HISTORY

Böhme (1575-1624) was a shoemaker in Görlitz, Silesia, whose humble activities were interspersed with ecstatic visions and profound speculations. His unorthodox ideas got him into trouble with the Lutheran pastors, and for six years he was virtually prohibited from writing. But the compelling force of his visions caused him to break his silence, and his last years (1612–1624) were his most productive.

Böhme is the pivotal link in the chain of thought which extends from Eckhart to Hegel. Böhme brought together ideas taken from Eckhart, Nicholas of Cues, Paracelsus, and Luther; he transformed them into a theosophy which, in the process of secularization from Leibniz to Hegel, assumed those characteristics which are generally regarded as the peculiar contribution of the German mind to philosophy. He is therefore frequently referred to as the "Teutonic Philosopher."

His basic idea was that the universe and everything in it are the self-revelation or self-realization of God. In its original state the divine is, so to speak, formless, a blank or nothing. Out of this "abyss of indifference" the divine will seeks self-realization by a process of differentiation into opposites. The appearance of the angels is followed by the falling away of Satan and his cohorts. Then the creation of Adam brings Eve. The Fall of Man leads to the second Adam, Christ the Redeemer.

A similar process of "falling away" and reunion is taking place in history. The decadence of Catholicism brings forth the messianic figure of Luther. Again decline ensues in the form of dogmatic confessionalism and the persecution of those who have kept alive the true faith during the "falling away."

The true church comprises the hidden community of the genuine spiritual believers. They are now scattered over the whole world among many sects and denominations. They will be gathered together in the "final hours" which usher in the reign of the Holy Spirit. In this period, the crowning revelation will be vouchsafed whereby the union of the mundane and transcendent worlds will be made visible. No longer will there be the separation which came with man's fall and exclusion from Paradise.

God thus becomes the self-realizing source of Christ and Satan, man and nature, good and evil, love and wrath. Altogether they constitute a dynamic totality which is all-inclusive and therefore has no windows to the outside, looking only inward to the divine will, which becomes manifest in the ceaseless conflict of opposites. This activity of the will can recognize no mediating degrees between good and evil, which in their absolute dualism are both to be found in God. The Lutheran concept of God as a creature of will received such radical formulation here as to transform the Deity virtually into a metaphysical principle.

There is still another aspect of Böhme's conception of God which gained increasing significance in the eighteenth and nineteenth centuries. God is no longer regarded as a static perfect being but as a continual becoming. The former conception went with the old idea of God as occupying a heaven above, which could be fitted into the Ptolemaic hierarchical view of the cosmos. But the Copernican view allowed in principle for no conceptions of *above* and *below*. It eventually dissolved the conception of a stationary heaven as well as of a stationary earth. Since there can be no fixed resting point in space there can be no heaven in a spatial sense.[1] Henceforth heaven becomes transformed into a "future state" and God becomes a process of revelation—that is, of self-realization in time.

Böhme was also influenced by the Joachimite conception, in which, as we have seen, a new historical perspective was projected, possibly as significant as the new cosmology. It became freighted with new meaning in the seventeenth and eighteenth centuries. The Trinity became the model for the process of divine self-realization in nature and history. Stress was consequently laid on the cumulative development of the three Ages of Father, Son, and Holy Spirit culminating in the last Age of the Spirit. Christ was thus no longer the fixed center of history but a stage toward the achievement of a purely spiritual religion.[2]

In place of a static heaven and earth with its distinct realms of spirit and nature the religion of the Copernican world of nature is permeated with the Spirit which now comes down to earth to illuminate the hearts and minds of men. The *inner word* or Spirit takes the place of the sacramental grace of the church. In place of looking back toward the lost *sacrum imperium*, as Cues still did, there is quest for a new *Reich*, thought of as the Age of the Spirit.

ALCHEMICAL SALVATION BY TECHNICAL KNOWLEDGE

Emphasis on the inner word reflected not only a revolt against the dominance of institution and sacrament in the old church and of scriptures and dogma in the Protestant church but also a revolt against man's imprisonment in the web of causal relationships, presented by the astrological view of the universe.

The thought of this early modern period pursued various ways to free man from the idea of a causal necessity, which made him subject to the movement of the heavenly bodies and which assigned him a fixed place in the structure of the universe and in the realization of the divine purpose in history.

We have already encountered the humanist view that man, created in the image of God, does not occupy a fixed place with respect to the heavens or the earth; nor is he bound by the limits of his own age but can seek new norms and values in all that man has thought and achieved in the past.

Astrology and alchemy, particularly, became definitely conceptualized and spiritualized and thus sloughed off the old demoniacal and magical notions which persisted among the lower orders of the population. They became transformed into a nature philosophy which exerted a great influence in German thought down to the middle of the nineteenth century.

By the seventeenth century this nature philosophy embodied three basic ideas whose general lineaments we have already encountered in Paracelsus: (1) The world is a self-sufficient universal harmony of forces imbued with a vital creative spirit. (2) The totality is reproduced in every particular; this is the macrocosm-microcosm relationship so prominently displayed in Paracelsus. And (3) man is obliged to seek a universal knowledge, comprising things both material and spiritual, which will produce an age of harmony in which the sciences will function for the general welfare.

This last idea introduced a new note, the product in part of the religious utopianism of the sectarian world but more so of the transmutation of alchemical notions into scientific-technological ones. The earlier pragmatic quest for gold, long life, and esoteric knowledge now turned to the extension of scientific, that is, public knowledge, and to the devising of technics for the betterment of mankind in general. The seventeenth century marked the beginning of scientific technology not only because of the invention of the telescope and microscope but because of the development of the *idea* that by increasing the human knowledge of nature man could achieve power over it.[3] This concept of knowledge was indeed an essential feature of alchemy, but there it had been associated with the magical notion of the acquisition of a special knowledge by the "gifted" individual (*adepta*), who would use it to enhance his own power. Modern science and technology seek to extend both the means of acquiring knowledge and its benefits to men in general.

The man whose thought expressed this transformation most characteristically was Francis Bacon (1561–1626). Bacon would not accept the discoveries of Copernicus and Galileo, and he ignored or did not understand Kepler, Harvey, and Gilbert. But he was the chief advocate of the idea that knowledge of nature is the way to power over nature, and in his *New Atlantis* he projected an ideal society based on science and technology. His emphasis on sense knowledge as the technical means to transform existing society into utopia revealed his basic alchemistic disposition. Bacon acknowledged his indebtedness to Paracelsus.

But unlike Paracelsus, Bacon regarded nature as fundamentally hostile.[4] Therefore his concern was with releasing, not the *anima mundi* from its materialistic chains but man from the bonds of a hostile nature. He sought to point the way to man's transcendence of the natural limits of space and time and of causality and substance. The knowledge by which antagonistic nature is to be overcome can be extracted from her only by a process of interrogation of the hostile witness similar to that followed in judicial procedure. Bacon, it should be noted, was a jurist. Thus man was to achieve the conquest of nature and his own salvation in a kingdom of peace and plenty here upon earth.

Bacon's *New Atlantis* and Thomas Campanella's *City of the Sun* (1602) were outstanding examples of utopias based on the conception fundamental to the "new alchemy," that a transmutation of society can be achieved through technology. Sir Thomas More's famous *Utopia* (1516) was based on humanistic values, but the most typical examples of this genre, including Aldous Huxley's *Brave New World*, are concerned with the transforming influence of technology.

It has been plausibly argued that modern technological development took over from alchemy its salvation motif, which alchemy derived from Christianity; introducing, however, the important difference that man becomes his own saviour. One might say that technics took the place of the sacraments as the transcendent world dissolved and man's hopes for salvation turned increasingly from subjective faith or conviction to the quest of new objective means.[5] It may also be contended that in our day Paracelsus is certainly triumphing over both Luther and Erasmus.

COMENIUS AND EDUCATION FOR UTOPIA

In the confused and polemical century from 1550 to 1650 the ideas of these great pathfinders of the modern age tended to interweave frequently in various odd ways. This is especially apparent in Johannes Amos Comenius (1592–1670), the great Bohemian educational reformer. He studied at the Calvinistic universities of Heidelberg and Herborn. As a member of the Bohemian or Moravian Brethren, an off-shoot of Hussitism, he was driven out of Bohemia when the Counter Reformation cast its shadow over that country. For some time he and his comrades found refuge in Poland, but there, too, they were forced out by the advancing tide of the Counter Reformation. His educational ideas were influential in both Sweden and England. He finally settled in Holland, the chief haven of the persecuted of the time.

The turmoil and tumult of the times may explain the appearance of many stories of wandering picaresque heroes and pilgrims, from Cervantes' *Don Quixote* (1605–1615) to Bunyan's *Pilgrim's Progress* (1678). Their German counterparts in the seventeenth century were the famous picaresque novel, *Simplicissimus* of Grimmelshausen (ca. 1668), and the less familiar pilgrim journeys pictured by Comenius and his friend, Johann Valentine Andreä (1586–1654). Andreä, who was a pastor in Wurtemberg, has his pilgrim travel through a fantastic world of allegorized good and evil forces until he ends up on an island where he encounters a utopian community modeled after Campanella's *City of the Sun*, but with a much more realistic atmosphere. In Comenius' *Labyrinth of the World* the quest has a more Faustian character since the pilgrim encounters all manner of sages, scholars, philosophers, alchemists, Rosicrucians, and exponents of diverse religions. But he seeks to go beyond all their special forms of knowledge to enter into the invisible church and there experience the vision of the Most High.

In these quests we see expressed the yearning for a world in which war and religious strife will be ended and man will use knowledge and technics for the betterment of all. The mystic vision of eternal harmony must be combined with universal knowledge to form what

Comenius called *pansophy*, which would embody knowledge of both God and nature and bring man out of the darkness into the light where the fusion of spirit and science brings both peace and enlightenment. Religion should stress the common elements in all faiths and thus reflect the vision of cosmic harmony. This return to original simplicity and harmony with God would bring about a rebirth and renewal of man and society.

Comenius was quite convinced that the world was growing old and that the secular order stood on the threshold of an apocalyptic *Reich* whose coming was imminent. To him the growth of science and the many new inventions all bespoke the great change already appearing on the horizon. There is manifested here the fusion of the expectancy of the millennium characteristic of the sectarian along with the utopian aspiration of the alchemist-scientist.

The Paracelsian and Baconian conception of the transforming power of scientific knowledge founded on observation and sense knowledge constituted the basis of Comenius' philosophy of education. Humanism and Protestantism had made the printed book the center of the training of youth as the means of understanding the ancient sources of culture and religion. Comenius recommended the teaching of the vernacular languages. Through them ideas and conceptions in the form of concrete images could be more easily transmitted to the child. Also like Bacon, he placed great emphasis on useful knowledge. The pupil was to be made to feel the growing creative character of nature and led to feel himself as an emerging creative personality brought into organic relationship with the development of plant and animal life. Education was thus to be based upon the direct approach both to nature and to the Scriptures without the intermediary of theoretical conceptions, whether embodied in mathematical formula or religious dogma.

It is obvious that there was no feeling of conflict between this natural philosophy and the Scriptures. Both were regarded as forms of revelation accessible to all who had faith in the divine creative process. But a real conflict developed when the relativity principle involved in the Copernican system was made the basis for a mathematical-mechanistic conception of the world.

THE COPERNICAN COSMOLOGY AND KEPLER

The modern mathematical-mechanistic conception of a soulless universe became juxtaposed to the spirituality of both God and man as emphasized by humanism and Protestantism. By the nineteenth century this polarity had become crystallized, on the one hand, in an objective physical mechanical order and, on the other, in a spiritual subjective observer and exploiter relatively free from the causal necessity which dominates the natural order. The foundations of this view were laid in the sixteenth and seventeenth centuries by Copernicus, Kepler, Galileo, and Newton.

Nicolaus Copernicus (1473–1543), the son of a German merchant, studied at the Polish University of Cracow and then in Italy at Padua and Bologna. In time he returned north to Frauenburg in East Prussia, where he served as a canon in the cathedral, practised medicine, and pursued astronomical studies. His work on the revolutions of the heavenly bodies was not published until after his death in 1543.

The introduction which a friend wrote to this work implied that what Copernicus intended was to propose a mathematical fiction convenient for purposes of calculation, but not a physical description. Thus one could still accept the apparent evidence of one's eyes that the sun and planets revolved about the earth. Copernicus had in fact supplied no observational data of his own as to the movement of heavenly bodies. These circumstances may explain why his conception encountered no opposition from ecclesiastical authorities until seventy-three years later, in 1616, when Galileo (1564–1642) encountered the censure of the church. With the telescope he had developed, Galileo observed sunspots, the rings of Saturn, and, in the revolving moons of Jupiter, "a miniature Copernican solar system." [6] There was no question in his mind of the correctness of the Copernican theory as a description of the solar system. From then on the march of the Copernican revolution could not be stopped.

It was Johann Kepler (1571–1630) who gave the Copernican system its mathematical basis. He was born of Lutheran parents in a predominantly Roman Catholic environment in Wurtemberg. He studied theology and mathematics at Tübingen, became a friend of Andreä, and thus came in contact with those who sought an intermediate way between Lutheranism and Calvinism. This middle-of-the-road position brought him into constant friction with ecclesiastical authority. He taught mathematics in Styria, and then he accepted the invitation of Tycho Brahe, the Danish astronomer, to come to Prague in 1600 to serve as his assistant. When Brahe died the following year, Kepler stepped into his place as court mathematician under Emperor Rudolph II. Kepler remained in the imperial service until the emperor's death in 1612, when he went to teach in the *Gymnasium* at Linz until 1628. The last years of his life were clouded by the charge of witchcraft brought against his mother and by his difficulty in getting compensation for his work from Emperor Ferdinand II, Wallenstein, and the *Reichstag* at Regensburg.

It was Kepler's good fortune to be able to utilize the great mass of astronomical observations which Tycho Brahe had gathered. On the basis of this data, Kepler arrived at the formulation of the mathematical laws of motion of the planets describing their elliptical orbits about the sun. He strongly urged Galileo to hold to the Copernican view of the universe. Kepler contributed most toward furthering the Copernican revolution by presenting the elliptical orbit formulas in place of the perfect circle conception, which had prevailed since the time of the Greeks. The latter assumed that the heavenly bodies embodied divine intelligence, which must therefore circumscribe circles, the most complete and perfect geometrical forms. This qualitative geometric view was now superseded by a quantitative one. Kepler established the validity of the Copernican conception on a definite measurable basis.

Although the mathematical mechanistic conception may have been foreshadowed by Kepler and Galileo and given definite formulation toward the end of the century by Newton, Kepler himself was still influenced by the astrological conception of the universe with Platonic and Pythagorean embroidery. The work which he prized most was his *Harmonicus Mundi libri V* (1619), in which, as the title indicated, "world harmony" is the great theme.[7] For him the universe was animated by a vital spirit or soul which united things celestial and terrestrial in one all-embracing energy. The energy flowed out from the sun to draw the planets in their courses and to manifest the universal harmony which the Creator had implanted in the universe. While this universal force suggests Newton's gravity, the latter was purely mechanical, knowable only in quantitative and functional terms, whereas Kepler's vital force still suggests a qualitative spiritual substance.

To view the universe in quantitative, mathematical terms meant seeing it in terms of mass, volume, energy, and motion rather than in terms of substance, essence, accident, and appearance which had dominated the Aristotelian medieval view. One can hardly exaggerate the fundamental transformation in men's views of man, the universe, and society that came about in the next three centuries as a consequence of this revolution in thought.

By the end of the seventeenth century the general attitude of the new science was (in summary) as follows: the universe is to be comprehended in quantitative rather than qualitative terms; the nature of all objects consists in matter in motion; and nature loves simplicity, that is, economy of effort. These basic underlying ideas projected a universe which was a self-sufficient mechanical order. Man, the spiritual being, develops a sense of distance and isolation from this soulless mechanism, which he can comprehend and control only through measurement and abstract mathematical formulae. Man is no longer concerned with releasing the imprisoned *spiritus mundi* but with unlimited mastery over the mechanism. Here we have embodied, in substance, the scientific technological ideal of the modern world.

COHESION IN STATE AND SOCIETY: ALTHUSIUS

As in natural science, so also in political thought the main drive was toward the discovery of a common force of cohesion in the community, like the force of gravity in the cosmos. Altruism, self-interest, and the struggle for survival were suggested as the motive forces which bind individuals together in communities called states. Speculation along these lines made the greatest headway in the Western countries, especially in England, where the revolutions of the seventeenth century created the favorable conditions for the appearance of Hobbes and Locke, who are better known than their continental contemporaries, Grotius and Althusius.

In the Germanies various forms of political aspiration and practices emerged out of the confusion of confessional conflicts. The first of these was the utopias, which, as we have already seen, were the projection of a medley of ideas drawn from natural philosophy and sectarianism. Andreä and Comenius were most representative of this line of thought. Their influence first centered particularly in the esoteric societies of Rosicrucians, Illuminati, and Free Masons and became generally pervasive among intellectuals during the eighteenth century.

More influential in a political, pragmatic sense were the conceptions of natural law as standing above rulers, of government based on contract between the ruler and the people, and of sovereignty as inhering in the people. These ideas went back to ancient times and had been influential among the medieval schoolmen. They were now revived especially by Jesuits and Calvinists to justify resistance to "ungodly rulers" who persecuted the adherents of the "true faith." The French Huguenots, the Scotch Presbyterians, and the Dutch Reformed—all Calvinists—used them in various ways to justify resistance, but, of course, not revolution. The right-of-resistance theory assumed that a contract existed between ruler and ruled which stipulated what interests and rights the ruler should safeguard.

Johannes Althusius (1557–1638) was the principal exponent of these ideas in the Germanies. Coming from near the Dutch border, he taught at the Calvinist school at Herborn, became a syndic of the imperial city of Emden, and then became the chief exponent of Calvinist political thought at the University of Leyden. His political ideas were much influenced, naturally, by the example of Dutch resistance against Spain and by the organization of the Dutch cities and provinces into a federal republic. The Calvinist church organization was also built up from below, beginning with the local congregation, then through provincial representative assemblies, and up to the national synod.

Althusius advocated what today we would call a pluralistic conception of the political community. Fundamental to his conception is the sovereignty of the whole people, expressed by them in the formation of a series of associations extending from the family through corporation, local community, and province to comprise finally what we call the state.[8] The important idea here is that the state is not made up of contracting individuals but of associations or communities. Resistance to tyranny thus should come only from the associations or communities through which the sovereignty of the people functions.

Again and again we encounter a resurgence of Althusius' multiple association idea, from Justus Möser in the eighteenth century to Otto von Gierke in the late nineteenth. A federal organization was suited to conditions along the whole Rhine with its variegated structure of political and social life. Unfortunately, the political communities, the Swiss Confederation and the Dutch Republic, which embodied this pluralistic and federal plan most fully, detached themselves completely from the *Reich* in the course of the seventeenth century. The center of political gravity then moved decisively to the states along the eastern border, where a paternalistic absolutism gained complete ascendancy.

ABSOLUTISM IN GOVERNMENT

Perhaps the most typical representatives of this absolutism were August I of Saxony (1553–1586), the leader of the Lutherans, and Maximilian I of Bavaria (1595–1651), the leader of the Catholics. These princes expanded bureaucratic organization and mercantilistic practices. Government by princely ordinance increasingly assumed priority over customary arrangements and resolutions of diets. Officials were recruited principally from the universities and the middle classes. Boot-licking servility and subserviency toward princely authority on the part of officials now became increasingly evident, although subservience to *Obrigkeit* did not assume its most nauseating forms until about a century later.

A mitigating factor in the century from 1550 to 1650 was that most princes and officials shared with their subjects a strong sense of duty and obligation, especially strong among the Lutherans. Subjects were, of course, enjoined to unconditional obedience to divinely instituted authorities. But both high and low had a sense of calling. Thus a personal sense of obligation and duty permeated the political and social order. It was not until the century after the Thirty Years' War (1618–1648) that bureaucratic functionalism and courtly ceremony created a wide chasm between the ruling classes and their subjects.

What strikes one most in the Germanies of the seventeenth century is the detachment of the thinker from the political and social scene. In France and England the intellectual was closely attached to chief currents of his time, as witness the participation of both Hobbes and Locke in the revolutions of that century. Of course the Western countries were undergoing profound constructive changes while the Germanies, at least in the first half of the century, suffered pronounced economic decline, social degradation, and political anarchy in the Thirty Years' War. It may also be argued, however, that this polarity of creative thought and political and social decline has been a continuing characteristic of German development and was the consequence fundamentally of the lack of a definite national mold.

In the period from 1550 to 1650 the French, Dutch, and English religious conflicts were really civil wars involving ideological conflicts between groups, both political and religious. In central Europe the Thirty Years' War involved mainly sovereign states. Out of these civil wars in the west emerged strongly unified national communities, whereas in the Germanies the religious conflicts accentuated the independence and sovereign power of individual states, large and small.

A most important difference lay also in the general cultural and material conditions which accompanied these struggles. The Western countries witnessed, in the course of the century, a golden age in literature and art. The economic life of the seaboard countries flowed into the current of overseas trade expansion which brought with it the foundation of vast colonial empires. But central Europe and the Italian peninsula were now isolated from these great movements of cultural and commercial expansion and state building. These areas thus lost both the cultural and economic ascendancy that they had held from the fourteenth to the middle of the sixteenth centuries. The Germanies entered another one of those periods of exhaustion and disintegration after a tremendous outburst of creative energy that seems to be a characteristic phenomenon of their development. The great wave of the upsurge trickled away in the hundreds of little rivulets of principalities and states.

Since the thirteenth century the cities in Germany had been the chief carriers of culture, and their populations had exhibited both initiative and independence in trade and politics. They had also given the chief impetus to the Lutheran movement in its early stages of enthusiastic expansion. The princes now became the chief props of religion, culture, and of economic life. Their dominant position was greatly fostered by the decline of all the local forces, knights, peasants, and towns. The towns entered a period of definite depression augmented by the Thirty Years' War. Though the war has lost some of its catastrophic character in the estimation of many historians, no one denies that it was a great disaster, comparable, as far as central Europe was concerned, to the Black Death.

In the long run, the shift in trade routes from the Mediterranean to the Atlantic had a decisive influence. The south German and Rhineland cities, while temporarily successful in shifting their operations to Spain and Portugal, eventually lost out, particularly to the Dutch and the English. The competition of the English even squeezed the Hansa cities out of their pre-eminent position in the North and Baltic seas.

Thus, while by 1600 the German cities still retained much of their outward splendor, they had declined greatly in economic importance. The Germanies had been the principal source of precious metals since the mining revolution of the fifteenth century. Now the mines of the New World provided a great competing source of wealth. Moreover, such great capitalistic families as the Fuggers and Welsers had suffered a body blow in the financial crises of the second half of the sixteenth century, especially with the repudiation of his debts by Philip II of Spain. The close alliance of the south German capitalists with the Hapsburgs, both in the Germanies and in Spain, initially brought them great prosperity, but in time these relations also involved them in the decline of Spanish wealth and power.

Capital now moved into lands and castles and avoided risk-taking ventures. Magnificent public buildings and residences were erected, but this outward splendor covered inner decay. There were, of course, exceptions such as Hamburg and Frankfort-on-the-Main, which, because of favorable location, continued to prosper greatly.

The princes exerted an increasing influence on economic life in the regulation of gild affairs and in the imposition of tolls and tariffs, which secured for them much greater revenues but which were often a hindrance to trade. In the countryside the peasants had not yet recovered from the disastrous revolt of the previous century. They were exploited everywhere.

All classes suffered from the terrific inflation of prices which reached its climax in the second half of the sixteenth and continued into the seventeenth century. It was the product of both business expansion and the influx of precious metals. It was also a symptom of a fundamental dislocation of economic life brought about by the transition to new forms of economic enterprise and control. The war tremendously accelerated these shifts, just as the Black Death had in the fourteenth century.

The Thirty Years' War presents another instance of that violent turmoil and chaotic confusion which characterized the Germanies in periods of crisis. It was not unlike the Time of Troubles (1598–1613) in Russia which, however, came about largely through the breakdown of royal power whose restoration led to the re-establishment of order. In the Germanies the lack of *any* central authority resulted, during crisis periods, in eddies and cross-currents of disorder. Foreign intervention brought no rallying around the crown or ruler as a center of resistance on the part of those who placed country above religious or class considerations. Whatever resistance did emerge appeared in innumerable local centers, particularly in the cities.

THE COALESCENCE OF FORCES IN THE THIRTY YEARS' WAR

Amidst the welter of routing armies engaged in sieges and sackings of cities, and of general devastation and ravishment of great areas by mercenary bands, one discerns three long-run trends which extend back into the previous century. Two of these trends, the conflict between Catholics and Protestants for supremacy and the drive of the Hapsburg emperors to establish a dominant political power in the *Reich*, came to a head in the course of the war. But the third trend, that of the interest of external powers, especially Sweden and France, in the affairs of the *Reich* became a continuing factor in the promotion of centrifugal forces. As a consequence territorial and dynastic interests superseded religious and confessional ones, and the war became a power conflict among European states and principalities. This last phase of the conflict marked the rise of two new territorial states on the eastern borders, Austria and Prussia.

Armies such as those recruited by Wallenstein and his fellow *condottiere* were largely drawn from the dregs of the population and lived off the country. They contributed not only to the unprecedented destructiveness of the war but also prolonged military operations. Time had to be taken out after each battle to forage for food. Most of the military expeditions, even those of the Swedes, were really great sorties for plunder rather than calculated campaigns directed toward a definite military objective.

The Peace of Westphalia (1648) brought about a compromise solution of the religious issue. The Germanies were divided about equally between Protestants and Roman Catholics. The arbitrary date of 1624 was set as a basis for establishing the lines between Catholicism and Protestantism. Protestant minorities who had been residing in Catholic territories previous to 1624—and likewise Catholics in Protestant territories—were accorded freedom of worship. Even those who had moved in after that date were given the right of individual freedom of conscience but could not form congregations or engage in public worship. These provisions marked great advances in the direction of religious toleration. Most important, during the following years Protestants and Catholics tended more and more to take each other for granted; the assumption died out gradually that religious unity would be re-established on the basis of the predominance of either religious confession.

The results were less happy with respect to the power and status of the *Reich*. It virtually ceased to exist as a political force in Europe.

First of all, the Empire lost the Swiss and the Dutch who had been the most active defenders of the western frontiers against the Spanish and French. The Swedes secured territories at the mouths of three important rivers flowing into the Baltic, the Oder, the Elbe, and the Weser, thus virtually closing off direct access to the Baltic except through territories controlled by them. France secured such cities as Metz, Toul, and Verdun and sovereignties in Alsace, which opened the way to French absorption of Alsace and Lorraine.

Second, the princes were now recognized as completely sovereign with the right to enter into treaties and alliances with foreign powers. This was a virtual ratification of the dissolution of the Empire as a sovereign entity. It now had decomposed into some three hundred or more fragments.

Even more important was the final liquidation of the idea projected by Maximilian and his grandson Charles V of making the imperial office stand above the princes as the supreme and dominant power and authority in the *Reich*. The Hapsburgs confined themselves exclusively to promoting the interests of Austria. However, they were confronted in central Europe by a new state power, Brandenburg-Prussia, which was to become the chief rival of Austria in the affairs of the *Reich* within the century following Westphalia.

THE MODERN CONSTELLATION OF FORCES

The new forces, utopia, science, and state, which dominated Europe in the modern age, all have a pronounced secular sound to us, although, as we have seen, they grew out of a magical and religious soil. Their secularization and general acceptance differed from country to country. In the Germanies the process of secularization was at least overtly slower than in France, where the mental climate seemed to change abruptly at the turn of the century from the seventeenth to the eighteenth. France was the intellectual pacemaker mainly because of her development of a full-fledged rationalistic point of view but also because she developed the means of its dissemination by way of salon and a dominant intellectual center, Paris. The Germanies lacked these agencies for the propagation of ideas and hence the process of secularization centered not in the formation of an activist public opinion but in the inner proliferation of ideas by more or less isolated individuals. This immanent form of the process was to distinguish the German mind, particularly in this phase of its history.

The new historical orientation of the self-realization of the Spirit brought about a change as fundamental in the German mental climate as the new view of the universe. The Age of the Spirit was to be the fulfillment of history and was not to be inaugurated by apocalyptic event and messianic deliverer. Utopia was also not to be the projection of a "moment" in history but the end-product of a long process of development.

The convergence of alchemical-astrological thinking with sectarian notions produced the conception of the unitary process of nature and history culminating in the release of the *spiritus mundi*. The prominence of this conception in much of German thinking deterred the development of that dualism of history and nature which dominated Western thinking, in which the Newtonian conception of the universe was victorious.

Conscious union with the evolutionary process through experiment produced technical knowledge. In Bacon's language this meant power over nature, and in the spiritualized alchemy of the Rosicrucians and in the pansophy of Comenius, union with the cosmic creative forces, but for both it meant utopia in terms of wealth, health, and wisdom.

Science, for contemporary man, has become both a means of salvation and a means of destruction. Initially, it provided assurance with respect to man's freedom from the fate of the stars or the caprice of supernatural beings. The reduction of the universe to a mechanistic order made it observable and measurable by the new instruments which the seventeenth century devised. The collaboration of mechanistic conception and instrumental agencies led to the recognition of the slow progress of scientific knowledge—that there are no alchemical short-cuts in the discovery of a key to the nature of the universe. The only key was the positive and non-metaphysical method of dealing with the universe provided by the fusion of science and technology—it would eventually bring man to utopia.

The invariable order of the universe came to be juxtaposed as an ideal to the caprice and arbitrary character of human relationships. But it was also felt that this divergence could be overcome. History could, in fact, be regarded as man's attempt to find rational means of overcoming the irrational tendencies among men at large. It revealed that the chief hope lay in the enlightened ruler who protects the rational few from the ignorant and superstitious rabble and gives rational form to man's behavior. Thus history as well as nature was to be exorcised, that is, deprived of external and arbitrary caprices and indelible and substantival qualities.

The state's means of organizing man's activities in a rational manner assumed two aspects. First, it provided a way of organizing conflicts between groups so as to prevent the war *à outrance*, leading to the progressive annihilation of groups. It achieved this for central Europe by way of the disastrous Thirty Years' War ending in the Peace of Westphalia. The latter may be said to have provided a constitutional and legal basis for the Germanies, the pivotal area of Europe for a long time to come, since that area was Europe's great power vacuum. Gradually, state relations were subjected to *raison d'état*, international law, and the practices of diplomacy so as to mitigate the conflict of states. On the high seas, the war of all against all continued unabated, leading eventually to the dominance of one power.

A second aspect concerned the conflicts of individuals within states. Here the state, first embodied in the ruler, gradually became impersonal, standing above factions and concerned not merely with war and finances but with the general welfare. This tendency culminated in the eighteenth century in "enlightened despotism," which attained its most characteristic expression in the Germanies. The state also came to be regarded as the agency through which a total change might be brought about in creating utopia.

Neither nature as science nor history as the state could, however, provide the German with a road to utopia. One was really the embodiment of mechanistic reason and the other of coercive power and hence could not furnish man freedom. Only the eventual breakthrough of the Spirit could overcome what were but modern forms of very ancient compulsive forces in human existence. Only being attuned to the fusion of nature and history in one vast unitary creative process culminating in that breakthrough could lead to salvation. This was the most characteristic line of the thinking of the Germans during this second phase of their history.

VII

The Baroque Synthesis and Its Disintegration

The epoch under consideration here is generally designated by historians as the Age of Louis XIV (1643–1715), and there is no doubt that, at least politically, the figure of that great king casts its shadow over most of the events of the age. However, from the German point of view one might call it the Age of Leibniz (1646–1716), who was the most active intellectual force among those who wished to marshal both the political and spiritual forces of the *Reich* against the attempt of Louis XIV to establish hegemony over Europe. Leibniz wished to reassert the unifying influence of the conception of the *Reich* in Europe. The *Reich* was to be restored as the central pole of Christendom to overcome both religious divisions and political power conflicts which were leading to periodic struggles for hegemony in Europe.

LEIBNIZ AND THE UNITY OF CHRISTENDOM

Although a Protestant, Leibniz began his active political and intellectual career in the employ of the Archbishop of Mainz. The

Archbishop was not only an imperial elector but also chancellor of the *Reich*—an office of high dignity but little authority. John Philip Schönborn (1605–1673), the reigning Archbishop, was also an active exponent of what may be called *Reich* union against the French menace on the Rhine. A Catholic ecclesiastical prince, he ruled over a city which was dominantly Protestant. Naturally inclined toward religious tolerance, he was, moreover, actively interested in Leibniz' schemes for religious union.

With the death of the Archbishop, Leibniz traveled abroad for some years (1672–1676), going to London and Paris and staying for some time in Holland. During these journeys he became acquainted with the chief philosophers and scientists of the day. From 1676 until his death in 1716 he was librarian and held other positions in the employ of the electors of Hanover. These sinecures allowed him to engage in a variety of activities, the best known of which are his mathematical and philosophical writings. But his main goal continued to be religious and intellectual unity.

At the Hanoverian court Leibniz had the sympathetic ear of the Electress, Sophia. This remarkable woman not only gathered about her a circle of enlightened minds, but her influence extended to the courts of other states, for example, to England and Prussia. Her daughter Dorothea was the mother of Frederick the Great, and her son George became King of England. Hanover's connections with England lifted this principality of the Guelfs above the general level of German *Kleinstaaterei* (small-state system). In the course of the eighteenth century its great university at Göttingen became an intellectual center of northern Germany; its only real rival was Halle in Prussia.

Leibniz bears many resemblances to Nicholas of Cues not only in his synthetic quality of mind and versatility of interests but also in his concern with the achievement of the unity of the *Reich* on a level higher than the political or even the specifically religious. Both were faced by a period of breakdown and confusion in which an old order was passing and a new one emerging. Cues was confronted by the general solvent of nominalism, Leibniz by the new mechanistic science. Both were interested in effecting a synthesis of politics, religion, science, and philosophy, not by an eclectic combination of elements from each but by projecting a new principle of unity: for Cues, through the coincidence of opposites; for Leibniz, through the concept of the monad.

Leibniz also regarded the *Reich* as the necessary axis of the unity of Christendom because it was the unique historical expression of this unity. Emperor and pope should work together for the restoration of the *Reich;* the emperor, as "his apostolic majesty," should hold the keys of St. Peter as the symbol of the highest center of unity directed against the enemies of Christendom.

Unity within was in fact to be achieved, as in the Middle Ages, by directing the energies of peoples and rulers toward the external tasks and missions of Christendom. Austria was to repel the Turks, the French should turn their urge for conquest in the direction of Egypt and the Levant. The destiny of England lay in America; the Dutch, of course, would look toward the Orient. As for Russia, she was to be feared as the emerging colossus who was beginning to cast a shadow over the Western world.

THE UNIVERSE AS UNITY WITHIN DIVERSITY

Again, as with Cues, Leibniz' thought was closely interwoven with the multifarious activities in which he engaged. He was more a journalist and publicist than a philosopher. His one independent work was the *Theodicy* (1710). The other works, including the *Monadology* (1714), appeared in journals late in his life. All his writing was in either French or Latin. Leibniz reflected the various interests and profusion of knowledge typical of the Baroque *polyhistor* before the age of specialization began to dawn in the eighteenth century. He was a jurist and theologian, scientist and historian, mathematician and philologist, and, of course, something of a philosopher. With all his vast erudition he was a creative thinker who, for one thing, disputed with Newton priority in the discovery of the differential calculus. His creativeness might well be called Faustian, the ceaseless quest for the harmonizing, unifying principle underlying all. This quest reflected in a more rarefied form the ancient alchemical urge to find the primal matter or the philosopher's stone.

Intellectually, Leibniz stood on the threshold between the Paracelsian alchemical world view and the natural scientific-mechanistic point of view. As a young man, he had been a secretary of an alchemical Rosicrucian society at Nuremberg. The world of the qualitative, the creative, and the purposeful stood juxtaposed in his thought to the world of quantitatively determined mechanistic forces. How could the mechanistic conception of the universe with its emphasis on the uniform and invariable operation of forces be reconciled with the religious-metaphysical and alchemical notion of creative purpose, that is, with movement toward an ideal goal?

In the monad, Leibniz projected a conception of the universe in which individual self-determination was combined with the relativity of the Copernican world view. The monad is distinguished from the atom by individuality, by the fact that each monad is unlike any other. Atoms are all alike because they are acted upon only by external forces. All atomic changes, therefore, come from without; all monadic changes come only from within. The monad has an individual quality because it is an expression of a creative force within itself. It has, so to speak, no windows to the outside.

Each monad, no matter how small, reflects within itself the total universe, which is also a monad. Each is impelled by an inner drive to self-consciousness, that is, toward a realization of its own unique role in the totality. Again we encounter the relation of microcosm and macrocosm so characteristic of this major trend of German thought.

In Leibniz we also meet the Paracelsian notion of God as the creative force of the universe. God is not merely the great engineer or mathematician who builds a machine which ever after runs without care, as the Deist assumed. God is immanent in the universe; He is the monad of all monads, each one of which is a little god within its own sphere. Each thinks both as a self-conscious *I* distinguished *from* the world and creatively along *with* God *in* the world. Each seeks realization in the clarity and order of a pre-established harmony implicit in this best of all possible worlds. This world is really the only possible one through which a divine creative spirit could realize itself. There are many things in the world we do not like, but we must remember that it was not created for us alone. Moreover, it is not finished, but moving toward the consummation of the kingdom of God.

THE IMPERIUM OF THE SPIRIT AND OF THE FLESH

Leibniz sought to achieve the rebirth of the *sacrum imperium* not as the old sacramental order but as a new order of the creative spirit. This was the dream, now spiritualized, of the alchemists and of many heretics. The monadic conception of diversity in unity would provide the new principle of harmony. Leibniz sought to give through this concept of the monad a spiritual representation of the old forms —*Reich*, emperor, pope, sacraments—to bring about a restoration of a unified and purified Christendom. He looked forward toward the coming of a "third great emperor" after Charlemagne and Otto the Great.[1]

Leibniz was in Vienna toward the end of his life, from 1712 to 1715. He had long been in correspondence with the leading Austrian statesman, Prince Eugene, who shared many of his aspirations and whose assistance he now sought in the realization of the new *sacrum imperium* of the Spirit. From the seat of imperial rule, he hoped to see achieved a world union of churches, peoples, and sciences. He envisaged first of all an imperial academy of the sciences and arts established at Vienna, which would serve as a central agency of world unity working through local academies in the chief capitals of Europe and eastward by way of Russia to China. Russia would thus be brought within the European cultural orbit, and cultural contact would be established between China and the West. The academy was to be the chief means of bringing together the best minds of Christendom for the achievement of harmony. It would provide a unified church in place of the old church, torn apart by theological controversy. Similar ideas had been expressed by previous thinkers, by Comenius, for example. However, the achievement fell far short of Leibniz' hopes; only the academy at Berlin was realized. The atmosphere of Counter Reformation of the Catholic south was unsympathetic to this spiritualistic rationalism which hovered on the intellectual borderland between Protestantism and Catholicism.

Within a much narrower compass than that contemplated by Leibniz, the Hapsburgs presented a union of peoples under one dynasty, a fusion of arts and sciences under royal and aristocratic patronage, and the maintenance of the one true faith under "His Apostolic Majesty." Thus they achieved to a certain extent one rule, one faith, and one artistic expression. Vienna established what has been called the "world theater" of the Baroque reflecting in its opera, pageants, and masques the magical and mythical world of past and present. The culture of aristocratic court and of village common were combined in this patriarchal society and archaic economy in which nobility and peasantry were still closely tied together. It was not until the nineteenth century that middle-class culture drove a wedge between them.[2]

As in Carolingian and Saxon art, so in the Baroque, architecture, sculpture, and painting served both as a stage setting for religious, political, and social ceremonialism and as a representation of the order of things. In the Baroque there was, of course, a much more self-conscious use of both than in the earlier art expressions. It can be argued, however, that the *ordo* of the *sacrum imperium* found its last great expression in Baroque forms.

Undoubtedly the Baroque may be regarded as the last great example of an international style, comparable to the Romanesque, Gothic, and Renaissance. It had its origin in Italy in the sixteenth century; it achieved a classic expression in France in the second half of the seventeenth century; and it attained its final and most distinctive phase in the palaces of the early eighteenth century in the Germanies. The great Baroque building era in the Germanies began in the 1680's, reaching its peak in the early decades of the eighteenth century. Never perhaps have so many great edifices been constructed in any part of Europe in so short a span of time. This building boom reflected the new consciousness of imperial destiny which emanated from Vienna, stimulated by the victories over the Turks and the French, and by the new sense of unity centering in dynasty, aristocracy, and church.

The mother church of the Jesuits in Rome, *Gesu* (1568–1584), became a kind of model for later Baroque churches and palaces. The older monastic orders also adopted the new dynamic forms. The consequent stimulus given to the Baroque may be surmised from the fact that the Austrian lands of the Hapsburgs alone comprised 2,163 monasteries with 65,000 monks and nuns.[3] While this great development of Baroque religious architecture was characteristic of the early and middle phases, in its last phase, toward the end of the seventeenth and beginning of the eighteenth centuries, the characteristic form of Baroque art was the great princely palace and aristocratic residence.

In the Baroque the tension between spiritualistic and naturalistic forces already noted in Leibniz' thought also became manifest. It grew out of the stress laid on an inner spiritual experience in the religious movements and the projection of a mechanistic conception of the universe which seemed to make man the puppet of impersonal forces. In the Baroque this tension was expressed through such naturalistic means as exaggerated contortion of features and muscles in sculpture, and the virtual obliteration of spatial boundaries. These effects could be achieved only by breaking through the static quality of Renaissance classical forms by a return to the spatial dynamism of the Gothic. This new space feeling emerged in the transition from the Romanesque to the late Gothic *Hallenkirche*. The Baroque represented a further extension of this notion of the dynamic unity of space.

BAROQUE SPACE DYNAMICS

The extraordinary fluidity of Baroque architecture was made possible first of all by the development of the open form of basic structure in place of the Renaissance closed form. The latter was in part a return to the centralized structure of the ancients with its great dome and its emphasis on the balance of spatial forms. It took the place of the longitudinal basilican structure which had dominated the Middle Ages. In the Baroque the two were fused to form an oval which, of course, had greater mobility than either the central or longitudinal forms. It was the counterpart of Kepler's dynamic elliptical orbit of the planets in place of the static circular form of the Ptolemaic system.

Sculpture and painting, having achieved complete independence from architecture in the Renaissance, now strove to dominate it and in so doing again became merged with it. The sculptured figures of gods and saints became indistinguishable in their plastic form from their pictorial backgrounds, which in turn merged with the structural forms. Painting became space-enlarging, creating the illusion of vanishing wall and ceiling. Each art expression thus lost its distinct function and served but to create a total impression on the beholder of grandeur or devotion, as it might be. Painting, with its greater capacity for illusion, tended to predominate by giving the impression of a world of forms like the scenery in a theater.

In its most typical building, the palace, two aspects of the Baroque tend to stand out: all parts are subordinated to a total conception or grand form, and the movement of the eye is directed along precise lines outward so as to give the impression of limitless space.[4]

The original form of the Baroque palace stemmed from the fusion of the Italian Renaissance *palazzo* and villa. The palace had a cube-like form looking in upon itself, that is, upon an inner court. It was built to suit the turbulent conditions of the late medieval city with its narrow thoroughfares and crowded living conditions. The villa, on the other hand, built outside the city walls, looked out upon gardens and landscaping, and therefore it offered opportunity for terraces, vistas, and fountains. The Baroque palace combined the features of both. It broke through the cube structure to assume an open *I* or *U* form, thus providing wings which looked out upon gardens.

The accent was placed on the center of the building comprising the central stairway, banquet hall, and ballroom. In the great south German palaces, such as the Vienna Belvedere and the Würzburg episcopal residence, the stair hall became the focus of the whole building. The magnificent, sweeping stairways communicated a sense of movement, both vertical and horizontal, and provided the opportunity to make a grand entrance to the banquet hall.

THE ARCHITECTURE OF LANDSCAPE

Baroque space composition revolved around moving spectators who saw their own image reflected not only in the vast expanses of mirror and water but also enhanced by the very grandeur of their surroundings. The grand stairways and great halls may seem to the visitor of today empty shells even with their original furnishings. But perhaps more than any architectural forms of the past, they were deliberately intended to provide background for assemblies of color-fully dressed ladies and gentlemen, always, so to speak, in costume and always conscious not only of being on a stage but of themselves observing this spectacle or pageant.

The Baroque palace looked out not upon the world of nature as forest and field and lake and river, but upon a landscape as definitely patterned to serve this function of background and scenery for the human spectacle as its interior. In fact, both palace and park were fused to form a courtly world secluded from both raw nature and the general barbarity of man.

Long rows of windows looked out upon gardens with clipped hedges and geometrically laid-out walks and paths. These in turn opened onto fountains and statuary, beyond which lay widening vistas. The great fountains from which radiated avenues of walks like the spokes of a wheel stood juxtaposed to the secluded grotto with its weirdly distorted shapes. Underneath the surface of social and cultural artifice there still lingered in the Baroque the awareness of the world of dark and demonic forces.

The Baroque made an enduring contribution to town planning. It projected the ideal city. The city was not to be merely the result of the accidents of chance settlement but the unified creation of a sovereign will.[5] New towns such as Karlsruhe and Mannheim were established and older ones reshaped and reformed. The medieval town had been laid out on the basis of the realistic considerations of growth and expansion within the walls protecting it from the feudal countryside. The Renaissance town initiated rational planning, but it was the Baroque which projected the total plan built around the idea of spatial orientation with respect to the surrounding environment. The Baroque town presented a star-shaped character, looking out upon the countryside as the palace looked out upon its gardens. The town was organized around the princely residence, which stood in the center of a great open space. Avenues radiated from this central circle like the spokes of a wheel. From it, also, vistas opened in various directions, limited only by the hardly visible triangular bastions of the fortifications. The fortified city served largely as a fixed anchor, both logistically and tactically, for the increasingly mobile warfare of maneuver.

Toward the end of the seventeenth and the beginning of the

eighteenth centuries a series of great native architects appeared, among whom the more important were Fischer von Erlach, Balthasar Neumann, Mathäus Daniel Pöppelmann, and Jacob Prandtauer. Although French influence now superseded that of the Italians, the south Germans achieved a native variation which like late Gothic exhibited an overripeness both as to exuberance of forms and as to the enhancement of spatial frames.

In addition to being the most populous and powerful country in Europe under Louis XIV, France was the chief source of inspiration for the classic phase of the Baroque in the second half of the seventeenth century. One great palace, Versailles, the symbol of the cult of majesty, dominated all others and became the model for princely residences elsewhere. Its form was distinctly classical, resembling the Roman imperial façade. Its predominant horizontal axis was also reflected in the great corridors, such as the Hall of Mirrors; Versailles lacked the monumental stairway characteristic of the German palaces. French society was more functionally organized with respect to crafts and services than elsewhere and had developed greater functional specialization of rooms such as salon, dining room, and bedroom. In the Germanies the French influence was strongest in the north—most so in Berlin, where the colony of Huguenots comprised approximately one-fourth of the population of the city.

THE REPRESENTATION OF A POLITICAL AND SOCIAL ORDER

In the Baroque we are conscious of dealing with an art which still represented a world order rather than one in which individual genius merely sought expression in art forms. The ancient Greeks were concerned with representing the cosmos as eternal recurrence; medieval man, with representing the transmission of divine authority and grace as a hierarchical order. Both gradually dissolved with the Renaissance projection of a new cosmic order and with the Reformation accent on faith as an inner assurance. Hence the Baroque turned to the representation of a divinely instituted political and social order, reviving the medieval sacred monarchy not as the projection of a heavenly order but deliberately instituted to maintain order and the true faith.[6]

The Baroque political and social order centered therefore in the charismatic ruler whose magic was communicated through the dynastic blood tie. Moreover, as the anointed of the Lord by divine delegation, he maintained the order of things as a reflection of the divine will. He accorded to each his place in the hierarchical order of the estates. Proximity to the king—the source of grace—determined one's rank and position.

This cult of majesty may be traced back, especially as far as its ceremonial forms are concerned, to the old Byzantine forms of sacred monarchy, which were communicated through Spain to the French monarchy and to the Hapsburgs.

The ceremonial centering in the person of the ruler came to be worked out with greatest comprehensiveness at the court of Louis XIV. There were two spheres of activity which absorbed the king: the affairs in *cabinet*, where he met with his bourgeois ministers to deal with the business of administering both the external and internal affairs of the kingdom; and the sphere of the *court*, equally important from the point of view of the time, in which there was represented an ideal projection of the political and social order. The *levée* and the *coucher*, the rising and the retiring of the king, presented the daily liturgical frame of the round of courtly functions. The heads of the great aristocratic houses felt no sense of humiliation nor loss of face in the rendering of services even of a menial character to the king. He was to them a charismatic symbol who prescribed gradations and precedence within the "sacred" order; consequently the services one rendered actually enhanced one's prominence.

In the Baroque this sacred order attained visible representation through the heightened effect of illusion and ideal form rather than through symbolism. The given order needed no justification on the basis of usefulness or ideology. Grand manner and elaborate dress were not merely decorative; they enhanced the effect of the ideal illusion. One lived always in a frame, that of rank or estate; to be one's self meant to be a wild man or barbarian.

Architecture was also directed specifically toward fashioning a physical frame which would itself achieve these heightened effects. We see little concern with the functional organization of living, nor in fact, for the most simple hygienic provisions. There might be hundreds of fountains in the gardens but not a bathroom in the whole palace. Moreover, the tendency to create the illusion of an ideal order contributed toward blurring the line between fiction and reality; hence, the charlatan, the quack, and the purveyor of the occult were frequently in evidence in this society.

THE WORLD AS ILLUSION

Emphasis should be placed on the Baroque *illusion* of an ideal order standing in juxtaposition not to a real but to an equally artificial or illusory human existence. The court with its daily liturgical round, its festivals, pageants, balls, and spectacles, presented, so to speak, a theater within the world theater. In the latter, men were the puppets of forces contending for man's salvation or damnation. Man stood on an earthly stage suspended between heaven and hell. The Baroque thus returned to the vertical axis of the Middle Ages but sought to represent the conflict of realms not symbolically but theatrically with all the illusionist devices reflected in its architecture, which, as indicated, was itself but a stage setting. One was always conscious of being both an actor and a spectator in the world theater.[7]

This conception of the world theater reflected the fundamental pessimism of the Baroque *Weltanschauung*. Baroque man had neither the faith in a divine *ordo* and providence of the Middle Ages nor had he achieved confidence in a mechanistic universe nor an optimistic conception of human development as the eighteenth-century Enlightenment did.

The Baroque reflected the declining world of the Counter Reformation. Religious conflicts had engendered widespread skepticism and disillusionment, culminating in world weariness. Nothing seemed to have substance or stability; the reign of Fortuna was supreme. In the life of the cavalier and courtier the whim or caprice of monarch or mistress determined one's fortune. Everything in the world was a masquerade. It was one grand illusion as were human integrity and sincerity. In the Baroque drama the most typical character was the prince disguised as the clown or servant, or the villain masquerading as the just ruler or grand aristocrat. Flight from this world was really possible only in the monastery in quest of eternity or in the theater where one immersed oneself in the moment. The moment was to be filled with festival or spectacle, for just as the Baroque abhorred empty space, so it also abhorred empty time.

Disillusionment with the Renaissance world of the senses is reflected in one of the chief philosophers of the seventeenth century, the Frenchman, Descartes. He sought to build philosophy not on sense knowledge but on a pure act of thought—"I think; therefore I am." This pure act of thought attributed to the world of things a rational character only with respect to their extension in space, that is, to objective relationships which are measurable; the qualitative world of color, texture, and vibrancy has no rational character and hence is really illusory since it is purely subjective. Both Descartes and Newton, while projecting a mechanistic world order, themselves remained devout Christians, thus setting up a dualism between the rational universe and irrational religious faith.

Leibniz, it will be recalled, sought to bring the worlds of sense and spirit into harmony by the dynamic totality of his monad, in which the self-realizing transformation from within was its dominant characteristic. The Baroque theater also sought to overcome this dualism by accepting neither a mechanistic world order nor a purely subjective standpoint, but the sense world, not as representing so-called reality but as a stage on which both the human spectacle and the supranatural drama might be represented.

Especially characteristic of the Baroque theater itself was its use of all the elaborate technics and machinery for the deception of eye and ear to demonstrate the illusory character of reality. The Renaissance had used perspective to create the illusion of reality, whereas the Baroque converted reality into an illusion. Its "invention" of scenery was therefore most characteristic as contrasted with the permanent backgrounds, built of stone and wood, of the Middle Ages and the Renaissance. It made possible the illusion of great depth, both horizontally and vertically. The walls of the stage and theater began to dematerialize and vanish. The Baroque concave stage moved into the audience in contrast with the Renaissance convex form which withdrew from it. The Baroque theater thus brought to conclusion the development of the stage from the public square of the Middle Ages by way of the Renaissance perspectival hole-in-the-wall to the virtual fusion of audience and actors.

The Baroque stage thus created a new space which neither belonged to the world of reality nor fitted into that of illusion, since actor and audience were conscious of occupying an intermediate zone where spirit and senses became so intermingled as to be indistinguishable. The Baroque renounced the sense world as illusory but at the same time developed the most sensuous art forms. It assumed that man is at once an actor and a spectator and in this ambivalent role the senses are so heightened that they virtually transcend themselves, without being relinquished, however. It is not surprising, therefore, that the Baroque produced a number of great mystics who also lived in this intermediate zone of heightened awareness of the worlds of sense and spirit.

Although it has been said that the Jesuits converted the church into a sacred theater, one could also maintain that the theater took the place of the church. Certainly, the theater in all its aspects, pageant, spectacle, festival, and opera, was the great intermediary between court and church. It offered the appropriate medium for the projection of the ideal illusion whose allegorical dress was woven of both pagan and Christian mythology. The fact that theatrical productions at the Hofburg in Vienna sometimes ran for eight hours indicates the predilection of this age for forms of illusion which actually but heightened that of the liturgical round of court and church.

The opera, conceived originally as a return to the Greek theater, was a typical Baroque total work of art, combining music, drama, and dancing. In it we also encounter the grand gesture and grandiloquent declamation which the Baroque loved. The immense expansion of the range of voices and of instruments in the seventeenth century made possible the production of these effects.

ROCOCO AS THE ART OF INTERIOR DECORATION

The Rococo, which is often regarded as merely a late and more elegant phase of the Baroque, actually marked the end of Baroque representation. King and aristocracy began to find the ceremonialism of court life burdensome; they preferred smaller residences where more intimate gatherings could take place. These were the matrices for the emergence of *society*, which came to center in the salon—a society which was no longer concerned with representation but with mutual amusement and edification, subject to conventions of behavior. Consequently, philosophers such as Rousseau began to preach a gospel of return to nature which was essentially a revolt against the artificiality of social convention since it did not represent an "order."

Although Rococo art no longer reflected a world order, it provided a decorative and functional frame for society. While it lacked the robustness and flamboyance of the Baroque it achieved elegance and grace. The minuet and the powdered wig were its symbols. Life lost its serious quality. It was meant for joyous frivolity, a *fête gallant*. In the salon, conversation, with its lightness, wit, and repartee, took the place of the pompous ceremonial and brilliant spectacle of the court.

Few great palaces were built after the mid-century. The two chief examples of Rococo architecture were the *Dresdener Zwinger* (1711–1722), a royal pleasure pavilion, and *Sans Souci* (1745–1747), Frederick's palace at Potsdam. In the latter, the elegance and lightness of Rococo decoration present an obvious contrast to the grandiose lavishness of the Baroque. The Rococo residences hug the ground and follow curved lines so as to almost enclose the gardens, which have largely lost their geometric lay-out and now follow the English fashion of allowing shrubs and trees to grow naturally and to provide secluded spots for the intimate tête-à-tête.

Interior decoration took precedence in the Rococo over the overall architectural planning of the Baroque. Furniture detached itself completely from walls and windows and became both deliberately decorative and more functional. In response to the growing concern with social functions, it assumed the specialized character which we take for granted today. For example, the commode had evolved from its medieval prototype, the chest, and the chair had assumed its present form as distinct from the backless stool or ceremonial throne. Bedrooms were separated from reception rooms. Windows no longer accented the contrast of light and shade, but suffused the interior with light. Delicate pastel shades of color in silk and porcelain took the place of the harsh contrasts of the Baroque.

Music also reflected the new interests and forms of the age. The Catholic south produced the greatest musical geniuses, not only of this period but perhaps of all time. German music attained its golden age in the second half of the eighteenth century. It became the medium of expression of universal values, not merely those of a particular religious faith or regional culture. Most typical were Gluck, Haydn, Mozart, and Beethoven. The chamber music of Mozart, provided for small gatherings, expressed the same qualities of lightness, elegance, and grace which characterized the Rococo in general.

THE TECHNOLOGIES OF SURFACE AND OF DEPTH

Baroque culture was based upon a wind, water, and wood technology. Holland, with its many windmills and canals, is the typical example. This technology exploited the surface forces: the movement of wind and water in turning wheels and sailing boats.[8] It contributed enormously toward the acceleration of movement along roads and waterways as, among other things, the building of turnpikes and the introduction of postal and coach services indicates.

In the Germanies there were still many restrictions on the movement of people and goods during the first half of the eighteenth century. Mercantilism added a multiplicity of tariffs and customs duties imposed on the borders of each of the three hundred or more states or at the gates of cities. Goods going approximately three hundred miles, from Strassburg to Holland, paid more than thirty different customs or tariffs. The roads were best in southern Europe and relatively poor in the north, perhaps kept deliberately so to keep foreign goods out and to keep people from moving away. The chief complaint of the economists of the time was the predilection of the Germans for French goods as well as for French culture.[9]

By the beginning of the eighteenth century this technology was confronted with a crisis in the exhaustion of wood resources. The clearing of the land for agricultural purposes and the use of wood for all manner of functions, even in machinery, and especially the great demand for its use as a fuel in the smelting of iron, threatened the depletion of the forests. A series of inventions, notably the development of the use of coal in the smelting of iron and the improvement of the steam engine, ushered in the new technology of the mine, first in England and later on the continent.

An even more basic modification of technology occurred with

the transformation of the underlying motivation of technical progress. In Baroque technology, extending far into the eighteenth century, technics were adapted largely to nonutilitarian purposes, except for the construction of instruments of war, cannon and small arms. The great spectacles called for automatons such as mechanical ducks and flute players and for elaborate water and firework displays which revealed a mechanical ingenuity beyond the contemporary English innovations in the spinning and weaving of cloth, which are associated with the beginnings of the Industrial Revolution.

In the Baroque, technics are closely associated with art, but in the eighteenth century the cleavage between the fine and useful arts widened decisively, as is evident in the thought of the *philosophes*, such as Voltaire. The distinction did not become of great aesthetic significance until the nineteenth century. The useful arts gained great prestige as they became associated in the Enlightenment with the progress toward human welfare and happiness. The fine arts, no longer representing an "order," became concerned in the Rococo with promoting intimacy and comfort.

That the technology of mining had its beginning in England has been attributed to her relative backwardness in the eighteenth century as compared with the continental countries such as France and the Germanies.[10] There were fewer restrictions in England in terms not only of gild and mercantilist regulations but of ideal considerations embodied in the artistic and social ethos. There the middle class had achieved a widening sphere of independence and influence in politics and religion as well as in commerce and industry. As far as technical know-how was concerned, however, the French and Germans were regarded as superior by contemporaries. The Germans, in Goethe's *Faust*, produced the first great work which not only envisaged the future of technological potentialities but also recognized its ambivalent significance for humanity.

THE CULTURAL SHIFT FROM SOUTH TO NORTH

Rococo culture and industrial technology undermined the Baroque synthesis from within most definitely in the north. Both reflected middle-class values, art as decoration and technology as utilitarian, which came to dominate the nineteenth century, primarily in northern Europe. The Baroque continued to lead a decaying existence in the south, especially in the Hapsburg domains. Vienna always continued to reflect its past glories in the pomp and ceremonial of the Hapsburg courts, in the prestige of its aristocratic houses, and in the brilliance of its opera and theater. While Romanticism and revolution brought some modifications, the basic forms and spirit of the Baroque persisted in the south until the time of Hitler.

While the religious conflict lost much of its old intensity, the cultural division between Protestant north and Catholic south tended to become more marked in the course of the eighteenth century. The Counter Reformation had largely purged the Catholic south of religious dissent, both Protestant and sectarian, removing a source of religious and intellectual ferment and placing the emphasis on conformity. In the north, on the other hand, spiritualism and sectarianism took on new forms after the Thirty Years' War and assumed a new vitality in Pietism and Enlightenment. In the south, pronounced secular forms of spiritualism and sectarianism appeared again in the nineteenth century with the burgeoning of nationalism there.

In the eighteenth century the center of intellectual and political ferment moved to the northern Germanies. There the Prussian state under Frederick the Great assumed a leading role not only in international affairs but in the shaping of the new enlightened despotism. Pietism and Enlightenment were northern middle-class movements. Their fusion produced, in the idealism of Herder, Kant, and Goethe, the chief source of German intellectual dominance in the nineteenth century.

The northern middle class acquired a sense of cultural demarcation. The Baroque nobility had moved their festivals and pageants from the town square and street into the princely residences. The lower orders, it is true, had maintained in the south a close cultural connection with the nobility. In the north the new sense of importance, acquired by the middle class, is manifest in the many paintings by Dutch artists depicting heads of gilds and foundations in their finest Sunday dress. While in Holland and England the middle-class differentiation both from the lowest orders and from the nobility became especially apparent, yet they continued as heretofore to ape the manners and fashions of the nobility.

The Protestant burghers of the north developed in Pietism and Enlightenment new intellectual and religious vantage points from which to view the world. The Baroque representation of the world as an illusion was not suited to the realistic and optimistic temper of this rising class.

SPIRITUAL ILLUMINATION AND RELIGIOUS SUBJECTIVITY

As we have seen, the mystic Böhme had presented church history as a continual falling away from the ideal spiritual relationship of the individual with God. Whereas Luther presented a new vision of this spiritual tie, the Reformation had merely developed a new dogmatic orthodoxy now under princely rather than papal authority. Gottfried Arnold (1666–1714) gave the chief historical justification for the spiritualist movement in his influential work, *Impartial History of Church and Heresy* (1699–1700). He argued that the heretics had kept the torch of true spiritual religion burning throughout the recurrent dark ages of orthodoxy. But he further contended that a rebirth was at hand which would bring to an end the periodic degradation of spirituality and would usher in a return to the innocence and harmony of Paradise. The fraternity and community of the saints would then be established.

Arnold obviously presents the historical perspective of the old sectarian spiritualism with its culminating third Age of the Spirit. At one time he shared the views of those religious radicals who would purge the world with fire and the sword. Now, however, he assumed that a rebirth would bring not the triumph of an elect but a general spiritual illumination. The emerging Pietism which completely sloughed off the revolutionary social aspiration of earlier times was passive. While it lost practically all of the militancy that characterized the spiritualism of the Reformation period, it gained in emotional depth and in the many-sided nuances of religious subjectivity.

The man generally regarded as the founder of Pietism was Philipp Jakob Spener (1635–1705) who worked first as pastor in Frankfort-on-the-Main, later in Dresden, and finally in Berlin. His mystical piety, like that of the *devotio moderna* of the late Middle Ages, found an outlet particularly in the formation of small circles of the laity, including the nobility, concerned with intimate religious devotion.

August Herman Francke (1663–1727) was much more influential through his work in organizing the movement and in overcoming the opposition of the orthodox clergy. Francke's chief center of activity was at the University of Halle, from which both his theological and organizational influence proceeded. For him faith was primarily an inward experience expressed in the process of conversion. By virtue of his own religious experience, he had arrived at the various psychological stages by means of which faith was transformed, through rebirth, regeneration, and justification, from the acceptance of mere dogmatic formulae into the living experience of the soul. One began with a recognition of the worldly bent of one's soul. The awareness of the danger of this condition was then brought to a climax by the trigger action of some "incident." This led to contrition, which culminated in the illumination of divine grace and the condition of blessedness. The emphasis here was placed upon penitence arising from a sense of sin and the decisive act of will to change one's life. Thus a new inner activism was introduced to supplant sheer dogmatic acceptance.

Through Francke, Pietism exerted a great influence upon theological instruction, first at Halle and later in other theological schools, until it permeated and transformed the orthodox churches. Theology was now focused on the Bible and disassociated from its old Aristotelian and scholastic frame. Emphasis came to be placed upon the training of devout and active pastors who would know the Bible forward and backward. They were to be thoroughly grounded in the ancient languages of Hebrew and Greek in order that they might proceed to textual criticism and exegesis.[11]

In the left-wing Pietist groups, the old hope of the coming Kingdom of the Spirit persisted. These groups retained the old sectarian emphasis on the inner spiritual illumination of the believer in opposition to bibliolatry, and on the community of saints in opposition to ecclesiasticism. Inspired by Böhme's idea of the falling away of the official churches, small communities of the "illumined" were formed, the majority of which soon broke up either as a consequence of inner disputes or because of pressure from the authorities.

A permanent and highly influential community, that of Herrnhut, was formed by Count Zinzendorf (1700–1760) in Upper Silesia around a nucleus of Moravian brethren. It became a kind of asylum for all manner of spiritualists and sectarians. The spiritually awakened sought to live here, according to a common rule, in a fashion more like the lay groups of the Franciscans than like the sectarian communities. Zinzendorf thought of his community as the active and holy church within the general church, which was to be revitalized by the new leaven; therefore he made many missionary journeys to found similar communities as far afield as America.

The highly personal experience of conversion characteristic of much of Pietism was supplanted in these communities by the contemplation of the blood and wounds of the crucified Saviour as the means of raising the group to the highest level of devotion. Ecstatic and mystical devotion was inspired by communal prayer and song. All people not completely absorbed in Christ were regarded by Zinzendorf as atheists. The similarity of this piety to later medieval devotion is apparent in its emphasis on the communal and almost sensual experience of the drama of the cross.[12] There are also many resemblances here to the baroque piety of the Jesuits.

This radical aspect of Pietism served merely to underscore its failure to achieve one of its most important objectives. It undoubtedly gave greater emotional depth to the religious life of the official churches, but it failed altogether to transform German Protestant churches from a princely directed and controlled state organization into a community of believers working through the basic cell, the congregation.

One achievement of Pietism should be especially mentioned: its great expansion of the inner dimension of sacred music. The fact that Protestantism was limited by the simplicity of its church ceremonial in the service which visual art could offer to worship made for an intense interest in the exploitation of the emotional range of music. In the music of Bach and Händel we see its highest expression. Both of these musicians came from the middle lands of the *Reich*, from Saxony and Thuringia, where the Baroque creative exuberance of the south encountered the Pietism and rationalism of the north and brought about a veritable musical revolution.

Johann Sebastian Bach (1685–1750) was one of a dynasty of Lutheran cantors of Saxony. He spent approximately the last twenty years of his life in Leipzig. Only indirectly influenced by the pietistic emotional current, his basic Lutheran love of music expressed itself in great cantatas in which the combination of Baroque colorism and mathematical structure are apparent. Georg Friedrich Händel (1685–1759) had a much more cosmopolitan career, ranging from Italy to England, where the most creative phase of his career took place. In him we see also the Baroque notion of the total work of art built up on the basis of melodic expression of individual emotional effects.[13]

RATIONAL ENLIGHTENMENT AND TOLERATION

Pietism, like the Reformation, proceeded from the native soil of the Germanies, but the chief impact of the Enlightenment, like that of the Renaissance, came from abroad. The Enlightenment achieved its most characteristic expression in France, where it was directed principally against the church and its dogmas. While Pietism collided with orthodoxy, it did not constitute an attack on the basic tenets of the Christian faith; it sought rather to give them a new emotional content. In the Germanies, Pietism and Enlightenment had much more in common than they did in France.

Although assuming a variety of intellectual hues, the Enlightenment carried the general basic notion that if the individual mind were liberated from the bondage of superstition, bigotry, and ignorance, illumination of the reason would follow. It may be argued that the inner light of spiritualism became secularized in the rational illumination of the Enlightenment.

However, the rationalism of the Enlightenment assumed a more positive content by taking over the new cosmology and the new scientific method and using these as a basis for a new *Weltanschauung* and a new social and political order. While Descartes and Newton combined a rationalistic view of the universe with religious orthodoxy, the leaders of the Enlightenment found this impossible—more so in France than in the Germanies, where Pietism provided a bridge.

How these negative and positive aspects of the Enlightenment were exemplified in the Germanies may be illustrated by its leaders, Christian Thomasius and Christian Wolff.

Christian Thomasius (1655–1728) is generally spoken of as the founder of the German Enlightenment. The son of a jurist, he was born in Leipzig and trained in law, philosophy, and mathematics. As a professor at the University of Leipzig, he got into trouble with the local Lutheran clergy over his defense of Pietism and popular sovereignty. He accepted an invitation to go to the newly founded Prussian University of Halle, where he sought to achieve a reconciliation of Pietism and Enlightenment. Both Pietism and Enlightenment had common foes in the orthodox clergy and in the erudite but largely antiquarian Baroque scholarship which pervaded most of the German universities. Though earlier he was an exponent of French aristocratic and cosmopolitan culture, Thomasius later lectured and wrote in German, advocating popular bourgeois values of welfare and education.

In Thomasius we see the common concern of the Enlightenment and of Pietism with freeing the mind from dogma and superstition. One should use the reason that God has given us in all matters except those that pertain to religion. Theology should confine itself to purely religious problems and not become involved in philosophy, within whose province all other matters lie. This distinction between religion and philosophy was of course a reflection of the Pietistic emphasis on a religion of sheer inwardness.

The chief obstacle to the illumination of reason, as Thomasius saw it, lay in the various forms of superstition that pervaded the mind of the populace. Not even an ordinary activity could be engaged in without considering whether it was auspicious to do so. Alchemy had degenerated into a collection of magical recipes for achieving wealth, love, or youth. It had lost its Renaissance association with philosophy, which became yoked with mathematical and mechanistic science. By 1700 most people still believed in demonic possession and witchcraft. Great knowledge of physical phenomena was still regarded by the ordinary man as evidence of being in league with the devil. Peculiarities of physique and eccentricity of manner likewise laid one open to the charge of demonic association. Witchcraft, while on the decline among the educated, was still a popular obsession.

Back in the fifteenth century it had been given ecclesiastical recognition by Pope Innocent VIII. The standard work on how to recognize a witch, *The Witch's Hammer* (1487), had gone through about twenty-eight editions by 1669. It is calculated that approximately a million people lost their lives in the period between 1575 and 1700 as a consequence of indictment for demonic possession or witchcraft. The last witchcraft burning in Germany took place in 1775.[14]

Thomasius began his attack upon this evil after his own conversion from a belief in witchcraft. While he continued to believe in the devil and in demons he became convinced, when investigation of various accusations of witchcraft revealed the spurious character of the charges made, that collaboration with the Evil One was not provable. His Pietistic conviction of the inviolability of the human soul led him to oppose the notion of external control by either demon or church. Pietism thus carried Luther's idea of the spontaneous and uncoerced inner experience of faith forward to the point where each person should be allowed to approach God in his own individual way.

A more influential exponent of Enlightenment was Christian Wolff (1679–1754), who also was a professor at Halle and a friend of Thomasius. Exiled by Frederick William I of Prussia, Wolff went to the University of Marburg but returned to Halle in 1740 at the invitation of Frederick the Great.

Wolff encountered the opposition of the orthodox clergy when he implied that the ethics of Confucius demonstrated that it did not require a special revelation to arrive at the highest moral code. Wolff's mode of thinking reflected not Pietism but the scholastic logic and encyclopedism which had infiltrated orthodox Lutheran theology. But he used them to transform the ideas of Descartes and particularly those of Leibniz into a comprehensive rational and logical system. He thereby squeezed much of the protean quality out of Leibniz' ideas. If reason was for Leibniz a creative process immanent in the world, for Wolff it was an instrument for bringing all concepts into rational unity. The best of all possible worlds was one in which all things had their rational, that is, utilitarian purpose. All things obviously exist for the good of man and are therefore intended for his use. It is the function of philosophy to reveal to men how the rational order of things is directed toward their happiness.

The fact that Wolff's philosophical works were written in German and seemingly provided an explanation for everything contributed to their widespread popularity, especially among the middle classes, whose movement toward a rational and secular orientation became especially evident in the eighteenth century. Wolff's ideas were widely disseminated throughout the Germanies, from the pulpit as well as in the university lecture hall.

EMERGENCE OF A MIDDLE-CLASS MIND

Wolff thus marks the transition to a phase of the German Enlightenment, generally called "popular philosophy." Up to the middle of the eighteenth century the Enlightenment had been promoted largely by professors and scholars; after that, it radiated from middle-class circles. This process was made possible by the new freedom of opinion which appeared with the accession of Frederick the Great (1740–1786), who was himself a chief promoter of enlightenment.

The middle class now broke with the Baroque and mercantilist conception that society reflects an order of things distinguished by definite social groups, each of which had its peculiar vocation. Thereby the burgher was allowed neither free economic enterprise, since the state here took the initiative, nor a voice in giving meaning to his own place in the total order of things. It is true he might be called upon to give the king or prince advice in cabinet and he might also serve in an administrative capacity, but he played no role at court, in which, as we have seen, the Baroque order expressed its meaning of existence. The superiority of the noble rested on the fact that he determined the order of things; he had, so to speak, a monopoly of the world and life view.[15]

In the Enlightenment the middle class sought to arrive at a new concept of the meaning and purpose of man which would stand above the particular roles of the classes. It desired a philosophy which would express the purpose of man in terms of their own increasingly rational and functional activities. This German middle class was in no sense revolutionary in its aims. It desired chiefly to bring reason down from the lofty throne on which it had been placed by the learned philosophers, who saw in it only an attribute shared by God and man and concerned therefore with the universal order. The popular philosophy of the middle class was conceived in terms of the individual human reason and oriented toward useful interests. It was thus more sympathetic to the empiricism and utilitarianism of the English Enlightenment than to the rationalism and skepticism of the French, which had its greatest encouragement from Frederick, who even appointed a Frenchman as head of the Berlin academy. This popular utilitarian Enlightenment, disseminated by such men as the Berlin book publisher, Friedrich Nicolai (1733–1811), gradually pervaded the middle classes.

There was little criticism of absolutism in the German Enlightenment. It was fashionable to attack tyrants, but this largely reflected a mode derived from the ancient classics. Criticism might be directed against rulers like Duke Charles Eugene of Wurtemberg, whose tyrannical practices Frederick also condemned. But the general restrictions on the freedom of criticism, even of abuses, is evident in the career of the chief publicist of the period, the Wurtemberger, John Jacob Möser (1701–1785). He was kicked about from pillar to post, and he spent about five years in prison for merely opposing, as councillor, the proposal of Duke Charles Eugene to send a contingent of troops to the aid of the French in the Seven Years' War (1756–1763). A real political consciousness did not develop in the German middle class until the French Revolution.

Even in that other domain, religion, which had dominated peoples' lives and thought for so many centuries, the German reaction to rationalistic criticism was a very tentative one. It was here that the attack of the Enlightenment in France was most determined. The traditional role of the universities as the guardians of the purity of doctrine inclined their theological and philosophical faculties to the defense of the basic Christian dogmas against rationalistic attack rather than to the whittling down of their supranatural presuppositions.

A few philosophers and theologians did appear who were critical of the idea of miraculous revelation. They argued that so-called sacred scripture must be viewed, like other literature, in terms of its own inner validity and excellence. The Bible must therefore be studied in the context of the general literature of the ancient world. Jesus was but a man like others. However, more significant than this negative rationalistic approach was the profound conception of revelation as a creative process propounded by Lessing and Herder, who will be dealt with in the next chapter.

Perhaps the most significant reflection of the expansion of secular interests was the creation of a general reading public interested in literature other than theological and devotional works. The falling off in the publication of works specifically religious, especially after the middle of the century, indicates that an intellectual society, standing above the confessional conflicts, was now definitely emerging in the Germanies. The main interests of this society were expressed through the so-called "moral weeklies," which imitated Addison's "Spectator." They reflected the current tendency to divorce morality from religion.

The horizon of middle-class existence in the Germanies thus began to widen perceptibly in spite of the provincialism engendered by many small states and the lack of a great capital as a focus of the national life. For one thing, interest in world history and geography contributed toward overcoming narrow horizons. Cook, the discoverer of Australia (1768–1771), became almost a household name. The study of history, influenced by Voltaire, became concerned with what today would be called civilization—with showing how the arts and sciences contributed to the happiness and moral improvement of mankind. Knowledge of other peoples and cultures naturally led to a comparative approach, which, applied to religion, supported the rationalistic critique of dogmatic orthodoxy. It suggested a natural and common-sense religion in which the supreme being was necessary only for the creation of the universe whose moral code was man's chief concern. The Masonic lodges, which numbered among their members Frederick the Great and Goethe, were the chief promoters of this rather cold, intellectual religion, generally called "Deism."

Intellectualism was not the only current of the age. There was also a strong movement of sentimentalism fostered mainly by the secularization of the characteristic features of Pietism: emphasis on the religion of the heart and an interest in forming small intimate gatherings of the devout. It was in the writing of letters, which became almost a mania in the second half of the century, that one could express one's innermost feelings, not only to a circle of intimate friends, but even to remote acquaintances. Sentimentalism indulged in pastel-shaded emotions; it lacked the melodramatic effects of Baroque passion. In the most popular novels of the time, such as those of the English author Richardson, tears were shed by the heroine at the slightest provocation, under the influence of moonlight or at the recollection of the death of a great-grandmother. This Rococo sentimentality was also evident in the new feeling for nature reflected in the prevailing interest in going on picnics in parklands and in the depiction of shepherds and shepherdesses amid idyllic rustic scenes.

Berlin played the chief role in intellectual enlightenment, but Leipzig and Dresden in Saxony were the chief centers of literature and art. Leipzig was famous for its great book mart; Dresden, the capital, was referred to as "The Little Paris" for its art and opera. Moreover, Saxony enjoyed great commercial prosperity through its connections eastward with Poland and westward with France, especially in the development and production of the chief luxury articles of the time: silken fabrics and porcelain.

THE DYNAMICS OF PRUSSIAN STATISM

The most typical figure of this age of reason and elegance was the great Prussian king, Frederick the Great (1740–1786). He was the embodiment of a spirit of political conduct which has been called *raison d'état*, in which politics detached itself from the old patriarchal and patrimonial forms of the Baroque world as the Rococo art forms were set free from the representational ethos of that world.

By virtue of Calvinistic upbringing and thorough association with the ideas of Wolff, Frederick came to a conception of a general rational order virtually deterministic in character. Juxtaposed to this view was his admiration of the great personality who broke through traditional bonds and set in motion a new train of circumstances by force of *virtù*—heroic hardihood and capacity.

Translated into political terms these attitudes represented the recognition of a European order based on the balance of power, always in a state of fluid equilibrium. This order was a matter of rational calculation in which each state must always be on the alert to guard its power interests; one could not rely on the mechanism of balance to insure one's position.

Prussia was, however, not just another European state. Her rise in a century from a secondary German state to the position of a major European power was not due to a dynasty, as in the case of Austria, but to the personal force of two rulers, the Great Elector and King Frederick William I, the father of Frederick the Great. They had raised Prussia to a pre-eminent military power in spite of meager resources which made necessary careful husbanding of revenues. They had used her very weaknesses, her exposed position on the north German plain and the scattered character of her territories, as a means of fashioning a highly mobile and well disciplined military-bureaucratic state under the absolute control of its ruler. Upstart Prussia, having no traditional position or prestige, must be eternally vigilant in the face of its neighbors, both large and small, who were bent upon reducing her to her former lowly status.

Fully conscious of the precariousness of Prussia's position, Frederick the Great realized that she could not remain content with the status quo nor merely seize upon the chances offered by wars between her neighbors to gain prestige and power, as the Great Elector had done. She must assume the initiative, and at the beginning of his reign Frederick judged that the constellation of powers was favorable to a lightning thrust. He invaded and seized Silesia from the Hapsburgs, thereby initiating a series of conflicts culminating in the Seven Years' War (1756–1763) in which Prussia stood arrayed against a coalition of powers comprising Austria, France, and Russia, and had only the financial assistance of England. The divisions among his opponents and the rapidity of his movements in fighting them one at a time, as well as luck, enabled him to come through with Silesia still in his grasp.

One can hardly exaggerate the impact of Frederick's personality upon the minds and imagination of Germans, both of his own age and later. It is not strange that he, like Charlemagne and Otto I, came to be called "the Great."

The contemporary attitude was more ambivalent than that of later times. The Germans might be impressed by the sheer demonic force of Frederick's personality as revealed in the struggle against the great coalition, but nevertheless they also abhorred the Prussian barrack state, which was, to men like Möser and Herder, but a machine without limits to its expansive power drive; its bureaucratic-military structure obviously lacked the organic roots which they were seeking in the realm of communal and cultural forms.

In the nineteenth century Frederick, who in language and tastes was essentially French and who referred to himself as ruling over barbarians, became a great national symbol. By the second half of that century his personality was no longer disassociated from but had been completely absorbed in the Prussian power state, which was then regarded as the necessary core of German national unity.

In the twentieth century, particularly in the experience of World War I, when Germany felt herself encircled by a great coalition, as Frederick had been, his type of personality again came to the fore. But in that era his tactics were reduced almost to a military formula —the lightning thrust into the enemy territory, the all-out effort against the encircling foes, the last stand, and the miracle of being saved from annihilation. The whole development of Prussia has been pictured by some recent interpreters as deriving from Frederick's tour de force methods.

In the eighteenth century, contemporary foreign admirers of Prussia frequently assumed that her success in war and diplomacy grew out of the progressive and enlightened character of her ruler. At the outset of his reign, Frederick introduced some typical enlightened reforms such as the abolition of the use of torture in judicial processes, the extension of the freedom of the press, and religious toleration. But he did very little to modify the basic structure of the state he had inherited from his father. This structure involved maintenance of the absolute authority of the ruler, the dominance in the government of military administration, the service role of all social groups in the state, and the mercantilist promotion of trade and commerce to gain revenues for the state. It was the close integration of army, finance, and foreign policy under one supreme director that carried Frederick through the Seven Years' War.

Perhaps Frederick's most important achievement was to give to this power-state a rational form both in theory and in practice. The old absolutism had stressed centralization of authority and revenues for the army, while the newer enlightened variety placed the accent on uniformity of law and administration for the economic and cultural welfare of the subjects. Most important, it undermined the sanctions on which the old patriarchal divine-right absolutism had rested. The latter assumed that there existed a God-given order of things, according to which society was divided into definite groups, each of which had its special calling, including even the ruler. Under Frederick's father the state was still merely a collection of military, fiscal, and bureaucratic agencies engaged in more or less perpetual competition with the representative officials and diets of the estates which, like the ruler, derived their authority directly by divine right and hence stood outside the state. But the rationalism of the Enlightenment ousted God, so to speak, not only from the cosmos but also from the political and social dwellings of men. In Frederick's conception, the state came to take God's place in standing above both ruler and subjects. Frederick still retained, it is true, the vague idea that Providence had designated him as head of the state through the process of dynastic succession. But even as the nobility served in army and diplomacy, the middle class in economic affairs and administration, and the peasant on the land and in the infantry, so Frederick was a servant of the state.

As "the first servant of the state" he had a special obligation to it. He would sacrifice all personal interests and comforts, as he had done in the Seven Years' War, to the good of the state. Nor was the state a mere instrument for contributing to the individual welfare or happiness of its citizens. It protected their life and property, and it sought to secure release of their energies. But it did so in order that they might serve the state more effectively.

That the real motive power in this Prussian state came from its ruler rather than from below or even from the nobility is indicated by the rapid decline of Prussia after the death of Frederick, when the direction of the state fell into mediocre hands. The service state by its very nature tends to crystallize in rigid forms unless supplied with an energizing personal force. The various service strata tend to fall back upon the defense of privileged positions when no longer carried forward by the *élan* of a ruling personality.

It has been pointed out that the very successes of enlightened despotism in central Europe proved in the end to be a liability. They retarded the emergence of liberal democratic forms and practices.[16]

In spite of this, many of the German states, especially Prussia, were looked upon by reformers in other countries as having the most enlightened governments and as contributing more to the welfare of their populations than did other governments. Undoubtedly these successes staved off revolutionary movements at the end of the century. But by attributing a rational function to the old hierarchy of classes—just as the rationalism of Wolff did to the universe at large—enlightened despotism hindered the decisive breakthrough of national and individual self-determination.

GERMAN CULTURAL AND SPIRITUAL DIFFERENTIATION

The most important consequence of the Baroque synthesis and its disintegration for the Germanies was the accentuation of the division between north and south Germans. Underlying it, of course, was the religious differentiation which was now reinforced by a cultural differentiation. Catholic south Germany continued to be influenced by the Baroque modified by Romanticism. Theater and music were its chief creations even in the nineteenth century. Northern Protestant Germany followed the Pietist and Rationalist roads to their fusion in Idealism and Classicism. Its great creative achievement was in philosophy and literature.

Europe as a whole was of course influenced by this north-south cultural axis, the consequence of the movement of the intellectual and industrial centers of gravity northward. It made southern Europe seem backward and decadent. France was not as greatly affected as the Germanies because its revolution brought about a final unification in terms of the triumph of a rational order. In the Germanies, however, and especially after the middle of the nineteenth century, Austria was viewed askance, not only because of her multinational character but also because of her apparent decadence. Bismarck therefore had little difficulty in severing her from the main body of Germans in the new united Germany which he set up under Prussian domination. Today there are three Germanies, the old colonial northeast within the Soviet zone, Austria to the south, and West Germany, with the Rhine as its backbone. The cultural centrifugal forces within the German complex proved much stronger than the centripetal tendencies induced by modern nation-state development, of which France is the prime example.

Another kind of differentiation proceeded from the Pietism, rationalism, and statism of the north. Rationalism as a philosophy of progress exerted much less influence than elsewhere, for example, in France. It was most concerned within middle-class circles with making things as they are appear right and thus contributed further to the passivity of the German middle class, at least as far as the appeal of reform and revolution was concerned.

However, the idealistic-spiritualist tendencies in Pietism and the rational functionalism implicit in Prussian statism were to become the two chief poles of German development during the nineteenth century and far into the twentieth.

One pole, Pietism, with its emphasis on the inwardness of spiritual illumination and conversion, gave religion a new impetus. It exerted its greatest direct influence on religious thinking in the nineteenth century through Schleiermacher and other Romantic writers. More immediately, the inner light of spiritualism may be said to have become secularized in the immanent creative spirit of Idealism. Also, the accent placed on the intimate community of those united by the same spirit provided a basis for the organic view of the national community and for the juxtaposition in German thought of community as based upon an inner imperative as against society based on outward convention. On the other hand, since it sloughed off the social revolutionary aspirations of the older spiritualist sectarians, the hope of a new order was taken over by the secular underground of Marxian socialism, for whom religion was the opium of the masses.

The other pole, that of rational-functional organization, was to have an equally important bearing on German development. As we have seen, under Frederick the Great the Prussian state provided a buttressing to the idea of a hierarchical order of society—only to the extent, of course, that each class has a functional role but no longer a symbolic significance, as it still had in the Baroque. It did this by continuing the military and bureaucratic functions of the nobility within its organization and giving these functions the highest prestige in society. The spirit of functional rationalism came to permeate the whole of society, and this may explain the decisive breakthrough of the technological point of view among the Germans earlier than elsewhere in Europe.

VIII

The Realm of Spirit

$\mathcal{W}$ hen we speak of the "realm of the spirit," we are referring to still another phase of the German quest for a religion of pure spirit (*Geist*) which had its sources in the spiritualization of the *sacrum imperium*. While Cues, Paracelsus, Böhme, and Leibniz contributed most to this spiritualization, many other spiritualist and sectarian thinkers provided new insights. The decline of the *Reich* as political entity reached its nadir in the eighteenth century just when a new *Reich* of *Geist* was conceived as standing above the contending powers and principalities. The building of this universal empire of the spirit, in which the individual could achieve inner freedom, became the chief goal of philosophic and religious quest in the second half of the eighteenth and early nineteenth centuries.

THE SPIRITUALIST TRADITION

A brief review of the religious and philosophic lineage of the conception of a realm of the spirit will serve to indicate some of its archetypical bases and the remarkable continuity of the spiritualist tradition. This tradition grew more by a kind of inner unfolding and proliferation than by the accretion of new ideas from the outside.

Its primal source was ancient Gnosticism, which put forward the following fundamental ideas: the exaltation of the immanent divine spirit in the universe, the conception of knowledge as an illumination of the mind whereby one rises up the hierarchical ladder of being to the contemplation of pure spirit, and the inspired prophet, philosopher, or sage as its chief transmitter. These archetypical ideas were transmitted through the centuries, especially through Neo-Platonic spiritualism and Renaissance nature philosophy. They flowed through the insights of Paracelsus, Böhme, and Leibniz into the Idealistic movement.

A fundamental reorientation began in the late Middle Ages with the impact of the Joachimite conception of the three ages of man's movement toward salvation. A spiritualist philosophy of history in terms of fulfillment in an Age of the Spirit took the place of the hierarchical ladder of contemplation.

This horizontal or historical orientation of the spiritualist aspiration pervaded the sectarian and spiritualist thought of the Reformation. Differences of belief now turned on the issue as to how the final Age of the Spirit was to be ushered in—by an apocalyptic event such as the coming of a divine deliverer or by a purging of the wicked from the world by the elect who thus set up the Kingdom of God or by a unitary process of development in nature and history culminating in the final release of the spirit from its material prison. These forms of salvation are both very ancient and also, in somewhat different garb, very modern.

A further modification occurred in the seventeenth and eighteenth centuries with the appearance of the new cosmic order from which not only God was excluded, except as the original architect, but also man, except as an observer. God and man thus no longer confronted each other in nature but only in history, from which God was soon also excluded.

To Baroque man, history was still essentially meaningless except as a record of God's plan for man's salvation. The Enlightenment, however, especially through Voltaire and Turgot, discovered in history the progressive development of rational enlightenment and the eventual triumph of reason over unreason. In general, it applied to the past the test of achievement in the arts and sciences as the yardstick of reason.

The German Idealistic movement, though influenced by this secular orientation, returned to the earlier spiritualist tradition in discerning in history an immanent creative process in which each age plays an individual role in the eventual fulfillment of the spirit. Just as Leibniz projected the closed universe of the windowless monad, so history was to be regarded as a completely self-sufficient realm from which all intervention from the outside by deity or human reason was to be excluded.

THE EIGHTEENTH-CENTURY GERMAN MATRIX

The culmination of the German spiritualist tradition in the late eighteenth and early nineteenth centuries may be attributed to a number of special circumstances then characterizing the German scene.

First, in the Germanies, the state, in both its old patriarchal form and in its new rational-functional form of enlightened despotism, allowed for little assurance of individual or group autonomy. The ruler could go as far as he liked in prescribing the vocations and careers of subjects, in controlling their travels, and in determining what books they might read or write. Much depended, of course, on the character of the ruler and the quality of his officials, who might themselves be petty tyrants. Though the Duke of Wurtemberg had the reputation of being a particularly atrocious tyrant, the Duke of Weimar was known for his enlightened patronage of the arts and sciences. The very existence of numerous states, both large and small, naturally allowed for wide differences in freedom with respect to opinion and belief.

In Prussia many of the middle-class officials were most receptive to the ideas of the Enlightenment, but this gave no enduring assurance of freedom of opinion. Under the mediocre successor of Frederick the Great, Frederick William II (1786–1797), a religious edict was issued at the instigation of an official by the name of Wöllner, which prohibited pastors from preaching ideas contrary to church dogma and subjected them to censorship. While the uproar this edict caused prevented effective enforcement, still it is evidence of the often arbitrary nature of government by bureaucratic officials who are under an absolute ruler.

A second circumstance was the combination of Pietism and Enlightenment, which together had brought about the dissolution of the Baroque order, at least in the north, by insisting that the relationship of the individual to church, state, and society should be an inner, vital one rather than an outer acceptance of dogma or of the external trappings of rank and ceremonial. But both had failed to achieve fundamental modification in the structure of the military-bureaucratic state or in its tool, the authoritarian church.

Pietism succumbed to an alliance with ecclesiastical orthodoxy directed against the enlightened critique of religious dogma and of biblical truth. The Enlightenment succumbed to the welfare policy, religious toleration, and patronage of the arts of enlightened despots, such as Frederick the Great. It envisaged but did not realize a state and society based on a dynamic public opinion.

Both Pietism and the Enlightenment had lost their original vision and *élan* by the second half of the eighteenth century and had degenerated, on the one hand, into mere sentimentalized devotion and, on the other, into viewing religion and even the arts as merely expedient for human happiness. Idealism, although nourished by the original creative spirit of Pietism and Enlightenment, turned from this later trivialization to the development of a new life of the spirit outside of the church and the state in which the mystical communalism of Pietism and the rational critique of the Enlightenment could be joined. Idealism was a true descendant of the Lutheran Reformation in that it did not harbor revolutionary, political, or social aspirations.

A third circumstance of significance was the dominant religious background of the leaders. They were either pastors, like Herder, or had studied theology, like Lessing and Winckelmann, or had come under the influence of Pietism, like Kant and Goethe. Even throughout the nineteenth century the sons of pastors continued to provide German leaders in philosophy, literature, and science. Here the middle class had a monopoly comparable to the gentry's monopoly of the upper ranks of the army. Naturally the talented sons of middle-class families sought careers in the church and particularly in the closely related academic pursuits. Social juxtaposition of the military and the bureaucracy to church and university thus re-enforced the polar tension of *Staat* and *Geist*.

The fourth circumstance is the reaction in German literature against the dominant French forms of rationalism and classicism. In the eighteenth century the new reading public was attracted to French books; the works of Goethe and Schiller received compara-tively little attention. The Germanies possessed nothing comparable to the salons of Paris. Goethe complained of his loneliness, of the lack of a general intellectual society in which ideas and attitudes could be exchanged. This comparative isolation of German thinkers and artists had its compensations, for it led them to emphasize the importance of genius and inspiration as against the rules and con-ventions dictated by salons or academies.

In the eighteenth century French literature was still mainly a function of society while German literature had already turned to the "revelation" of the inner creative forces which was to reach its culmination in Romanticism. The key word, *Geist*, suggesting orig-inality and spontaneity, expressed itself in variety and individuality. It was also expressed as "inward form" achieved through a harmo-nious relationship between inner creative spirit and its outward pro-jection in the forms of religion, art, and institution. The archetype of *Geist* was the monad.

The realization of this free creativity was itself a matter of growth and development. This is apparent if we compare the thought of the three pioneers, Lessing (1729–1781), Winckelmann (1717–1768), and Möser (1720–1794), with that of the three giants of the mature Idealism, Herder (1744–1803), Kant (1724–1804), and Goethe (1749–1832). The pioneers were in quest of inward form in the historical development of religion, art, and institutions, but the culminators turned first to the creative force within man which molds and shapes religious faiths, artistic styles, and institu-tional forms. In between lay the meteoric revolt against tradition and convention known as *Sturm und Drang* (Storm and Stress).

REVELATION AS EDUCATION

The career of Gotthold Ephraim Lessing testifies to the difficulties encountered by those who sought to make letters a career and to avoid dependence on princely patronage and French literary precedent. As the son of a Saxon pastor, he went to the University of Leipzig in 1741 to study theology, but neither theology nor medicine attracted him as did literature, especially drama. At Leipzig the celebrated Professor Gottsched was the dictator of the form and taste of the prevailing French pseudo-classicism. As against such artificialities, Lessing came to recommend the "natural" genius of Sophocles and Shakespeare. This tendency of turning from the French to the English and ancient Greeks was to become characteristic of the Idealistic movement.

In the seventeenth century, the Baroque theater had catered largely to the interest of courtly and aristocratic circles in spectacle and pageantry. At the famous Dresden opera house the presentation of one opera involved the use of eight thousand candles and the service of two hundred and fifty people to operate the machinery that produced the complicated scenic effects.[1] In the eighteenth century, these grand Baroque exhibitions gradually lost favor and were displaced by interest in the dramatic development of character and plot centering in moral problems.

Lessing is generally regarded as the real creator of the German theater by virtue of a series of plays that he wrote beginning with *Miss Sarah Simpson*, presented at Frankfort-on-the-Oder in 1755, and culminating in *Nathan the Wise* in 1779. In them he tried to show that the middle classes also have their seductions, suicides, and murders, which are fit subjects for the drama. In *Nathan*, he used the ancient story of the three rings to preach toleration. In this way he made the stage a pulpit for preaching middle-class virtues and enlightenment. For the educated middle classes of his time, the theater virtually took the place of the church as the medium of moral improvement.

Lessing's career oscillated between the poles of the pursuit of these new values and the quest for economic security. Among other pursuits he managed an ill-fated theatrical company in Hamburg, served as secretary to the military governor of Silesia, and toward the end of his life, as librarian to the Duke of Brunswick at Wolfenbüttel. For a time he enjoyed considerable security and happiness there; later he became involved in a bitter religious controversy.

This controversy revolved around the very critical attitude taken toward revelation in a hitherto unpublished work by a Professor Reimarus of Hamburg, of whose work Lessing published fragments between 1774 and 1778. The professor went so far as to argue that Christianity started with a deception practiced by the disciples when they hid the body of Jesus to make it appear that he had been "raised from the dead." The publication of this attack on what may be regarded as the basic tenet of orthodox Christianity raised such a storm of protest from the clergy as to almost sweep Lessing out of his job. His general response, although ambiguous with respect to the particular issue of the resurrection, was that revelation involved not the acceptance of prescribed dogmas but a continuous quest for the truth. This attitude he presented both in his best-known drama, *Nathan the Wise*, and, in philosophic terms, in the *Education of the Human Race*, published in 1780, the year before his death.

Lessing was critical of both the Deist position of his friends among the popular philosophers, Nicolai and Moses Mendelssohn, and of the supranatural position of his orthodox critics. He argued that God does not reveal himself, as assumed by the current Deism, merely in the order and design of the universe. He is not merely the great architect and law-giver of the universe, who, after having accomplished His task in a perfect creation, had gone on a perpetual holiday, leaving it more or less for fortuitous discoveries to reveal the superlative harmony of His handiwork. Nor on the other hand, as the orthodox assumed, did God reveal His purpose with regard to man and the universe once and for all in certain sacred writings which therefore mark the end of revelation. For both orthodoxy and Deism the basic assumption was that God's creative activity took place in a particular time situation and worked, so to speak, from the outside.

To Lessing God was immanent in both nature and history, revealing Himself continuously in the growing self-knowledge of man.

Reason and revelation are one and therefore progressive in that God becomes known in the self-education of the human race.

Such education proceeds by stages, each of which provides the means appropriate to the advance made by the pupil. Initially, God chose a particular people, the Hebrews, to serve as the teachers of mankind. Out of their religious experience came two basic primers, the Old and New Testaments, as well as the greatest teacher of all, Jesus, who embodied the conception of an ethical god as against the earlier jealous tribal deity. Each age has, therefore, a conception of God appropriate to its stage of development. Modern man may regard Him as the great mathematician and engineer, a notion which appeals to man's sense of the rational order of things; but again this is merely another stage in the development of man as a rational being.

Revelation as reason is a quest by which mankind seeks God by various avenues, and, in the very seeking, finds a god appropriate to its own aspirations. Yet, in achieving its own ideal conception, mankind goes beyond the previous age and aspires to the next higher level. The whole education of humanity thus moves toward a kind of final consummation.

In Lessing we also see the notion of the coming of the Age of the Spirit, the fulfillment now of the education of humanity. He refers to the fact that Joachim of Flora and the Franciscan spirituals, with their notion of three ages, were wrong only in assuming that the last Age of the Eternal Gospel was at hand. This last age, as Lessing envisioned it, does not come by any apocalyptic or revolutionary political and social event but in the minds and hearts of men. The Eternal Gospel does not, therefore, present a new order—a utopia—but an expectancy, a looking forward. Thus the notion of the coming Kingdom of God becomes completely interiorized and spiritualized.[2]

FREEDOM AND THE CLASSICAL NORM

Winckelmann and Möser looked backward rather than forward in order to provide norms for the present and future. They assumed, generally speaking, that the art and institutions of their own time were degenerate in comparison with the ancient past. Winckelmann measured his own age by the yardstick of Greek classical art; Möser likewise used the institutions of the early Germans. They discovered among the ancient Greeks and Germans the ideal relationship between the style of life of a society and the spirit of freedom which animates it. Both the lavish artifice of Baroque and Rococo and the uniformity of a few rules proposed by rationalism and pseudo-classicism were, to them, expressions of the prevailing lack of freedom under despotism. Winckelmann sought to show how the "noble simplicity and quiet grandeur" of classical Greek art was a manifestation of city-state freedom; Möser, that the dynamic relation of liberty and property was a function of the principle of free association among the early Germans.

Some scholars have argued that Winckelmann and Möser ushered in what is called the "tyranny of Greece and Germania over the German mind." It should be noted, however, that both still belonged to the rationalist and classical eighteenth century in that they were concerned with finding the ideal norms of art and institutions in Greece and Germania. In other words, they were still occupied with universally valid golden ages rather than with the genetic origins of a particular culture, as the later Romantics were.

Both also reflected the concern of an emerging German cultural nationalism in its reaction against French cultural hegemony to link itself with an ideal past age. The dominant motif was not, however, return to cultural sources as such but a nostalgic yearning for simplicity and sincerity as against the artificialities of existing culture and society such as we have already encountered in humanism and Reformation. In this respect they were influenced by Rousseau, with his gospel of return to the spontaneity and simplicity of nature; but Rousseau was in no sense the soul-stirring experience to them that he was to the younger generation of the *Sturm und Drang*.

Art criticism in the Germanies may be said to have made its first definite statement of the ideal norm of beauty in Johann Joachim Winckelmann's *Thoughts on the Imitation of Greek Works* in 1755. It marked a decisive break with Baroque representation and ushered in the series of classical and Gothic revivals which characterize much of the late eighteenth and most of the nineteenth century. As a consequence the works of art acquired a self-contained character juxtaposed to the subjective creative *élan* of individuals and peoples. The superlative works of art of the past may then be detached from their original creative matrices and exhibited in museums so as to present the various stages in the evolution of art. Art objects may also be studied on a comparative basis to discover stylistic trends and cycles. Winckelmann contributed unintentionally toward this historicizing of artistic styles through the influence of his famous work, *History of the Art of Antiquity* (1764).

Winckelmann himself felt that he was continuing the work of the Renaissance in purifying art of the excesses and extravagances it had fallen into since the days of Raphael. He had left Prussia and abandoned theology to turn to history and art when he became librarian in 1748 for Count Heinrich von Bunau, whose estate lay near Dresden and who possessed one of the greatest libraries in Europe.

Dresden had become, under August the Strong (1694-1733), the chief art center of Europe. The *Zwinger* (1711-1722), an amusement pavilion, the work of the architect Pöppelmann, was the most famous example of Rococo art in the north. But the great art collections of Dresden, which included the works of Raphael, introduced Winckelmann to the classical quality of Renaissance art and turned his eye back to the original fount of classicism.

Winckelmann was given a pension in 1755 by Frederick August II of Saxony, to whom he had dedicated his early work, and sent to Rome, where he spent the remainder of his life as a kind of caretaker of ruins. He had become a convert to Catholicism, and he always contended that only in Rome did he find the cultural and social atmosphere in which both freedom of the mind and a sense of form were joined. He was among the first of many who made the pilgrimage to Italy instead of to France and discovered that the south was by no means decadent.

In the *History* which he composed while in Rome, Winckelmann sought to show that the great Greek achievement could be attributed neither entirely to environmental circumstances nor to the genius of individual artists. The ideal qualities of the classical style were the culmination of a process of development which coincided with the fruition of Greek democratic freedom in the fifth and fourth centuries.

The superlative qualities of classical art were therefore not the mere product of the native genius of a people but of a process of progressive education whereby art was stripped of archaic conventions and rules and came to follow nature. The culmination was the joyous freedom of naked forms of the time of Phidias and Praxiteles. Classical Greek art did not, of course, merely copy nature; it recognized that art, as Plato argued, must also transcend nature in order to arrive at purity of form. Since this classical art of "noble simplicity and quiet grandeur" reflects a condition of soul, there is no movement in it—only an ideal "being." The tensions of the Baroque are therefore completely absent.

As an organic part of the life of the people and not merely a decorative function of a court, Greek art naturally responded to the changing political and social structure of the Greek world. As the city-states lost their freedom, both internally and externally, art gradually lapsed into the distortions of realism which reached their peak under the imperial despotism of Alexander and his successors. Winckelmann also accepted the idea, common in his time, that real freedom is possible only in small states and is the necessary basis of great art.

While Winckelmann thus presented a conception of Greek art as the expression of a total historical development of a particular people never to be excelled, nevertheless, the ideal qualities of beauty which evolved could serve as a norm for all ages. Thus the dogma of an ideal beauty was projected which was to provide a canon of art criticism for approximately a century. Contemporary artistic creation itself reflected an archaeological classicism in the rather cold and severe simplicity manifest in its productions, as contrasted with the lavish forms and vehement emotionalism of the Baroque.

The increasing interest of the eighteenth century in going back to the ancient sources of culture is evident in the archaeological and historical studies of the time. In the second half of the century the new University of Göttingen, in Hanover, became the chief center of historical and philological study. The controversy over whether the *Iliad* and the *Odyssey* were a product of an individual genius or a collective product of the Greek folk genius in a barbaric but heroic stage of its development reflected a growing disposition to view history in terms of individuality and development rather than as a progressive sloughing off of superstition and barbarism.

HIERARCHICAL STRUCTURE AND GERMANIC FREEDOM

Although Justus Möser appears both in background and interests to be the complete opposite of Winckelmann, his basic approach to history was very much like that of his older contemporary. Möser acknowledged that Winckelmann had shown him how the style of an age is expressed not only in its art but in its institutions and in its mode of life.

Möser viewed the world not from the vantage point of the cosmopolitan society and culture of a great capital city but from within the small ecclesiastical principality of Osnabrück near the Dutch border, where he spent practically the whole of his life except for a short stay in England. Osnabrück might be called a museum of medieval antiquities. It retained such vestiges of the medieval hierarchical structure as prince-bishop, estates, gilds, manorial regime, and serfdom. Hence it might also be regarded as a microcosm of the old *Reich*. It had one important bridge to the outside: at this time the English king, in addition to being the Elector of Hanover, was also the Prince-Bishop of Osnabrück.

By virtue of his outstanding ability, particularly along legal and juristic lines, Möser rose to a position wherein he became the most influential man in the affairs of Osnabrück. As the legal representative of both the nobility and the British king, he came to occupy virtually the position of a prime minister.

Möser was the only one among those considered here with whom practical affairs came first. He published a weekly in which he devoted himself particularly to defending the medieval complexities of Osnabrück against the ideas of the French *philosophes* of the Enlightenment, whose notion of a uniform code of law based on rational principles would contribute to the leveling of the hierarchical structure inherited from the past. Möser himself was influenced by the Enlightenment, at least to the extent that he sought to defend that structure on utilitarian grounds rather than on traditionalist or religious grounds. He argued that the various forms of that structure had arisen in response to concrete needs and should be abandoned only when the needs no longer existed, not on the basis of theoretical principles.

The hierarchical structure arose, Möser contended, in response to the desire for security, liberty, and status. These should not be separated from each other and isolated from a concrete historical situation in accordance with the analytical method of the rationalists. The rationalists atomized society into individuals presumably animated by uniform interests and appetites which should be subordinated to the general ideals of liberty and justice for all. But does man really desire liberty and equality above all? Haven't these been merely attributed to him by the abstract philosophers of the present? Judging from the past, he seems to have been more concerned with status than with equality; in other words, with looking both up and down from a position on the hierarchical ladder. He has associated liberty with the possession of the rights and duties which derive from a particular rung of the ladder and whose exercise assures him a positive role in the community. The liberty and equality that the *philosophes* desired would tend to liquidate this substantival basis of man's freedom and thereby remove the very guarantees against despotism. Uniformity, Möser contended, was the surest road to despotism.

He shared with early liberalism the notion that the association of the ownership of land with the rendering of public service, especially of military service, provided the surest guarantee of liberty. In early Germanic society this association was, according to Möser, most ideally presented. The alliance of these two pillars of freedom down to Möser's own day furnished the real basis of liberty as against constitutions, universal suffrage, or declarations of human rights. Only the possessors of a stake in society in the form of property, preferably landed property, could be relied upon to defend the community against oppression and conquest. Only they, therefore, should form the association known as the state; only they should be regarded as citizens.

In his *History of Osnabrück* (1768ff.) Möser made this realistic notion of liberty the norm of German constitutional development. He held that the changing fortunes of this liberty provided the dynamic inward form of the development of the *Reich* rather than the traditional conception of the transference of imperial authority from the Romans to the Germans. As he saw it, liberty was, as a matter of fact, almost extinguished by the imperialistic ventures of Charlemagne, especially by the conquest and conversion of the Saxons, among all the German peoples, its most ardent defenders. The breakdown of Charles's empire led to the crystallization of a feudal state, wherein military service was no longer associated with the *ownership* of land but became instead a class privilege.

Only in the later Middle Ages, when the breakdown of both feudalism and imperial authority allowed for the emergence of many corporations and associations such as leagues of cities, nobles, and peasants, do we see the original liberty coming to the surface again. Since then, Möser argued, the development of the military-bureaucratic state had undermined liberty, except in such countries as England and the Netherlands and in the ecclesiastical principalities and imperial cities of the *Reich*. The process of rationalization in social development now made necessary the deliberate formation of such associations as gilds of doctors and lawyers, animated by common economic interest and concern with public service to counteract the growing danger of despotism from the throne and from the mob.

Möser's conception of an organic society built up from below by associations based on a community of interest and service was to exert great influence on later statesmen and thinkers. It provided the fundamental ideas which Stein and the "old liberals" later sought to embody in the constitutional reform of both Prussia and the *Reich*. It also provided the National Liberal Frederick List, the father of the *Zollverein* (union of German states for the maintenance of a uniform tariff), with his basic economic and political philosophy. Both Justus Möser and Edmund Burke represented a trend in liberalism which venerated ancient institutions and habits because their emergence revealed a higher expediency, that is, a fitness and appropriateness to human needs which would serve as the best cement to bind men together in communities against the atomization of revolutionary rationalism.

The publication of a work on the character of German art in 1773 brought together three essays which represented a kind of declaration of independence from the prevailing conceptions. They comprised the introduction to Möser's *History of Osnabrück,* an interpretation of Shakespeare by Herder, and an interpretation of Gothic art as represented in the Strassburg Cathedral, by Goethe. Two points of view predominated: an appreciation of the creative variety of the culture of the Middle Ages as something other than an age of barbarism and superstition, and consequently the assumption that diversity and multiplicity of forms arise out of spontaneous natural creativity within a matrix of common values and aspirations. It is not rules that determine great art but common cultural values, from which genius must derive its sustenance.

STURM UND DRANG AND ROUSSEAU

This new conception of the natural in terms of creative spontaneity, which is at the same time rooted in a cultural soil, was expressed vividly in the movement known as *Sturm und Drang.* As this term suggests, it was an explosive movement of short duration, culminating in the 1770's and 1780's and then rapidly burning out. It was chiefly a literary movement of young authors, among whom the best known are Herder, Schiller, and Goethe. It was a highly emotional rebellion against both the provincialism and caste consciousness of German society and the artificiality and cold intellectualism of the dominant French culture. The drama was the chief means of preaching revolt, not against particular political and social abuses but against general social and cultural impediments to the free expression of inner values. It carried the banner of Rousseau's revolt of the individual against society and civilization. The most popular heroes were leaders of robber bands or robber knights such as Goethe's Götz von Berlichingen. The Renaissance Faust myth provided a favorite theme. Not only was it used by Goethe but also by other writers of the movement as symbolic of the attempt to transcend the limitations imposed by church and society.

Jean Jacques Rousseau (1712–1778), provided the trigger action which released this pent-up sense of inner revolt. He was the chief critic of what was coming to be called "civilization" in his day. It signified high achievements in the sciences and arts. He argued, however, that culture really was unnatural, since both sciences and arts, as well as social conventions, created molds which prevented man from expressing his true self. Everything in civilization seemed to minister to the intellect, nothing to the feelings and convictions.

Rousseau offered a way of return to the natural man in his most influential books, especially in *Émile,* which dealt with education, and in the *Social Contract,* which concerned the basis of the community. He began with the assumption that man in the state of nature lived a life of spontaneous free impulse. But once man had eaten of the tree of knowledge, there was no return to this paradise of naive and instinctive existence. Nevertheless, man could now rise to what might be called a third higher level where he used reason to recognize the limits of reason. In the *Social Contract* Rousseau posed the problem of how man could achieve a self-conscious freedom whereby he imposed laws of his own choosing upon himself. Rousseau's pattern of salvation was obviously a kind of secularized version of the Judaic-Christian epic.

Nowhere was the influence of this frame of thought greater than in Germany. In France Rousseau became the prophet of popular sovereignty, but in the Germanies he became the symbol of inner freedom from the artificial molds of civilization and pointed the way to organic growth and development leading to the consciousness of dynamic inward form.

Naturally there were many variations of this basic theme in a movement so rich in creative personalities. Generally speaking, the Idealist movement is regarded as falling between 1770, the year in which Goethe and Herder encountered each other at Strassburg, and the death of Goethe in 1832. Within these six decades the movement went through three phases which overlap and intermingle both as to the generations involved and the currents of thought. The classical phase lay in the three decades from 1770 to 1800; that of the romantic from 1795 to 1805; and finally, the nationalist from 1805 to 1815. These chronological brackets represent in each case the peak creative phases of the movement. Romanticism and nationalism, arising as reactions to the explosions of the French Revolution and Napoleonic imperialism, turned the movement in new directions, which will be dealt with in the next chapter.

Herder, Kant, and Goethe possessed a much more marked spiritualistic syncretism than the pioneers of Idealism. They juxtaposed the individual's inner creative freedom to civilization (taste and toleration) and to a mechanistic universe whose network of causal relationships threatened the individual. Erasmian, Lutheran, and particularly Paracelsian motifs were blended in the thinking of the time, although the supernatural frame of sixteenth-century thought was of course almost obliterated. Both Herder and Goethe viewed man and the universe as a dynamic totality of forces, while Kant followed Luther in stressing a dualism, not of sinful man and a Holy God, but of subjective man and the world out there.

Each stood in opposition to certain aspects of French rationalism: Herder to its conception of civilization as a progressive movement from barbarism to enlightenment, Kant to the assumption that science provides the universal key to knowledge and morality, and Goethe to the conception of the cosmos as a mere mathematical-mechanistic order.

THE PROTEAN UNIVERSE AND THE NATION

Both Herder and Kant were East Prussians. The much younger Herder studied under his fellow countryman at the University of Königsberg. Following his theological studies, Herder became a pastor at Riga on the Baltic; then he traveled widely in England, France, and Holland. The journal he kept during the sea voyage from Riga to France in 1769 reflected the widening horizon of his thinking, which received a new impulse from his friendship with Goethe. Goethe induced Herder to go to Weimar, where he occupied the office of general superintendent of ecclesiastical affairs.

We find in Herder a universality of interests comparable to that in Leibniz, and Herder's ideas had a similar suggestive power. He was a theologian, historian, poet, and philosopher. He also had a Faustian drive, a sense of the limitless power to penetrate to the secret of all things—especially characteristic of the line of German theosophical thought from Paracelsus to Jakob Böhme.

Like Paracelsus, Herder felt that the universe was a vital living organism animated by a creative spirit. Nature and culture are inhabited by the same divine protean spirit. All things in the universe therefore respond to the same laws of growth and decay. In his work on the philosophy of the history of mankind, man and nature are presented as one great evolutionary development. Its distinguishing feature is spontaneous creativeness manifesting itself in the production of a multiplicity of forms.

Culture shows this characteristic most conspicuously in the variety of singular forms called "nations." In developing its individual character, each national culture reveals a facet of humanity. Each manifests its unique quality, especially in the springtime of its existence, before contamination by alien influences and before hardening of the cultural arteries has set in. This last stage is revealed in civilization, with its scholastic-intellectual molds, artificial social and literary conventions, and machine-like bureaucratic-military states.

Herder found in early ballad and song, myth and saga, custom and ritual, the keys to the discovery of the pure national spirit. He thereby opened the way for the Romantics to seek origins and influenced the development of nationalism in the nineteenth century, especially among the Slavic peoples just then rising to national self-consciousness.

There is, for Herder, an inner urge in each people to realize its own distinct cultural individuality. It can do this best by continually returning to its own literary and artistic genesis where national self-consciousness first appears in naive and instinctive forms, which have not yet been abstracted by the process of rationalization. This search for roots is a kind of historization of Rousseau's gospel of return to nature.

With Herder the conception of national cultures definitely emerged. Each culture makes its appearance on the stage of history at the appropriate time, and reveals a facet of that ideal humanity toward which mankind is moving. The concept of the subordination of the nation to humanity was a characteristic of German thought far into the nineteenth century.

Herder was repelled by the cold and abstract quality of Kant's thought, which detached the individual from his roots in the national soil and made him apparently both the creator and creature of an abstract moral imperative, thereby incarcerating him in a new and more rigid mold. There is no doubt that Kant stood deeper in the rationalistic current of the Enlightenment than Herder. Kant's point of departure was the new view of the universe portrayed by the mathematical sciences. In fact, he had made a contribution in an early work to the theory of planetary evolution. But he was also influenced by the more irrational currents present in Pietism and Rousseau.

COSMIC ORDER AND THE COMMITMENT OF REASON

Immanuel Kant's career presents a complete contrast to that of Herder. He never left East Prussia nor, for that matter, Königsberg. He studied at the university, began teaching in 1755, and, for the remainder of a long career until 1804, served as a professor of philosophy there. He never departed from the regular pattern of teaching, study, and writing. The iron regularity of his habits is attested by the fact that housewives set their clocks by the daily walk he invariably took at a particular time. The only break in this routine came on the day he began reading Rousseau's *Social Contract*, which he could not lay down; Rousseau's portrait hung on the wall of Kant's study. The only other incident which seems to have ruffled the calm of his life was Wöllner's censure of him, in 1794, for having contributed to the depreciation of the fundamental teachings of Christianity.

Kant presented the philosopher with three questions which the development of the sciences had made most pertinent. What can I know? What ought I to do? What may I hope? For Kant, the second and third questions definitely derived from the first. The very formulation of these questions implied a departure from the optimistic belief of the Enlightenment that human reason can push back the limits of knowledge indefinitely. It was assumed that, since there exist no limits to the extension of knowledge, there exist no limits to the moral improvement and increasing happiness of mankind. All things in the universe were provided by a beneficent creator for the good of man if he will only discover their proper use as intended by that creator. Thus, in the popular philosophy of the period, ethics became merely an extension of knowledge.

Kant dealt a body blow to these conceptions first of all in showing the limitations of our knowledge of the world about us. The English philosopher Hume had already argued that the prevailing notion of the universe as a causal nexus was an illusion growing out of the habit of assuming that since events seem to follow each other in regular succession, there is a necessary causal relationship between them. Kant went beyond him in contending that causality, whereby we impute necessary relationships, is but a frame of human thinking. *Space* and *time* are also such theoretical frames or molds of thinking which are, so to speak, imposed on the phenomena by the reason. We actually fill these frames with concrete material communicated by the senses; the ideas which we tend to attribute to the *out there* are really in our minds. But we cannot know the out there in itself; we only know it as appearances communicated by the senses.

Kant thus shifted the center of gravity of knowledge from an external objective world to the subjective world within the individual; but he did not make knowledge merely an arbitrary matter, for thought has its own laws of logic.

This new point of view constituted for Kant and his contemporaries a liberation of man, who now became the molder of the universe rather than an almost passive recipient of influences impinging from the outside. Consequently, he could see the universe from the point of view of purpose and goals rather than merely as a network of cause and effect relationships. Man was thus rendered less secure because what he could know of the universe by way of science came to have a problematical character. He could not know it in itself but only as phenomena. Hence he could find no moral support in an external order.

With respect to the problem of morality, Kant had an even more revolutionary significance. Here he was greatly influenced by Rousseau. Once having rendered the theoretical reason autonomous with respect to the out there, what is then the position of the practical reason which is concerned with human conduct? Are there objective moral laws? If so, man is not really free, since these laws come from the outside. In essence morality demands that if man is responsible, he must also legislate for himself. In fact, the freer he is from outside compulsion, the greater is his responsibility. Responsibility also demands that he follow not only his individual appetites and desires, but that he legislate for the common good. This, however, is not a mere matter of providing theories of morality on an intellectual level, for, in concocting these, he will have no real sense of responsibility. Only in action, when he is completely involved, can he propose maxims or rules of universal validity. This is the categorical imperative according to which man should so act in each instance that the universal application of his action might lead to the establishment of a moral rule or maxim. Only in this way can he rise to that complete sense of responsibility which his own inner moral nature demands.

Although Rousseau, through the *Social Contract*, may have exerted the most immediate influence upon Kant, there is no doubt of Luther's impact here, reinforced by Pietism, especially in the emphasis placed by Kant on the freedom of the inner moral experience. In Kant this is obviously put in moral and rational terms; in Luther, in religious and emotional forms. It follows that for Kant only a society in which the individual can exercise this autonomous act of moral legislation can be said to offer man real freedom. The state must therefore embody not merely power but the laws imposed on men by themselves. Kant goes so far as to argue for a world state in which force and war will be eliminated as unnecessary to the moral nature of man. He was optimistic about its eventual establishment.

The profound philosophic questions raised by Kant inaugurated a revolutionary movement in modern philosophy by freeing it not only from religious traditionalism but also from the rigid rationalism of the Enlightenment.

ORGANIC FORM AND INDIVIDUAL ASPIRATION

It is through philosophers like Kant that the Germans have exerted their greatest influence upon the Western mind. In the field of literature and the visual arts Germany's influence has in general fallen far below that of other countries. However, in the period we are here considering there appeared one superlative literary artist, Goethe, who is generally ranked with Dante and Shakespeare. He so far outshone other German writers, with the possible exception of Schiller, that they are almost totally eclipsed, at least to non-German peoples. But even Goethe's pre-eminence may be attributed to the fact that art was for him indistinguishable from science and religion. It was his philosophy of man and nature, transmitted through a variety of literary media, that accounts for his pervasive influence.

We have already encountered Goethe in association with the older Herder, whom Goethe brought to Weimar and who was undoubtedly, in the years of the *Sturm und Drang*, his chief inspiration toward creative spontaneity and diversity. But later, as Goethe gained a sense of aesthetic integrity and of organic harmony, the roles were reversed. Famous also, in spite of very different temperaments and conceptions as to the role of the artist, was the friendship between Goethe and Schiller. Goethe had the valuable capacity of being able to enter into the interests and enthusiasms of others even though these ran counter to his own tastes. At Weimar he had the opportunity to render aid and stimulation to many writers and thinkers. Under the enlightened patronage of its ruler, who was Goethe's friend and patron, Weimar became a kind of German Athens or Florence. Too small to play a role in the power politics of the time, Weimar became for a time, perhaps because of the fortunate friendship of ruler and genius, the chief literary center of the Germanies.

Johann Wolfgang von Goethe was the son of a well-to-do middle-class family in Frankfort-on-the-Main, a city with a cosmopolitan, intellectual atmosphere. He first studied law at Strassburg but abandoned the prospects of a legal career to enter the service of the Archduke Karl August of Weimar. He became a kind of prime minister of the small principality and was able to combine practical pursuits with intellectual and artistic creation. His position was somewhat like that of his older contemporary, Möser, whose integrity of personality and views Goethe admired greatly.

The long sojourn at Weimar from 1788 to 1832 almost without interruption was disturbed inwardly hardly at all by the great events of the French Revolution and the Napoleonic conquests. Like Möser, Goethe became convinced that pure rationalism as exemplified in the Revolution was a solvent of the natural organic bonds of public order and society. It led to the atomized masses and the man on horseback. Napoleon he regarded as a necessary force to bring turmoil to an end and restore a minimum of order on the basis of which organic growth could again proceed.

One discovers no inner crises in the uniform unfolding of Goethe's personality and artistic creativeness. The only event of importance which may be said to have provided a marked change in his values and interests was a journey to Italy (1786–1788). It revealed to him the incomparable harmony of ancient art, which Winckelmann had already disclosed in his great work on Greek art. Here also he came upon the first clues to the morphological structure of the world of plant and animal life.

Seeking a return to that natural spontaneous freedom which Rousseau had presented in such alluring form, Goethe found that the way was neither through return to genetic sources nor through moral imperative but through art, in which man's striving and creation can find an end in itself without ulterior considerations of utilitarianism or transcendentalism. Greek culture presented the model of what was both natural—that is, naive and spontaneous—and of what, at the same time, embodied an ideal norm. Greece became an "inner fatherland," suffused somewhat by the idyllic atmosphere of the Rococo landscape.

Goethe's development presents a slow unfolding of creative personality. His writings cover a vast range of subject matter, philosophical, scientific, literary, and artistic, presented in a variety of forms. Each marks a steppingstone in a conscious quest to achieve an ever wider range of interest and mastery over form. His whole career as a writer presents a process of self-education and self-fulfillment. In his chief works, *Wilhelm Meister* and *Faust*, the quest becomes a self-portrayal.[3] Goethe called his own works "fragments of a great confession."

Goethe was primarily concerned with bringing individual aspiration into harmony with the inner form of the world of culture and nature. Basic to his artistic ethos was the conception of the work of art as a self-sufficient entity expressed in its own inner form, not dependent on outward or so-called real circumstances. Likewise, the Faustian striving to transcend the limits of ordinary knowledge was bounded by the final impenetrable mystery of the universe—like the Kantian thing-in-itself. For Goethe, man's autobiography began with the constellation of the stars at his birth, implying the closed universe of astrology rather than the infinite one of Newton.[4]

Goethe's quest was not a search for a moral imperative, as was that of Kant, but a search for form expressed in his own personality as well as in the universe. His scientific interests especially revealed this facet of his mind. As against the prevailing Newtonian mechanistic and mathematical conception, Goethe conceived of the universe as an organic totality. Man was a living part of it and should not stand outside of it as a mere observer and exploiter. Only the understanding eye of the artist could really discern its creative processes in the unfolding of organic forms. The artist could discover the archetypical forms of plant and animal life, from which all others were derived. Existing structures were but transformations of the primordial forms which, however, never lost their identity in the multiplicity and diversity of a protean universe.

We are here in the presence again of a type of thinking which goes back to Leibniz and beyond him to Paracelsus and Nicholas of Cues in which "inner form" has become a principle of development for both the personality and the universe.

A synthetic approach toward the universe is particularly apparent in Goethe's work on color theory, which he regarded in later years as his most significant achievement.[5] In it, he adopted a hypothesis directly opposite to that of Newton's optics, which assumed that what seems like colorless light is in fact composed of all the strands of color in the spectrum. Goethe, on the basis of an ancient metaphor of Neo-Platonism, saw in light the original source of all life and hence of all unity in the physical universe comparable to the primordial plant form. Goethe's objection to Newton's color synthesis revealed yet another facet of his approach to nature. Goethe relied on the sensation of light coming through the eye rather than through a prism or grating, as Newton did. This reveals Goethe's feeling that if an apparatus were allowed to stand between man and nature, man would be an onlooker; he would cease to be a participant and hence would lose reverence for nature's forms.

In German culture Goethe was a towering figure. Although he has been much quoted and almost worshipped, he seldom has been completely appreciated or sympathetically understood. In this respect he resembles Erasmus. Both were concerned with man's inner freedom of development. Both sought in ironical detachment a means of avoiding an *either-or* confrontation. In neither do we see the soul struggle of a Luther nor the moral tension manifest in a

Kant. Herder's Dionysian creativity is balanced by Apollonian harmony in Goethe. Goethe's Olympian calm and universality of point of view raised him above the ordinary political and religious quarrels of his day, which may account for his countrymen's ambivalent attitude toward him.

Goethe himself was conscious in his old age (he died at eighty-two) of having lived far beyond his time. Great events were ushering in a new Europe of political and social change for which he had no sympathy. He stood for the old Europe of the cultured aristocracy and patriciate, of polite society and of ideal classical norms. In the latter parts of both *Wilhelm Meister* and *Faust*, he envisioned a utopian future of technological and scientific achievement involving the domination of nature, mass organization, great material welfare, and subjective freedom.

THE PHILOSOPHY OF HISTORY AS REDEMPTION

It is apparent from the foregoing that two basic ideas shaped the German conception of the freedom of the creative spirit.

(1) The persistence of the spiritualist tradition influenced by Leibniz' monadology and Spinoza's pantheism led to the retention of the notion of the union of God and the world in a great creative process resulting in the endless multiplication of individualized forms, in both nature and culture. While a differentiation was made between nature and history it was assumed that these represented polarities in the self-realization of the spirit or reason. Basic to this unitary conception was the notion that man should not be reduced to the role of an observer or onlooker of nature and history. Both God and man were to engage, so to speak, in an active co-partnership in the evolution of humanity and cosmos to their highest potentialities.

(2) The sense of participation was enormously enhanced by the impact of Rousseau's secularization of the Christian epic of salvation. His ideas were converted into a revolutionary ideology in the course of the French Revolution, but in the Germanies they became the core of an evolutionary philosophy of history. Not until Marxism, in the middle of the nineteenth century, was an attempt

made to fuse revolutionary ideology proposing a program of action with an evolutionary philosophy of history presenting an inevitable development.

The German idealistic philosophy of history was a product of two sets of ideas, one representing the continuity of a spiritual tradition, the other rising out of the individual feeling of the need of moral redemption in the face of a fundamental crisis brought on by the impact of the impersonal forces of science and state. The fusion of the two attained its last great expression in Hegel.

In Herder, this fusion first became explicit when he historicized the process of redemption in the three phases of primitive spontaneity, artificial civilization, and eventual spiritual humanity. The nation, juxtaposed to cosmopolitan rationalistic civilization, is the cultural bridge between the primordial *Volk* rooted in nature and the ideal humanity of the future. In this new conception of the three ages the middle period of present civilization assumes an almost negative character, leading later, for example in Marx, to the conception of a dialectical process. In Hegel, the idea of fulfillment in the *present*, consummated in the Prussian state, was restored as it was in the St. Simonian notion of the impending triumph of a scientific technological order. In both, the present acquires a positive role in the onward march of reason.

Herder inaugurated the Romantic escape from the present into the past and its turning to the nation as the ideal community in which past, present, and future are fused as a dynamic totality. The Neo-Romanticism of the late nineteenth and early twentieth centuries went a step farther in identifying *Urzeit* and *Spätzeit* as essentially non-historical and therefore mythical, the one in primordial terms and the other as the technological civilization of the masses.

Unlike Herder's virtual rejection of the present, Kant sought to make it the point of departure for human freedom. Indeed, he juxtaposed civilization to nature as an advance in the direction of self-conscious freedom. Man in the state of nature may have lived a paradisal existence of naive sense-life, but he transcends this with the life of reason as civilization, in which history emerges as the deliberate setting of goals. It is the rule of law embodied in the state and created by the citizens which eventually will bring peace to mankind with its extension to the society of nations. This marks the supreme goal of civilization.

In Kant's philosophy of history the basis is laid for the characteristic idealistic assumption that the redemption of mankind can come only through the life of reason as a commitment and not merely as an accretional evolution in knowledge of and mastery over nature. Fichte, in his exaltation of the nation-state as the fusion of nature and reason, went beyond Kant in asserting that it is the national group rather than the individual which commits itself to the life of reason in setting up the state.

While Goethe's thought revolved in the same general matrix as that of Kant and Herder, he was much less conscious of the dualism of nature and reason. The world of nature and culture for Goethe are both dominated by a ceaseless creative flux. Since they are self-contained, they move only in cyclical and polar rhythms. This timeless recurrence is, however, broken through by the Faustian striving of man who seeks to transcend these natural and normative limits ending in tragic frustration or the serenity of resignation.

Nietzsche and Spengler were later the avowed exponents of this Goethean philosophy of history. Both were critics of the European civilization of their day but saw no Third Age looming on the horizon. For both, faced by civilization as decadence, there was at most the nostalgic memory of the primordial and mythical. Hence, man must sink himself in that total present in which he accepts his fate.

In these philosophies of history the center of gravity obviously had moved from expectancy of future fulfillment to concern with the manner or mode of redemption from the anomalies of the present. In the French Revolution this concern proceeded from a traditional national frame, but the German, lacking this orientation, went over to a universal philosophy of history. Marxism sought to unite this philosophy of history with the idea of revolution within a class matrix. In our day, expectancy and breakthrough are becoming fused in the technological revolution.

IX

Revolution, Romanticism, and Nationalism

In the course of the eighteenth century a new catchword became prominent on the European intellectual horizon: "revolution." We have seen that "renaissance" or "rebirth" during the late Middle Ages expressed the desire for fundamental change, first of all in the church and then in culture, by a return to their ancient sources. In the eighteenth and nineteenth centuries, "revolution" came to express both a desire for a fundamental change and the mode by which such a change might be brought about. The displacement of "renaissance" by "revolution" marked a basic transformation in Western man's conception of the rationale of change in human affairs and in his view of history.

RENAISSANCE AND THE IDEA OF PROGRESS

The concept of rebirth went back to an early medieval word, *renovatio*, which referred to a renewal or restoration of the Roman Empire and with it the peace and culture that had come to be associated with it. "Renaissance" came to mean something more than restoration. It reflected a desire to return to the ancient sources of culture and religion for the purpose of renewing their dynamic promise with respect to both the norms of art and the prophetic quality of religion. The notion of rebirth was associated with a fundamental change in epochal self-consciousness whereby the humanists thought of themselves as marking the dawn of a new age which was a repudiation of the intervening ages (Middle Ages) between them and the glorified ancient times.

The feeling of having ushered in a new age called "modern" provided the West with its characteristic intellectual temper. Increasingly the consciousness of modernity was directed not toward a return to the ancient past but definitely toward the future development of man. Symptoms of this reorientation were noted in connection with the impact of the new science and cosmology in the sixteenth and seventeenth centuries. Man was to be no longer subject to the astrological fate of nature nor to the fortuitous happenings of history. The revolutions of the heavenly bodies reflected the reason that was at the heart of the universe which should become the directing force in human affairs as well.

In the seventeenth century the new orientation also became manifest in the quarrel between the ancients and the moderns. The defenders of the ancients argued that the ancients had produced philosophies and works of art of such superiority and excellence that they would never be surpassed and should therefore serve as models for future ages. Basic to this notion was the emphasis on continuity within the Hellenic-Roman community of culture. The advocates of the moderns, on the other hand, contended that the achievements of the last centuries in art, literature, and philosophy were at least the equals of those of the ancients. Surely modern man, by standing on the shoulders of the ancients, could look farther ahead than they could.

The fusion of the conception of revolution with the idea of progress began with the Enlightenment and attained its climax in the revolutionary period from 1789 to 1848.[1]

On the face of it, the conception of revolution and the idea of progress seem irreconcilable because to us "progress" means gradual continuous linear development, without the abrupt violent change connoted by "revolution." Only very recently in the current phrase "permanent revolution" as applied to economic planning and technological change has a rather unstable fusion of the two apparent incompatibles of revolution and progress been projected.

In the eighteenth century, except for the German Idealist thinkers who came late in the century and then were largely isolated figures, most intellectuals did not conceive of progress as meaning development because they regarded the past largely as a record of errors, the product of ignorance and superstition. The future opened up the possibility of regulated change in the application of the method of science, in which the critical reason in man attained highest expression. The consequent expansion of knowledge and enlightenment had, it was recognized, a progressive, that is, cumulative character; but did the advance of knowledge provide assurance of the improvement of human relationships in the face of capricious despotisms and the passions of the rabble? How could freedom in the pursuit of knowledge itself be achieved except on the rare occasions when an enlightened ruler appeared? Voltaire's conception of the history of civilization was in fact based on the notion of the coincidence of enlightened rulers and the flourishing of the arts and sciences.

The question as to how the populace in general could be induced either to follow along or at least to permit innovations was never answered by the eighteenth-century *philosophes*. They were generally contemptuous of what today are called the "masses." Another related and very pertinent question for the late eighteenth century was how *hoi polloi* could be induced to wait upon the gradual accumulation of knowledge to solve public problems rather than "jump the gun" in an irrational rebellion and insurrection.

Without a conception of development which integrated past, present, and future,—skeptical with regard to the extension of enlightenment to the general populace—the intellectuals before 1789 found it virtually impossible to reconcile the apparent need for an immediate and total transformation of state and society with the gradual and progressive expansion of knowledge and enlightenment. Their juxtaposition of a natural and ideal political and social order to the anomalies and abuses of the existing situation suggested not a piecemeal and gradual change but total transformation.

THE IDEA OF REVOLUTION

The varying content of the word "revolution" will perhaps make clear the difficulty of reconciling revolution and progress which was actually resolved only in the end by revolution itself.

(1) "Revolution" designated a change in political regime brought on by rebellions, insurrections, or civil wars. No fundamental structural change of state or society was assumed to be involved and therefore no suggestion of what might be called progress toward democratic forms. Here was a notion comparable to that of the Baroque conception of state actions as emanating from intrigues and conspiracies and the caprices of kings and mistresses. As a result political changes were still regarded as largely fortuitous.

(2) "Revolution" was also applied to fundamental changes in human development growing out of natural phenomena such as earthquakes or volcanic action or out of cultural changes such as inventions, or again, as Voltaire assumed, out of religious transformations such as the papal imperialism of the eleventh and twelfth centuries, or the Reformation of the sixteenth century.

We still distinguish today between political happenings involving violent change such as the French or Russian revolutions and transformations of long enduring character such as the industrial and scientific revolutions, a distinction which is itself evidence of the fact that we still have not reconciled revolution with progress.

(3) Most significant was Voltaire's allusion to a fundamental change in attitude of mind which had come with the Enlightenment and which would in the future break through to a new way of looking at the world and provide a new set of laws to govern men. There was a feeling prevalent among intellectuals of standing on the brink of a new order of things in which the intellectual would become the ruling force in society and displace kings and priests, certainly the latter. The notion of intellectuals taking the place of priests was to play a very important part in the nineteenth-century development of the idea of progress.

The sense of importance of the intellectual had been greatly enhanced by the ferment of ideas centering in Masonic lodges, clubs,

coffee houses, and salons, and expressed in the tremendous efflores-
cence of periodical literature of all kinds. It was further enhanced
by the alliance between enlightened despots and intellectuals, especially in Prussia under Frederick the Great. Berlin was the focus of
enlightened opinion, promoted by its large colony of Frenchmen
and Frederick's own predilection for French culture. Enlightened
rulers seemed to be the only guarantee against the suppression of
freedom of opinion, always threatened by ecclesiastical authorities,
and the general ignorance of the lower orders. Moreover, by virtue
of its establishment of uniform legal codes and by its welfare projects in behalf of peasants and townsmen, enlightened despotism
seemed to be pointing in the direction of progress. But the alliance
between ruler and intellectual was at best a tenuous one, as was
demonstrated by the reaction under Frederick's successor when a
campaign against "subversive" societies was instituted.

The resistance movements in Corsica, Poland, and finally in
America were regarded as harbingers of the coming change and
called forth widespread interest and discussion. The discussion revolved mainly around the right of resistance to tyranny rather than
the right of revolution, although the distinction was beginning to
be recognized, especially in connection with the American war of
independence. To many German intellectuals in the decade before
1789, the movements were portents of a revolution which might
destroy the very foundations of the historic order. The partition of
Poland in 1772 by its powerful neighbors rendered all small states
insecure. Both from above and below there were threats to the existing order of things. Accompanying this feeling of the imminence
of fundamental change was the fear of anarchy from below and the
growing disillusionment with reform under enlightened despotism.[2]

THE IDEALISTIC REACTION TO THE FRENCH REVOLUTION

The abrupt reversal of mood which attended the news of the
events in 1789 in France was itself indicative of the highly unstable
atmosphere of intellectual opinion. German intellectuals greeted the
events as marking a new era in human development. The inital enthusiasm was not so much a reaction to revolution as to a utopian

image of mankind's struggle toward freedom. The *Declaration of the Rights of Man* was hailed as opening up a new vista of mankind's ascent to liberty, equality, and fraternity. The three young friends, Hegel, Schelling, and Hölderlin, then studying theology at Tübingen, were caught up in the general jubilation and joined "the dance about the tree of freedom." [3]

The enthusiasm was wholly idealistic and romantic rather than based on a real sense of common cause with the French Third Estate. Thoughts and feelings were garbed in the ancient classical notion of the uprising against the despot or tyrant. The assertion and declaration of the principles of freedom in resounding statements meant much more to this rhetorical generation than its embodiment in concrete institutions and processes of government. To some it seemed actually that they stood on the very threshold of the Third Age. Not just ancient rights lost through usurpation by kings or nobility were to be recovered, but for the first time in the history of man a new order was to be erected on the basis of the fundamental principles of human rights.

As the Revolution entered its more violent phase beginning with the September massacres of 1792 and culminating in the reign of the guillotine during the Terror of 1793–94, there was a gradual reversal of attitude.

The struggle of parties for dominance finally resulted in the ascendancy of one party, the Jacobins, who employed techniques of terror and propaganda to liquidate opponents in the name of "a republic of reason and virtue." Both king and constitutional government were done away with in order to make the will of the nation supreme. Eventually, weariness with innovation and turmoil, as well as desire for order within and conquest and booty without, led to displacement of the Jacobins by the military leader as the instrument of the national will.

It was this violent phase which produced such divergent responses. To many it seemed that the Revolution had fallen into the hands of the radical sectarians, who were virtually converting France into one gigantic *Münster*. To others this phase seemed but the logical application of the gospel according to Jean Jacques Rousseau, whereby one proceeds from the society of the free play of individual self-interest to the community of mutualism and solidarity.

GOETHE, KANT, AND THE REVOLUTION

Of the three intellectual leaders of the Idealist movement, Herder in the main followed the cycle described above. Goethe and Kant, however, reflected departures. The former approached the Revolution from its very beginning with objective detachment while the latter was a supporter of its ideals throughout.

Goethe was, by sheer proximity, in closer touch with the revolutionary events than Kant. He participated in the campaign of the coalition against revolutionary France in 1792 and took part in the siege of Mainz (1793) which had gone over to the Revolution. Weimar became a center of counter revolutionary activity directed toward organizing the western lands and Rhineland areas into a kind of Third Germany for resistance to the Revolution.

The concrete and integral character of Goethe's philosophy of life is apparent in his attitude toward the Revolution. Above all, he was imbued with a reverence for the individuality of existing life forms manifest in both nature and history. He did not view them from the perspective of the idea of progress. Abstract political principles merely interpose a barrier between man and the understanding of such living structures as monarchy and aristocracy just as the prism does in the study of light. Nature, however, has both creative and destructive aspects. The Revolution was a natural phenomenon which would run its course and in so doing would probably destroy the foundations of historic Europe. It was a manifestation of underground forces represented by the masses coming to the surface. The upper classes, both aristocratic and patriciate, were in part responsible for this eruption in that they had played with abstract principles of justice and with progressivist ideas of reform and thus undermined the very organic forms in which their existence was rooted.

Goethe regarded the Revolution as not just an insurrection or rebellion nor as a breakthrough to a new age of freedom but as an occurrence which, once initiated, goes through its natural course of development. The insurgence of the masses, its most characteristic positive manifestation, revealed the appearance of a new historical matrix, which in turn would follow its cycle of development.

This conception of the Revolution as a self-contained dynamic entity found an echo in the thinking of conservative Romantics both in the Germanies and in France. But with many of these Romantics the Revolution virtually became an apocalyptic judgment let loose upon mankind for abandoning altar and throne. Goethe, however, much as he disapproved of its destruction of old Europe, yet recognized in it an "emergent" which was contributing to the enhancement of the creative processes of the spiritual and natural cosmos. He associated freedom with the universal creative processes in the universe, rather than with the moral improvement of mankind, as Kant did.[4]

Although living in far away Königsberg and teaching at its university, Kant gave close attention to all the available reports of what was transpiring in France. He was a great admirer of the French and an advocate of the kind of rapprochement between the German and French peoples that he saw projected in the Prussian withdrawal in 1795 from the coalition of powers directed against the Revolution.

In Kant, therefore, we find a view of the Revolution diametrically opposed to that of Goethe, again not in terms of a superficial reaction to its idealism or its violence, but a consequence of a definitely formulated philosophical point of view. A defender of the Revolution throughout, he saw it as a stage in the long development of mankind from the original natural condition of the species to a rational maturity, whereby man might live in accordance with self-imposed laws. Revolution to Kant was philosophy achieving practical consequences. Enlightened despotism, while it might provide uniformity of law, did nothing to promote human initiative and responsibility. Consequently, it remained a despotism. The life of reason was a commitment and not just a natural or cultural phenomenon and the French people had made that commitment in their revolution.

Nevertheless, within the frame of eighteenth-century thinking, this conception of reason as an active and dynamic force posed basic contradictions in the attempt to reconcile progress with revolution.

On the one hand, the idea of progress as enlightenment connoted a gradual and peaceful development indefinitely extending into the future and therefore never really coming to fruition. On the other, the French Revolution proceeded in its radical phase to the almost apocalyptic assumption that the Kingdom of God could be established in the here and now as the republic of reason and virtue. The attempt to overcome this antinomy lay at the basis of much of the ideological conflict of the nineteenth and twentieth centuries.

THE RISE OF IDEOLOGIES

Three frames of opinion, radical, liberal, and conservative, arose in response to the question raised by the Revolution as to how change was to be brought about in human affairs. That change was inevitable as a historical phenomenon came to be accepted; differences of opinion centered mainly around the question of the tactics of change posed by the Revolution.

George Forster (1754–1794), the renowned world traveler who became a leader of the revolutionary movement in Mainz and a delegate to the French National Convention, exemplified the radical position. He recognized in the French movement something much more than a rebellion or insurrection; it was a movement for the liquidation of the old regime, a movement which would envelop the whole of Europe. The French Revolution was but the beginning of an epoch of revolutions. The raw energies of the masses were being released against the privileged classes.

Public opinion during the Revolution was embodied in the will of the French people. The unity of will of the people was the enduring force, not either the excesses of violence or institutional reforms. But surrender to the insurgency of the movement actually involved capitulation to its violent course, which ran counter to the moralistic idealism of the intellectuals—a paradox which was to characterize the radicalism of the early nineteenth century.[5]

A second group of intellectuals looked mainly to England as the model of development. The chief center of the English influence was in Hanover, where professors at the University of Göttingen and officials in the government became the chief advocates of the views of Justus Möser and of the Englishman, Edmund Burke, especially, on reform and revolution.

Möser and Burke agreed that the uniformitarian tendency of rationalism, whether as enlightened despotism or as revolution, broke the organic continuity with the past. Burke contended that the Frenchmen of that day had no right on the basis of the claim of popular sovereignty to destroy a political and social edifice built up by countless preceding generations. The twenty-five million living Frenchmen were after all but a link in the endless chain of generations. They might modify but not liquidate their heritage. Liberty is a matter of the concrete rights acquired by individuals in the course of a community's history. It is not to be derived from the abstract principles of constitutional provisions. The American revolt was justified because the colonists were fighting for their ancient rights as Englishmen, but the revolutionary French turned their backs completely on the past.

Neither Burke nor Möser were merely defenders of the status quo; they recognized the necessity for reform but believed it should be piecemeal and pragmatic. They came to represent the chief source of liberal opposition to the radicalism of the Revolution and the imperialism of Napoleon. Burke's work, *Reflections on the Revolution in France*, was published in 1790 and translated into German by 1793. Its intellectual influence in the Germanies was perhaps greater than in its homeland. Its translator, Friedrich Gentz (1764–1832) was a Prussian who became in the first decade of the next century the chief German publicist writing against the Revolution and Napoleon.

Influenced by the French circle in Berlin, then by Kant and finally by Burke, he sought to unite the ideas basic to natural rights, the Kantian moral imperative, and the British constitution. A realist who sought to combine new and old principles and institutions, he recognized that the idea of natural rights was the necessary foundation of freedom in the new civil order and that the balance of power was its counterpart in the relations between states. The Revolution was not only destructive of the historic order; it was a solvent of the very rational order which its initiators had established. It was also a menace to the political order of Europe in that it led to the appearance of the man on horseback, Napoleon, who destroyed the state system on which the liberties of people rested.

The third group grew out of Romanticism, the German counterpart of the French Revolution. It had its roots in the eighteenth-century idealistic reaction against French rationalism, but it developed in polar tension to the Revolution.

Like the Revolution, Romanticism had two phases. First, there was the attempt to free the artistic personality and liberate through it the protean spirit in the universe. The early Romantics certainly regarded the French Revolution as a stimulus or, as they called it, an "incitation" to this liberation. Romanticism was to them the "German Revolution." In its second phase, however, Romanticism turned to the national community as the means of restoring continuity with the past after the Revolution and Napoleon seemed to be cutting European man loose from all his ancient moorings. Return to the medieval sources of European culture became a main tenet of its conservative phase.

THE SOURCES OF ROMANTICISM

Romanticism had its inception in the north in Berlin and at the University of Jena near Weimar during the decade from 1795 to 1805. A powerful factor shaping its early development was the isolation of the northern Germanies during that decade of tumultuous events which attended the rise and conquests of Napoleon Bonaparte.

The coalition formed by the Prussian, Austrian, and Russian rulers to defend central Europe against the Revolution began to crack under the pressure of conflicts over Poland and the resumption of the old rivalry between Prussia and Austria.

Prussia left the coalition and made a separate peace with France. In the peace of Basel (1795) she conceded to France the whole left bank of the Rhine. She was joined in this action by the northern German states, Hanover, Saxony, and Hesse-Cassel, which closed off the whole of the northern Germanies as a neutral zone in the conflict between France and what remained of the coalition.

The western lands of the *Reich* now completely collapsed under French pressure; princes and cities in effect became French satellites.

Prussia was to receive compensation for losses on the west bank by the contemplated liquidation of the ecclesiastical principalities, the symbols of the old *Reich*, to the east of the Rhine. As a consequence, the Treaty of Basel was a decisive act in the process which was to result in the liquidation of the *Reich*.

From 1795 to 1805 isolation from direct participation in the main stream of events had a most important effect on the intellectual climate of the north. Herder, Kant, and Goethe were enabled to complete their creative work unhampered by the immediate impact of war. Most important, the German mind could now turn wholly inward to the discovery of new dimensions of feeling and imagination, which were in turn to lead to a new appreciation, in fact, to a rediscovery of the irrational values of faith, community, and history. Even in the *Sturm und Drang* the accent had been placed on overcoming intractable, external conditions by emotional insurgency. But Romanticism was less a revolt against the tyranny of rule, convention, and custom than a positive expression of the creative artistic personality. To the very stirring events and innovations inaugurated by the Revolution, its response was the accentuation of inner fluidity and mobility.

In addition to the impact of political circumstance, the development of Romanticism derived much of its singular character from the economic and social situation. The general lag in economic development in central Europe in the eighteenth century undoubtedly had contributed to the diversion of talent into government jobs and intellectual and literary pursuits. Many of the leaders of the Enlightenment and the Idealistic movement occupied posts in government, church and university. But for the generation of young people who attained adulthood in the 1790's, these were difficult to obtain.

The reforming drive of enlightened despotism had drained away; in any case it was overwhelmed by the radical changes in France. These seemed to prophesy that everything formerly regarded as rooted in the natural and traditional order of things was passing. Although northern Germany, after 1795, was removed from the arena of great events, it responded to the emotional and intellectual fluidity of the times and created among young intellectuals a feeling of uprootedness, uncertainty, and frustration.

Young artists, writers, and thinkers prided themselves on their detachment from what the bourgeoisie called the "actualities of life." Defense of the middle-class way of life was no longer an important consideration as it was with the Enlightenment and even with the *Sturm und Drang.* Circles of close friendships and semibohemian modes of life manifested a definite reaction against the prosaic and pedestrian middle-class life. The salon now assumed an important role in German literary and artistic movements. In the new creative life women played an equal and positive role both as writers and personalities. Marriage rested on intellectual and artistic affinity; "souls were to be in tune with each other," which meant that marriages were often entered into easily and dissolved with equal facility.

Altogether, we sense here the emergence of a much more intensely emotional and subjective life than existed in the circle around Goethe at Weimar, where the great genius towered. Romanticism developed within circles of intimate, though often ephemeral, friendship, suffused by a common subjective mood, esthetic vision, and spiritual value. One might call Romanticism a kind of artistic and intellectual Pietism.

Highly transient as to participants, the Romantic circles spread by a process like that of cellular fission. From the original group at Berlin, comprising among others the two brothers Schlegel, Schleiermacher, and Novalis, some of the leaders soon split off to form a very influential group at Jena, a short distance from Weimar. The middle of the first decade of the new century saw the formation of still other groups at Vienna and Heidelberg. In its last phase the movement assumed a completely diffuse character and scattered its seeds far and wide.

Poetry and philosophy were the principal vehicles of Romantic expression in the Germanies, although music and painting also exhibited the new imaginative vision and feeling. The founders of the movement, Friedrich Schlegel (1772–1828) and Friedrich von Hardenberg (1772–1801), who called himself Novalis, were both poets and philosophers. They provided a theory of, and a program for, Romanticism in the periodical, the *Athenaeum*, published from 1796 to 1800. The close association of poetry and philosophy contributed most perhaps toward the creation of a total world and life view which distinguished German Romanticism from its more narrowly artistic and stylistic counterparts elsewhere.

At the University of Jena Romanticism underwent a cross-fertilization with the Idealistic movement in philosophy inaugurated by Kant. Fichte was there from 1794 to 1798, Schelling from 1797 to 1806, and Hegel from 1801 to 1806. Fichte and Schelling were brought to Jena at Goethe's prompting. Only Schelling can rightly be called a Romantic philosopher. Fichte provided the bridge between Kant and Romanticism, whereas Hegel created the great synthesis between rationalism and Romanticism which was to serve as the point of departure for much of the thought of the nineteenth century.

LIBERATION OF THE CREATIVE SPIRIT IN NATURE AND CULTURE

In following the basic German strand of thinking from Eckhart, Paracelsus, and Böhme to Leibniz, Herder, and Goethe, we have seen the emergence of a conception of the universe as a living organic process with which man must put himself in tune in order that the immanent creative spirit may become conscious and that man may collaborate with it in realizing its divine purpose. God and man encounter each other in the all-inclusive creative process, which is both nature and spirit. Dualism was overcome by regarding nature and spirit as polarities within the universal creative process.

A new dualism was projected by Kant between the knowing mind and the unknowable thing-in-itself. Nature presumably provides only the raw material through sense experience which the mind shapes and forms in accordance with its own categories of thought. In the realm of conduct man is allowed freedom of choice, but he should act in accordance with the imperative that humanity acts in him.

Kant's pupil, Fichte (1762–1814), now took the further step of arguing that the world outside the individual mind exists only to provide materials for the self-creative activity of the ego. The I is in a continual state of coming to complete self-consciousness not only by projecting the non-I but by overcoming the alien non-I and so arriving at the absolute subject. The affirmation of the I, its denial in the non-I and the reaffirmation of the I thus constitute a dialectical process.[6] There is therefore no substance nor category, nor is there a contemplative sinking in a state of rest in static being but a continual activity arising out of the affirmation by the ego of its own pure self. The procedure is analogous to that whereby the mystic Meister Eckhart found God in the abyss of the soul by turning the eye completely inward to the exclusion of the out there.

The implication of this dialectical point of view is that the world can be known only to the extent that the knowing subject is continually involved in its creation, and that this creative activity arises out of the complete self-consciousness of the subjective ego. These were the basic philosophic assumptions of Romanticism.

Romantic youth saw in Fichte's creative ego, as presented in his early work *Principles of Knowledge* (1794), not only a release of man from bondage to an objective world of nature with its own laws and principles but a program of action. While Fichte centered everything in the intellectual quality (*Geist*) of the ego and objected to the spiritualizing of nature, the Romantic shifted the center of gravity somewhat by fashioning nature in the image of his own creative ego.

The notion of a universal protean spirit was fundamental to Romanticism. The life of the universe is like a great ocean whose waves and tidal sweeps throw up new forms in inexhaustible abundance from the creative depths. In this Dionysian view of life, reminiscent of Herder, the creative urge expresses itself in the rhythm of opposites which produces new and higher unities, out of which new opposites appear. The spirit manifests itself in movement from an original unity to the polarity of light and shadow, spirit and matter, soul and body, which in turn seek reunion in a higher unity. Since it is a dynamic total development, it can be grasped only by intuitive insight and not by analysis.

Romanticism thus sought to restore the intimate bond between man and nature, which scientific rationalism had broken. The latter, as we have seen, conceived of nature as a dead, soulless mechanism existing only for man's exploitation. This point of view ushered in what has been aptly called "technological hubris."[7] It was Schelling in particular who, following Paracelsus and Böhme, sought to overcome the alienation of nature from spirit. Nature and spirit present a dynamic polarity whereby the creative Absolute seeks to achieve self-consciousness. Only art can achieve a fundamental harmony between the individual consciousness and the total creative process.

The artist is really a magician in whom the spirit in nature is evoked and thereby released from its material, inert bonds. All of nature seeks to become self-conscious and raise itself to complete freedom. Man is that part of nature in which spirit has become most completely self-conscious and is therefore most free from the cyclical fate of nature.

In the artist, self-consciousness may be described as the complete inner mobility of the subjective self. At all costs it seeks to avoid projection in definite forms. The poem, the painting, and the musical composition are but sparks thrown off by the inner flame. Consequently, the Romantics produced no finished artistic products such as those of the classical period. The Romantics believed that the creative personality cannot be imprisoned by being made one with its own creations. It is as protean as life itself, which is a never-ending stream. Creative subjectivity manifests itself characteristically in the romantic yearning for the limitless and boundless.

The Romantics sought to bring the feelings and the imagination under the control of reason without merely damming them up. Reflection was to serve as a guide to the feelings. The rational was to serve as a vehicle for the expression of the irrational but not as a means of suppressing or overcoming the irrational.

The Romantics were the first to come to an appreciation of the depths of the unconscious, especially of what is now called the "collective unconscious," whose fundamental drives and yearnings express themselves in the legends and folk tales of the youth of the race. Since the Renaissance, people had been turning to the past, especially to antiquity, for the discovery of cultural and religious norms. But Romanticism was concerned with reaching back into the obscure mists of the origin of peoples to find the archetypal bases of cultures.

Although antiquity also exercised its sway over the minds and feelings of the early Romantics, Greece did not present to them primarily the evolution of an ideal norm culminating in incomparable works of art in the classical high noon, as it did for Winckelmann. But following Herder, they thought of Greek culture as having its sources of creation in the dark and mysterious depths of the Dionysian fertility cults. In the bacchanalian frenzy of the rites of these cults was expressed that holy intoxication in which lay the creative source of all poetry and art. In them the Greek really manifested his oneness with spontaneous nature, whereas classical art was the reflection of "society" and based on rational rules. This polarity of Apollonian harmony and Dionysian creativity, already suggested by Herder and Goethe, later came to play a very important role in the thought of Nietzsche and his disciples.

In their quest for sources, the Romantics even went back to the obscure pre-Homeric ages, and from these to the Orient to discover the springs not only of Greek culture but of Western culture in general. This quest reached its culmination in Friedrich Schlegel's *Language and Wisdom of the Indians* (1808). Orientalism, it has been said, was just a different word for Romanticism.

The Romantics actually knew little about the Orient in any realistic historical sense. What attracted them was its very remoteness. They did not seek it so much for its own sake but as a realm of infinite imaginative possibilities; a land of magic free from that aesthetic and archeological study of monuments and remains which had attached itself to classical Greece. Asia was to them the eternal mother of myth and religion.

For Joseph Görres (1776–1848) this return to the primordial brought to consciousness in man the polarity of his two natures. One nature represents night, symbolized by the mother, which is dark, brooding, creative; the other is the masculine day, representing light and activity. As man's life oscillates between sleeping and waking, birth and death, so he oscillates between despotism, which is night, and republic, which is day.

It must not be assumed that the Romantic interest in mythical origins was motivated merely by the desire to escape, as has been argued, from an unpleasant present into a glamorous past. Many also associate absorption in the Middle Ages, "when knighthood was in flower," with Romanticism. The Romantics were actually concerned with doing something about a specific present which, they thought, was moving toward a progressive annihilation of all values. In their view the French Revolution demonstrated the destructive force of rationalism in its curve of development from utopian idealism through sectarian utopianism to a militaristic nihilism which threatened to destroy the organic basis of the European order.

ROMANTIC RELIGIOSITY

In the search for the roots of the nihilistic tendencies of the times, the Romantics re-examined religion. They found these first of all in the religious divisions brought about by the Reformation, which had broken up the basic unity of the Middle Ages and contributed thus to a progressive secularization. Now this interpretation did not necessarily mean to them the reunion of Protestantism with what remained of the mother church. It is true, a number of the Romantics —initially most of them were of Protestant derivation—went over to Roman Catholicism. Friedrich von Schlegel and Adam Müller were such converts. But by and large they longed for a new Catholicism in which reconciliation of differences would be achieved on the basis of a higher unity.

Novalis in his celebrated essay, *Christianity or Europe* (1799), thought of the new Christian unity both as hierarchical and evangelical and as a restoration of Christian mystical solidarity in an over-all arching *sacrum imperium*. Schelling would bring about the synthesis of the Petrine principle of Roman Catholic solidarity with the Pauline principle of Protestant subjective dynamism in a third, the Johannine, church of the spirit. Here we encounter again the conception of a Third Age. In fact, these Romantics felt that they were standing on the brink of a new unity in which all opposites such as myth and logos, mythology and revelation, paganism and Christianity, Middle Ages and modern age would be reconciled.[8] The destructive nihilism of the times was a necessary wandering in the wilderness in order that mankind might be led into the promised land where all conflicts would be resolved in a spiritual unity.

Lessing had asked whether religion had any character of its own outside of philosophy and ethics. The rationalists, in stripping religion of practically all of its supranatural elements, had left little but belief in a deity who was necessary to explain the creation of the world. Lessing, however, accorded to what is ordinarily regarded as religion a positive role in the continuous process of revelation, which is the education of humanity. It was not just something to be sloughed off as superstition. Both the Idealists and the Romantics had a concept of God as an all-pervading creative spirit which obviously assigned a positive and continuing role to deity. Furthermore, the Romantics "discovered" the genesis of culture in the very irrational aspects of the earliest religious forms. It was Friedrich Schleiermacher (1768–1834) who took a long stride ahead by arguing that religions have a character of their own, derived from unique inward experiences. He thus returned, in a sense, to Luther's position, stripped of its dogmatic notions.

The son of a pastor, Schleiermacher was educated in the schools of Zinzendorf's Moravian Brethren. At eighteen he broke away from his sectarian isolation into the broad intellectual world, first in theological studies at the University of Halle, then in 1796 at Berlin, where he served as chaplain of a hospital and where he entered the circle of Romantics. He became, in fact, the close friend of Friedrich Schlegel, with whom he shared an apartment.

This world of intellectual and artistic ferment did not capture him entirely. While he shared the disdain of the early Romantics for the aridity of rationalistic Deism and dogmatic orthodoxy, his mind continued to dwell on the youthful impressions derived from the fervid and Christ-centered religiosity of the Zinzendorf community.

His reflections produced the famous *Addresses on Religion* (*Reden über die Religion*), published anonymously in 1799 and dedicated to the "cultured deriders of religion." The great impression made by these *Addresses* has been pointed out repeatedly. Their obvious counterpart were the equally famous *Addresses to the German Nation* (1807–1808) by Fichte in which a new conception of the nation was projected.

The significance of Schleiermacher's work lay in his attempt to avoid defining religion in terms of philosophy or ethics or revelation or mythology or nature or *Geist;* to him it was a moment of "clear insight" when the eternal "impinges upon the individual soul." It might also be described as the immediate and original activity of God within man expressed through the feelings. Most important, the eternal has a mysterious and hidden quality which arouses in man a sense of dependence.[9] God is not mentioned, although he is referred to in such allusions as *universum, eternity,* and *world-spirit.* The church is the community of those who share the individual religious experience.

Schleiermacher sought to go beyond the rationalist conception of religion as the irreducible minimum of the unknown to the uniqueness of the unknown in religion, without which there can be no religion. He stressed the fact that religious experience in its true character as awareness of the eternal is vouchsafed to only a few select heroes of the spirit. Jesus particularly had a clear insight into His role of mediating the religious experience to others.

The nature of religion is revealed not in rational formulas but in its positive historical forms, which reflect the experiences of mankind in quest of the eternal. Christianity as one of these experiences may, however, be displaced in time by a new and higher form of religion. The eternal and boundless are not expressed as a total apprehension of the creative spirit in nature nor in a mere subjective religiosity but are unveiled in the various historic forms arising out of the experiences of a great individual or a people.

THE DISCOVERY OF THE VOLKSGEIST

The rediscovery of nature and of religion was accompanied by the rediscovery of the community, which took the form of a newly awakened insight into the sources of rebirth and regeneration, which are to be found in the great community—Christendom and its component, the nation. Following in the footsteps of Möser, Herder, and Burke, the Romantics discovered that the nation was something more than a power complex or an association of interests or a natural organism—it was in fact a *spiritual entity* because it was a member of a *spiritual ecumene.*

What contributed to this insight in part was the Romantics' tendency to subjectivize not only nature and religion but also the community. This extreme subjectivism when carried to its outer limits seemed to undergo a transmutation into a quest for objective rootedness in living historic forms. Undoubtedly the ebbing of the revolutionary tide and the reaction against Napoleonic aggression in the Germanies were important formative influences. The search for roots in an objective tradition took the place of the cultivation of subjective rootlessness. Friedrich Schlegel in 1808 led the way for many into the Roman Catholic church.

The Romantics thus made the full swing around the circle. In their youth, influenced by the acid of rationalism, which dissolved all traditional forms of religion, culture, and politics, they had ended up with an extreme subjectivism. They sought to achieve a pure inner mobility tuned to primordial sources. But the increasing emphasis on return to the sources of culture, especially in religion, inevitably led them back to a consideration of the sources of Western culture in Christianity and even more specifically to the traditional springs of Germanic-Christian culture in the Middle Ages.

Some Romantics thought that Napoleon performed a necessary role in his defeat of the Prussian military-bureaucratic state (1806–1807) which Frederick the Great and his predecessors had fashioned. Its destruction was necessary in order that a national rebirth and regeneration might take place.

Rebirth was not to be achieved, however, by giving the nation a different political structure, as the revolutionaries did in France or as the Prussian reformers, Fichte and Scharnhorst, contemplated for the Germanies. The French revolutionaries thought merely of a particular class, the Third Estate, and the Prussians of a particular state as the nucleus of the nation. The Romantics, however, projected the idea of the *Volk*, influenced certainly by Herder's organic conception of the community growing like a plant and rooted in the soil of a definite region and Burke's idea of the continuity of generations. But perhaps Pietism, with its conception of the religious community united by inner mystical bonds came closest to what the Romantics were looking for when they propounded the conception of the *Volksgeist* (folk soul).

Volk in the past had referred generally to the subjects of a ruler, the people. It also had a derogatory implication, meaning the vulgar rabble. Now the Romantics raised *Volk* to a new dignity by uniting the cultural community with the bonds of common ancestors, language, and native soil. In this way the *Volk* was juxtaposed to the prevailing French conception of the nation, which was viewed as a sovereign association based on common rights and interests and achieved through a great event, a war of liberation or a revolution.

The Romantic concept of the *Volk* is perhaps best illustrated by two historians of law and language, Friedrich Karl von Savigny (1779–1861) and Jacob Grimm (1785–1863). Savigny in 1814 became involved in a controversy over the question of whether Germany should be provided with a general code of laws such as the Napoleonic Code. It was argued that, since a new society was coming into being based on conceptions of natural rights and natural law, a new general legal code embodying the acceptance of uniform principles should take the place of the local and historic diversities and complexities of existing law. We have already noted that eighteenth-century rulers such as Frederick the Great had been moving in this direction. Savigny, however, argued that the idea of a general code was based on two false implications: that uniformity of laws was desirable and that law proceeded from state power. These assumptions were of recent origin, attributable to enlightened despotism and revolution, both of which exalted the state at the expense of the community. Law, Savigny held, is as old as the language and customs of a people and is not the product of the ideas or political power of a particular age. Law lives in the consciousness of a people and not in codes any more than faith does in dogma. Tradition preserves law through the continuity of generations. Emphasis was thus placed by Savigny on the unconscious evolution rather than on the deliberate creation of law and constitutions either by lawgiver, ruler, or constitutional convention.

Law and language emanate from the *Volksgeist,* the creative spirit of a people which in the Romantic conception seems to retain an indelible character throughout its history. It is the bond of continuity which unites the endless chain of generations arising in the obscure mists of the past and disappearing into eternity. It is an inexhaustible spring from which flows all that is original and unique in a people's culture.

Like Herder, the Romantic school of historians turned to the youth or springtime of the *Volksgeist* to find the authentic sources of national culture before alien influences entered. The world of saga, myth, and custom presents the creative soil of all that a culture later produces. When conscious and deliberate artistry enters in, then real poetry, which is folk poetry, is forced to descend to a warped existence among the common people.

The Romantic quest for the sources of language, law, and literature contributed to the ferreting out of an enormous body of folklore, fairy tale, and legend. Its popular influence is reflected in the famous collection of fairy tales published by the Grimm brothers in 1812. The unveiling of national cultural sources absorbed much of the historical interest of the nineteenth century, which has been called the century of history. Publication of the oldest monuments of law and literature also greatly promoted the rising nationalism of that century, fostering delusions of national uniqueness and peculiarity. It should be pointed out, however, that the conception of national mission was fostered rather more by the Jacobin revolutionary current than by the Romantic absorption in genesis.

THE MIDDLE AGES AS THE SOURCE OF EUROPEAN UNITY AND LIBERTY

In the search for roots, the increasing conservative trend in Romanticism turned to a less remote and more realistic past, the Middle Ages. The medieval past was, of course, closely tied in with national origins. In their glorification of the medieval empire, church, and feudalism, the conservative Romantics contributed enormously toward providing the German people with a specific historical background. While both antiquity and early Germanic society had about them a mythical and legendary remoteness, the vestiges of the Middle Ages lingered everywhere. Hence, the Romantics turned to such concrete historical institutions as the Roman Catholic church and the Holy Roman Empire rather than to such mystical entelechies as the *Volksgeist*. The Middle Ages, as the great creative phase of the West, came in fact to have an almost normative character.

To Renaissance humanists, to religious reformers, and to enlightened rationalists alike, the Middle Ages had thus far assumed a mere negative character. Romanticism now gave the age a positive quality. It came to represent the antithesis of the dominant tendencies of the time: rationalism, classicism, and bureaucracy, which the Romantics abhorred.

259

But everybody did not see the Middle Ages in terms of empire and church. Followers of Möser, such as Stein, who were particularly opposed to bureaucratic absolutism and the revolutionary conception of popular sovereignty, saw in it an age in which all manner of associations and corporations such as estates, gilds, and orders of chivalry expressed those community ties and loyalties characteristic of Germanic freedom. This kind of corporate and communal freedom was assumed to be the basis of English liberty as represented by parliament and jury.

A few saw medieval remains best preserved in the Catholic south and moved to Vienna and Munich to seek employment in a congenial atmosphere. It was their influence that contributed in part to making Austria the symbol of conservative reaction.

Among those who migrated to Vienna was the leading social theorist of conservative Romanticism, Adam Müller (1779–1829), who was also a convert to Roman Catholicism. He particularly opposed the liberal notion of Adam Smith that the competition of individual interests, if allowed free rein, would lead to an actual harmony. Conflicts of economic interests were best reconciled, according to Müller, in such medieval creations as gilds and feudalism, in which the rights of property were subordinated to the interests of the whole community. Likewise, national states should not be regarded as independent sovereign entities but as members of an ecumenical community united by a common Christian faith.

To the real conservative Romanticist, the Middle Ages was the great age of Christian unity, in contrast to the contemporary anarchy of individualism and power conflicts. A few looked back to the *sacrum imperium* based on an organic hierarchical social order and a charismatic ruler. But most glorified the union of feudalism and church as expressed in the religious character of knighthood and in the great movement of the Crusades.

In the long run, the dynamic concept of *Volkstum* (nationality) was much more influential than this religious conception of the relation of nation and ecumene for which there existed no real material or spiritual basis in the Europe of the day. The idea of *Volkstum*, however, expressed the German's feeling of cultural individuality in the face of the threat of French cultural and political domination. Moreover, in the *Volkstum*, Romanticism propounded, in place of the Western conception of society as a fabric of common rights and interests, the notion of the organic community of spiritual and cultural values. Culture was no longer to be viewed as the product of society, reflecting refinement of taste and manners but had to be approached with awe and reverence as the mystical expression of the soul of a people. It was to take on a new dynamic significance in the nineteenth and twentieth centuries as it assumed a naturalistic coloration in the concept of race.

NAPOLEON AND THE RISE OF NATIONAL SELF-CONSCIOUSNESS

It may be said that German national consciousness was developed from within by the Idealists and the Romantics; from without by resistance to Napoleon. From within came the concept of the *Volk* as the spontaneous creative source from which flowed the forms of a cultural individuality. The pressure coming from without, from Napoleonic conquest and imperial rule, gave to the state a new significance; it was no longer merely a source of order and the base of conquest, but the fortress within which the *Volk* safeguarded its individuality.

Napoleon contributed both positively and negatively to the movement for unity. He reorganized a great part of the Germanies that came under his control, reducing some three-hundred states to thirty-nine. On the other hand, he aroused intense opposition, especially after 1806–07, by his subordination of German interests, both political and economic, to the war against England, and to the goal of complete French hegemony.

The reduction of the number of states naturally affected most the western part of the *Reich* because *Kleinstaaterei* had been most prevalent and imperial sentiment was strongest there. Thus the basis of the old *Reich*, the old medieval pattern of imperial knights, cities, and ecclesiastical principalities, which had persisted there alongside of the modernized states of Prussia and Austria, was effaced with one stroke by an outside power.

This reorganization along the right bank of the Rhine did not stop with mere territorial consolidations. Internal structures were reshaped in accordance with the Napoleonic model in France. The "Third Germany" was created, to be distinguished from the Germanies of Prussia and Austria. Provided with a modern system of administration, courts, and financial organization, and with professions and vocations open to all, it was even more advanced and modern than the other Germanies. A new class of officials, lawyers, and jurists emerged with a broader national and international horizon, since they were no longer confined within the narrow boundaries of *Kleinstaaterei.* They became the core of the liberal and national movement which culminated in the revolution of 1848.

The passing of ecclesiastical principalities, imperial cities, and knights, and the formation of the Confederation of the Rhine by Napoleon in 1806 rendered the Holy Roman Empire completely superfluous. Emperor Francis II laid aside the ancient imperial crown in that year and adopted the imperial title for the Hapsburg lands only. While the Empire ceased to exist as a political entity, it continued as a nostalgic memory.

Napoleon's drive into central and eastern Europe was not halted by his virtual conquest of the western Germanies. In two battles, at Jena and Auerstadt in 1806, the Prussian army was decisively defeated. Complete collapse followed. With a couple of exceptions—for example, the defense of Kolberg under Gneisenau—the Prussian fortresses surrendered almost without resistance, and Napoleon marched into Berlin. Lacking the staying qualities that traditionalist Austria showed again and again, this military-bureaucratic state collapsed like a house of cards.

Most dangerous to the Napoleonic Empire, which by the treaty of Tilsit (1807) comprised the greater part of central and southern Europe, was the mounting national feeling which was beginning to appear in various sections of Europe. The French intervention in Spain (1808) was followed by continuous guerilla warfare proceeding from local centers of resistance. In Austria this new force of national feeling and the news of Napoleon's Spanish defeats even led Emperor Francis II to issue a call for a popular uprising against the French. But only in the mountainous Tyrol did the peasants, under Andreas Hofer, rise to drive out the alien and godless French. The Archduke Charles defeated Napoleon at Aspern in 1809, and then in that year was himself defeated at Wagram. These events marked the end of the very short association of the Hapsburgs with the national movement. Resistance against the French continued locally in the Tyrol, but Hofer was finally captured and shot. The chief center of the national movement against the French now moved to the northern Germanies.

In Prussia the strongest stimulus to nationalist opposition came not from dynasty or peasants but from professors and officials. It was pointed out that the expression of cultural individuality was not enough, that the *Volk* could attain its complete fulfillment only in the state. But it was also recognized that freedom from French political hegemony could not be achieved through the old military-bureaucratic state. Stein and Arndt argued that this state was out of touch with the springs of the emerging national consciousness, which must find expression through appropriate popular forms of political participation rooted in the historical soil. The so-called Prussian Jacobins, Fichte and Scharnhorst, laid emphasis on the assertion of the collective national will in the manner of the French revolutionaries through national conscription and public education.

Both Fichte and Schleiermacher, as noted above, made the transition from Idealistic and Romantic subjectivism to a recognition of the importance of the external forms of historical action and development. Schleiermacher stressed the Christian experience of salvation and hence the necessity of freeing its embodiment, the church, from state control to make it an agency of national regeneration. Fichte, on the other hand, turned to the state as the means of educating the *Volk* to its tasks in behalf of humanity. Both were called to teach at the newly founded University of Berlin (1810) which became the leading center of historical studies in the nineteenth century.

THE STATE AS NATIONAL WILL

Fichte, the son of a humble Saxon weaver, imbued with a hatred of aristocracy, was an enthusiastic supporter of the French Revolution. He even wanted to teach at a French university and become a French citizen because he was convinced that France was the nation destined to free mankind. Although in time he lost his fervor and assumed a critical attitude toward the Revolution, he recognized its great significance, particularly in its second, or Jacobin, phase.

The early revolutionary emphasis on the achievement of individual liberty by way of the recognition of natural rights he came to regard as an inadequate goal. Natural rights for him had only a negative character; they merely placed limitations on the state's sphere of action. In doing so, they actually deprived the state of its real function, which was to give positive content to human freedom. Fichte advocated state socialism for the promotion of general education and communal work as the means of inspiring the highest ethical development of the citizens. The state was not to become a welfare institution as under enlightened despotism, but a school of citizenship, such as Rousseau had suggested, in which the collective will becomes energized.

Fichte was also concerned with the corruption of public and private life brought about by the revolutionary changes which, though they removed traditional institutional controls, had put nothing in their place and had merely released the struggle between egotistical interests. Like Machiavelli, whom he "rediscovered," Fichte also felt that the restoration of the state as lawgiver was, as among the Romans, necessary in order to restore in people the recognition of the pre-eminence of the community. But the law was not to come from the outside by the fiat of a ruler or be the product of the vegetative growth of custom; it should rather express the collective will of the German people as they became conscious of their own peculiar mission.

Though internally the nation-state was concerned with an ethical mission, externally it was still confronted by the power conflict for survival. By virtue of this very emphasis on the fact that the nation-state must set its task or mission from within, Fichte was led to rule out the existence of an objective order among states based either on a natural and harmonious order of interests or on the historic order of the Christian ecumene. This extraordinary emphasis on the inner ethical motive to the exclusion of an external order was to have dire consequences for German liberal thinking in the nineteenth and twentieth centuries.

The theoretical basis of the conception of the state as embodying a moral imperative was provided by a philosophy or metaphysics of history in which the fusion of Kantian Idealism and Romanticism becomes apparent.

According to Fichte, mankind proceeds by stages to the achievement of the highest moral consciousness. These stages are reminiscent of Rousseau's conception of moral ascent. First, man is a creature of instinct and impulse. Then reason, deriving its sanction from external sources, guides man first by authoritative principles as in the Middle Ages, then in the Enlightenment it becomes the means of throwing off that authority to allow individual freedom. Finally, man follows moral law as a product of his own conscience. He wills the good deliberately, and he follows it willingly because it is imposed by his inner self.

This moral imperative assumed, in the Third Age, on whose threshold mankind stood, the form of a task or mission for the welfare of humanity, which a community sets for itself. Here the collective will of the community was to rise above the mere vegetative level of cultural nationalism.

In the *Addresses to the German Nation*, Fichte contended that the Germans were the one people through whom humanity could express this highest moral ideal. Among all European peoples they were an original people (*Urvolk*); they had not been corrupted by civilization. The idea of Herder that civilization constituted the rigid mold in which the original spontaneous creativity of a people eventually became hardened was employed by Fichte with a new twist. The Latin peoples were not original because they were derivatives of the ancient Roman community, as their languages demonstrated. The Germans occupied their original homeland and had an original language uncorrupted by terms borrowed from the political arsenal of another state. Because their language did not have a second-hand character, the Germans were closest to the sources of humanity. To serve as the nation of humanity, they should purify themselves of Latin importations and develop a political language expressing their own self-consciousness as a group. They must throw off both the cultural and political yokes of the French conqueror to achieve nationhood and assume their messianic role in behalf of humanity.

Fichte's call to action was directed toward all Germans, but more specifically it was aimed at Prussia as the one state which under Frederick the Great had been the effective military-bureaucratic instrument of a ruling genius and now was capable of moral leadership if it would but reform itself to become the embodiment of the will of the people. Also the reformers, Stein, Scharnhorst, and Humboldt were not interested in enhancing Prussian power for its own sake. They saw in her regeneration the means of throwing off the French yoke if she would but abandon her strictly military-bureaucratic organization, her social caste system and royal cabinet politics, and base the state on the moral will of the community, having its roots in the creative forces of the *Volk*.

THE STATE AS FORTRESS OF THE VOLK

Another facet of the emerging German national idea was presented by Ernst Moritz Arndt (1769–1860). He approached the national problem from the perspective of the German landscape as the most important frame of the *Volk*.

Arndt was the son of emancipated peasant folk on the Baltic island of Rügen, who had risen to some degree of material welfare, at least beyond that of their own station in life. Arndt developed, therefore, an early interest in peasant emancipation. He argued that Roman law and the territorial state had contributed most to the depression of the peasant in modern times. Rooted in the soil, the peasant was the basis of the *Volk*, and he must be brought into organic relation with the state.

Although serving as a professor first at Greifswald and later at Bonn, Arndt never reflected the typical academic mind nor developed a systematic body of ideas. He wrote poetry of the folkish variety and engaged in polemics against the abuses of his time, particularly those concerned with French influence and domination. To begin with, he had been attracted to the policy of peasant emancipation pursued by the Revolution, and he had even regarded Napoleon as a great hero, necessary to lead a people out of the wilderness. A journey through France, south Germany, and Italy brought a widening of national horizons. The national movement in Austria, which culminated in the Austrian war against Napoleon in 1809, for a time led him to hope for a restoration of the *Reich* under Hapsburg leadership and caused him to lean toward Catholicism, with its appreciation of peasant culture. But under the influence of Stein and the War of Liberation against Napoleon (1813–1814), he became a supporter of German national unity under Prussian leadership and a devout Lutheran. These permutations reflect, among other things, the close linkage of political points of view with religious faiths.

Arndt had a concrete appreciation of the German landscape, which we miss in his more philosophic contemporaries. For him, Germany was represented by its important rivers, the Elbe, Danube, and Rhine. That he sensed their political significance is evident from a pamphlet he wrote, "The Rhine: Germany's Stream but not Her Frontier." With him the Rhine began to serve as a symbol of national antagonism toward the French. In including the Danube among the rivers of Germany, he brought in the bordering lands and also envisaged the great central European area of German settlement and expansion.

His geopolitical orientation naturally led him to sense the cultural significance of the middle position of the Germans. Confronted with alien currents bearing upon them from all sides, the Germans were naturally placed on the defensive with respect to maintaining their cultural individuality. The state as power, he felt, should serve as the fortress of national individuality, but to do so it should have its roots in the folkish community and not be merely a bureaucratic-military machine. Arndt contributed particularly toward popularizing the Romantic conception of *Volksgeist* by giving it a concrete character in terms of landscape and of peasant culture.

In Arndt's grass-roots nationalism and Fichte's rather abstract conception concerning the moral imperative of the nation-state, we already see reflected the two chief poles between which the German national idea oscillated for more than a century. Fichte proceeded from the Kantian imperative of mission in behalf of humanity, whereas Arndt's point of departure was Herder's and the Romantic's emphasis on the release of the creative forces in the *Volk* with its roots in a particular landscape.

Arndt's influence was more immediate. He joined Baron Stein in exile in Russia where he became Stein's secretary and propagandist for his reform ideas, which had the most direct bearing on the revitalization of Prussia. After being forced to resign as Prussian minister of state in 1808, Stein entered the service of Czar Alexander, then the chief adversary of Napoleon.

THE STATE AND THE RELEASE OF NATIONAL ENERGIES

Karl Freiherr von Stein (1757–1831) came from a very old family of imperial knights of the Rhineland area. He, unlike others of his class and family, sought service, not with Austria, but first in the Hanoverian government, then in the Prussian administration in 1780. Educated at the University of Göttingen, he had come in contact there with admirers of English institutions and the liberal conservatism of Möser and Burke.

Unlike most of the enlightened officials of his time, Stein was very critical of the tendency of enlightened despotism to emphasize uniformity and welfare. He sought to stimulate the local initiative of the nobility, middle class, and peasantry as against the prevailing tendency toward the extension of the sphere of centralized bureaucratic action. He looked to the English forms of parliamentary government involving ministerial responsibility, separation of functions —judicial, administrative, and legislative—and a forceful public opinion as the model for the Germans.

While recognizing the French Revolution as a great boon to the French people in delivering them from corrupt rulers, Stein opposed the Revolution's excesses, its social leveling, state centralism, and terrorism. The equalitarian tendencies of the revolutionary movement paved the way, he thought, for the upstart and adventurer, Napoleon, and promoted the self-interest of the subservient masses in getting the bread of state doles and the circuses of military glory. He became the determined and unremitting foe of the French when they proceeded, in their career of imperial conquest, to scrap the whole corporative structure of the old *Reich* on both banks of the Rhine.

He was a bitter critic of Prussia's policy of neutrality and selfish isolation from the general concerns of the *Reich* after 1795, and again and again he advocated collaboration with Austria in resistance against French imperialism. The disastrous defeat of Prussia was due, Stein felt, to this policy of isolation from the *Reich* and to the fact that the military-bureaucratic state of the old regime had separated itself from the people and could not stand up against the French revolutionary nation, embodying as it did the collective energies of a people. His dominant idea was to restore the vitality of the component social groups, peasantry, middle class, and nobility, and so create an organic political community in Prussia which could assume its role in a strengthened and revitalized *Reich*.

Because Prussia found itself in a state of almost complete prostration, Stein and his fellow reformers, Scharnhorst, Gneisenau, and Humboldt, were able to launch reforms in spite of a reluctant sovereign and the opposition of most of the East Elbian Junkers. Confronted by a ruthless conqueror who might at any time, in the interests of his grandiose imperial plans, completely wipe out what was left of Prussia, the king was forced in the interests of mere self-preservation to call on these reformers, whom his conservative intimates regarded as Jacobins, to restore Prussia. A bureaucratic-military state of the Prussian type without a reservoir of tradition must in defeat resort to extraordinary means to restore its prestige and power. What the state now lacked in material means was to be made up by the release of the spiritual energies of the people.

Stein was the chief driving force behind a program of reform, some features of which harked back to enlightened despotism, whose general purpose was the creation of a body politic of moral and spiritual ferment and activation. The various social groups, nobility, middle class, and peasants were to be granted equality and freedom before the law in the choice of professions and in the exchange of lands and goods. In proposing local self-government for the towns and a certain degree of popular control of administration, he reflected Möser's admiration for the corporate structure of the Middle Ages. Finally, Stein also had in mind, as the capstone of the new body politic, the creation of a representative legislative body and ministerial responsibility, perhaps along the lines of the English parliament and cabinet system.

These proposals represented neither revolution from above nor from below. But the Prussian king, who viewed them all with distaste, within a year after the beginning of Stein's reform ministry took advantage of Napoleon's increasing distrust of Stein to dismiss him. In general, the nobility, especially the East Elbian Junkers, opposed the reforms, and a good many of the burghers and peasants proved apathetic. The reform proposals actually stemmed from a small group of idealistic officials, a number of whom were non-Prussians and most of whom placed the general welfare of the *Reich* above Prussian interests. Although they came from various ranks of society, they reflected perhaps most the general values of a narrow strata of the middle class, the propertied and cultured upper *Bürgertum.* Influenced by the idealistic philosophy of Kant, Schelling, and Fichte, they sought to liberate the state from old patriarchal and welfare notions and to permeate it with the dynamic of a new moral imperative.

Just as many of Stein's reforms were circumvented, so the aim of Scharnhorst, Gneisenau, and others to follow the French example of creating a nation in arms proved abortive in the long run. Though universal military service was established, the army continued to be dominated during the nineteenth century by the Junker officer class.

This had an important bearing on the maintenance of their political and social pre-eminence, because armies came to be regarded increasingly as schools of citizenship and the Prussian kings were inclined to look to the army as the chief basis of the throne.

HUMANIST EDUCATION AND NATIONAL LIBERATION

Educational reforms are associated with the name of Wilhelm von Humboldt (1767–1835). Humboldt had oscillated between the holding of diplomatic posts—for example at Rome and Vienna—and the scholarly world of linguistics and humanistic studies until called into the government by Stein.

He had written a book arguing that the sphere of action of the state should be limited to the absolute minimum of maintaining defense and order so that the greatest amount of elbow room might be allowed for the harmonious development of the individual personality. This was to be no self-sufficient isolated individualism, however, for he argued that the citizen is best off when united by as many ties as possible to his fellow-citizens and by as few as possible to the state. The close-knit community of the ancient Greek *polis* allowed for the free development of creative personality; the bureaucratic-military welfare state of Frederick the Great did not. The organic community should express itself in diverse associations, standing juxtaposed to the state and allowing for the development of personality through free and mutual efforts in behalf of the common good.

The most important organs of national self-expression were education and the army. The army was necessary to the maintenance of a strong state without, while education promoted the free creative activity of the *Geist* within. Here again was the German dichotomy between the strong state without and freedom within.

Two movements contributed particularly to bringing education into vital relationship with the nation and with the rebirth of *Geist*. The one, proceeding from Rousseau, implemented in the Germanies particularly by the Swiss reformer, Pestalozzi (1745–1827), aimed at reducing the emphasis on discipline of intellect and emotion. The accent was to be placed on the free unfolding of personality through the rebirth of the community and its cultural heritage. Fichte had recommended Pestalozzi in his *Addresses*, and Humboldt now proposed introducing his ideas and methods.

In the other, the unfolding of personality was achieved in exemplary fashion in the ancient Greek ideal of the harmonious development of personality. The norms and values of Hellenic culture rather than the rigid molds of the so-called classical rules were to become a source of inspiration. This turning to the Greeks as models was promoted by the writings of Winckelmann and Friedrich A. Wolff of the University of Halle, who is generally regarded as the father of philology.

These humanistic ideals, along with the fact that Napoleon had suppressed the University of Halle in 1806 for its pro-Prussianism, provided the background for the establishment in 1810 of the University of Berlin. In the first half of the nineteenth century it became the chief center of philological and philosophical studies in Europe. Not until the second half of that century did the natural sciences assume a place of equal importance. Philology enjoyed an extraordinary significance. The techniques developed by German scholars for the careful examination and elucidation of ancient texts served as models of objective research for the scholars of other nations. The University of Berlin came to provide the ideal of academic scholarship in its emphasis on the fusion of teaching and research, thus providing the chief energizing force in the enormous expansion of historical and scientific knowledge in the nineteenth century.

In secondary education, the classical *Gymnasium*, which emphasized Latin and Greek studies, and secondarily German and mathematics, as preparation for the professions, came to be distinguished from the *real Gymnasium*, which aimed at vocational education. This division tended to sharpen the difference between social classes, especially before the natural sciences came into prominence in the second half of the nineteenth century. In general the reforms in education favored the middle classes who flocked to the universities. As formal education became increasingly the test of competence in both public and private life, their social importance was greatly enhanced. They lost the narrow horizons peculiar to their class during much of the eighteenth century.

The reformers were, of course, not attuned to the long-run effects of their achievements. They were immediately concerned with driving out the French. This, they thought, could be achieved only by a national resurrection. Some, such as Stein and even the old soldier Gneisenau, advocated an uprising of the people from below against the hated French. But the rulers of Prussia and Austria were most reluctant to resort to revolutionary means to overcome the French. The remedy might well have been worse than the disease. Even after the disastrous losses suffered by Napoleon in the Russian campaign of 1812, the Prussian and Austrian governments moved slowly. The movement of national feeling was far ahead, as manifested in sporadic revolts here and there and in the calls to action issued by leading patriots, mostly writers and publicists. Some of the reformers, such as Stein, Arndt, and Clausewitz, went over to the Russians as the best hope against Napoleon. Stein became a close advisor of Alexander I and a continual goad to carry the war against the French beyond the borders of Russia into western Europe.

The War of Liberation (1813–1814), leading to the defeat of Napoleon, was achieved by a coalition of rulers and a carefully worked out military campaign. But to German historians of the late nineteenth and twentieth centuries, it came to be regarded as a national resurrection extending from 1806 to 1814. It came to loom larger than the abortive revolution of 1848 or even the later Prussian unification of Germany. It came to symbolize the unfulfilled promise of a real German unity forged in the crucible of war against the alien invader.

THE DYNAMICS OF CULTURAL NATIONALISM

For the German, national self-consciousness did not appear within a historic mold or assume a sense of mission, as it did for the French and English. It had its source in reactions against the French rationalistic Enlightenment, against the Revolution, and particularly against Napoleon. Since German national feeling did not develop within a political mold and had this negative character, it assumed a peculiar cultural complexion. It was not concerned mainly with how the collective national will might be realized but how the unique cultural character of a people might be safeguarded. The German was inclined to apply as the yardstick of nationality the test of cultural individuality involving the peculiarities of language, literature, and religion rather than political self-determination by the individuals of the state they belong to or wish to join. The latter is called national self-determination, whereas the German point of view may be designated as "cultural determinism."

As we have seen, Romanticism, like the Revolution, presented both individualistic and collectivistic aspects. The artistic personality was to be brought into tune with the spontaneous creative forces of a protean nature. It also sought to provide the *Volk* with roots in this creative nature. But in the face of Napoleonic France it needed also to be provided with a fortress in the state to safeguard its individuality. As the accent on the state came to predominate in German political thinking in the nineteenth century, the cultural roots of the *Volk* tended to be lost sight of except by isolated thinkers. In the twentieth century the conception of the *Volk* as a unique collective individuality, rooted in a landscape and having a peculiar destiny, was given radical expression in National Socialism.

The Revolution in its radical phase attempted to achieve utopia not as embodied in particular institutions, but as the dynamic of the collective will. Romanticism likewise was concerned not with cultural products but with the creative spirit which disregarded rational and classical rules and was imbued with a reverence for the organic and spontaneous development of culture and nature. This revolutionary and Romantic dynamism was the chief motive force in the ideological and cultural conflicts of the nineteenth and twentieth centuries.

X

The Clash of Ideologies

The peace negotiated at Vienna (1814–1815) demonstrated, at least outwardly, that the coalition of rulers rather than the insurgence of peoples had been most effective in defeating Napoleon. Middle Europe retained the state structure established by Napoleon; the Germanies were organized in a loose confederation. In the individual states the old dynasties and aristocracies were restored, but in most states the reforms introduced during the Napoleonic supremacy were retained. In the period from 1815 to 1830 the rulers of Europe, led by the Austrian statesman Metternich relied upon the collaboration of the great powers not only to prevent another French attempt at continental hegemony but also to repress popular aspirations toward unity and freedom.

RESTORATIONS BY WAY OF STATE SYSTEM, REICH, AND ECUMENE

At Vienna the English and Austrian interest in stability and order on the continent prevailed. Both Alexander I of Russia, having in mind a project for a new Christian fellowship of rulers and peoples, and the Prussian reformers, concerned with achieving some form of German unity, were suspect. It was of course a meeting of kings and aristocrats and not of representatives of peoples. The gathering at Vienna sought to revive the grandeur and splendor of the old regime, but there was an air of decadence about this refurbished magnificence. Peoples and territories were shuffled about amidst balls and banquets accompanied by the usual backstairs intrigue, diplomatic maneuvering, and crises, the principal crisis being occasioned by the attempted comeback of Napoleon.

Prince Metternich, who had been the chief organizer of the coalition which had defeated Napoleon, was himself a typical carry-over of the eighteenth-century diplomat: suave, elegant, charming, and a philanderer of the old style. Unlike many conservatives of his time, he had not become an advocate of the alliance of altar and throne as the chief means of restoring a Christian organic society. He remained an enlightened and skeptical aristocrat for whom political expediency was the main consideration. Monarchy, aristocracy, and church did not have the intrinsic appeal to him that they did to such a conservative Romantic as Adam Müller, though he recognized that these institutions were necessary in a state like Austria as counter forces to nationalism and liberalism.

The first essential, however, to the maintenance of (the existing) order in central Europe was the collaboration of the great powers. The old balance of power system, founded on the cosmopolitan forces of monarchy and aristocracy, was to be restored along with a high degree of local self-government as bulwarks against revolution and nationalism. Metternich was quite willing to abandon the old Hapsburg imperial role, involving among other things the cultural and religious mission of defending the Rhine against the French and the Danube against the Turks, because these policies had lost their significance in an age of secular power politics.

German patriots such as Stein, Humboldt, Görres, and Arndt advocated the restoration of the old *Reich* under the Hapsburg emperor as a means of maintaining the unity of central Europe. They had in mind not the creation of a power state but the restoration of a symbol of German cultural mission and the establishment of a legal and constitutional frame within which the moral forces of the *Volk*,

276

now aroused, could surmount the drives of state egoisms. The nation could then also sink its roots in a particular historical and cultural landscape rather than be the mere expression of a subjective drive for national self-determination. Moreover, the *Volk* meant to them not the more or less mystical entity of Romanticism nor the broad mass of the populace but the landowning gentry and the upper middle class of education and property.

Only in historic orientation did the attitudes of Stein, Humboldt, Görres and Arndt bear some resemblance to the current conservative Romanticism of Friedrich Schlegel and Adam Müller, who were concerned with the restoration of a European Christian ecumenical order and not with the release of German national energies, which they associated with revolution and the dissolution of the Christian community.

Alexander I (1777–1825) of Russia came forward with a similar idea. He proposed the establishment of a union of European monarchs called the Holy Alliance. In place of the competition of power interests, these rulers were to dedicate themselves jointly to rule over their peoples in the spirit of Christian brotherhood. Therefore each of the sovereigns was to fix his own personal signature to the treaty rather than sign through a minister or diplomatic envoy, as was customary with such documents.

The Holy Alliance has been variously referred to as a "sonorous nothing," as the chief instrument of reaction in modern times, and even as a somewhat nebulous anticipation of the League of Nations. It was a typical expression of the romantic religiosity which surcharged the atmosphere of this phase of conservatism and restoration. Alexander had in his youth been influenced by the rationalistic humanitarianism of a Swiss tutor by the name of De la Harpe. But the great events of the Napoleonic invasion, the burning of Moscow, and the catastrophic retreat of the alien invader had turned Alexander's very susceptible mind into the channel of religious and mystical speculation. His association with a Madame Krüdener, a leading Swiss pietist and mystic of the time, served to reinforce this trend; it was her influence that led to the proposal of the Holy Alliance.

The Alliance was to be the forefront of an ecumenical union of Christian rulers and peoples in which Greek Orthodoxy would be joined with Roman Catholicism and Protestantism. Such proposals for the restoration of the unity of Christendom go back to Nicholas of Cues and Leibniz and were renewed again by Romantics like Novalis and Schelling. The pantheist philosopher Schelling, while professor at Münich, became associated with a Catholic Romantic theosophist by the name of Franz von Baader (1765-1841) who received his chief inspiration from Böhme and Leibniz. Both Schelling and Baader sought a non-dogmatic Christianity which would serve as a basis for the union of faiths, end the confessional conflicts, and present a united front to the atheistic rationalism of revolution and dictatorship. Baader was especially conscious of the middle position of the Germanies between the mystical East and the rationalistic West. He was in close contact with Alexander Golitzin, the friend of Czar Alexander and procurator of the Holy Synod and thereby the political head of the Russian church.

RELIGIOUS AND NATIONALISTIC FERMENT

These proposals for the restoration of the unity and vitality of Christendom were accompanied by a religious ferment coming from below which swept over the whole of middle Europe. The eastern Germanic borderlands extending southward from the Baltic through Saxony, Bohemia, and Austria were particularly involved, although the whole of Germany experienced a new pietistic awakening. From the borderlands, the ferment spread eastward into Russia, especially by way of the colonies of south German dissenters established in the Ukraine, many of whom came from Catholic Bavaria and Protestant Wurtemberg. This religious insurgence showed a variegated pattern of ideas and aspirations; it was shot through with flashes of utopian vision, mystical and orgiastic ecstasy, and fanatical bigotry. As it became secularized in the course of the nineteenth and twentieth centuries, it came to assume a political and social dynamism whose explosive force we have recently witnessed.

Intertwined with these Romantic religious aspirations in various curious ways and similarly variegated was the contemporary nationalistic insurgence. It was most vocal among university students and professors. The spirit of nationalistic insurgency had welled up for the first time during the War of Liberation with the appeal for a national uprising against the foreign invader. It was not positively, that is, rationalistically, revolutionary in the Western sense of having as its goal a new order on the basis of universal principles of liberty and equality. It was romantically anti-rational in that it eschewed all universal notions and sought to appeal to heroic individuality in terms of "deed" and "sentiment," all enveloped in the rather grandiloquent phrases of "honor, freedom, fatherland."

There was also a very radical fringe of insurgency with revolutionary republican ideals, which in its advocacy of tyrannicide was hardly to be distinguished from anarchistic terrorism. In the Germanies it was confined mainly to students and writers; but in Spain, Italy, and Russia around 1820 army officers were its chief carriers.

The German movement was greatly influenced by Fichte's notion of the Germans as an original *Volk* and especially by Arndt's sentimental poetry about the Fatherland. But most immediately influential was the agitation of Friedrich Ludwig Jahn (1778–1852), the founder of gymnastic clubs (*Turnverein*). He sought to counteract the one-sided intellectualism of education with Swedish gymnastic exercises and the promotion of national sentiment. Typical, as with Arndt, was the fusion of nationalism with folkish democracy, whereby the peasants were presented as the chief basis of the *Reich*. The members of his gymnastic clubs went around in what they regarded as ancient Germanic garb—gray jackets with dagger on hip and open collars and long hair. As a member of a volunteer company in the recent war, Jahn had found guns and gunpowder quite at variance with his romantic medieval visions of individual combat with lance, ax, and dagger, and was soon mustered out.

Jahn was also one of the main promoters of certain student associations (*Burschenschaften*) at many universities, the first of which was founded at Jena in 1815. They were intended to overcome the evils which had grown up around the old student associations dating back to the Middle Ages, which had a regional rather than national representation and were concerned principally with drinking bouts and the subjection of underclassmen. The *Burschenschaften* were the product of the national idealism pervasive among students returning from the war against Napoleon—the particularism and provincialism of German life was to be surmounted by the establishment of patriotic associations at the university level which were combined in 1818 in a national German organization.

To the traits already noted which the nationalistic insurgency had in common with that which succeeded World War I must be added anti-Semitism, which swept over the Germanies after the Napoleonic wars and was promoted by intellectuals of all stripes, especially in the *Burschenschaften.* In the tolerant atmosphere of the Enlightenment Jews had attained a large degree of intellectual and social equality, although they were still prohibited from becoming army officers, university professors, and judges. Both Joseph II and the Prussian reformers had sought to extend the scope of their legal equality. The introduction of the Napoleonic Code in the Rhineland area carried with it the achievement of rights of full citizenship for Jews. Both the Austrian and Prussian governments sought to have their legal equality affirmed in the provisions establishing the German Confederation. Failure to carry through with this proposal marked the resurgence of anti-Semitism in the postwar period.

Jews were generally excluded from the *Burschenschaften,* and the free cities of Hamburg, Bremen, Lübeck, and Frankfort deprived the Jews of such rights as they had acquired. In fact, in Lübeck and Bremen Jewish families were expelled from the city. Here and there attacks on Jews by mobs occurred, although there were also notable instances of their defense such as at Heidelberg, where the famous jurist, Anton Thibaut, an advocate of legal reform against Savigny, prevailed upon the students to come to the rescue of the Jews.[1]

The writings against the Jews argued either that they be reduced to a ghetto-like existence by a distinctive marking of dress, or that they be forced to assimilation by abandonment of their religion and by intermarriage with gentiles. While there was implicit in Romantic nationalism the idea of purification of the *Volk* of alien ingredients, the chief motivation here was religious and not racial; it was stimulated by the prevailing religious and nationalistic ferment.

Undoubtedly the severe economic depression following the wars, marked particularly by a catastrophically bad harvest in 1816 with consequent famine and great fluctuations in prices, contributed to the waves of popular hysteria which periodically swept through the streets of the towns. The conditions were similar to those in the late Middle Ages which had led to the destruction of many prosperous Jewish communities scattered through central Europe.

This intermixture of Romantic nationalism, religious revivalism, and democratic aspiration attained characteristic expression in the celebration held at the Wartburg in 1817 in memory of Luther's publication of his *Ninety-five Theses*. Here *Burschenschaft* students and members of Jahn's gymnastic clubs built a huge fire and threw into it non-*Volk* symbols of both reaction and liberalism: pigtailed hair, corporals' canes, and such diverse books as the "liberal" *Code Napoléon* and the conservative Kotzebue's history of Germany. This act may be regarded as a travesty of Luther's burning of the papal bull. But it was also a concrete expression of the belief that all cultural forms should come from within, from the *Volksgeist;* they should be the creation of the national genius purified of alien elements.

What caused the greatest disturbance, however, was the murder of Kotzebue in 1819 by the student, Karl Sand. August von Kotzebue, a very popular writer of rather mediocre plays, had spent some four decades in Russia and returned as a kind of political and cultural observer for the Russian government. Of a skeptical but conservative turn of mind, he had ridiculed the nationalistic intolerance and the excesses of the students. His murder was hailed as an act of tyrannicide in university circles.

Back of Sand, as his chief ideological influence, stood a Robespierre-like character such as we seldom encounter among the Germans. He was Karl Follen (1795–1840), the founder of the *Burschenschaft* at the University of Giessen, where he taught before he went to Jena. Influenced first by Arndt and Jahn, and then by Fichte, he became the leader of a radical wing of the *Burschenschaften*, the Unlimited (*Unbedingten*). He preached an equalitarian democracy and absolute subservience of the individual will to the general will of the group without regard to considerations of life or morality. After the assassination he fled first to Switzerland and then to America, where he became a professor of German literature at Harvard and also, in keeping with his background, a zealous crusader against slavery in this country. He was significant as the exponent of a Fichtean radicalism of thought and action involving the fusion of individual wills in the collective will through the crucible of action in behalf of the radical ideal. There were many of his kind in the Russian terrorist movement of the second half of the century and a few in its German counterpart in the period of the Weimar Republic.

REPRESSION AND THE CONSERVATIVE MIND

In the eyes of the governments, the murder of Kotzebue seemed to indicate the existence of a widespread conspiracy to overthrow the established order of things by revolutionary terrorism. The heads of the Austrian and Prussian governments now got together to push through the Diet of the Confederation a set of resolutions known from their place of publication as the Karlsbad Decrees (1819). They provided for the dissolution of the *Burschenschaften* and imposed a general system of censorship on the universities and on the publication of books and periodicals.

The movement for the suppression of liberal and nationalist opinion reached its greatest intensity in the so-called "harrassing of the demagogs," especially with the 1820 disturbances. Görres was forced to suspend publication of his famous paper, *Der Rheinische Merkur*. Schleiermacher and Arndt came under police observation and Arndt was dismissed from his professorship at Bonn. Jahn was imprisoned and his gymnastic clubs were dissolved. Wilhelm von Humboldt and Boyen were dismissed from the Prussian service. The first emigration of intellectuals to Switzerland and France now took place.

Revolutionary Romanticism, driven underground, lost much of its spontaneous insurgency. It was to appear in a new guise in the twentieth century.

During the decade after 1820, the conservative mood came to prevail more or less completely over the revolutionary tendencies stemming from both rationalism and Romanticism. This conservative frame of mind sank deep roots in the religious, cultural, and ideological soil of the Germanies. It exerted a greater influence there than elsewhere because it had a more enduring class basis in the gentry and upper middle class, who dominated political life, and in the professional groups of officials and academicians, who set the tone of intellectual life. Liberals and radicals represented only a fringe of political and social life, although they captured the sympathy of historians of a later, more liberal and democratic era.

Protestant and Roman Catholic churches remained the chief conservative buttresses of society. The religious ferment contributed little in the end toward the vitality of the "community of believers" as against ecclesiastical or state authority. Indeed, in the course of the next century the community of believers came to be transmuted into the solidarity of the proletariat and of the *völkisch* community—the church was relegated to the background.

Conservative Romanticism turned, as we have seen, to the Middle Ages as the ideal age when Christendom was united and when religious values attained supreme expression in crusade and cathedral. But the new Catholic religiosity had a distinctly subjective character; it was a rather singular compound of the aesthetic and emotional. The very influential works of the French writer and statesman Chateaubriand (1768–1845) gave a romantic aesthetic coloration to the splendor of liturgy and to the fervor of devotion. Thus the new religiosity was rendered palatable to those who, like Chateaubriand himself, had in their earlier years come under the sway of rationalistic skepticism but who now saw in religion a safeguard of the social order.

In Protestantism a similar fusion took place of the new emotional values of religion fostered by the pietistic awakening with the conservative political and social trends. The religious revival was stimulated by the War of Liberation, by the religion of the heart preached by Schleiermacher, and by the evangelical emphasis on pietistic and mystical devotion. But after some sporadic and sectarian insurgence, it flowed into the orthodox ecclesiastical molds, though permeating, as had early Pietism, ancient dogmas and beliefs with a new fervor and spiritual devotion. It thus gave up the idea of promoting a communal life of the faithful, independent of the state church.

The period immediately after the Napoleonic wars was also marked, as we have already noted, by economic and social phenomena which enhanced greatly both the intellectual and political ferment, and at the same time, promoted conservative reaction.

These phenomena were the product of dislocations arising out of war, natural catastrophe, and population growth. The conditions for widespread political and social unrest coming from below, such as a dominant urban society and industrial economy, did not as yet exist.

The population of central Europe increased greatly—by five million from 1816 to 1830, to a total of about thirty million, approximately 85 to 90 per cent of which might be classed as rural. There were only one or two cities of any considerable size; Berlin had a population of around 200,000 and Hamburg, the next largest city, about 100,000, but fully half the urban population lived in towns of less than 20,000.[2] In these small towns the gild economy, modified by the domestic system, still prevailed and agriculture was of course the chief basis of the economy. The agrarian crisis, greatly aggravated by the disastrous harvests of 1816 and 1817 and by very bountiful yields in subsequent years, produced tremendous fluctuations in the price of agricultural products and a complete dislocation of the rural economy. Stabilization, ushering in a period of general prosperity, did not set in until the late 1820's.

In general the large landowners of the eastern borderlands came out of the disturbances of war and economic crisis better off than they were before. The agrarian crisis forced some of the Junker landlords to sell out, but those that survived until the return of prosperity and adopted new agricultural technics stood on much sounder economic ground. The substitution of a cash relationship for the old patriarchal tie between landlord and peasant relieved the landlord of the old obligation of caring for his peasants.

The Prussian gentry also developed a class ideology with which they sought to buttress their new economic and political status. They came to form a conservative agrarian bloc which viewed the monarchy with some distrust since it had succumbed at one time to the pressure of the reformers. They were, of course, opposed to the emerging middle-class liberalism. Throughout most of the nineteenth century they supported collaboration with Austria as the best means of counteracting the forces which threatened the established order.

Their best and most influential representative during this period was the Junker landlord, Friedrich August Ludwig von der Marwitz (1777–1837). He came from a family which had furnished Prussia with six generals. He ascribed Prussian collapse in 1806–07 not to military inadequacy but to the corrosive influence on the Prussian state of Free Masons and middle-class liberals who sought to imitate the French. His deep Lutheran piety was affronted by the presumptuous rationalism of these movements, which undermined man's sense of dependence on God. He vigorously opposed the reforms of Stein and Hardenberg, the former for contributing to the uprooting of the peasantry and the nobility and the latter for promoting a bureaucratic government at the sole command of the monarch.

The influence of Möser is evident in Marwitz's basing the preeminence of the nobility on land and military service and in his reservation of the spheres of trade, learning, and the arts for the middle classes. Only by this functional division could these classes be prevented from becoming mere special interest groups. His brand of conservatism, like that of Möser, was pragmatic and opposed to that of Müller and Hegel, whose ideas he regarded as doctrinaire.

BIEDERMEIER

Except for a narrow but vocal fringe of intellectuals, the middle classes tended to sink back into their old provincial and traditional passivity. Their horizons were limited to family, friends, and economic pursuits. Complacency with the restoration of the good old times was combined with a general attitude of sociability and cheerfulness—the proverbial *Gemütlichkeit*.

The sentimentalism and classicism of the literature and art of the period from 1815 to 1848 is often referred to as *Biedermeier*, from a well-known comic literary character of the time. It attained its most characteristic expression in Austria, especially in Vienna. Austrian culture has always shown strong assimilative powers. In *Biedermeier* were incorporated baroque, romantic, and classical elements. Conservative Romantics had, as we have seen, found a most sympathetic climate in the southern Germanies. Classical elements predominated, not in the grand style of Weimar, however, but in a sober middle-class fashion. Baroque elements persisted most of all in the theater, which was throughout the nineteenth century the chief vehicle for Austrian cultural expression. Such great writers as Franz

Grillparzer (1792–1872) followed the models of the Spanish dramatists of the Golden Age, but without their baroque flamboyance. Grillparzer thought that the chief mission of Austria was to encourage the nationalities under her protection to develop their own native literatures and cultural individuality.

It was characteristic of *Biedermeier* that music, a real rival of the theater, moved into the middle-class home, where participation centered in the family circle. Its popularization is reflected in the works of Schubert, Strauss, and Mendelssohn. The great masters of the late eighteenth century, Mozart and Beethoven, were still influential; but, in general, music descended from the high flights of the baroque and classical to the level of a sentimentalism already foreshadowed in Rococo.

While the old aristocratic society continued with much brilliant splendor in salon and banquet hall, middle-class society, as it moved into the home, became definitely separated from it. Bourgeois interests centered in interior decoration, modes of dress, and the conviviality of the family circle and friends. Moreover, interest in language, song, and art as national or folk creations took the place of concern with the tension between ideal and real which had been expressed in baroque and classical art and literature. The popularization of fairy tale and legend by the Grimm brothers, the interest in ancient custom and usage, and the preoccupation with historical scene and pageantry in literature and art show that Romanticism had come down to earth.

CONSERVATIVE VERSUS RADICAL IDEOLOGY

Conservatism was still but a mood or at most a body of general attitudes and not the program of a party. It was opposed to "revolution from above and below"; that is, to the bureaucratic absolute state and to the democracy of popular sovereignty. Both, it was felt, undermined religious values and the corporative forms of society represented in church, estates, and gilds. Both contributed to the "atomization" of society, with its consequent leveling of traditional institutions and structures.

Conservatism in general lacked political and social dynamism, since it held to the organic view of slow growth and development. But Karl Ludwig Haller (1768–1854) gave it a new slant by arguing that feudal society arose on the basis of property seized by the strong, who thus came to rule over the weak. Since political power rested on property, it should be restored to the estates which had possessed it before monarchical absolutism set in. Haller appealed not to historical tradition, but to the natural instincts of competition. This naturalistic tendency did not become decisive in conservatism till the end of the nineteenth century when the idea of maintenance of medieval corporative forms and the restoration of a Christian ecumenical order had dissolved under the impact of industrialism and science.

It may be argued that the distinction between conservatism and radicalism was less significant for German ideological development than the cleavage between those who saw in the *Volk* the great creative source of cultural and institutional development and those who stressed the role of the state as the chief rational instrument for the attainment of human goals. This cleavage was implicit in Idealism—for example, between Herder and Kant, between Arndt and Fichte—and indeed was made most explicit in the polarity of Romanticism and Revolution. It was, moreover, a polarity to be found in both the conservative and radical camps.

The Romantic conservative wished to maintain the medieval corporative form, custom, and usage because these had made their appearance before the alien state arose and were therefore the product of spontaneous growth emanating from the *Volksgeist*. The Romantic radical was imbued with an almost fanatical devotion to what was peculiarly German and therefore to the purification of the *völkisch* community.

Among those who stressed the pre-eminence of the state there were some who, like the conservatives Metternich and Gentz, saw in it the means of containing social and cultural forces which threatened the order based on the state system and the equilibrium of classes. On the other hand, the radical Fichtean conception viewed the state as the embodiment of the collective moral will of the community which had come to rational self-consciousness.

EXALTATION OF THE STATE: RANKE AND HEGEL

The old Idealist polarity of *Geist* and *Staat*, of course, began to blur when *Geist* achieved virtual embodiment in the *Volk*, losing much of its universal moral implications, and conversely, when *Staat* acquired an ethical role in behalf of the realization of human freedom and so sloughed off much of its particularistic connotations. This very significant change was fostered especially by the historian Leopold von Ranke and the philosopher Georg Wilhelm Friedrich Hegel who contributed most perhaps toward bringing *Volk* and *Staat* into closer union in new syntheses of historical development which were to have a determining influence on German thinking during the remaining two-thirds of the century. Each contributed toward giving the state a dominant role in both conservative and radical thought.

Both Hegel (1770–1831) and his younger contemporary Ranke (1795–1886), came from the study of theology to a historical perspective—the one by way of Kantian philosophy and the other by way of classical philology. Both came to teach at the University of Berlin: Hegel in 1818 and Ranke in 1825. Here they represented opposing points of view from which to approach history.

Ranke approached the historical scene from the point of view of the individual destinies of the communities comprising the European family of states. Hegel sought to present the grand unfolding of the universal reason toward the achievement of its most complete self-consciousness and freedom in the Prussian state. In the attempt to unite the universal and the particular, both had as their underlying point of view the notion of an immanent divine providence in history; both regarded the Western community of peoples as the culminating goal of history; and both viewed the state as the rational frame within which a people must realize its peculiar destiny.

In dealing with the development of the European state system since the fifteenth century, Ranke viewed the idea and practice of reasons of state not merely in terms of the power requirements of a state, but also as its attempt to achieve a distinct national individuality by realizing its own peculiar interests within the western European cultural community. Struggles between states over power interests tended to be expressed in terms of issues stated on an idealistic level, thus avoiding at least the appearance of a naked power conflict. This European community, based on a fusion of Germanic and Latin values and institutions, constituted, therefore, the necessary idealistic frame within which the state system could operate.

The state system recognized, at least implicitly, the inviolable character of the individual communities to be guarded against annihilation or domination by maintaining a balance of power among the various states. Religious or ideological wars are bad because they subordinate individual state interests to universal considerations, in this way producing international civil wars which threaten the very existence of the independent sovereign states.

Ranke's many histories, written during a long lifetime of uninterrupted scholarship and covering many different countries, concentrated particularly upon the centuries between the fifteenth and the nineteenth when the European community of states was emerging. These histories have been regarded as the supreme literary and critical models in the realm of political history by German historians down to the present.

Two points of view which Ranke stressed have influenced later German historians particularly. One, by arguing that "each age stands immediate to God," Ranke virtually repudiated the notion that past ages should be measured by the yardstick of progress to determine their contribution to the present. Each age should be viewed in terms of its own values and each nation should also be so regarded. His historical relativism was contrary to Hegel's assumption of an all-enveloping purpose running through history. To Ranke history revealed only a plurality of individual goals whose total significance was hidden.

In the other, he subordinated the internal affairs of countries to their external relations on the ground that the primary concern of a state should be the maintenance of its sovereignty and power in order that it might be able to safeguard its own individual ethos. This idea contributed to the stress laid by later German historians on the primacy of foreign over internal affairs in the interpretation of the development of a nation. Both the revolutionary and the romantic doctrines had held that the external relations should stem from the inner drive toward freedom expressed through constitutional guarantees and democratic participation, or through the cultural creativity of the *Volksgeist*.

Hegel was also concerned with the state, not primarily in terms of the particular reasons of state but as the highest expression of the development of the universal reason. The cosmic reason in its march through history had brought to the fore the Greeks, the Romans, and the Germans as its peculiar embodiment during their appearance on the stage of history. Each of these peoples, during its appearance on the world stage, made its contribution to the advancement of the universal reason by virtue of its peculiar political and cultural achievements. The whole process, he assumed, reached its consummation in the present in that rational ideal order which was the essence of the Prussian bureaucratic-military state.

Hegel sought especially to demonstrate that reason does not express itself in ideal static forms which are suspended above the concrete events of history. It becomes embodied in the individual concrete historical states, empires, artistic styles, philosophies, and religions. The process by which the reason manifests itself is through the union of opposites which operates in historical development as it does in the logic of the individual's reasoning. It assumes that any position taken with regard to any problem has only a partial and not an absolute character and therefore immediately calls forth a negative position. The reconciliation of opposites takes place in the dialectical fusion of thesis and antithesis to form a third higher level of synthesis. This process is continuous in history and leads to a progressive unfolding of all the potentialities implicit in the universal reason.

Hegel agreed with Ranke that whatever form of state and culture is achieved at a given time is appropriate to that age but, contrary to Ranke, he also regarded each age as a stage in the onward march of the universal reason toward its consummation: hence, the ambiguity of the famous Hegelian formula: "what is real is rational and what is rational is real." To emphasize the real—the historical existent—as the rational would please the conservative interested in justifying the status quo. Conversely, the radical would stress the other half of the formula: "that the rational is the real" as the embodiment of his revolutionary principle, that history is undoubtedly moving toward the ideal society. The Prussian conservatives stressed the first, while radicals such as Karl Marx appropriated the second along with the conception of an inevitable dialectical process in history moving not toward the Prussian state but toward proletarian society.

Hegel's projected synthesis of the unfolding of the reason in history with the expression of individuality in peoples and cultures marks the end of the great creative phase of German idealistic thought. After him there seemed nothing else to do but to examine the historical processes themselves to see how the reason was manifesting itself. Only the radicals such as Marx and his followers dealt explicitly with the question of the reconciliation of the revolutionary leap with organic historical development. Most conservative and liberal historians after the middle of the nineteenth century adopted a counter-revolutionary stance in assuming that all historical development takes place by minute steps. However, between 1830 and 1850, when the middle class was still striving for political and social liberty and equality, revolutionary insurgency still loomed large on its horizon.

REVOLUTIONARY AND LIBERAL FERMENT

The twenty years from 1830 to 1850 began and ended with waves of revolution. Revolution supplanted Romanticism as the main motive force. The chief impulse to political and social agitation in the Germanies came from France. The mood of reaction against alien influences which had characterized the *Burschenschaften* movement was almost wholly absent. An internationale of societies, clubs, and intellectuals emerged during the 1830's and 1840's in opposition to the conservative internationale of monarchy, aristocracy, and church, which thus far had been dominant. Vienna was the headquarters of the latter; Paris that of the former.

The chief intellectual movements, Young Germany and the Left Hegelians, aimed at the emancipation of man from convention, tradition, and religion. Railroad building and customs unions created a new economic atmosphere of liberation of trade and industry from the confinement of *Kleinstaaterei* and paved the way for the Industrial Revolution and national unification.

These movements provided the chief drives in early liberalism which took a middle position between conservatism and radicalism, aiming more at removing traditional shackles than at preserving or creating positive forms of community life.

The establishment of middle-class rule in France by the July-Revolution of 1830 and in England by the Reform Act of 1832 was achieved virtually without bloodshed and violent disturbance of the political and social order. This result may be attributed to the fact that the changes involved went no farther than the establishment of the political pre-eminence of the upper middle class, comprising people of culture and property, and the continued exclusion of the great mass of the lower population who had by their agitation and demonstrations contributed greatly to the transformation. The lower middle-class groups and workers of the towns naturally felt themselves betrayed. But middle-class liberal opinion in general felt confident that fundamental reforms could be achieved without far-reaching disturbances in the social order. Revolution was after all a two-edged sword; it might bring overthrow of reactionary government and establishment of constitutional freedoms, but, as the French Revolution had demonstrated, it might also go beyond the intention of those who initiated it and bring mob action, dictatorship, and war.

In the Germanies there were no uprisings of importance, only incidents like those immediately after 1815. Comparable to the Wartburg Festival was the Hambach gathering in the Rhineland in 1832 where some 25,000 people assembled to listen to speeches dealing with freedom and national unity. Unlike the Wartburg scene, the Hambach gathering reflected a prevailing interest in republicanism and European confederation.

In the following year a heterogeneous band of students, townsmen, and fugitives attacked the guard at Frankfort in a demonstration which they hoped would spark a revolution. New measures of repression of liberals and democratic sympathizers were inaugurated which, however, hit the small fry more than the prominent literary figures and academicians.

In 1837, however, seven professors at the University of Göttingen were dismissed for protesting against the suspension of the constitution by the new Hanoverian ruler. Their dismissal and the banishment of three of them from the country, including Jacob Grimm, aroused a storm of protest. The predominance of the academic element in these and other incidents is indicative of how thin the veneer of liberal opinion was; the bulk of the populace remained passive.

The chief organ of liberal thought was the *Encyclopedia of Political Science*, published by Karl von Rotteck and Karl Welcker, which exerted widespread influence between 1834 and 1848. Both were professors at the University of Freiburg in Baden, which had the most liberal government among the middle states. Both also served as representatives in the lower house of the legislature. Rotteck considered the cause of freedom involving liberty of the press, the liquidation of peasant burdens, and constitutional government as more important than the cause of national unity. This accent distinguished the left-wing liberal from the right-wing.

The *Encyclopedia* was the first work of its kind in the Germanies which avoided the extremes of conservative reaction and of radical revolution and sought to find a middle ground. Intended as an instrument of political education, it shows, however, in its incoherence and lack of clarity, the confusions of liberal opinion at the time. After all, liberalism, like conservatism, was still a state of mind and did not become the program of a political party until after the revolution of 1848. Liberal ideas were therefore still in a state of suspension. Uppermost in liberal minds was the rather ingenuous notion of the conflict between the ideal of freedom and equality and the reality of despotism and aristocratic privilege.

One source of confusion lay in the fact that liberals, in their admiration of the Western countries, were divided as to their preference for France or England. France stood for the revolutionary leap, for natural rights and constitutions framed by conventions. England was the symbol of organic growth through custom and parliamentary usages. Those inclined toward republicanism naturally turned toward France, while those under the strong influence of the historical school of Savigny and Grimm looked in the direction of England.

YOUNG GERMANY

Much more radical was the association known as Young Germany, which was inspired by the Italian nationalist Mazzini, who formed Young Italy for the purpose of enlisting the youth in the cause of revolution. The German counterpart had its center in Switzerland among the fugitives driven from the Germanies by the new repressive measures. Its sporadic agitation and even terrorist action directed against tyranny and treason within its ranks is reminiscent of the left wing of the *Burschenschaften.*

More significant and to be distinguished from the above political association was the other Young Germany movement comprising a group of young writers bound together by literary friendships and by a common interest in the emancipation of man from the bonds of conventional morality, orthodox religion, and the political censor. Like the writers of the *Sturm und Drang,* whom they greatly admired, they were rampantly individualistic and shunned rootedness in a particular social situation or vocation. In opposition to the attachment of conservative romantics to the cultural and historical heritage of a particular country or region, they exhibited a radical cosmopolitanism.

Their two most influential writers, Heinrich Heine (1797–1856) and Ludwig Börne (1786–1837), made Paris their headquarters. To these young Jews from the Rhineland, the *Biedermeier* atmosphere and political reaction in the Germanies was stifling. In Paris there was freedom of expression; literature and politics served as mutually fructifying forces. In the Germanies there was no politics, and literature was still dominated by the serene classicism of Goethe or the stodgy romanticism of *Biedermeier.* Both Heine and Börne became what today might be called foreign correspondents, in that they reported in letters to friends and newspapers the news on art, literature, and politics from the cultural capital of Europe. They presented events graphically in a journalistic manner, and their novels were written in the form of letters and diaries. Descriptions of journeys served frequently as vehicles for highly realistic portrayals of national and class peculiarities.

In place of the Olympian detachment of Idealism and the absorption in a glorified past by Romanticism, literature was now to become the means of political and social transformation. Outside of Heine, most of what the young generation produced had little permanent aesthetic value or interest. But they were seriously concerned with galvanizing the moribund political and social life of the Germanies into action and were willing to suffer suppression of their writings and even imprisonment to bring down the citadels of absolutism, orthodoxy, and social convention. The cultivation of an aesthetic personality combined with social radicalism contributed to a tension between the poles of anarchical individualism and a yearning for communal solidarity. They came out particularly for the emancipation of women and Jews, who were to be accorded equal rights. They derived their catch-phrase, "emancipation of the flesh," from French Saint Simonian socialism.

Saint Simonian socialism became the religion of this Young Germany. It combined notions to be found both in the French Enlightenment and German Idealistic philosophy. Pantheistic religion, socialistic mutualism, and technocratic industrialism were to be combined to produce the new heaven on earth which this utopian generation envisioned. Above all, the dualism of spirit and matter by which Christianity had come to condemn the life of the senses was to be overcome in a functionally organized society in which all peoples would be united in a universal religion of humanity. Saint Simonianism assumed that this age of solidarity and harmony would mark the fulfillment of the previous ages in which man had looked at the world first through the eyes of myth and legend and then through the abstractions of theology and metaphysics. Man stood on the threshold of a Third Age of positive concrete knowledge devoted to human welfare.

A tremendous optimism prevailed toward the possibilities of human perfection—if only the bonds which shackled man's good impulses could be thrown off. It represented generally throughout Europe a great resurgence of the eighteenth-century rationalistic point of view. In Germany, it collided not only with the conservative tendency to emphasize historical organic development through custom and tradition, but with that romantic Christian-Germanic nationalism of the revived *Burschenschaften* which hated the internationalisms of liberalism, socialism, and Catholicism. In Wolfgang Menzel (1798–1873), who for a time set himself up as literary arbiter, we see this radical romantic nationalism moving toward amalgamation with the conservative right. At one time associated in the *Burschenschaften* with the radical republicanism of Karl Follen, he had fled to Switzerland, but upon return, and particularly after the July Revolution, he turned increasingly against his erstwhile friends among the Young Germany writers. He denounced them in 1835 before the Diet as purveyors of subversive ideas against the Christian-Germanic religion, social order, and morality.[3] His literary criticism was inclined toward a *völkisch* and racial point of view, which was later to find acceptance on the extreme right.

Those to the left of center who favored, in varying degree, political democracy along with social and economic solidarity felt that their hopes had been betrayed by the upper middle class, whose chief concern now was for the protection of property and humanistic culture as evidences of man's spiritual progress. The consequent sense of resentment toward and isolation from bourgeois society led to a deliberate attack upon the religious and philosophic presuppositions of its *Weltanschauung*. In the Germanies this attack along with that coming from the romantic-conservative right greatly contributed to the failure of characteristic bourgeois political and social values in achieving the ascendancy they did in France and England.

THE LEFT HEGELIANS

In this opposition, the most radical in philosophic point of view and influential in the long run were the Young or Left Hegelians. Most prominent were Ludwig Feuerbach, Bruno Bauer, Max Stirner, David Friedrich Strauss, Karl Marx, and Sören Kierkegaard. Their attack upon the religious assumptions of the existing order was to have the most far-reaching effects in the development of a radical secularism and existentialism, expressed variously as idealistic agnosticism, materialistic socialism, or spiritual anarchism. There emerged a new underground of sectarian opposition which threatened not only the conservative world based on religious sanction but the liberal-bourgeois society based on the autonomy of the spiritual sphere.

Many reflective minds were aware that the demon of revolution had been exorcized neither by the conservative restoration nor by liberal reformism but presented new and terrifying possibilities, through rationalism, of the dissolution of all political and social bonds. Both Goethe and Hegel had at the basis of their thought the notion of a rightful order, represented for Goethe in the organic harmony and unity of nature and, for Hegel, in the organic revelation of the reason in history. The new radical point of view, how-ever, was being oriented increasingly toward polar extremes between which one continually oscillated, with no fixed position from which one could see the world and man in perspective. Reaction toward polar extremes threatened to become the determining influence rather than an orientation from a stable humanist middle position, one which would be taken for granted by all intellectuals.[4]

The Left Hegelians have been compared with the late medieval Spirituals who, it will be recalled, had derived revolutionary conse-quences from Joachim of Flora's conception of a coming Third Age, the fulfillment of the whole course of history.[5] So also Hegel's dialectical process was lifted out of its own theological matrix by his followers and applied as a technic of undermining the presump-tions of church, class, and nation. The Spirituals had been driven into an underground opposition by their attack on the basic assump-tion that the existing church would usher in the end-situation. Like-wise the Left Hegelians attacked the presumption of bourgeois so-ciety that it was a reflection of a divinely sanctioned cosmic order toward which all history had been moving and were driven into a foxhole existence. Feuerbach, Bauer, and Stirner were dismissed from their teaching positions, and, in the case of the last two, reduced to the direst circumstances. Marx, among others, was forced into exile to live always in jeopardy of the police. The most lonely figure among them was probably Kierkegaard, a Dane, who had first come under the spell of Hegel and then turned against him and religious orthodoxy to turn inward, as Luther had, to find God in the isolation of human solitariness.

The significant writings of this group of radical thinkers were concentrated in the 1840's and reveal a remarkable unity of outlook, especially in the repudiation of the presuppositions of the bourgeois *Weltanschauung*. Their general point of departure was the second half of Hegel's formula, namely, that the "rational is the real." All institutions, religions, and philosophies, as the expression of the on-ward march of reason, have no special sanctity in themselves; they only mark the transition to its next creations. Christianity, capital-ism, and the state are but way stations on the road toward the even-tual consummation of the reason. For every positive historical form its negative future creation can be projected.

The attack on contemporary values and institutions was directed first against religion as the source of the sanctity of historical, political, and social forms. Religion had of course been closely yoked with the state since the Reformation. Now Hegel cemented the union by making the universal reason culminate in Protestant Christianity and the Prussian state. In them was achieved both the coincidence and consummation of the historical development and of the dialectical process of the reason.

Hegel also equated the Third Age with the modern epoch as the consummation of the ancient and medieval ages. Thus the Age of the Spirit was virtually realized and no longer to be awaited. The philosopher gave up his role as prophet and became a mere functionary in the existing order. Hegel brought to an end the spiritualistic and idealistic quest which had been the motive force in German thought for centuries.[6]

The Left Hegelians, however, employed Hegel's own logic to disrupt this identity of reason and actuality and in so doing contributed greatly not only toward undermining faith in historical Christianity but also to the unmasking of religious-philosophical illusions in general.

David Friedrich Strauss, in his *Life of Jesus,* published in 1835, pointed out that what we have before us in the orthodox portrayal is the mythical conception of Jesus originally derived from contemporary Jewish Messianism but greatly elaborated in the course of history. The Jesus of history and the Christ of faith are not to be confused. The latter, as an afterthought of a later time, has a history of its own, independent of the actual person whose meaning it ostensibly seeks to assess.

Ludwig Feuerbach, in his *Nature of Christianity* (1841), proceeded even more radically in declaring that religion arises out of man's egotistical impulses on which man builds a superstructure of theological ideas which are illusory. Only the general idea of humanity has any reality by virtue of its ethical consequences, which contribute to tolerance and human brotherhood.

Max Stirner, in his *The Ego and His Own* (1844), in which the theoretical foundations of anarchism are laid down, went beyond Feuerbach in arguing that all ideals are illusory. There is no reality but the ego and the objectives it sets itself.

For Karl Marx (1818–1883), ideals and ideas were merely egoistical reflexes of classes. He was the son of a Jewish family of rabbinical background who had gone over to Protestantism. He studied law and philosophy at Bonn, Berlin, and Jena. In his doctoral dissertation he presented a critical approach to Hegelian Idealism by way of a consideration of ancient Epicureanism. He joined the circle of Young Hegelians around Bruno Bauer. Failure to gain a teaching position at the University of Berlin because of his radical ideas led him into newspaper work. When the authorities suppressed the *Rheinishen Zeitung,* which he edited, Marx and his wife migrated to Paris in 1842. There he came in contact with socialist and communist circles and began his very fruitful theoretical and polemical labors. There also he began his lifelong friendship with Friedrich Engels (1820–1895).

Hegel's dialectical conception of the historical process and Feuerbach's criticism of religion were the chief points of departure for Marx. He argued that Feuerbach was right in making an attack upon religion the springboard for the freeing of men's minds. This was necessary before one could proceed to a criticism of society. Religion had throughout history served dominant groups as the chief means of turning the exploited away from remedying their circumstances in the here and now by holding out the prospect of a heavenly paradise. It had thus served as "the opium for the people."

However, Marx also argued that Feuerbach had set up another illusion in his conception of the brotherhood of humanity. This was only another religion. In the dialectical process of history, capitalists and workers represent opposite poles; the former are bound to be superseded by the latter as a consequence of economic and technological progress. Marx was singularly persuasive in his clarion call to revolution, *The Communist Manifesto,* which he began to compose in 1847 in collaboration with Engels at the suggestion of a communist group in Brussels. Marx had found refuge there after being ousted from Paris by the police at the instigation of the Prussian authorities.

ECONOMIC LIBERATION

The theme of liberation and emancipation in thought was the dominant motif in the movement which culminated in the revolutions of 1848. Reference should be made, however, to certain de-

velopments such as the customs union and railway building as forces
which sought to liberate economic enterprise within a national frame.

Adam Smith (1723–1790) had gained increasing recognition in
Germany since the publication of his *Wealth of Nations* in 1776. His
ideas acquired general currency in the Germanies in the early nineteenth century, mainly through university professors and administrative officials. Economic conditions favored liberation from the
multiplicity of tariffs and tolls associated with *Kleinstaaterei*. While
no tariff duties were imposed on the borders of the German Confederation, at least ten different ones were exacted on goods trans-
ported from Berlin to Switzerland. Along with the corporal's cane,
the beam of the toll gate had become another symbol of *Kleinstaaterei*
and tyranny.

The real drive for a customs union came from Prussia. Here the
influence of Smith's ideas among upper officials and her special economic needs promoted the movement. The scattered character of
the Prussian territories, separated from each other by other states or
enveloping islands of foreign territory, made the customs restrictions
especially onerous.

Another stimulus came from railroad building. The first German
railway was constructed in 1839 between Leipzig and Dresden. Most
of the rolling stock of the early railroads was secured from England.
In the 1840's, however, construction of locomotives began to make
headway. The consequent demand for iron stimulated heavy industry. Also, the steamboat was brought into increasing use on the
Rhine, especially to haul barges. The telegraph developed in 1830 by
Gauss and Weber at Göttingen and Werner von Siemens' production
of gutta-percha for covering wires were indicative of German participation in the great strides made by technological progress at the
time.

The chief intellectual agitator for railways and for customs union, Friedrich List (1789–1846), was also the most eloquent exponent
of a national economy which embodied the basic idea of free trade
and free enterprise within a national tariff wall raised against foreigners.

List, a Wurtemberger, had risen from the position of a minor
bureaucrat to professor of political science at Tübingen. He soon
found himself at odds with the dominant economic philosophy at the

university, which unreservedly favored the free trade ideas of Adam Smith. List was an advocate of free trade within states but not between states. He argued that Smith's idea of free trade in a world market based on the specialized needs and capacities of particular regions was merely a rationalization of the existing dominant industrial position of Great Britain. By virtue of her advanced machine industry, she could dominate a free world market and the Germanies might remain a largely agrarian country, an economic colony of Britain.

The enthusiastic and often aggressive way in which he put forward these ideas caused him to run afoul of the authorities. He was not only forced out of Tübingen but compelled to leave the country. He eventually found asylum, like a considerable number of his compatriots, in the United States. There he came in contact with a young and vigorous country engaged in building up an infant industry under the effective shelter of a protective tariff. On his return to Germany as United States consul at Leipzig he resumed his agitation and presented his chief ideas in the very influential work, *A National System of Economy*, published in 1841.

List argued that a national economy should be built up as a means of promoting a harmonious development of the creative powers of a people. Here he leaned on the ideas of the conservative Romantic Adam Müller, rather than on those of Adam Smith. Müller viewed economic development not as autonomous, as Smith did, but as an integral part of the national culture. List took over this Romantic conception of totality but laid stress on the dynamic release of creative forces within the frame of political and economic unity rather than on the perpetuation of a medieval corporate structure. The nation-state, as the chief carrier of culture, should serve as a mediator between the individual and humanity. His nationalism, like that of Fichte and Wilhelm von Humboldt, stressed the idea that it is a people which makes its peculiar contribution to the total cultural progress of humanity, and not individuals in the competition of the world arena.

List died a frustrated suicide in 1846, but his ideas of a national economy were to have a great influence later—modified greatly, it is true, to suit the needs of the Bismarckian *Reich*. In his enthusiastic faith in ideas as the motive forces in human affairs and in his optimistic belief in the capacity of mankind to see the way to a better society, he exemplified the dominant idealistic character of the liberalism of this period.

Most liberals and radicals of the time lacked a realistic program of social and economic action, partly because the Germanies were suspended between the old agrarian and corporative world and a new industrial capitalist order, just on the horizon. There were plenty of advocates of various types of social utopia, but these had only a sporadic effect upon public opinion. Even *The Communist Manifesto* of 1848 was utopian as far as the Germanies were concerned because its appeal to the worker to throw off his chains could find little response in a land as yet without a real proletariat.

With respect to the national question there was the same ambiguous state of mind. Enthusiasm for Western liberalism and cosmopolitanism appeared cheek by jowl with outbursts of nationalistic fervor, such as occurred when the French seemed to be advancing on the Rhine in 1840. This advance produced the two most famous national hymns, *Die Wacht am Rhine* and *Deutschland über Alles*. Both were the work of poets belonging to Young Germany.

Liberalism found itself confronted by the persistence of the old hierarchical social order reinforced by the fact that each strata was becoming class conscious and developing its own ideology. On the one hand, there was the conservative order, buttressed by the state and by a romantic ideology, and entrenched in the ruling classes in church and society. On the other hand, from below came the rising forces of social discontent among artisans, peasants, and industrial workers rendered articulate by radical intellectuals. In the end it was the tragic fate of German liberalism to be crushed between these upper and nether millstones.

THE FAILURE OF LIBERAL REVOLUTION

Before the mid-century there was no general consciousness of a menace from below among middle-class liberals. The alliance with popular forces in the achievement of human freedom and national self-determination had been implicitly accepted. Only in the course of the revolution of 1848 and especially in its aftermath of disillusionment and sense of betrayal on both sides did the cleavage become completely manifest.

The European revolutions which began in February of 1848 were not unexpected. Among conservatives and liberals alike there was the feeling that the atmosphere was charged with impending revolutionary change. The conflagration was set off by the insurrection of the 24th of February in Paris. Uprisings spread like a chain reaction through middle Europe during March, April, and May. The widespread character of these revolutionary disturbances were probably due to a common frame of mind induced by the dominance of intellectuals in the social and cultural life of the times.[7] The consequent common field of revolutionary forces and ideas may also account for the spontaneity of the movement when compared with the twentieth-century revolutions.

Likewise the sudden collapse of the established regimes may be attributed to the divided state of mind among conservatives, arising out of the conflict between the reverence for historical and traditional institutions and the necessity of appealing to the power of the state when these forms ceased to hold their own.

The liberals were caught in a similar dilemma. The sudden collapse of the old state powers was disconcerting to liberal intellectuals. It left a vacuum of power and authority into which revolutionary forces from below might flow, accompanied by the threat of intervention from abroad. Constitutional and parliamentary forms of government were to be achieved only within the frame of the established order of royal power and administrative organization. The energies of the people, both economic and political, were to be released, but within the frame of a state strong enough to maintain order within and safeguard the national integrity.

Sudden collapse of state authority and popular insurgence were identified in memory with the War of Liberation against Napoleon. Then they were both reactions against foreign domination; now popular insurgence had contributed to the very collapse of state power. Many conservatives and certainly all liberals came to romanticize the episode of the War of Liberation without fully realizing this distinction. Both groups were motivated by the supreme desire to recapture the sense of a common great effort which would fuse divergent groups and classes into a united national self-determination. The *Volk* would thus come to self-consciousness in the crystallization of common aspiration and action.

Many liberals soon became uncomfortably aware, however, that national insurgence directed against the government rather than a foreign power had revolutionary implications beyond their intentions. Left-wing liberals and most radicals thought in terms of revolutionary action by the Third or Fourth Estates which now would declare themselves to be the sovereign nation, as in the French Revolution. But most Germans, both conservative and liberal, thought of the nation in the Romantic sense of *Volk*, that is, as a cultural individuality rather than in the revolutionary sense of popular sovereignty.

Their idealistic reliance upon the moral forces of the *Volk* and their consequent lack of a realistic appreciation of political power undermined the liberals' position in the course of the revolutionary disturbances. They approved the suppression of radical democratic and socialist movements in Cologne, Baden, Vienna, and Frankfort as necessary to the maintenance of order; they assumed that the spontaneous expression of moral and spiritual forces could only take place under such instituted order. They gave their approval for much the same reason that Luther approved the suppression of the peasant revolts: only within instituted order could the freedom of faith be realized.

The liberals did not realize that state power is never neutral but rather the instrument of group interests and that their turn was coming next. They were more concerned, in the last analysis, with maintaining the two props of liberal middle-class existence, property and culture, than with freedom under constitutional and parliamentary government. The radical movements in their eyes presented the chief menace to these props and the prospect of the arbitrary tyranny of the vulgar mob.

The collapse of the great hopes of 1848 marked also the beginning of the great exodus to the New World from central Europe. More than a million Germans left in the years 1849 to 1851. During the middle decades of the nineteenth century the United States came to be regarded as utopia by the people of western Europe. Its competing utopia was that presented to the workers by Karl Marx in *The Communist Manifesto*. Marx and his associate, Engels, felt that the workers' turn had come with the debacle of the hopes of the liberal bourgeoisie in central Europe. They did not appreciate the new vitality given to the power state by Bismarck nor did they recognize the dynamic qualities embodied in the notion of the *Volk* as it came to be divorced from liberal idealism and yoked with myth and race, as in the music and writings of Richard Wagner.

THE ACCENTUATION OF CENTRIFUGAL FORCES

When we compare the ideological clashes of the first half of the nineteenth century with the comparable confessional conflicts of the Reformation period we are struck by one fundamental resemblance, namely, their inconclusive character. In the confessional conflicts none of the various reform movements—Erasmian, Lutheran, or sectarian—achieved any decisive victory. So also none of the ideologies which emanated from revolution and Romanticism succeeded in attaining ascendancy. Like the confessions, they failed to overcome the centrifugal tendencies within the hierarchical social structure and those of state particularism.

By the mid-nineteenth century these centrifugal forces had been in fact accentuated by ideological drives, and the obstacles to political and cultural unification seemed insurmountable.

The Napoleonic reorganization had led to the liquidation of a whole mélange of ecclesiastical principalities, free cities, and feudal structures, and consolidated some three hundred of them, leaving thirty-nine states. Along with this amalgamation had come the final dissolution of the Holy Roman Empire. But instead of promoting national unity, power politics merely gained complete ascendency with the wiping out of gradations of sovereignty by the submergence of princes, bishops, and free cities in the individual states. Central Europe was thus completely integrated with the general European state system. Ranke and Hegel provided historical and philosophical justification for the pre-eminence of the state as power by arguing that it was the necessary vehicle for the realization of the highest moral goals of a people.

The conception of *Volk* as *Geist* had arisen in the attempt to find a binding force above and beyond state particularism. But the Romantic idea of *Volksgeist* as inner creativity seemed incompatible with the state as power. Ranke and Hegel in trying to bridge the chasm ended up by according to the existing power states a predominant rational and historical role. Could a Prussian or Austrian state patriotism be made the basis of German union? If so, what happened then to the *Volk* as *Geist*, which presumably stood above state particularism? Two opposing answers appeared during the next century: the Bismarckian *Reich* sought to achieve unity around the axis of the Prussian state with the exclusion of Austria; and the brief and explosive Third *Reich* sought to make the German *Volk* the dynamic unifying force of a greater Germany. Both failed because a one-sided emphasis either on a particular state or on a unique *Volk* generated hegemonial drives which led to disastrous wars with great coalitions of powers.

The problem was made even more complex by the persistence of two traditional forces juxtaposed to state and *Volk:* the ideal of *Reich* and the hierarchical class structure.

Though the Holy Roman Empire had been officially dissolved and supplanted by the anemic German Confederation, the ideal of *Reich* had been revitalized by the Romantic return to the medieval notion of an ecumenical union of peoples to overcome the existing rivalries of states and nations. The mid-century revolutions had shown that the German manifestation of national consciousness provoked similar reactions among the peoples along the eastern border who had been cultural protégés of the Germans since the early *sacrum imperium.* The Czechs, the most completely Germanized, had been in the forefront in promoting a Slavic renaissance directed against German hegemony. How could national unification be reconciled with the German cultural hegemony and mission to the east?

The traditional hierarchical class structure remained intact largely because the gentry retained a pre-eminent political and military position and social prestige. Consequently, the middle class, sandwiched between them and the lower orders, peasants and workers, did not have the feeling of being the embodiment of the nation as the politically and socially dominant French bourgeoisie did. Lutheranism in particular stressed the importance of being content with and active in one's divinely ordained station in the hierarchical social order.

Marx's anti-religious propaganda was directed not toward national unification but toward the accentuation of class cleavage. The worker, he contended, has neither church nor fatherland—no more than he has property—and thus has no common bond with the sacrosanct social order. Marxism succeeded to a marked degree in dissolving the religious tie but not the national one, as National Socialism later demonstrated.

State, *Volk, Reich,* and class increasingly ceased to be regarded as expressions of such universal forces as moral imperative, protean world spirit, and sacred *ordo* and became merely manifestations of the spirit of an age (*Zeitgeist*). Bismarck, Marx, Wagner, and their successors down to the present were to be mainly guided by this historical orientation of their mutual appropriateness to the needs of the time. Concentration upon the needs of the present seen against a historical background eventually led to the great technological breakthrough of the twentieth century, with its accent on obsolescence.

3

From Historicism to Technical Existenz
1850-1950

XI

Ideas: Myth, Reasons of State, and Economic Determinism

The ideological conflict lost much of its intensity after the midcentury revolutions: first, because a new era of repression and reaction set in during which the former leaders of liberal and radical opinion were scattered and driven underground or into exile; second, the ideologies lost much of their idealistic drive by being embodied in the programs of political parties concerned with problems of organization, parliamentary tactics, and propaganda.

THE STIMULATION OF ARTISTIC, SOCIAL, AND POLITICAL ACTION

A corresponding change in accent occurred with respect to *Volk*, state, and class from a concern with their substantival character to how they might be energized to counteract either German decadence, Prussian extinction, or proletarian degradation. Richard Wagner sought to revitalize the German *Volk* through the combination of a racial myth with a fusion of music and the arts of the theater. Karl Marx sought to instill a sense of mission in the proletariat, who would be the inevitable heirs of all technical progress. Otto von Bismarck sought to imbue the Prussian body politic with the same will to ascendancy that had animated its great rulers, and thus contain the forces of nationalism and democracy which threatened its very existence.

It is apparent that these tendencies within *Volk*, state, and class promoted divergence. This was the consequence of a deliberate adjustment of means to ends in attempting to make the Baroque theater a cult center, the socialist party the means of arousing the proletariat to self-consciousness, and the Prussian state the focus of a national patriotism. As the old spiritual and idealistic matrix was pushed to the background, the primacy of means over ends was the natural result.

While Wagner was oriented toward the past as myth and Marx toward the future as utopia, Bismarck lived most completely in the historical present. Consequently, the influence of Wagner and Marx was, of course, generally pervasive and long range rather than politically immediate. In the end the proletarian socialist movement and the more incoherent body of racial notions and myths were to undermine the Bismarckian *Reich*.

The early ideological careers of Richard Wagner (1813–1883) and Karl Marx (1818–1883) followed a somewhat similar pattern. Both were influenced by the anti-Christian point of view of Feuerbach, and both originally subscribed to a revolutionary republicanism which they later abandoned for a more "fundamental" point of view which would overcome the alienation of modern man from the basic racial or communal sources of humanity. Both participated in the turbulent events of 1848–49 and were afterward forced into exile. But here the similarity ends. Marx continued while in exile in England to agitate for the revolutionary overthrow of the existing social order. Wagner, returning to Germany, greeted the new Bismarckian *Reich* with enthusiasm at first, then followed Nietzsche in being disillusioned by its materialistic pursuit of power. Wagner's basic notions about race and myth, which were at variance with the fundamental premises of the Second *Reich*, prepared the way for the Third *Reich*.

THE TOTAL WORK OF ART AND RACIAL MYTH

After 1848, Wagner's revolutionary *élan* flowed into the creation of a new art form through which the regeneration of German culture might be achieved. He became absorbed in the development of the *Gesamtkunstwerk*, the total work of art, which, as in ancient Greek tragedy and Baroque opera, would combine music and drama. These, as we have seen, were the dominant arts of the nineteenth century, but, like the contemporary visual arts—painting, sculpture, and architecture—they had become separated from each other. Painting and sculpture had become independent of architecture, the great public and organic art. Now, in the bourgeois age, the autonomy of the arts made them serve a merely private and decorative function. Analogically, Marx argued that the deliberate separation of the bourgeois capitalistic order—that is, the economic functions of production and exchange of goods—from politics and society caused the latter to lose their real function and become merely decorative, at least for the mass of the population.

In his *Gesamtkunstwerk*, Wagner would not link music and drama, as in the Baroque opera, so that music would serve mainly a decorative function with respect to the dramatic action. He wanted to achieve an organic union in which each mode of expression retained its individuality, with no subordination of one to the other. In his great music dramas, especially in *The Ring of the Nibelung*, both music and dramatic action carry the theme. In the tone poems music reflects the mood and passion. The leitmotiv is the special musical theme associated with an individual character or a dramatic idea throughout an opera. Nonetheless, music becomes the medium of the sensuous form, while the drama carries the action.

Wagner was also greatly influenced by the idea that Western culture was decadent—an idea which gained increasing acceptance among literati and intellectuals as the century drew to a close. The Romantics had already argued that increasing rationalism would cause Western culture to lose contact with its grass-roots sources in the myths of the race. In this connection Wagner began his association with Friedrich Nietzsche, then a young professor of the classics at Basel, Switzerland. Nietzsche emphasized in his work, *The Birth of Tragedy out of the Spirit of Music* (1873) the Dionysian myth of creative intoxication, in which were to be found the origins of Greek drama, as the Romantics had assumed. Greek drama was not only a total work of art, but because it drew most directly on mythical sources, it was also the supreme inspiration of Greek culture in general. In contrast, as Nietzsche saw it, the idealistic philosophy of Socrates and Plato had removed itself by a process of abstraction from mythic sources and contributed thereby to the decline of ancient culture. Myth must therefore be revived as a source of regeneration.

In transforming race into a spiritual entity, Wagner was also greatly influenced by the theories of his French friend, Count Gobineau. For Gobineau, race as a spiritual entity was continually subject to bastardization by the influx of alien racial elements and to decadence by the rationalizing process of civilization.

Wagner concluded that only in its own racial myths were to be found the sources for the regeneration of the German people. Because the music drama was the medium for tapping these sources, it should not merely present the ordinary loves and hates of men dressed up in the flamboyant forms of Baroque opera but should give form to the racial epic of salvation through heroic pessimism.

Some of Wagner's music dramas combined the mythic spirit of pessimism with political and social beliefs of a pre-1848 utopian revolutionary character. They were re-enforced by the long conversations he held with his friend, the famous Russian revolutionary anarchist, Mikhail Bakunin. The myths of the *Ring* were really intended to express disillusionment with intellectual progress, contempt for the capitalistic and materialistic bourgeoisie, and abhorrence of the growing omnipotence of the state. The Jew was the outstanding symbol of the bourgeois decadence of which society should be purged. It was to be swept away by a kind of political and social *Götterdämmerung* inaugurated by a new god-man deliverer, Siegfried. This was to be achieved not by the abstractions of a liberal constitutionalism or by proletarian collectivism but by the actual creative freedom of work in the community of solidarity and mutualism.

Wagner remained basically an optimist who dreamed of using

the heroic pessimism of myth and philosophical skepticism to brush away the illusions of middle-class liberalism. He never really succumbed to the cyclical fatalism of the racial doctrine, as did some of his later followers. What attracted some National Socialists was the vision of a clean sweep brought about by a deliverer who would inaugurate a new *sacrum imperium*.

PESSIMISM AND THE ARTISTIC TOUR DE FORCE

The pessimism of some of Wagner's later works has been attributed to the impact of the writings of the philosopher Arthur Schopenhauer, which he began to read during the last stages of the composition of the *Ring*. He read and re-read Schopenhauer's *The World as Will and Idea* (1819). In it he discovered philosophic justification for his own ideas.

Schopenhauer's (1788–1860) philosophy of pessimism was, in the beginning at least, less popular than the rationalistic optimism of his academic rival, Hegel. But after the revolution of 1848, his pessimism suited the changed mood, and for a while Schopenhauer became the fashion.

His philosophy was in harmony with the prevailing notion that the fundamental creative spiritual forces had been exhausted, leaving materialistic interests. It was felt that rationalism and idealism had merely glided over the surface of human existence. Hegel had been concerned with the relationships of things and with consequences, never with the thing-in-itself. Schopenhauer sought to probe the deep currents of life, in which he saw only suffering and tragedy. The tragic character of human existence, he argued, arose out of the insatiable striving of the will which seeks preservation in a world of forms which are really illusory. The sex drive is one of the most compelling. The only escape is in art, where we are concerned with ends in themselves, not with mere means as in a rational order. For Schopenhauer art became a kind of Nirvana wherein the impelling drives of the will could be sublimated and find a passive quiescence. History has, of course, no meaning in terms of progress. It takes the great isolated genius to really transcend the limits of existence set by the will.

This frame of thought suited the temper of Wagner's mind and it furnished his ideas with philosophical buttressing. Schopenhauer provided a metaphysical cloak for the idea of tragic fate in *The Götterdämmerung* and for the sexual sublimation of *Tristan* and *Parsifal*.

Moreover, in a country where the philosopher had displaced the theologian as the popular idol, it was especially important to attach oneself to him. Wagner's own flamboyant personality and unconventional habits brought upon him a great deal of ridicule. Many people did not take him seriously; they thought of him as a showman of spectacular proportions.

Due to the grandiose character of his artistic schemes, which had a kind of Cecil B. De Mille flavor, and to his rather extravagant and bizarre mode of life, Wagner was generally in debt. He was fortunate in securing the aid of such a highly-placed patron as young King Ludwig II of Bavaria, his friend and financial supporter, who built the Bayreuth playhouse for his productions.

Wagner achieved more than a revolution in music; he became the founder of a cult. His music became the subtle and enduring medium for arousing those basic irrational urges and drives which were poorly communicated in his garbled writings. His son-in-law, Houston Chamberlain, later gave his ideas more systematic intellectual form. The great playhouse at Bayreuth, erected specifically for the purpose of the production of his colossal *Ring* and opened in 1876, became the temple of the Wagnerian cult. His widow and son Siegfried, along with many devoted disciples, have maintained this shrine of pure Germanic music.

Wagner's significance lies not alone in his conception that the total work of art, through a return to the mythical and eternal sources of creativity, was the vehicle of regeneration of the race; he was also the supreme exemplification of the artist of the late nineteenth and early twentieth centuries—the artist who, breaking away from both the social and moral conventions, freed himself from bourgeois sentimentalism and from the current conception of a grand form or style in order to manipulate the new art forms to achieve a particular effect.

Wagner's total work of art was the tour de force of an artistic personality with a superlative sense of showmanship. He wrote the words, composed the music, created the scenery, trained the singers, staged the whole production, and supervised the performances of his great operas. In him the genius of the theater reached its peak; he knew exactly what stops to pull in order to sway his audiences. In essence he expressed the *Führer* principle in the arts, a principle which later attracted Hitler as much as did Wagner's specific racial ideas. Hitler, the demagog, had a Wagnerian feeling for showmanship and the theatrical.

APPEARANCE OF INDUSTRIAL CAPITALISM

The second half of the century also marked the appearance of new economic and social forces which sought assimilation in the German organism. The development of industrial capitalism brought with it the emergence of a class of industrial workers.

Up to the middle of the century Germany had been a predominantly agrarian country, but by 1870 a balance had already been achieved between agriculture and industry. In Prussia the same shift in population from the country to the city took place as had occurred earlier in England. Between 1816 and 1871 the agrarian east increased 91 per cent in population, while the south and west added only 23 per cent. Between 1871 and 1890 the trend was reversed; the East Elbian areas increased by only 26 per cent while the industrial areas of the south and west increased by 79 per cent. This shift in population was accompanied by a great general upward surge of the population curve for the whole country.

The idealistic liberalism of the early nineteenth century was based on home industry and upon the artisan, who was inclined to look to the intellectual bourgeoisie for leadership. But the industrial worker, who became an important social and political factor after 1850, was more inclined to look for direction in his own organizations of trade union and labor party. In the 1860's the worker achieved the right to form trade unions. At about the same time industrial strikes made their appearance, and consumers' cooperatives were formed similar to those in England.

The organization of industrial capitalism also made very rapid progress in Germany after the middle of the century. Banks and credit institutions were established. Railroads increased their mileage from 2,000 kilometres in 1845 to about 28,000 in 1875. The greatest of the German steamship lines, the North German Lloyd, was established in 1857. The 1850's saw the founding of a great number of stock companies; some fifty-nine were established in the mining and iron industries. The introduction of the machine made rapid strides, first in the textile industry, then in coal and iron. In the 1850's the chemical industry had already become a major force in the German economy and a competitive factor in international trade.

The rather sudden appearance in large numbers of the two new social types, the industrial entrepreneur and the factory worker, had a disturbing effect on German society. There was no opportunity to absorb them gradually through the course of a century or more, as in England. The old type of merchant entrepreneur made money to use in buying land. The new industrial entrepreneur was often solely motivated by an expansive drive to promote his business. The same lack of social obligation characterized industrial workers, who, deprived of the tools of a trade, had only their labor to sell. As a result the worker's relationship to his employer assumed an increasingly impersonal character, bringing to an end the old patriarchal ties.

The new entrepreneur was primarily concerned with the economic realities of an expanding industrial enterprise. He naturally linked himself with the Prussian power-state, for whose expansive drive he had an affinity. In contrast, alienated both from Prussian statism and liberal constitutionalism, the worker found a meaning for his existence in the new Social-Democratic party, based on the ideas of Karl Marx and Friedrich Engels.

PROLETARIAN CONSCIOUSNESS AND ECONOMIC DETERMINISM

The new socialism, called "scientific" by its chief promoters, was a typical product of the German intellectual climate. Its ideological founder, Karl Marx, had received a university education and might have followed an academic career if he had not become involved in the revolutionary movement through the publication of a radical journal and *The Communist Manifesto* in 1848. After the collapse of 1848 he went to England, expecting to return soon to the continent to participate in the next and decisive wave of revolutionary insurgence. Actually, he remained in England until his death in 1883.

Marx and his growing family often faced dire poverty and indeed managed to survive only with the intermittent help of Engels, who went to work in his father's textile business in Manchester in order to secure the means to subsidize Marx in his socialist writings. With Engels' aid and with hack work for various newspapers and periodicals, including a job as military correspondent for a New York paper, Marx managed to keep body and soul together for himself and his family. He spent most of his time working in the library of the British Museum, gathering materials for his great work, *Das Kapital*, the first volume of which was published in 1867. Volumes two and three were issued after his death, under Engels' supervision.

While somewhat disillusioned about the immediacy of the proletarian revolution, Marx continued throughout the remainder of his life to be steadfast in his faith in the eventual victory of the worker's cause. This attitude is reflected in *Das Kapital*, in which he attempts to show the inevitable debacle of capitalism. The accent is placed on historical development as contrasted with revolutionary fervor and the immediacy of victory as reflected in *The Communist Manifesto*. In *Das Kapital*, in addition to presenting a description of economic and social developments, he sought to inspire the workers with a sense of mission by showing them that history is on their side and that capitalism would destroy itself by virtue of its own inner contradictions. Marx himself was imbued with the prophetic vision of a chosen people who would inherit the earth.

Throughout the period of his exile, Marx expectantly scanned the continental skies for signs of the coming revolution. France, the heartland of revolution, was the logical place for the outbreak. The Paris Commune and its suppression in 1870–71 was evidence of the capitalist masters' mounting fear of the rising insurgence of the exploited masses.

In spite of disappointment in the abortive uprisings and the stupidity of the workers' leaders, Marx felt that the end was inexorable. His major writings were directed toward proving, by a painstaking analysis of its end phases, which mark also the emergence of the classless society, that the collapse of capitalism was inevitable. Particularly striking is the driving logic of the argument which conclusively arrives at the certain triumph of the proletariat.

The force of Marx's logic is exemplified in the following classic statement from *A Contribution to the Critique of Political Economy* (1859):

> In the social production which men carry on, they enter into definite relations that are indispensable and independent of their will; these relations of production correspond to a definite stage of development of their material powers of production. The sum total of these productive relations constitutes the economic structure of society—the real foundation on which rise legal and political superstructures, and to which correspond definite forms of social consciousness. The mode of production in material life determines the general character of the social, political and spiritual processes of life. It is not the consciousness of men that determines their existence, but on the contrary their social existence that determines their consciousness. At a certain stage of their development, the material forces of production in society come into conflict with the existing relations of production, or—what is but a legal expression for the same thing—with the property relations within which they had been at work before. From forms of development of the productive forces these relations turn into their fetters. Then comes the period of social revolution. With the change of the economic foundation the whole vast superstructure is sooner or later entirely transformed. But in considering such transformations the distinction should always be made between the material transformation of the economic conditions of production, which can be determined with the precision of natural science, and the legal, political, religious, aesthetic or philosophic —in short the ideological forms in which men become conscious of the conflict and fight it out.[1]

Here is presented Marx's law of social development, as irreversible in Marxist doctrine as the second law of thermodynamics, or as Darwin's law of natural selection. In the past it produced great social transformations; for example, from a society based on master-slave to one based on a lord-serf productive relationship. In Marx's time its operation was bringing about the transition from the capitalist-proletarian society to a new phase in man's development, the classless society. He assumed that mankind's development proceeded through three phases: first, that of a primitive communism; second, that of the class struggle; and third, that of the rise of the most oppressed and exploited of all classes, the proletariat. The victory of the proletariat would be the inevitable result of the new technology, which could overcome scarcity and make the struggle for existence meaningless.

What determined the workers' victory, therefore, was the fact that they were merely the product of the historical development. Their very condition—that of being, in comparison with all previous classes, deprived of everything—will inevitably lead to their victory when the means of production makes possible a complete plenitude for all. The bourgeois capitalists have dug their own graves by making everything hinge on market value—even art and literature. As a consequence, they have deprived the proletariat of creative participation in culture and have created a class which has been exploited to the utmost. Therefore, since the proletariat is at the very bottom of the heap its triumph must usher in the classless society.

What delays the transition is that the proletariat is not aware of its role, that is, of its own inevitable victory. It is not necessary to furnish it with an ideal or even a program in the liberal sense of promoting a cause. Its very historical existence is enough; all that must be done is to arouse it to an awareness of that existence.

SOCIALIST POLITICAL ORGANIZATION

In conformity with these ideas, Marx abandoned after 1848 the notion of awaiting a spontaneous revolution from below. Instead, he adopted the deliberate tactics of organization and propaganda to bring the proletariat to an awareness of its peculiar role. First, he emphasized that there was to be no cooperation with the middle-class revolution in the general movement toward democratic forms of government. Such cooperation would merely lead to sops being thrown out to the workers and to a threat of assimilation. Second, and most significant, he saw the necessity of organizing workers' parties. He turned against the trade unions, which were just getting under way during the fifties and sixties, because their limited aims of securing better hours and wages were sure to blunt the edge of lower-class militancy. On the other hand, he was convinced that the earlier aim of creating an elite of revolutionary leaders who would lead the workers to revolutionary action must be abandoned. The earlier plan had proved unsuccessful because the proletariat were not yet conscious of their role. The great necessity lay, therefore, in organizing parties to educate the proletariat to their mission.

The organization of a German workers' party was really begun by Ferdinand Lassalle (1825–1864). A brilliant young Jew, he was led to socialism by way of Hegel's philosophy, Heine's influence, the example of French socialists, and finally by the impact of the ideas of Marx and Engels. Only his brilliant oratorical defense in court kept him from serving more than repeated short sentences in jail for running head-on against police and law because of revolutionary agitation. Perhaps only the fact that he happened to be in jail during the radical uprisings of 1849 prevented his being exiled later during the reaction.

Lassalle was not only a brilliant orator but also a very able organizer. A speaking tour through German industrial areas in 1859 contributed to the organization of workers' party cells and finally to the founding of a social-democratic party. Lassalle's aim was, by force of sheer numbers and cohesive organization, to capture control of the state through democratic constitutional processes.

The socialism of Lassalle marks a transition from pre-1848 idealism to Marxian realism. It reflected the economic conditions in the Germanies of the 1860's. There were then in Prussia only about 750,000 industrial workers among about a million handicraft artisans and three and a half million peasants. Hence the industrial workers, the backbone of the proletariat, as defined by Marx, were still a relatively small minority.

Lassalle leaned in the direction of the humanist notion that thought can determine social action rather than, as Marx assumed, that thought is a reflection of class interests. Lassalle followed Fichte in his projection of the three stages of man's ascent to freedom. Up to the French Revolution, solidarity among men was enforced by authority. Then the bourgeois era of negative and abstract freedom —that is, of freedom from various restraints—was ushered in. The triumph of the workers would bring the final concrete freedom of the producer based on a union of freedom and solidarity. For

Lassalle, also, the state was to be the means of achieving this positive freedom by becoming the "corporation of the workers."

Lassalle was actually an advocate of state socialism and corresponded with Bismarck over the possibility of joining forces against bourgeois liberalism. He was an advocate of German unification under Prussian leadership, by which means he hoped to create a nation-state which the workers could eventually take over. Marx, although initially friendly, came to distrust Lassalle's very brilliant gifts and his very definite nationalistic leanings.

Marx was also concerned about the influence that such an imposing personality was likely to have on the workers' consciousness. Devotion to a leader was likely to take the place of the all-important feeling of proletarian mission. The premature death of Lassalle in a duel in 1864 removed his "dangerous personality" and made way for Marxian leadership. Although Marx's ideas came to dominate the thought of the German socialist movement, the movement continued to be more completely swayed by powerful leaders than either English or French socialism.

The formation of national parties and the threat of fragmentation of the proletarian movement impelled Marx to come out of the isolation of his study to definitely participate in its organization. He took an active part in the founding of the International Workers' Association (First International) in 1864. Internal dissension provoked by the discipline which Marx sought to impose and the national antagonisms awakened by the Franco-Prussian war (1870–1871) contributed to its dissolution in 1876. Marx's chief opponent was Bakunin (1814–1876), who proposed what may be called total revolution: the destruction of the whole existing political and social order so as to permit the new to rise spontaneously in its place. He, of course, opposed party organization and its parliamentary tactics. Bakunin marked the point of departure for the syndicalist movement in the Latin countries. But the German and Russian Marxist social-democratic parties were to assume the leadership of the proletarian movement both locally and abroad.

The great influence of Marxism in Germany and Russia may be ascribed to the fact that, in both of these semi-feudal and military-bureaucratic countries, not only the church but also big industry became closely yoked to the state. Both had a weak upper middle class, and the development of big business contributed there especially to the widening of the chasm between the upper and lower middle-class groups. Because both countries lacked real parliamentary forms of government, the workers and many from the lower middle class were driven to form counter organizations, social-democratic parties. These parties expressed a militant spirit of opposition to the state and the capitalistic order associated with it. This intransigence was a major source of weakness in the new imperial order established by Bismarck.

The basic cleavages created by all the forces considered in this chapter may be attributed to the fundamental secularization of Western society, which among the Germans happened abruptly and in a most aggravated form. Wagner's association of art with racial myth, Marx's association of class with technics, and (to be considered later) the liberals' association of liberty with science were all radical expressions of this process of secularization. In them the divergent tendencies of theater, party, and university took the place of the unifying force once exercised by the church. In his exaltation of the Prussian state, Bismarck merely raised another secular force by the side of these others.

NATIONALISM AND PARTY IDEOLOGY

The most important development in both Austria and Prussia with the subsidence of the furore of peoples after 1848 was the reassertion of state power. Nationalism increasingly lost its earlier revolutionary implications and became associated with the existing states. National unification came to depend upon the use of diplomatic and military methods rather than upon constitutional assemblies and barricades. This transformation was quite in harmony with the intellectual temper engendered by the new empirical sciences and the new historical realism.

Both conservativism and liberalism now assumed a much more doctrinaire complexion. Both emphasized institutional molds: the former, monarchical-aristocratic order; the latter, constitutional-parliamentary procedure. Both lacked the social dynamic approach of men like Marwitz, Stein, or Marx, who were much less concerned with institutional frames and legal formulas than with the vital functional role of social groups in the life of the community.

But there were also important differences in coloration and content. Conservativism combined pietistic religious orthodoxy with the conception of the state as the guardian of the corporative traditional order involving monarchy, landed aristocracy, and church. Liberalism, on the other hand, emphasized the individual private conscience in matters of religion along with the legal state as the frame within which individual liberty and self-government were to be promoted, particularly through dependence of the crown on the majority in parliament. They differed most radically with respect to nationalism, which to most conservatives was a revolutionary and subversive force. The liberals, though aware of nationalism's radical potentialities, yet thought it necessary to the realization of the highest potentialities of individual peoples. This distinction was of crucial significance in the relation of Bismarck to the conservatives and liberals.

Most Germans of the upper classes were, of course, much more sensitive to drastic changes coming from below than from above. Moreover, the old frames of *Reich, Staat,* and *Volk* had been lifted out of their traditional historical molds during the 1848 upheaval and were more amenable to manipulation from above as well as below.

Among the Germans there existed no national traditional frame as in France, England, and Russia within which new forces could flow and provide a sense of continuity and direction. The old mold of the *Reich* as the *sacrum imperium* had become anachronistic in a world of secularism and the many molds of the individual states seemed too parochial even in their great power forms, such as Prussia and Austria. Neither the attenuated universalism of the *Reich* tradition nor the accentuated particularism of the states could contain the new mission of the *Volk* opened up by technological and industrial vistas. To bring about a fusion of the free-wheeling elements of *Reich, Staat,* and *Volk* required the catalytic action of a great personality.

RELIGION AND REASONS OF STATE

Otto von Bismarck (1815–1898), by reviving the Prussian power tradition of the great Hohenzollerns (from the Great Elector to Frederick the Great), provided the axis around which German national existence revolved for a time. He agreed with Ranke that the interests of states had been distorted by being subordinated to universal aims during the era of revolution. Like Frederick the Great, he aimed to reassert Prussia's power interests, while recognizing the existence of such new forces as liberalism and nationalism, which should be entrained in the service of the state.

Bismarck came to this point of view only as a consequence of two conversions. Originally, he shared the legitimist conservatism of the Prussian gentry but departed from them and from the liberals because of their assumption that politics should be oriented toward *Weltanschauung* principles rather than toward power interests.

On his father's side Bismarck came from an old Brandenburg Junker family, so ancient that it regarded the Hohenzollerns as interlopers and upstarts. His mother, however, came from a middle-class jurist family. In the university, first at Göttingen and then at Berlin, he studied law, and in 1836 entered government service. But after three years, dissatisfied with the life of officialdom, he turned to the management of the family estate in Pomerania. Under the influence of pietistic religious circles, he abandoned his wildness and atheism, and married Johanna von Puttkamer, who moved in these circles.

Historians are inclined to accord to Bismarck's religious conversion a major influence in determining his whole attitude toward the problems of politics. Initially, the pietistic influence provided him with a stable center for his emotional life, whose violent expression in drinking bouts and wild rides through the countryside had led people to refer to him as that "mad Bismarck." It also introduced him to that combination of unreserved trust in God and absolute loyalty to the monarch which represented the psychological mainstays of conservatism. But, unlike that of most conservatives, his religious faith lacked altogether dogmatic or ecclesiastical overtones;

it had a highly personal and even mystical coloration and had little connection with the official church. In religion as in politics he shied away from an objective order.

Bismarck originally shared the political views of his class, for whom the liberal and national movement, which culminated in 1848, was anathema. He was a member of the Prussian Diet in 1847, then (1849–1851) a deputy to the lower house of the newly established Prussian parliament. He argued vehemently for the maintenance of monarchical power within and Prussian interests without. He contended that Austria was the real buttress of conservative order against the forces of revolution and that cooperation with her should be a fundamental basis of Prussian policy.

His political conversion took place in the period between 1851 and 1859, when Bismarck served as Prussian envoy to the Diet of the German Confederation at Frankfort. Here he soon came to sense that a war between Austria and Prussia over hegemony in the Germanies was inevitable. He saw that after 1848 Austria definitely aimed at the expansion of her power within the Confederation and its subversion to Austrian interests. He also became aware that the force of nationalism both among the Germans and the other peoples of middle Europe was not to be suppressed, that it was moreover driving a wedge between Prussia and Austria since it confronted them with quite different problems. Austria faced dissolution into component nationalities while Prussia faced assimilation into a German national state. His recognition of the basic power conflict between Austria and Prussia and of the fact that nationalism must be dealt with positively marked his conversion from a conservative to a *Realpolitiker*, placing the interests of state above considerations of *Weltanschauung*.

In advocating a policy of state egoism, Bismarck stood practically alone. The conservatives adhered to the traditional friendship with Austria. The liberals, though they felt Austria to be an obstacle to German unity, thought that unity would be realized by the slow but cumulative pressure of public opinion, which would bring about the dissolution of the Hapsburg empire and the assimilation of Prussia into a national union. Bismarck, on the other hand, now stood for the assertion of Prussian power interests by resort to war if necessary.

He provided no idealizations for his position. He was convinced that it was the responsibility of a statesman to concern himself only with the interests of his particular state and not with considerations of international order. For him to think otherwise—that is, to rely on an international order or on a traditional friendship—would really mean seeking reliance upon human forms of support rather than upon God. As he saw it, the power embodied in the state and the authority centered in the monarch were the appropriate means God had provided for the maintenance of order in the world of politics. The liberal notion of a progressive transformation of the world in the direction of a rational order of things was an illusion.

THE PRIMACY OF STATISM OVER NATIONALISM

It follows that for Bismarck the external relations of a state were primary. For Prussia the first consideration was the conflict with Austria over domination in middle Europe and over leadership of the national movement. Prussian leadership of it could not only prevent her own liquidation but that of the other states, including Austria. Prussian leadership in collaboration with Russia could also hold in check the revolutionary forces of nationalism among the peoples on the eastern borders which threatened the landed gentry and German cultural pre-eminence. A strong state could hold these disruptive forces in line but not just by building a dam. As Bismarck came to see it, the state must make positive use of the force of nationalism as an instrument in the creation of German political unity without sacrificing the monarchical-artistocratic order or Prussian pre-eminence.

The events from the Schleswig-Holstein War of 1864 to the Franco-Prussian War of 1870–71 reveal particularly Bismarck's great skill in keeping each war both an isolated event and a local affair. It seems in retrospect that Bismarck had a definite set of moves which he calculated ahead, like a chess player. Actually in conformity with his religiosity, he was a complete opportunist in dealing with events. Unlike the liberals, he did not view events as inevitable in the course of development toward a desired end. Neither a traditionalist nor a doctrinaire, he could take advantage of events as they occurred.

Bismarck's unexpected success in virtually pushing Austria out of German affairs and in laying the foundations of German unity under Prussian aegis brought its reward in popular acclaim. Whereas once he had been the most hated man in Prussia and the Germanies, he now came to be regarded as something like a demigod. So complete a reversal of attitude was indicative of the increasing admiration of pragmatic success.

For Bismarck nationalism was a kind of elemental force to be controlled and directed into the proper channels. He always viewed it with detachment and never was caught up in its emotionalism. But to direct it, he felt compelled to take over from Louis Napoleon the tactic of democratic Caesarism—a tactic which by-passed liberal public opinion and took the road of adroit appeals to the populace, whose hates and prejudices could be easily played upon. The success of this tactic was demonstrated particularly in the years between 1866 and 1870 in his manipulation of the mounting national feeling which culminated in the war with France.

During the middle decades of the nineteenth century the French were great admirers of German culture; it was the period when German Romantic literature, Idealistic philosophy, and critical historiography began to exert great influence in Europe. But by the 1860's the emotionally surcharged nationalism on both sides of the Rhine had lost its earlier idealistic balance wheel and was capable of very rapid and capricious changes. Among the Germans the idea even became prevalent that a sacrifice of blood in a war with France was desirable as a unifying force.

The constitution of the new German Empire, which was born with the Franco-Prussian War, was quite obviously the expression of power politics. It was not the embodiment of theoretical principles like the early French constitutions, nor the product of the slow development of community forms like the English political structure—it was not what Stein and the early reformers had envisaged. It had a contrived and eclectic character comprising traditional federal, nationalist unitary, and particularistic power elements intrinsically incompatible but brought together by a great political impresario whose mind revolved almost exclusively in the diplomatic constellations of power forces. The fact that it was a power complex rather than a real constitutional dwelling perhaps explains its relatively short duration.

In spite of superficial similarities, the Bismarckian empire bore little resemblance in either structure or ethos to the *sacrum imperium;* it was the product of historical accretions. Its real axis was the particularistic and functional rational ethos of the Prussian state. In its structure were to be found vestiges of the old *Reich,* much state particularism, and a very large dose of nationalism. The *Reichstag* as the representative of the German people was in a sense but a reincarnation of the Frankfort Assembly. The real innovation was the position of the imperial chancellor who was the essential unifying force during the first two decades of the second *Reich.* During that time the sheer force of mind and personality of Bismarck kept the other governmental agencies revolving in their respective orbits.

THE STATE VERSUS ITS ENEMIES WITHIN AND WITHOUT

In the first years Bismarck was confronted in the *Reichstag* by two parties, the Conservatives and the Liberals. The majority in both groups were at least partially satisfied with the new imperial edifice, but for different reasons. On the one hand, the National Liberals found satisfaction in national union and in the *Reichstag;* on the other, the Conservatives approved of the federal arrangement and monarchical hegemony. But neither Liberals nor Conservatives accepted the politically irresponsible position of the chancellor by virtue of which he could play off the *Reichstag* against the emperor and vice versa.

However, in spite of the rather qualified approval which many Liberals and Conservatives accorded to the structure of the new empire, they became much more enthusiastic supporters as the empire demonstrated apparent success in achieving economic prosperity and a greatly enhanced power position. Though large groups in each party came to approve of the Bismarckian empire, the splitting off of minority elements who clung to the defense of principles was a constant reminder of the decline of political integrity. As a consequence the conflict between material interests and success and basic social and political principles and values was enormously accentuated.

The two other parties, the Catholic Center and the Marxist Social Democrats, were, to begin with, actually parties of opposition to the regime itself because they were pivoted upon church and class, which had an international rather than a national orientation.

The emergence of the new Germany organized around Prussia coincided with the appearance of ideological parties organized around Roman Catholicism, proletarian socialism, and rationalistic liberalism. The basic particularism and Lutheran ethos of Prussianism ran counter to the recognition of an objective international order of values which these ideologies represented; Prussianism insisted on the primacy of state interests, both within and without. Bismarck saw in these ideological forces, principally Catholicism and socialism, foes of the state to be dealt with by much the same diplomatic tactics that he employed against foreign powers. Although he and his successors might effect a reconciliation with one or the other of them, the relationship would be in the nature of an alliance; the opposing forces were not really integrated within the frame of the new nation-state.

The conflict for survival with Bismarck served to throw these blocs back upon their *Weltanschauung* positions and mass appeal. Roman Catholicism returned to its medieval tradition of the freedom of the church, and Marxian socialism to the sectarian view of a coming new age, now to be ushered in by a revolution. They sought to establish the chief focus of values outside both the state and culture: the one in the church, the other in the factory. Catholicism and socialism became organized as vast pressure groups to influence mass opinion and to combat the Prussian bureaucratic-military state.

This conflict produced an inner fragmentation of German political and cultural life much worse than the earlier *Kleinstaaterei*, since it culminated in a warfare of ideologies when, under the Weimar Republic, the Prussian state was obliterated and the parties turned upon each other. Victory in the name of the *Volksgemeinschaft* (folk community) of that wholly opportunistic ideology, National Socialism, seemed at the time to most Germans the only way of restoring unity within and strength without.

To protect the new *Reich* Bismarck constructed a great web of alliances at the center of which lay the Austro-German alliance. In the next circle lay Italy, and beyond her on the periphery, Russia and England. Only a master of diplomacy such as Bismarck could keep the various planets moving in their appropriate orbits. Neither ideology nor sentiment held them there, but rather the mutual attraction and repulsion of state interests. It was too cunningly contrived, too much the great tour de force of a diplomatic genius. It depended too much for its successful operation upon the agile mind and cold calculation of one individual. When his hand left the helm, the storms of nationalism and imperialism broke it asunder.

THE CREATIVE PERSONALITY AND HISTORY

The dominance of the great personality and the definite subordination of other personalities perhaps equally capable but less forceful and ruthless was a characteristic of the European scene in general and of the German one in particular during the second half of the nineteenth century. The creative individual was no longer regarded as the vehicle of a grand form or of *Geist*. Grand form made its last appearance in the Baroque, and after the middle of the century creativity was no longer derived from the protean character of a world spirit but from individual originality which renders articulate the novel needs or tastes of the time. This creativity was most manifest in the consciousness of individuals that they served as a bridge between past and future.

Such historical consciousness became manifest in two ways. One, there was the revival of old styles of architecture, the interest of scholars and publicists in finding historical precedents for all manner of institutions, and the concern of philosophers with the restoration of old frames of thought. The other, some artists and a few philosophers sought to transcend this dependence on the historic past by striving for an art and philosophy expressing the vitalistic and functional energies of life itself rather than the revitalization of past forms. For the French it was the art of Manet and Cézanne, and for the Germans, the philosophy of Nietzsche and Dilthey, which most characteristically expressed this reassertion of creative personality as a revolt against middle-class appropriation of precedents

—as if heritage were a species of property. It was a revolt against the middle-class assumption that the whole of history had been moving toward the realization of the values it stood for. A new kind of revolution, that of the creative individual, appeared alongside the proletarian revolt. It was directed against the middle-class expropriation of the past as well as of the present.

The great personality of the nineteenth and especially of the twentieth century was very much aware that his creative force depended on his identification with the moment of history in which he was placed and not upon tradition arising out of an original national matrix nor upon the expectancy of a new order. Both the complete immanence and transcendence of the great individual were achieved in the twentieth century by Lenin and Hitler, who regarded themselves as the movement of history itself and not as being placed in history.

XII

Scientific Technology, Power-State History, and Kultur

The middle decades of the nineteenth century form an intellectual water-shed in the development of the European mind. They mark the turn from an idealistic and speculative outlook ✳ on life to a realistic and materialistic attitude toward both nature and history and to a preponderant interest in the exact procedures of the special sciences. This change was very abrupt in the Germanies because there idealistic and romantic forms of thought had largely obliterated the rationalistic attitude of the Enlightenment whose strong influence was still manifest in France and England in the nineteenth century.

The swing of German thought to the opposite extreme of realism and materialism was another example of the German tendency toward radical thought. Seeking to develop all the possibilities implicit in a new point of view, the Germans tended to convert it into a total world and life view. The new point of view was impelled to become totalitarian in practice by permeating the whole intellectual, political, and social life. Secularism became an immanent force. Conversely, in the Western countries the secular emerged as a natural order juxtaposed to a spiritual order, each of which sought to maintain its autonomy.

THE INSURGENCY OF POSITIVISTIC SCIENCE

During the second half of the nineteenth century the natural sciences definitely took the lead over such humanistic disciplines as philosophy and philology, which had constituted the glory of the German universities during the previous epoch. The empirical approach of the specialized sciences superseded the earlier speculative approach of natural philosophy. The study of particular phenomena took the place of the quest for an all-embracing pattern of the universe. The clinic in medicine, the experimental laboratory in physics and chemistry, and the seminar in historical-philological studies emphasized the search for particular facts.

The last really great encyclopedic work was *Cosmos* (5 vols., 1845–1858) by Alexander von Humboldt, the brother of Wilhelm, the humanist educational reformer. But even this attempt to achieve a coherent view of the universe was based mainly on particular investigations of positive phenomena, principally in the realm of geography. The two most important generalizations of the period, that of the conservation of energy by Robert Mayer (1842) and Charles Darwin's conception of evolution by natural selection (1859), are indicative of the limited and tentative character of the ideas propounded by the scientists of the time. The great physicist and physiologist, Hermann von Helmholz (1821–1894), repudiated the total organic point of view of Paracelsus for the mechanistic approach emphasized by Descartes. He sought to unite physics and physiology on a common mechanistic basis, for which he set about devising appropriate instruments of precise measurement.

Philosophy followed the lead of the sciences toward presenting the universe as a causal-mechanical order. With Hegel, the idealistic and speculative movement had run into the ground. It is true that in the second half of the century important revivals occurred in Neo-Hegelian and Neo-Kantian movements, but these opened up no new vistas. As their names indicate, they presented variations on the themes handed down by the great masters. Philosophy in the main became either a handmaiden of the empirical sciences, as it had been of theology in the Middle Ages, or stood in sterile opposition to them.

The vogue of mechanistic and materialistic conceptions during the 1850's, 1860's, and 1870's is particularly apparent in the popularity of the works of Jacob Moleschott (1822–1893) and Ludwig Büchner (1824–1899). In them philosophy and science were regarded as indistinguishable. Chemical reactions, mechanical law, and environmental adaptation served to explain all phenomena, not only of physical nature but also of the psychical character of man.

The popularity of this materialistic world and life view began to wane during the last quarter of the century. In a celebrated lecture given in 1880 the famous physiologist Emil du Bois-Reymond argued that half the so-called riddles of the universe pertaining to the nature of matter and energy and the origins of motion and life were unsolvable by science. But as late as 1899 the very popular and influential book of Ernst Haeckel, *The Riddle of the Universe*, still projected a comprehensive solution.

GERMAN LEADERSHIP IN THE FUSION OF SCIENCE AND TECHNOLOGY

Perhaps the most remarkable characteristic of the development of science during the century after 1850 was its increasingly close connection with technics. Technology, in fact, became applied science. Early in the nineteenth century the Germans assumed leadership in the application of science to the practical problems of agriculture and industry. This was natural in view of the radical swing from an idealistic and speculative attitude to an empirical and pragmatic approach in the specialized sciences. Also there was in the Germany no underpinning of the sciences by a dominant philosophy of natural law, such as existed in France and England.

In France and England the empirical sciences exerted a dominating intellectual role during the seventeenth and eighteenth centuries. Consequently, in France the sciences were linked with the Enlightenment and the Revolution; in England, with the liberal concern for the freedom of the individual and the development of a world market. But in Germany the dominance of the specialized empirical sciences coincided with the industrial upsurge and the emergence of Bismarck's power-state. The assumption that mastery over nature was being realized, which pervaded late nineteenth century science, came to be closely associated with the new industrial processes and the imperialistic power motif of the new national state.

The development of chemistry in Germany has been most typical of the close practical association of science with industry and agriculture, perhaps because chemistry has lacked the tendency toward theory promoted in physics by broad unifying mechanistic generalizations. The work of Justus von Liebig (1803–1873) laid the basis of this association, especially for agriculture. He went to Paris in 1822 to study under the famous chemist, Gay-Lussac, from whom he acquired a mastery of the experimental method. On his return he became professor at Giessen, where he established the first experimental laboratory devoted to the education of chemists.

The total view of nature derived from his admiration of Paracelsus certainly contributed to Liebig's association of chemistry with the growth of plants. The prevailing opinion among agriculturalists was that only the earth could restore its own natural balance; conversely, Liebig argued that man is an exploiter of nature and must recompense her for the losses he has occasioned her. He contended, moreover, that the decline of empires, peoples, and races might be ascribed to sheer exploitation and depletion of the earth's resources. Chemistry could come to the aid of nature and replenish her exhausted stores by artificial fertilizers, which would make possible the unlimited development of food resources and population.

The middle decades of the nineteenth century, marking the heroic age of modern industrial technology, were filled with optimism as to man's eventually overcoming both the drudgery of manual labor and the niggardliness of nature. Few shared the reverence for nature that still actuated Liebig. The prevailing scientific and technological view was that of a dead soulless mechanism, to be exploited at will. The exploitation of the earth, the forests, and the seas now set in with an enthusiasm never equaled. The psychology of mining with its slag heaps and gashes cut into the earth was not conducive to the achievement of a new sense of cultural form. In fact, in architecture there was a "mining of the past" in the use of classic and Gothic elements to contrive the highly eclectic style of the second half of the century. Only in painting, music, and the novel, where the notion of individual genius predominated over the recollection of great historic forms, was there any considerable creativeness.

Germany's industrial development toward the end of the nineteenth century became phenomenal. It coincided with the second phase of the industrial revolution, which presented the following prominent developments: a revolution in transportation; the rise of large-scale corporate enterprise and mass production; and the application of scientific technology to production by the conjunction of laboratory and factory. In these developments Germany took a leading role, but she was outstanding in the application of scientific research to technological development. The necessary material for this great industrial advance lay in the very abundant coal of the Ruhr and the iron of Lorraine. But even more important was the fact that her working class had a strong sense of discipline and duty and of obedience to authority. Though the German worker might join the Social-Democratic party, he showed little inclination to resort to work stoppage and sabotage, as compared with the French worker, who was much more disposed toward the syndicalist emphasis upon direct action, which played no role in German economic life.

The great advances in the electrical and chemical industries were a peculiar product of the alliance of laboratory and factory. The bases of both the electrical and chemical industries were laid by Siemens and Liebig: the former, by inventions in the electrical realm, and the latter, by chemical research.

Like Edison, Werner von Siemens (1816–1892) combined great inventive genius with business capacity. Even more than Edison, he reflected the temper of the age in its conversion of scientific knowledge to practical uses. He was the real father of the German electrical industry. His greatest invention was the dynamo. He founded the Siemens-Halske electrical business in 1867, from which developed the gigantic electrical trust known as the *Allgemeine Elektrizitätzgesellschaft* (A.E.G.).

The chemical industry had an equally phenomenal development. As a great industry, it was virtually an original creation of the Germans. Though basic discoveries were made elsewhere, it was the

Germans who gave them industrial application. Bayer, by the development of synthetic indigo, laid the basis of the analin dye manufacture from coal-tar, which also came to be organized as a great syndicate. The commercially successful extraction of nitrogen from the air made possible great improvements in agriculture. German leadership in the chemical industry extended far into the twentieth century.

THE UNIVERSITIES BECOME RESEARCH CENTERS

As with the humanistic disciplines, so the sciences found their chief arena in the universities which they transformed. Since the days of Luther the professor had been the chief arbiter in theological controversies and legal disputes. The German conscience may be said to have become lodged in the universities. In the second half of the nineteenth century the professor's role as arbiter in matters pertaining to moral and cultural values began to wane as he came to be looked upon as an expert in particular fields of knowledege.

It should be underlined that *Kleinstaaterei* had at least prevented that uniformity in formal education characteristic of France. Universities were founded in Germany in almost every state; as a consequence, they developed a certain local color and individuality. The divided religious situation also contributed to diversity in point of view. The Protestant foundations in general adapted themselves to the new intellectual attitudes more readily than the Catholic centers, which eventually found in Neo-Thomism a means of reconciliation with the new currents without abandonment of fundamental religious positions.

There was a close relationship between bureaucracy and scholarship. The university professor generally received his appointment through some minister of state. But, in spite of this link with the state, German universities enjoyed a high degree of self-government with which the state seldom interfered. It was still assumed that learning lay in the area of *Geist* and should be free from state power. The early nineteenth-century idealistic and humanistic point of view thus left an enduring impress on the universities.

Scholars were drawn, as heretofore, mainly from the middle class, especially from the lower ranks of that class. As before, the sons of

Lutheran pastors furnished recruits for university chairs; but in these middle decades an increasing number came from peasant and artisan families. They communicated to scholarship the spirit of discipline and industry which pervaded their social groups. Also, their strong sense of occupying a subordinate niche in the social hierarchy prompted them to seek anonymity in the exploration of a narrow field of research.

What continued to lend a dynamic quality to German scholarship were the old academic feuds now revolving principally around questions of historical interpretation of such movements as the Renaissance and the Reformation rather than of theological issues. The great historians, philosophers, and philologists—Savigny, Ranke, Hegel, Sybel, and Wilamowitz-Moellendorff—stirred up the great controversies which rocked the academic world. The academic wars expressed the freedom of *Geist,* of which the universities were presumed to be the guardians. An enormous number of learned journals appeared which presented the results of research and the often acrimonious reviews of academic critics. The lesser lights lined up behind the champions. While downright vilification often marred these learned jousts, they nevertheless gave German scholarship a vital and intense spirit, lacking in most other countries.

The growing emphasis on specialization and methodical research often led to mere industrious mediocrity, concerned with gathering factual materials within a narrow area. Teaching and research came to be closely linked; the professor was chiefly concerned with presenting the results of research to his students rather than with the forming of norms and values. The whole system of examinations and dissertations for doctoral degrees served principally to test the qualifications of those who proposed to engage in this meticulous research. Scholars from other countries, especially England and America, came to drink at the German founts of learning, and they carried German methods back to their own countries.

PREDOMINANCE OF HISTORICAL POSITIVISM

The domination of the empirical and realistic approach was also apparent in historical scholarship. In the Germanies, the historical approach tended to take precedence over the rational or natural point of view in law and economics as well as in the general areas of culture and politics. We have already dealt with the Romantic interest in the origins of law and language, as presented especially by Friedrich von Savigny and Jacob Grimm. Both Friedrich List and Karl Marx, from opposite points of the ideological spectrum, were concerned with the position of the emerging industrial capitalism in either the development of the German nation or the worker's proletariat.

The historical approach, applied to these various areas, led to an emphasis on the relation of law and economics to other cultural manifestations rather than on their individual autonomy; on the presentation of descriptive historical materials rather than on theoretical principles, and on the embodiment of common ethical and group goals in the pursuit of economic or legal policy rather than on considerations of competition and individual self-interest.

These emphases played an even stronger role in the most influential school of historians of the mid-century, the national-liberal, or, as they are more frequently called, the Prussian historians. The chief representatives of this school were Friedrich Christoph Dahlmann (d. 1860), Johann Gustav Droysen (d. 1884), Heinrich von Sybel (d. 1895), and Heinrich von Treitschke (d. 1896). Being more active in public affairs than their colleagues in other countries, they exemplify another salient characteristic of German scholars. Dahlmann and Droysen were leaders in the deliberations of the Frankfort Parliament of 1848. All played a leading role in the formation of national and liberal points of view in politics.

The national-liberal historians were chiefly concerned with emphasizing the importance of power in history; to them, not moral forces but state power and class interests were the determining factors in historical development. The revolution of 1848 had apparently demonstrated the decisive pre-eminence of these factors over spiritual forces in human affairs. Droysen, in dealing with the ancient world, centered his attention on the Hellenistic and Roman periods, where the power state was important, rather than on Periclean Athens, where culture and liberty were regarded as the dominant forces. Alexander the Great and Julius Caesar no longer appeared as destroyers of liberty and the product of decadent cultures, but as great creative geniuses who combined the promotion of culture and the general welfare with political power interests. The realistic and empirical spirit of art and learning of Hellenistic-Roman culture was praised. In his account of the French Revolution, Sybel sought to show that the property interests of the bourgeoisie and peasants rather than the party ideologies and politics of assemblies were the important factors.

These historians were wary of grand speculative conceptions of history, such as Hegel presented. Their histories also shied away from the romantic probing of the obscure origins of custom and community in the *Volksgeist;* they inclined toward the sober presentation of political forms and forces on the basis of a careful analysis of the primary sources. They might eschew Ranke's colorful portrayal of personalities and events, but they placed great stress on the careful methods of research he emphasized in his seminar.

THE HISTORIANS SUPPORT THE POWER-STATE

Most important was their departure from Ranke's conception that the historian should not sit in judgment on an age, including his own. They argued that a historian must assume a position since he is ethically bound to commit himself to the cause of liberty and national unity in his writings as well as in his activities as a citizen. They stated that one cannot and should not assume a mere contemplative attitude. This question was implicit in the controversy between the Prussian historian, Sybel, and the Austrian, Julius von Ficker, over the significance of the medieval *Reich*. The controversy (1861–1862) broke just when the question of natural unity was again becoming a hot issue, after a decade of comparative quiet.

The Holy Roman Empire was, for Ficker, really the embodiment of the national German tradition and mission. It had generated those imponderable values which were perpetuated by the Hapsburgs and Austria. German culture had become, as a consequence of the *Reich*, the dominant influence in the whole middle European area.

On the other hand, Sybel contended that the medieval emperors should not have gone on imperialistic adventures in Italy. Like the Capetians in France, they should have stayed at home and built up

343

the nucleus of a strong royal power around their house lands, thus contributing to German national unification. As it was, the Germanies had succumbed to *Kleinstaaterei*. A strong German nation could be built now only around the hard core of a particular state. It is obvious that Sybel was thinking of Prussia as the nucleus of a united Germany. To him and his like-minded colleagues, Austria, because she was Catholic and comprised so many non-Germans and because of her imperial heritage, was the chief obstacle to German unification.

These political nationalistic historians, while they most definitely desired a strong state to the outside, also wanted freedom within built upon a constitutional and parliamentary foundation. About the time of his controversy with Ficker, Sybel, as a member of the Prussian parliament, was vigorously resisting Bismarck's strong-arm methods of dealing with that legislature. As indicated, England was regarded as the great model of constitutional evolution, and it was assumed that Germany would follow a similar course of development. This conception, which took on an almost doctrinaire character with many nineteenth-century liberal historians, had its origin in the assumption we have already encountered: that the peculiar form of English liberty was born among the early Germans and was common to all the Teutonic peoples. In the gradual unfolding of English common law and parliamentary practices, primordial liberty had made itself manifest as against the revolutionary popular sovereignty idea of Latin origin considered as embodied in the French state. The increasing emphasis on slow legal and political development is a reflection of the growing counter-revolutionary temper of mind of the middle-class liberals.

Significant also was the changed conception of nationality among German scholars. In the early nineteenth century it had been assumed that national unity was to be attained by a slow and peaceful growth of national self-consciousness, either by the spread of constitutional and parliamentary institutions or by the organic expression of the *Volksgeist* within the molds of historic institutions. But now a large number from both liberal and conservative camps were converted by Bismarckian diplomatic and military successes to the worship of the state as power.

The chief exponent at the time of this power conception of the state was the historian, Heinrich von Treitschke (1834–1896). The son of a Saxon general, he had turned to the academic life when increasing deafness precluded a military career. He had been stirred especially by the national and liberal insurgence of 1848 and had opposed Bismarck's roughshod parliamentary tactics. But the Schleswig-Holstein and Austro-Prussian wars revealed to him the meaning of Bismarck's effort to make the Prussian state the frame within which German national unity was to be realized. He argued that both liberty and culture could be realized only within this frame. And he sought to show in his numerous writings and lectures, especially at the University of Berlin after 1874, that the Prussian state was the embodiment of the manifest destiny of German greatness.

It must be emphasized that neither to Treitschke nor to the National Liberals (the liberal supporters of Bismarck), was the state an end in itself. It was the matrix for the development of liberty and culture. Though the National Liberals did not abandon the idea that inner freedom on a parliamentary basis was a necessary development, they did, however, place the achievement of state unity ahead of the realization of self-government within. Regarding the state, there developed in their thinking a sharp distinction between an irrational force of power politics without and the rule of law within, the latter involving deliberation and discussion in the parliamentary arena. An increasing emphasis, however, on the primacy of external state affairs over domestic politics led to the consequent assumption that the state demanded a strong authoritarian government within.

THE CHARISMA OF REICH AND VOLK VERSUS THE POWER-STATE

The Prussian state had derived its dynamic in the past largely from the driving force of a great ruling personality. For Bismarck, the state was not an abstract entity but an expression of the concrete individual will of the ruler. Its ethos was embodied in the political testaments of the Hohenzollern rulers; these rather than the constitutional-legal order provided the real continuity of the state will.

In itself, the state represented only a structure and a function, not an idea such as France's advancement of civilization, or England's the white man's burden, or Russia's the Third Rome. In Germany, only *Reich* embodied the idea of mission. It will be recalled that the political form of *Reich* had long lost its medieval embodiment of a Christianizing and civilizing mission to the east. It retained only a vestige of its earlier significance in the idea of a German living-space (*Lebensraum*) in middle Europe. It lost all religious universalism in the Bismarckian *Reich*, which was actually built on a narrow Protestant Lutheran basis, and stood in polar tension to Roman Catholicism and to its secularized form, the French Enlightenment.

Almost with the establishment of the second *Reich* there had appeared criticisms because it had emasculated both *Reich* and *Volk* of their universal and spiritual implications by subordinating them to the state. The chief critics who sought to revive the charisma of *Reich* and *Volk* were isolated individuals, for example, Constantin Frantz (1817–1891) and Paul de Lagarde (1827–1891), who came from the middle classes and represented points of view neither distinctly conservative nor liberal. Frantz and Lagarde did most of their writing in the first two decades (1870–1890) of the Bismarckian *Reich*, but their influence was not really felt until later. Their point of view was definitely colored by a return to Romantic conceptions of *Reich* and *Volk*. Neo-romantic political and social philosophy sought to restore to the *Reich* some of its ancient spiritual aura, to revitalize the *Volksgemeinschaft*, and so to bring about a rebirth of that corporate and community feeling and sense of mission which had enabled Germans to play a great role in the Middle Ages.

For the conservative and very perceptive Prussian publicist, Constantin Frantz, federalism represented the key to the problem of middle Europe. Frantz juxtaposed federalism to nationalism and statism, since it expressed a natural growth as against the obviously contrived character of the Bismarckian *Reich*. Moreover, federalism was truly Christian in spirit, whereas both nationalism and statism had egocentric drives. In federalism both the power motif of statism and the individuality motif of nationalism could achieve harmony in a third, higher form.

The new harmony had already been foreshadowed in the Holy Roman Empire. It had provided a thousand years of relative tranquillity largely because it united both the spiritual and the temporal whose separation in modern times has been the chief source of strife. The head of the Empire had been such by virtue both of divine right and election. Election had been not by individuals, as modern liberalism and democracy advocated, but by corporations and communities.

Frantz argued that Germany was the natural core of a European federation by virtue of her middle position and her tradition of *sacrum imperium.* She had been the mother of dynasties and hence was able to supply the necessary monarchical headship. Monarchy was essential because it supplied the charismatic element without which political power becomes a naked force or degenerates into party expediency. Since France was the chief exponent of rationalism, which was the principal modern solvent of the bonds of community, she should not assume leadership. Neither England nor Russia, strictly speaking, belonged to the European community of peoples. In fact, both Russia and America, because of their vast continental proportions and resources, constituted a potential menace in the face of which Europe should now unite in a federation. A European federation to endure should develop a super-confessional type of Christianity which could again serve as the cement of the ecumenical community.[1]

Paul de Lagarde was concerned principally with finding a religious basis for German nationalism. As an Oriental philologist he was well known for his researches in the *Septuagint.* His greatest aspiration was the publication of an edition of the Bible, but most of his energies in later life came to flow into writing essays and articles on what the Germans call *Kulturphilosophie* (philosophy of culture).

Lagarde's chief criticism of Bismarck was that he followed a line, inaugurated by Luther and continued by Hegel, leading to the deification of the state. The German *Volk* was thereby deprived of a role in history. In order that it might be recovered, the German would have to develop a religion of his own. Lagarde's studies of the Hebraic messianic idea had revealed to him the importance of this drive in the life of a people. But he was all for purging the Jewish influence from contemporary Christianity. His pronounced anti-Semitism may perhaps be ascribed to the fact that he saw, in the rapid rise of the Jew in all spheres of German life, the effects of a competing messianism. In any case, this secularized messianism was a menace to the German with his docile acceptance of *Obrigkeit*.

Lagarde was also strongly imbued with the seventeenth century theosophist notion that what was needed was a new world religion, purged of both the Roman and Jewish elements and restored to original Christianity. Luther's direct approach to God was advocated, but in the manner of the earliest Christians, for whom God was pure spirit speaking directly in nature and in the hearts of men. For Lagarde the Gospels presented the great revelation of this religion of the spirit.

Here again was the resurgence of the old mystical-speculative faith extending from Meister Eckhart and Jakob Böhme through Schelling into the nineteenth century. But with Lagarde, it came to assume a German national coloration which later became most pronounced in Alfred Rosenberg.

According to Lagarde, Bismarck's deification of the state led him to think only in terms of expediency. Bismarck did not go far enough; he should have rid Europe of the two pre-eminently militaristic nations, France and Russia. He should have extended his conquests eastward and westward so as to create a new *sacrum imperium* under German aegis.

Frantz and Lagarde are nineteenth-century examples of those characteristically German thinkers whom we have encountered before, whose ideas seek to render articulate those subterranean currents of yearnings and aspirations toward unity and immediacy which depart from the normal dictates of expediency and practical conduct in political affairs. They are the real German revolutionaries. They are not projectors of a new political and social order based on rational principles but generally hark back to an assumed early condition of harmony and solidarity such as the *sacrum imperium* of which they desire a rebirth.

Two features distinguish this yearning for utopia in reverse. First, it represented a reaction against the current functional rationalism, which was concerned principally with the problem of the relation of means to ends, exemplified in the increasing emphasis on technics and organization. Both writers sought, in the face of the rationalist solvent, whether of Bismarck's *raison d'état*, liberal constitutionalism or Marxian economic determinism, to find political and social roots in a new religious consciousness. Both sought a rebirth of a purely spiritual religion which would not need ecclesiastical forms but would permeate the whole life of the community. They reflected the resurgence of a current of irrationalism which was to break through decisively in the period between the two world wars.

Second, these writers mark the appearance of a rising concern among intellectuals with the question of the German's role or mission in Western society. A like concern appears at the same time in other countries, most clearly in Russia, where we encounter in Danilevski and Dostoevski a similar questioning attitude. But the Germans did not share with the Russians that complete absorption in the problem as to whether they belonged to the East or the West which so dominated Russian thought in the nineteenth and twentieth centuries as to almost exclude consideration of all objective problems. Nevertheless, the German also began to feel that he faced two cultural fronts, especially evident in the controversy over *Kultur* which appeared in the last decades of the century.

THE SOURCES OF GERMAN KULTUR CONSCIOUSNESS

We must reconsider briefly the distinctive meaning of German *Kultur* as contrasted with French *civilization*. It will be recalled that in the eighteenth century Herder stressed the fact that each people produces its own unique cultural forms and that these arise spontaneously out of the spiritual consciousness of a people. For Romanticism, also, *Kultur* was an expression of the creative force of the *Volksgeist*. On the other hand, the eighteenth-century French, with their salon conception of civilization, regarded cultural forms as arising out of social intercourse promoted by tolerance and taste. Thus, civilization had a cosmopolitan character.

Differences pertaining to the creative matrix of culture were accentuated in the nineteenth century by two factors. First, the tremendous expansion of the historical point of view, pre-eminently in Germany, led to the assumption that cultural forms can be judged only in terms of the *Zeitgeist*, the spirit of the age in which they appear. Each society and each age must be judged by the unique character of the values it produces. This point of view was quite in harmony with the growing national consciousness of the time. But it seemed to do away with any general standards or norms by which cultural ideals or values might be judged.

A second and contrary factor was the great scientific and technological development, which obviously recognized neither the creative peculiarities of a particular people nor those of an age. It seemed to be an impersonal and irresistible force extending into the limitless future and destined to be world-wide in its effects.

The conflict between these two developments was particularly felt in Germany because the historical approach had deep roots in the Idealistic and Romantic period of philosophic, literary, and artistic creativeness, whereas scientific-technological progress had burst on the scene in the middle of the nineteenth century. We have noted that the characteristic values arising from the scientific conception of progress—expressed through human enlightenment and betterment—had exerted only a limited influence in the Germanies of the eighteenth century and were submerged by the Idealistic and Romantic movements with their emphasis on the spontaneous creative spirit common to man and nature. Even the technological point of view, in the tradition of Paracelsus and continued in Liebig, was not based on a dead soulless mechanism, but was imbued with a titanic faith in the divine creativeness immanent in the universe.[2]

But in the second half of the nineteenth century, experimental science hit the German mind simultaneously with the debut of machine industry, and the two became, as indicated, very closely associated. Mechanistic science, which had originated in the seventeenth and eighteenth centuries, principally in England and France, now acquired its devotees among German thinkers who built up, as we have seen, monistic philosophies of man and the universe on the basis of mechanistic and materialistic laws. The most popular and somewhat belated exposition of this point of view was Ernst Haeckel's famous *The Riddle of the Universe*, which appeared in 1899 and of which 400,000 copies had been published by 1926. It had also appeared in twenty-five translations. Haeckel's popularity may be ascribed to the fact that, when he answered questions as to the nature of matter and energy, the origins of life, the process of evolution, and the development of language and knowledge, he wrote in optimistic evolutionary and materialistic terms which were comprehensible to the layman; he did not drag in abstruse metaphysical or theological notions.

The last decades of the century were marked by a decided movement away from the official churches toward the quest for a philosophy or faith which would be in harmony with the latest findings of science or would bring about a rebirth of spiritual values, as we noted in the case of Lagarde.

The *Kultur* question was also raised by the increasing prominence of the great city with its inclination toward uniformity and standardization of dress, habits, and forms of recreation. The invasion of the countryside by these tendencies made it evident that the traditional diversity of forms was doomed to extinction. Many intellectuals found it difficult to accept the innovations in spite of the greater abundance of material things, the progressive elimination of numerous diseases and ailments, and the great enhancement in power and prestige that accrued to Germany from her scientific and industrial progress.

Nowhere was the consciousness of contrast between old and new and the longing for genuineness and inner freedom more explicitly presented than in the Youth Movement, inaugurated with the organization of the *Wandervogel* in 1897. It had some of the characteristics of rebellion against discipline and conventional modes of thought that had characterized the *Sturm und Drang* of the eighteenth century and the Young Germany movement of the early nineteenth century. But the phase of the Youth Movement which began at the end of that century was not confined to literati and intellectuals; it was distinctly a mass movement of youth from all walks of life who went in for sports, long hikes, and somewhat uninhibited speech and behavior. It had a distinctly back-to-nature and return-to-the-people aspect, with a revival of old German songs, dances, and festivities.

To begin with, the Youth Movement was most decidedly in revolt against that banal kind of romanticism in which the lower middle-class white collar worker indulged, filling his house with all manner of picturesque bric-a-brac along with a leather-backed representation of the classics, and who, on the occasion of gymnastic festivities, wore old German costumes and assumed the names of ancient

351

heroes. Here we have the real sources of the cultural background of the Nazis, and not in the Youth Movement in its early phases.

The reaction of the Youth Movement against bourgeois artificiality and Philistinism was expressed, in part, in bizarre forms of dress and speech. Many of its participants also read Nietzsche, Langbehn, and Chamberlain, going in for Dionysian myth and the *Führer* idea.

THE QUESTION OF THE HISTORICAL SOURCES OF KULTUR

The new *Kultur* consciousness which arose as a reaction to the new "barbarism" of mechanistic science, mass society, and power-state manifested various intellectual strands.

The idealistic reaction went back to Kant, who had attempted to indicate the relative limits of reason and of sense experience, just as St. Thomas Aquinas had indicated those of reason with respect to faith. Kant brought to the fore the creative function of the mind, especially in the realm of values. It was this aspect of Kant's philosophy that aroused opinion against the pre-eminence of materialistic and mechanistic conceptions toward the end of the century. Characteristic of this reaction were the various neo-movements such as Neo-Kantianism, Neo-Hegelianism, and Neo-romanticism, all going back to the Idealistic age of philosophy and all seeking to be freed from the dominance of the natural sciences.

In 1891 the historian Karl Lamprecht aroused a major controversy when he began the publication of his monumental German history, completed in 1909. It was not his unified view of German development at which historians and philosophers took umbrage. It was rather the projection of a progressive development of German self-consciousness by successive and definitely determined psychological stages. These stages presumably are also applicable to the development of the national psychology of other peoples. The critics argued that the generalizing methods of the natural sciences, which seek uniformities and regularities to project physical laws, are not applicable to the development of culture. The historical approach was concerned not with the repetitious character of phenomena in order to be able to predict, but with the unique and the individual in the expressions of the human spirit.

The conflict between the method of the natural sciences and that of the historical approach assumed almost the proportions of the struggle between reason and faith among the medieval schoolmen. History, it may be argued, was of great importance to the nineteenth-century German because he was essentially traditionless. His connection with the past was not something he took for granted because he was embedded in a national historical and cultural mold but had to be reinterpreted again and again by returning to the alternative values of either Antiquity or the Middle Ages. The distinctively German movements, Reformation and Romanticism, both sought to return to an original matrix in order to effect a rebirth; they looked backward toward a mythical utopia rather than forward toward a rational utopia, as was the predominant tendency of Renaissance and revolution.

The question of the sources of rebirth was of special concern to Jakob Burckhardt (1818–1897) and Friedrich Nietzsche (1844–1900). Both, in a sense, stood outside of the general German development and observed it critically as Europeans first and Germans second. Burckhardt, although born and reared in Basel, Switzerland, where he spent practically his whole life, was educated in the German universities and thought of himself as belonging to the German cultural complex. However, he refused an invitation to occupy the chair at Berlin vacated by the death of his master, Ranke, in 1886. The much younger Nietzsche, born in Germany, started out as a teacher of classical languages at Basel, where he became a citizen and where he came under the influence of Burckhardt. After illness forced him to give up teaching, he felt himself more and more isolated from his fellow Germans and, in fact, from his fellow men. Much of the later years of his life were spent in Italy. In his last decade his mind clouded over completely.

These men regarded the Bismarckian *Reich* as a combination of Prussian statism and bourgeois Philistinism, fundamentally hostile to a *geistige Kultur*. Yet they were equally critical of the tendencies in Western democracy toward a mass society and its nihilistic leveling of values. Statism and nationalism threatened to smother the creative individual in bureaucratic regimentation and an ethnic patriotism. They admired the small city-states in which the most creative cultural developments had taken place, as witness Periclean Athens and Renaissance Florence.

Burckhardt is known especially for his history of the culture of the Italian Renaissance, but he also wrote on the Rome of Constantine and the Athens of Pericles. He deliberately chose periods when the old constraining bonds of custom and tradition were breaking down. He also deliberately avoided the current evolutionary approach because he thought it was implicitly deterministic; Hegel's great construct of the development of the universal reason was the prime example of trying to compress the creative human spirit into a mold. Burckhardt's own method was analytical. In dealing with Italian society of the Quatrocento, he presented a cross-section to show how the crumbling of the old compulsions, such as the medieval empire and church, left elbow-room everywhere for the emergence of the creative individual, no longer bound by the old corporate and religious fetters.

As Renaissance men no longer viewed man and the world "through a veil woven of superstition and ignorance" they became aware of their own inherent creative dynamism. They became conscious of the infinite possibilities for molding and shaping culture to conform to the newly acquired sense of proportion and harmony, which they also discovered in the ancient world.

This interpretation of the Renaissance as marking a rebirth of culture and the great divide between the Middle Ages and the modern secular age aroused a remarkable controversy among German scholars and intellectuals over the origins of modern culture. While the controversy produced some repercussions among scholars elsewhere, its storm center was in Germany, where it became a *Kulturkampf* involving the basic question of the peculiarity and individuality of German culture. It reached its culmination in the decade after World War I.

Various questions arose as to the relation of the Renaissance to the Middle Ages, the great age of the Holy Roman Empire, which then extended its sway over Italy, and to the Reformation, the distinctively German religious movement. A significant school of interpreters argued that the Renaissance had its sources in the movement for a general cultural and spiritual rebirth or renewal stimulated by Franciscanism, particularly in its later spiritualist phase with its projection of the three ages of man's salvation. The yearning for spiritual rebirth culminated in the Reformation, if not specifically in Luther, at least in the sectarian and spiritualist movements, which looked forward to a coming third Age of the Spirit, of harmony and concord among men, and of oneness with the creative spirit of the universe. It was also pointed out that yearning for rebirth and the dawn of a new order became henceforth a persistent aspiration in German development strongly reflected in much of Pietism, Idealism, and Romanticism.

THE VITALISTIC SOURCES OF REBIRTH

Nietzsche had shared with Wagner the romantic notion of bringing about a rebirth of the Greek spirit of tragedy in the German soul. Music, that peculiarly German art akin to the Greek drama in its original form, was to be the chief vehicle through which this rebirth was to be effected. But Wagner disappointed Nietzsche by proving to be, as Nietzsche thought, merely theatrical, in the modern sense of the word, and by smuggling in, as in *Parsifal*, all the old unheroic and therefore non-Greek virtues derived from Christianity, such as humility, resignation, and asceticism. The attempt to find a modern substitute for religion in the idea of progress, in pacifism and toleration, which were really only idealistic distillations of decrepit ancient faiths, was for Nietzsche the worst kind of decadence. The Dionysian affirmation of life which he exalted derived its content from various sources: from the early Greek fertility cult and its intoxication with the creativeness of life; from the Darwinian struggle for survival with its drive toward mastery of the environment; and from the heroic vitalism revealed in Renaissance characters like Cesare Borgia, whose ruthless will to power might have purged the world of idealistic phantoms if Luther hadn't come along to again throw the apple of religious discord into the arena.

Biological science, according to Nietzsche, performed one invaluable function; it showed that man, who has maintained himself

355

wholly by his successful development of tools, is an integral part of nature. But eventually he is doomed to extinction like all other species and the universe will not be either better or worse for his passing. In fact, man's situation is most precarious since he relies not on instinct but on intellect, which makes him very self-conscious and thereby robs him of that sense of security which the other species have. There are for men no "eternal horizons or perspectives," either transcendental or biological. Hence man should always live as if the hourglass of his existence were about to be turned again to confront him with a wholly new situation, or even with extinction.[3]

The German in particular, Nietzsche implied, has turned to history as an escape from this essentially tragic view of human existence. In so doing, he has transformed history from a monumental art, concerned with portraying the great deeds and actions of men, into a science devoted to cataloguing the microscopic steps of man's progress toward the security of law and order. Great individual men and great individual events are emasculated of their creative force if they are reduced in stature to a common mediocrity. This kind of reflection on the past obviously leads to passivity and resignation in the face of the precariousness of human existence.

Nietzsche has been dealt with particularly as a critic of the *Kultur* of his times; his positive philosophy of eternal recurrence, of the superman and the transvaluation of all values, whereby nihilism may be overcome, will be dealt with later. Not until after the catastrophe of World War I did Nietzsche become a positive influence; before that he was more often an intellectual rage than a world and life experience.

THE INDELIBLE QUALITIES OF RACE

The rebirth of *Kultur* was also sought in a return to the Romantic conception of the *Volk*, now stripped of much of its earlier idealistic and humanitarian content and given a predominantly naturalistic and egotistical coloration.

Since he lacked political unity and power to buttress his sense of cultural individuality, the German had earlier sought support in the notion that, in realizing national cultural individuality as a facet of the potentialities of humanity, he was engaged in the common enterprise of the European community of peoples. But having acquired the outward appurtenances of political unity and power, he became, toward the end of the century, increasingly uncertain about that common enterprise as he became aware of two cultural fronts, the Western liberal and rationalistic and the Eastern autocratic and spiritualistic. Increasingly conscious of lying in the middle, his sense of cultural individuality turned completely inward to the search for so-called indelible qualities of national character and race.

The change occurred under the impact of the realism of the second half of the century reflected in the empiricism of the sciences, the *Realpolitik* of Bismarck, and the scientific socialism of Marx and Engels. The power conflicts of states and classes came to be regarded as the chief formative forces in society.

The most influential scientific generalization of the time was Darwin's conception of evolution by natural selection. It embodied three basic ideas: first, that all species tend to increase up to the very limits of food supply, producing the struggle for subsistence; second, that extensive environmental changes accentuate this struggle to the point where survival of whole species is involved; and third, under these conditions the apparently minute differences among individuals which favor survival are perpetuated and extended to produce new species.

These ideas, while generally not applied directly to social evolution, created a frame of thinking whose pervasive influence was second only to that of Marx. Many people found justification for inequalities among men on what were apparently scientific grounds, and the phrase "survival of the fittest" became the favorite slogan of imperialists, nationalists, and racialists.

Colonials were the natural advocates of racial distinctions and inequalities because they were removed from the homeland, and hence their tie with their compatriots was in terms of culture or race. Also, those Germans living in the eastern borderlands surrounded by Slavs were inclined to think of nationality in terms of the indelible qualities of race existing entirely apart from the fatherland and its national institutions.

In 1890 there appeared an anonymous work called *Rembrandt*

as Educator (*Rembrandt als Erzieher*) which aroused great attention. It was by Julius Langbehn, an art historian, who, influenced by Lagarde and Nietzsche, was very critical of the current scientific interest in the extension of empirical knowledge at the expense of character. Character had been formed in the past by dynamic elites —such as those of Venice, of the Dutch city republics, and of the Teutonic Order—which utilized a particular landscape to achieve creative cultures. This kind of culture rooted in a particular landscape achieved its highest expression in the art of Rembrandt. The growing emphasis on rootedness in the soil became especially evident in the increasing number of regional studies in literature and art.

About ten years later another work appeared of similar significance; it was Houston Stewart Chamberlain's *Foundations of the Nineteenth Century*, in which not soil but race was proposed as the basis of cultural pre-eminence. Chamberlain, originally an Englishman, came to live in Germany and became wholly devoted to its culture. He was an enthusiastic disciple of Wagner and, indeed, married Wagner's daughter. He wrote biographies of Wagner and Goethe, but he is best known for the *Foundations*, which was widely read by people who have been called "the half-educated." *Foundations* was also a favorite of William II.

Like *Rembrandt as Educator*, the ideas of the *Foundations* were mostly borrowed from others, principally from Gobineau, Lagarde, and Wagner. It presents the evolution of Western culture as the creative achievement of the Aryan peoples, all of whom have a common ancestry in one folk. These Aryan peoples include Greeks, Latins, Slavs, and the predominant Germanic group. The Jews are excluded as perhaps the chief enemies of the Christian-Germanic culture. Jesus, coming from the Palestinian borderland, was assumed to be an Aryan. The Roman Catholic church in its Counter Reformation incarnation was also an enemy. Again, Chamberlain sought a new faith for the German—a non-dogmatic religion which would experience God in the immediacy of nature. This combination of nature pantheism and mysticism was assumed to have been characteristic also of the ancient Aryans.

The appeal of these ideas to many Germans, especially among the middle classes, may be attributed to the fact that in mass societies myth takes the place of history. History had come to be thought of as a process of evolution in which such impersonal forces as economic conditions, power politics, and intellectual tendencies hold sway over peoples who appear to be mere puppets. Myth suggests rebirth by return to a primordial situation in which the individual and group are bound together by the mystic ties of blood relationships. It also suggests the tribal friend-foe relationship which means the exclusion from the group of the stranger who has customs which are alien.

The most obvious alien was the Jew, since he was assumed to have preserved more or less intact his own tribal customs and religion, which he carried with him wherever he went. As religion ceased to be a factor in distinguishing the Jew from others because of the general enlightenment and indifference to theology and dogma, another distinction appeared—race. Anti-Semitism began to gather momentum in Germany in the late nineteenth century just when the Germans were becoming *Kultur* conscious.

The *Kultur* problem, projected by scientific-technical progress and national-power politics, shifted the accent from the question of the creative sources of culture in spiritual universals, personality, and *Volksgeist* to their historic embodiments in classical idealism, Renaissance individualism, and Aryan dominance. *Kultur* was regarded as a cumulative product of these creative moments of history. It acquired an almost autonomous development, independent of the creative force of individual personality and of *Volksgeist*. Hence it came to be regarded as having its own built-in dynamic, provided by science, state, and capitalism as the motive forces of its progressive development. For the German, this point of view acquired particular relevance by virtue of the tremendous advances made by the union of science with industrial technology and of *Reich* with Prussian statism. To the generation preceding World War I *Kultur* consciousness seemed to be the culmination of all previous German development.

XIII

The Breakthrough of Irrationalism in Politics and Thought

The controversy over *Kultur* was still largely carried on within the old frames of Idealism and Romanticism. It reflected a questioning attitude toward science and a materialistic and mechanistic view of the universe, but Haeckel's very popular work at the end of the century still assumed that the problem of the universe was on the way to being solved within the framework of that view. The German felt that history demonstrated that the Second *Reich* was the structure within which he was destined to finally realize national unity.

THE CRISIS IN POLITICAL ETHOS AND IN WELTANSCHAUUNG

Along with most other Western peoples at the turn of the century, the Germans believed that the great advances of science and technology would contribute to human welfare in the extension of leisure and culture. Also, they assumed that the hundred years of peace since the Napoleonic Wars marred only by "necessary" local wars in behalf of national unity were evidence of this progress.

But the first two decades of the twentieth century definitely demonstrated that these notions were illusory. Two factors in particular contributed to the disillusionment. First, the German rulers seemed to lose sight of the political factors (of reasons of state) involved in the rise of Germany to a dominant position in central Europe; that the peaceful acceptance of a strong power unifying most of that area was largely due to the skill of one man, Bismarck, who declared the new Germany to be a satiated state.

The fact that the Germans lost sight of the fundamental precariousness of European peace and of the German position may be attributed to an illusion founded upon their continued and accelerated economic advance, which by 1914 had put them in the forefront among European states in steel production. The expansion of German industries, the establishment of her great steamship lines, and the appearance of products labeled "Made in Germany" in all the markets of the world served to conceal the real situation. It was even assumed that Germany by virtue of these advances was entitled to a place in the sun alongside the old imperialist powers who were staking out claims in Africa and Asia.

The hegemonial drive of the newly established German *Reich* was the major factor in the great wars of the twentieth century and contributed enormously toward the mounting technological fury of these wars and their revolutionary disturbance.[1]

The second factor was the fundamental reorientation in thought which took place simultaneously with this accentuation of national hubris. The older assumptions with regard to the universe and man were undermined. Both science and history sought to divorce themselves from the naively held conception of causal determinism. The subatomic and subconscious worlds were now juxtaposed to the traditional rational order and shown to be not amenable to the old conceptions of time, space, and causality. Philosophically speaking, the old cosmic order had provided a fairly well-mapped-out field of operations for the conquest of nature. Now the liquidation of this philosophic heritage had two results: it gave an added impetus to experimental-technological interests which were enhanced by the needs of war, and it rendered scientific knowledge problematical in spite of tremendous advances.

The coincidence of these political and intellectual crises in Germany made her a focus of world interest in the twentieth century. Although the Germans suffered defeat and dismemberment, their intellectual achievements, particularly in philosophy, science, and technology, have continued to exert a world-wide influence.

FROM BISMARCKIAN CONTAINMENT TO IMPERIALISM

When Germany became dissatisfied in the late nineteenth century with her narrow continental European position and entered the arena of world politics, she was confronted by such giants as the British oceanic empire and the great Eurasian empire of the Russians, who, along with the French, resented Germany's intrusion. Bismarck had been satisfied with maintaining the security of her position in the middle of Europe. He had acquiesced, it is true, in the acquisition of several thousand square miles of territory in Africa, but largely as a matter of political expediency. For him these acquisitions were still in the mercantilist tradition, to provide tropical products such as tea, tobacco, and cotton for the homeland. He did not anticipate that these meager colonies were to serve as a symbol in the German drive toward a place in the sun.

In general the Germans in the decades before World War I showed little interest in the expansion of the national frontiers in Europe, say, by the possible inclusion of the large block of Germans in Austria. Such union, later called *Anschluss*, would have meant the virtual dissolution of Austria-Hungary. Moreover, since predominantly Protestant Germany wanted no more Catholics, there were very definite limitations on expansion in middle Europe.

There were those who, like Frantz and Lagarde, criticized Bismarck for his containment policy in central and eastern Europe. The Pan-German League, which made its appearance in 1890 and which comprised a very small but vociferous group of imperialists, agitated for both overseas and middle European expansion. All in all, however, the Bismarckian policy in middle Europe was adhered to in government circles, which left the door open only to expansion abroad.

It was the upper middle class who were the chief exponents of the new imperialism—not the conservative agrarians nor the Marxist Social Democrats. The liberals, from the right-wing Nationals to the left-wing Progressives, were the chief supporters of the enhancement of Germany's prestige and power position. Among them were many such as Friedrich Naumann and Paul Rohrbach, who were in effect social imperialists. By the end of the century these social imperialists had succeeded in capturing about one-third of the total vote.

Naumann was a pastor concerned with preaching the social gospel among the underprivileged and with effecting a positive reconciliation of the Social Democrats with the Bismarckian *Reich*. He organized the National Socialist Association in 1896, which, it was hoped, would serve as the nucleus of a mass political party. It attracted a number of leading liberal intellectual lights but very few workers. Nevertheless, it marked the first real attempt to link nationalism with socialism. By their union Naumann hoped to bring to an end the futile opposition against the state which the Social Democrats carried on—an opposition which made no sense any more, since they had virtually abandoned the idea of working for revolution.

Naumann spoke of himself as being a Christian in his religious views, a Darwinian in his conception of the world of nature, and an imperialist in his political attitudes.[2] This constellation of rather disparate convictions indicates that the old logical coherence of liberalism was crumbling. It had centered on the notion that power must at all costs be contained and counterbalanced. The National Liberals had already made a concession to Bismarck's use of power to gain national unity. Now even the left-wing Progressives, whose leader Naumann virtually became, began to think positively about power. With Germany united under the leadership of a "social and democratic" emperor, which Naumann hoped William II would become, the conflict of classes and factions could be overcome. Political power would then serve as the means of securing democratic and social gains. In the very influential work entitled *Mitteleuropa*, published during and relevant to World War I, he presented this conception of a unified political and economic movement applied to the whole area of middle Europe.

An example of liberal positive thinking toward colonialism was presented in the books of Paul Rohrbach, a member of the Naumann circle who had traveled widely in the Orient and Africa. His *Germany Among the Peoples of the World* (1906) and the *German Idea in the World* (1912) argued that colonies were not necessary to Germany for dumping surplus population or manufactured products, nor as sources of raw materials. German emigration was declining, and, from an economic point of view, there were better markets and more abundant sources of essential raw materials elsewhere than in the colonial areas. Rohrbach had an idea not unlike that of Wakefield and the English imperial reformers of the early nineteenth century who wished to establish "Little Englands" in the colonies by planned colonization. In like manner, Rohrbach wished to transplant all manner of experts and technicians—administrative, agricultural, and industrial—of which the technical schools and universities threatened to create a surplus. Far away from the old caste pretensions and class antagonisms a new human type might thus be created.[3] The actual experience of German colonization in Africa, however, ran quite opposite to his aspirations. The bureaucratic-military Prussian virtues were accentuated in all their harshness and brutality, and provoked native unrest and rebellion in the Herrera insurrections (1904–1908).

These idealistic motivations in the German imperialistic drive of the late nineteenth and early twentieth centuries must be taken into consideration as well as the brash appeals to outright chauvinism of the Pan-German League, which generally impressed foreigners more than it did the Germans. The idealism explains why many prominent liberals, particularly in academic circles and among the literati, felt attracted by, or at least condoned, the often blatant talk of German destiny overseas.

GERMAN CONSCIOUSNESS OF MIDDLE EUROPEAN CONFINEMENT

Unlike the English and the French, the Germans had never held overseas territories. Their expansion had been a movement outward from the boundaries of the *Reich* to include adjoining lands and peoples, particularly to the east. Now in these adjacent areas German cultural influence was receding, reflecting the sense of lost creativity in *Kultur*. Naumann even argued that the Germans had nothing more to offer the Slavs, and that territorial conquests to the east were out of order since the frontiers of Europe were acquiring an almost "sacrosanct character."

Much of the expansive and even missionary zeal which had once found an outlet on the eastern frontiers now turned overseas. Though not without an idealist tincture, such as we have encountered in Naumann and Rohrbach, the emphasis was largely on prestige politics. Coming late on the world scene, Germany had no interests to protect or specific goals to attain, such as Constantinople, Suez, Singapore, Syria, and the Sudan which had been acquired by other countries in earlier phases of European expansion. By the late nineteenth century the backward areas all over the world had been either appropriated or claimed. Having neither specific interests to defend nor feasible outlets for expansion, Germany was thrown back on the assertion of national prestige in her encounter with the other powers in the world arena.

Unwilling to accept the given historical situation, Germany was inclined to play with the idea of a diplomatic breakthrough without going as far as an offensive action which would result in war. She was confronted with the frustrating situation that, although possessing economic and military power beyond her neighbors, she was, by virtue of coming late on the scene, confined to the cramping boundaries of middle Europe.

In judging Germany's behavior, we must bear in mind her suddenly acquired sense of power and with it her abrupt realization of the narrowness of her European position.

Under these circumstances Germany was regarded as an interloper in world affairs and a disturber of the peace. Her manners were often, indeed, very bad. Lacking the sense of security of an established position, she was always afraid that she would be overlooked. As a result she was frequently assertive and aggressive in claiming the right to participate—in pushing what little claim to an interest she may have had and in trying to drive a hard bargain. This became most apparent in the Morocco incidents of 1905 and 1911, which made Germany's international position worse.

To the consciousness of the narrowness of their land base in the middle of Europe, the Germans added the growing feeling of being encircled by their enemies. It took World War I and its aftermath to bring this notion to full realization. The feeling of encirclement was greatly accentuated by the retreat of the Germans in the eastern borderlands when a new aggressive form of nationalism swept over the peoples of those areas.

While the Germans were newcomers in the Orient and Africa, they were old hands as colonizers to the east in the borderlands extending from the eastern shores of the Baltic to the head of the Adriatic. Colonies of Germans had been thrust far northeastward along the shores of the Baltic and southeastward as far as Transylvania and along the Volga. Everywhere islands of Germans were interspersed among other nationalities. Only along the southern shores of the Baltic in East Prussia and to the southeast along the Danube in the Austrian lands had fairly solid blocks of German settlement been achieved.

The economic and cultural pre-eminence of the Germans enabled them to establish themselves among the Slavic peasant communities, where they often formed the urban centers of traders and artisans. Their cultural superiority and the lack of nationalistic prejudice before the nineteenth century had contributed to the Germanization of many of the more enterprising individuals among the indigenous population. In rising from the peasantry to the new social status of an official, a teacher, a doctor or lawyer, a person adopted the German language and probably took a Germanized name, which brought superior social prestige. German naturally became the language of culture in Prague and even in Budapest. Universities, such as that at Prague, were almost completely German.

Among the Germans known as Balts, who settled the lands along the eastern shores of the Baltic, members of the landed aristocracy played a leading role in Russian affairs, as the names of many prominent Russian soldiers and statesmen far into the nineteenth century indicate. The large communities of Jews, who generally predominated in trade and shopkeeping, were also German in culture.

SLAVIC MASS NATIONALISM

Earlier reactions against the Germans had been largely religious and political, but in the nineteenth century the nationalistic reactions began to assume a total cultural character. The first important nationalist wave came in the revolutions of 1848. Even these early nationalist movements were, however, inspired by the ideas first of Herder and then of Hegel. But toward the end of the nineteenth and the beginning of the twentieth century the nationalism of the border peoples acquired a much broader social basis. The early idealistic phase of nationalism had been largely confined to intellectuals and to a very thin layer of upper bourgeoisie. Now it percolated downward into the lower social strata—the lower middle class and the peasantry. Industrialization contributed toward the movement to the cities, which were the chief centers of the nationalist agitation. But even the peasantry of the countryside became infected with the national virus as a reaction against exploitation by alien landowners and by Jewish and German traders.

As nationalism assumed a mass character, it obviously lost its earlier idealistic complexion and became freighted with economic and social grievances. It tended to lose universal humanitarian aims and acquire a regional rootedness. It was more and more concerned with local autonomy and even national independence, which explains the decline of Pan-Slavism toward the end of the nineteenth century. This grass-roots nationalism ran counter to the centralism which had been the cornerstone of state power since the development of monarchical authority had undermined the local autonomy of the great feudal landowners.

Bismarck recognized that nationalism in the West was a unifying factor but that to the east it was a divisive and revolutionary force which might undermine the public order established for centuries. This explains his very definite concern with the maintenance of the monarchical authority in the three states, Germany, Russia, and Austria-Hungary, which comprised within their frontiers the whole of middle Europe. Like Metternich, he felt that the cooperation of the three sovereign rulers of these states was the best means of keeping intact the European public order in middle Europe. To the West, he appeared as a nationalist concerned primarily with German unity; to the East, however, he was the conservative Prussian Junker for whom the containment of the forces which threatened a centuries-old social order was the chief function of the state.

Bismarck apparently lacked concern for the plight of the Balts and other German groups abroad who were caught in the wheels of national assimilation processes. He was not fully aware of the elemental forces lodged in the new nationalism, which were threatening the dissolution, in his own time, of one of the three state props on which the order of middle Europe rested.

The state could no longer maintain its position of being above the nationalities, at least not in Austria-Hungary. Even in Germany with the relatively simple problem of having to deal only with a Polish minority, it became necessary for the state to intervene positively in behalf of the Germans in areas where they constituted a minority. Moreover, it was becoming harder to maintain the old social order whereby an aristocratic landowning class ruled over peasants of different nationality and a mercantile and industrial class of German culture exploited Slav workers. When these "lower" orders fused their social and national grievances through party and ballot, the Slav numbers began to speak louder than German culture and social prestige. The German both at home and abroad showed himself inept at dealing with the new Slavic nationalism. This has been ascribed to the fact that the Slav shows a greater aptitude for grass-roots communal solidarity than the German, who looks upward to state organization for cohesion.

SECTARIAN NATIONALISM IN AUSTRIA-HUNGARY

The situation of the Germans in Austria became most ambiguous. On the one hand, they had inherited the tradition of a ruling elite which had stood for the order and prestige represented by state, property, and culture as against the "inferior" peoples over whom they ruled. On the other hand, the creation of a national German state opened up the vista of a reunion of all Germans in a great national *Reich*.

The conflict between the ruling Germans and the most advanced people culturally and economically among the subject nationalities, the Czechs, became significant for the development not only of Austria-Hungary but also for the history of the Germans in general. The Czechs had been the leaders in the Pan-Slav reaction against Germanism in 1848. Their older Romanticist historians had not only promoted the conception of the brotherhood of all Slavs as descendants of a single people, but the notion of the pacific nature of the Slav as compared with conquering Germans. Their young historians, however, emphasized the historic unity of the Bohemian lands and that, in the Hussite wars, the Czechs had achieved for a time both political autonomy and religious individuality against the Hapsburgs. The Czechs thus provided themselves with a fully developed national past in which the villains were the Germans under Hapsburg championship.

In the second half of the nineteenth century, the Czechs, like the Poles, proceeded to the development of mass associations to promote national self-help and unity from below. Here we encounter what may be called sectarian nationalism, which was a total nationalism and which organized the populace from top to bottom and thus broke down the old distinctions between the classes upon which German superiority in terms of *Kultur* and property had been based. This nationalism thus ran counter to the tendency of intellectual or well-to-do Czechs to pass over, so to speak, into the ranks of the ruling group.

Much later than most of the other nationalities, the Germans began to develop a nationalist sectarianism involving mass organization, ethnic intransigence, and the tactics of obstruction. While antipathy to other nationalities was taken for granted, a more dangerous concomitant was the pronounced hostility to all forms of internationalism, such as financial capitalism, Marxian socialism, and Roman Catholic clericalism. In the Austrian Pan-Germanist and irredentist agitator, George Schönerer (1842–1921), opposition to these forms of internationalism was not a matter of principle but of concrete Germanism reflected in lower middle-class and peasant biases arrayed against the alien worlds of Pan-Slavism, Romanism, and Judaism. The Jews were regarded as a great danger by the lower middle-class shopkeepers and tradesmen and peasants because they represented big business capitalism and proletarian socialism, as the names of Rothschild and Marx testified. But the greatest danger was that Austria would be Slavified, aided and abetted by Roman Catholic clericalism. Schönerer turned Protestant and advocated a "free-from-Rome" strategy as well as a free-from-the-Hapsburgs movement. This predominantly *anti* point of view aimed at the union or *Anschluss* of Austrian territories with Germany to complete German national unity. A Germanized Bohemia would also be included, but the remaining Hapsburg territories, with such Germans as they might include, would be left to the Magyars.

These ideas, floating about in the emotionally surcharged atmosphere of Vienna in the decade before World War I, exerted a great influence upon the young Hitler, who spent the formative period of his intellectual and emotional life in Vienna from 1906 to 1913. Hitler was of German ancestry, coming from the Slavic border. His father had risen from the peasantry to the position of a lower official and had achieved middle-class status. The attitudes that Schönerer and other extremists like him reflected were to become the core of the Nazi ideology. National Socialism derived its mass organization, its friend-foe psychology, and its tactics of constitutional and legal sabotage from the nationalist sectarianism of the borderlands.

Along with the new imperialistic conflicts, the nationalistic animosities launched Europe upon a series of great wars which destroyed the very foundations of the middle European historic order. World War I marks the beginning of the revolutionary phase in the development of the continental peoples, just as the end of the eighteenth and early nineteenth centuries had marked that of the seaboard peoples.

FROM MILITARY BREAKTHROUGH TO MASS WARFARE

World War I, by converting Germany into a besieged fortress, forcibly brought home the fact of complete encirclement and the necessity of achieving a breakthrough. It was the urge to break out of the constricting limits of her central European position rather than the desire for specific territories which characterized the hegemonic drive of the Germans.

The increasing momentum of this drive during the war, along with mechanization, led to the complete dominance of the technical-military point of view over the political. Emperor, chancellor, and *Reichstag* were all pushed aside. Political considerations no longer played a restraining role; military victory at all costs became virtually an obsession. Consequently, there was little sense of moderation and practically no recognition of the limits of attainable ends, both with respect to the power of the enemy and with respect to what the German nationals would do.

The German military had developed a formula, called the "Schlieffen plan," to overcome what seemed to be the inevitable danger of a two-front war against a coalition. It was a military solution to compensate for a series of diplomatic blunders which had aligned Russia, France, and England against Germany and Austria-Hungary. It represented in itself a terrific gamble. All the chips were placed on German ability to deliver a knockout blow against France before the Russians could really get started. However, the relative quickness of the Russian mobilization and the invasion of East Prussian territories caused the shifting of divisions from the western front, depriving it of the necessary punch to carry through to its objective.

It may be argued that the whole plan relied too much on historical precedent—upon Frederick the Great's war with the great coalition and more particularly upon the elder Von Moltke's brilliant strategy in bringing about the defeat of France at Sedan in a single great battle. It was not recognized that the conditions of war had changed fundamentally with the development of the nation in arms. It also was not recognized that, even though the Marne might become a second Sedan, this would not necessarily mean the collapse of France, certainly not that of England. Hitler later achieved this very breakthrough and destruction of French military power, but he did not thereby win the war. The obsession of the military with the idea of a breakthrough and with a great battle of annihilation referred to as a "Cannae"—Hannibal's great battle against the Romans—continued to run like a red thread through the military thinking of the General Staff. As a consequence, the general strategy of the war was lost sight of. The failure of the Schlieffen plan seems to have left the German military without any other alternative than a mere exchange of blows with the enemy.

The war was not one of decisive battles, but rather a prolonged and continuous four-year struggle between masses of men occupying fortified positions in lines of trenches. The fighting fronts were stabilized in an intricate network of trenches and barbed wire entanglements. The soldier virtually went underground, conforming, so to speak, to the mining economy of which the war had become an expression. Periodic attacks involved the loss or gain of a few hundred yards at most but at the expense of thousands of lives. The fronts in the west did not vary by more than twelve miles in the four years of warfare. The rapid fire-power of machine guns and artillery accounted largely for the predominance of the defense and hence for a static type of warfare. Gas could also be used because of the relatively fixed fronts.

Essentially this warfare consisted in hurling masses of men and material at each other, making mass production count for everything. The fighting front of rapid consumption was, in a sense, but an extension of the home front production line, where tightening of belts prevailed as far as consumers' goods and food were concerned. Germany found it necessary, as early as 1915 when the prospect of rapid victory vanished, to conserve materials and foodstuffs. As the war continued, all foodstuffs and raw materials came to be placed on a priority list, which made necessary a careful coordination of finance, industry, and agriculture. In fact, many of the essential features of a planned economy appeared in what was called "war socialism."

WAR SOCIALISM AND FORTRESS MIDDLE EUROPE

The chief architect of the new war socialism was Walther Rathenau (1867–1922), the son of the founder of the great electric trust, the AEG, of which he became the head. Although a civilian and a Jew, he convinced the General Staff that the planned conservation of raw materials was important, and he became the head of a new division of the War Ministry devoted to that task. The General Staff gradually came to realize that it was up against a war for which there existed no precedent in the books on military strategy and tactics. Consequently, they were reluctantly forced to admit Rathenau and other civilians to their military councils.

Rathenau was not only an organizational genius but also had the philosophic mind to appreciate the implications of the new political and economic trends. The books he had written showed a profound appreciation of the emerging problem of the relation of technology to *Geist*. He was especially concerned with the cramping effect of mechanization and bureaucratization on man's spirit. He was also quick to appreciate that a new economic and social order was being born out of the war. Though convinced that return to the old laissez-faire economy of the prewar days would be extremely difficult, he still appreciated its emphasis on individual enterprise. But how could total bureaucratization be avoided under increasing state control and supervision?

The *Weltanschauung* of this enlightened capitalist recognized the polarity of two increasingly dominant forces: that of rational functionalism in technology and economics, and that of irrationalist values in politics and propaganda. Rathenau was a pronounced nationalist and statist. Mass democracy was to be combined with monarchy, which embodied an essential charismatic element. Frederick the Great, as the first servant of the state, was his ideal ruler. He recognized, however, that somehow in the twentieth century it would be necessary to fuse the Prussian organizational genius with the Romantic irrationalism of the *Volk*. These notions became prevalent among the more perceptive leaders of the new industrial middle class in the course of the war as it became more apparent that the Bismarckian *Reich* lacked roots in the populace.

In creating fortress Germany, the war naturally brought to sharp awareness the configuration of the land base of German power. The economic and military unity of the middle European area came to be clearly perceived. It was recognized that the Austrian territories and those of the German empire formed a natural geographical unity. Moreover, by virtue of their middle position, the Germans needed not only greater living space, but a fusion of the economic, cultural, and political sectors of this area.

This whole conception was most idealistically and forcefully presented in Friedrich Naumann's *Mitteleuropa* (1915). It was the most widely read book of its kind. War, it averred, opens up new horizons because it rips off political disguises and brings to consciousness the true nature of things.

Naumann envisaged a middle European unity extending from the Adriatic to the Baltic and eastward to the borders of Russia and westward to the Rhine. This unity was not to be formed out of regions pieced together like a crazy quilt in a mere political organization. It was to constitute a conscious fusion of military, cultural, and economic forces produced by the new awareness of space and time that the war created: the trenches, not mere physical forms such as rivers or mountains, idealized by Arndt, constituted its natural walls. The Romans and Chinese had also built such walls; so had the first great *Reich*, from Otto the Great to Frederick Barbarossa. These great historic precedents disclosed the German cultural mission in this area.

In the modern period, Germany had, by her economic and technological development, demonstrated the possibility of a new integration of society in a functional economy. It meant for Naumann the realization of socialism not on a class basis but as an expression of the communal solidarity of the *Volk*. In the war Prussian organizational discipline was permeating the *Volk* from top to bottom. The closed commercial state of Fichte could now be realized and a reconciliation achieved between the bourgeois nationalistic and the worker's socialistic conceptions of economy.

CONSCIOUSNESS OF GERMAN CULTURAL UNIQUENESS

War lost all heroic qualities and glory in the mud and slime of the trenches and the ghastly desolation of no man's land. The great sacrifices in lives demanded, moreover, that the war be presented not as a power struggle, but as one in behalf of ideal values. To the Western peoples, it naturally became a war in which democracy was arrayed against autocracy and militarism. Great numbers of books and pamphlets written by publicists and propagandists of the Allies sought to show that the roots of the German authoritarian and militaristic spirit were to be found in the Idealistic and Romantic movements and even in Luther. By way of the philosophers Kant and Hegel and the historians Ranke and Treitschke, the exaltation of might and force over right and reason had been forged in German thought. Even the much vaunted German universities, at whose wells of learning generations of English, French, and American scholars had drunk, now came to be regarded as sources of the glorification of the power-state.

It is apparent that total mass warfare demands the complete defamation of the thought and culture of a foe just as it seeks his complete annihilation in battle. Seen in the perspective of the past two decades, this was a distortion of German development built upon a series of partial truths. It was not appreciated, apparently, that the thought of all profound thinkers has an ambiguous character. In fact, it may be argued that the Germans, possessed by the notion of the eternal conflict of *Macht* and *Geist,* had merely gone farther in distinguishing the elements of force and power from those of values and ideals and in recognizing that *Macht* can no more be expunged from the world than *Geist.*

Made a pariah among the peoples of the earth and unable to appeal to the universal claims of liberalism and democracy, the German naturally turned to his own traditions, especially to those now attacked by the West—to the Idealism and Romanticism of the great classical age. In them he found justification for the peculiarity of his own culture. This point of view was expressed by a number of German writers, most convincingly in a series of essays by the novelist Thomas Mann, some of which were later published under the characteristic title, *Reflections of a Non-Political Mind* (1918). In his novels Mann portrayed searchingly and vividly the erosion of the ideals and values of the middle class.

Mann's basic assumption was that the peculiarity of Germany derived from her middle position between the East and the West. This point of view was also expressed in his greatest novel, *The Magic Mountain* (1924). For Mann the German stood between the mystically inclined East and the rationally intellectual West, a situation which produced the basic polarity in German thinking and its continual striving to bring about a conjunction or coincidence of opposites. Nowhere was this more characteristically manifest than in German Romanticism.

Mann's chief concern was with the polarity between the German idea of *Kultur* and the Western idea of civilization. *Kultur* in the Idealistic and Romantic tradition was the creative product of a *Volk.* Its roots lay deep in the communal values produced by the mythical and sacred associations of aristocracy with peasantry. Civilization, on the other hand, implied politics and technics, which are mass creations and the product of rationalization. Another polarity lay in community (*Gemeinschaft*) and society (*Gesellschaft*), the former being concerned with ends in themselves, at one time on the level of primordial tribal urges, now refined and elevated by *Geist;*

the latter being concerned with the adjustment of means to ends in associations founded for specific purposes, as exemplified in politics and conventions. The *Volk* was the highest form of German community, as the Western nation was that of society.

Mann was aware of the dangers which lurked in the Neo-romantic turning backward to the primitive and Dionysian irrational roots of *Kultur*. Nevertheless, he was powerfully influenced by the suggestive force of the ideas of Wagner and Nietzsche, as well as of Goethe. They expressed his own aversion to Western democratic, humanitarian values, although he was always aware that his own sense of irony was rooted in the world of Western rationalism.

These three middle-class thinkers, Rathenau, Naumann, and Mann, in their awareness of the polar tension between the Prussian organizational genius and the Romantic folk community (*Volksgemeinschaft*) reflected the tendency during war to abstract these polar entities from their specific historical forms for propaganda purposes. The polarities were thus imbued with a dynamism and revolutionary *élan* not characteristic of them in their traditional molds. Also, war socialism, fortress middle Europe, and communal culture were later given a new dynamism under the impact of defeat, national humiliation, and social crisis in autarchy, *Lebensraum*, and racialism as they appear in the ideological frame of National Socialism.

PRIMACY OF MILITARY OVER POLITICAL CONSIDERATIONS

In European wars since the seventeenth century, the political objectives which culminated in peace treaties and which, in turn, established power relationships had been the chief consideration. Now, in World War I, the military efforts were no longer an instrument of policy but became disassociated from politics and linked with the values of *Kultur* and *Geist* for the Germans and with civilization and democracy for the Western powers.

The pre-eminence of military over political considerations and especially the association of military with ideological factors became most apparent as the war entered its last phase in the fall of 1916, when the military dictatorship of Hindenburg and Ludendorff was virtually established.

Hindenburg was chosen as Chief of Staff, with Ludendorff, the real brains, associated with him in the high command. Hindenburg was generally credited with the victories on the eastern front. His big, bulky figure, whose wooden image was set up in public places all over Germany, became the symbol of victory. Public faith in political leadership had apparently completely collapsed.

Ludendorff, trained in the Prussian General Staff tradition, was opposed to an outright military dictatorship. He was a narrow militarist without any breadth of cultural background and with little understanding of political matters. He hoped for the appearance of a German Lloyd George from the people who would arouse them to a supreme effort toward victory. This point of view explains in considerable part his later association with Hitler. It certainly may be said that this man, who was the dominant figure in German affairs for two years, was much more a German nationalist than a Prussian; he differed from Hindenburg, who was distinctly inclined toward the traditions of Prussian monarchy and aristocracy involving limited ends and objectives.[4]

Ludendorff aimed at total mobilization as a means of fighting a mass war. All manpower up to sixty years of age was to be mobilized. Women were to work in the factories, and labor was to be recruited from the subject peoples. All resources were to be mobilized by ruthlessly carrying through a policy of war socialism. In the face of public inertia and opposition, most of these proposals could be carried through only in a half-hearted fashion.

The new phase of the war marked the end also of the *Burgfrieden*, literally, "fortress-peace," which actually meant a cessation of party strife. At the beginning of the conflict the Kaiser said that he recognized no parties, only Germans. Even the Social Democrats, whose leaders stood in some danger of being thrown into jail as suspected traitors, in general voted for the military credits. This unity, which was later looked back to with nostalgia and was assumed to be like that attained during the War of Liberation, grew out of the feeling of the Germans that they had been deliberately encircled and attacked.

However, the controversy over war aims, which became rife in the second half of 1916, brought about a fundamental split in the public mind. The ruling groups favored a decisive victory with annexations. Their opponents were convinced that Germany in a protracted war inevitably faced defeat and that therefore a negotiated peace should be arranged while her military power could still be used as a bargaining base. Both factions turned out to be unrealistic; not only was victory impossible but a negotiated peace was not feasible in the face of the mounting ideological and technological fury of the war.

The annexationists were inclined to regard those opposed to them as traitors. Consequently, a deep fissure began to divide the German body politic which was to have consequences of far-reaching importance, especially when the stab-in-the-back myth was developed in the course of the Weimar Republic. The growing tendency on the part of both the extreme right and the extreme left to emphasize the enemy within rather than the foe without also anticipated the position from which they later attacked that republic.

The new combination of factors which appeared in 1917–18, with the entrance of the United States into the war and with the Russian Revolution, pointed to a new world in the making. The war changed from a European power conflict into one having a worldwide orientation. The change portended the end of that conservative Europe which had centered in the three great empires of Germany, Russia, and Austria-Hungary, with their monarchical-aristocratic societies. It was this conservative Europe which the chancellor Bethmann-Hollweg and his associates, who were opposed to both annexationists and radicals, sought to preserve by entering into peace talks in 1916 with Russia and the United States.

Conservative Europe represented a world of diverse social, political, and cultural forms which had been developing since the Middle Ages. It was naturally concerned with defending its diversity, which it regarded as the basis of freedom against the equalitarian and leveling processes of Western democracy, war socialism, and Communist dictatorship. The diverse interests did not see eye to eye and consequently contributed toward the frustration of each other's efforts; but peace on a negotiated basis leading to the restoration of the status quo was the primary consideration.

Ludendorff's gamble—risking what remained of German re-

sources and hopes in one last great offensive in the spring of 1918—
and its failure not only contributed to the sudden collapse of German
morale but deprived the Germans of the means of bargaining with
the Allies. In the armistice negotiations the Allies insisted on the
complete disarmament of Germany, which placed her absolutely at
the mercy of her foes. Though the German army was still intact, the
war weariness, not only of the army but of the whole country, was
manifest in revolts and separatist movements. The proposals made by
Rathenau and Ludendorff for a last-ditch stand seemed merely a
flamboyant gesture.

SURFACE RATIONALISM AND DEPTH IRRATIONALISM

Along with the hegemonic drive involving finally war and defeat, there occurred a fundamental change in historical outlook and
in the conception of the universe. Although this intellectual transformation of the first half of the twentieth century was a general
European phenomenon, it assumed its most radical form among the
Germans. It had a significance comparable to the intellectual transformation in the first half of the sixteenth century in which the
Germans also took a leading part.

In the twentieth century we are again witnessing the dissolution
of a rational edifice, built up since the seventeenth and eighteenth
centuries. A new orientation toward the universe and man has appeared in the subatomic and subconscious worlds, which in their
indeterminacy and discontinuity stand in dynamic juxtaposition to
the surface world of rationalistic determinism. There is a tension
between these worlds. The eruption of the lower world may mark
the return of the demonic forces formerly exorcised by the rationalism which was inaugurated by the Enlightenment.

Depth consciousness seeks to find a new unifying basis beneath the
surface of rationalism and mechanism. It discovers there a vitalistic
life-force or an existential situation which leads again to metaphysical and metahistorical points of view having very ancient philosophical roots.

That this revolution in thought was first of all a German affair is
indicated by the names of the participants. The chief names in the
natural sciences were Einstein and Planck; in psychology, Freud and

Jung; in the social sciences, Karl Marx and Max Weber; in philosophy, Nietzsche and Heidegger; and in theology, Kierkegaard and Karl Barth.

Since history played the chief formative role in the development of German thought in the nineteenth century, there emerged a strong consciousness of historical distance involving the giving of a depth dimension to the cultural forms of the past, whereby they virtually acquired their own individual time situations. Thereby each age, era, and epoch acquired its own historic individuality and played its unique role in the perspective of mankind's development. This quality of uniqueness attributed to each age and movement seemed to render the notions of restoration and renaissance, and even of revolution, meaningless. This was the essence of nineteenth-century historicism.

Nature and history, as a causal network of forces, seemed to make unnecessary the consideration of such ultimate questions as the whence and wherefore of man and the universe. It was sufficient to accumulate the factual materials necessary to build the edifice of the universe, whose blueprints had been projected by Newton and Darwin. The order of nature presented by these thinkers, with its regular, uniform, and invariable changes in the arrangement of particles or in the development of species, furnished the backdrop to history. Historians continued to recognize the fortuitous in human development and to emphasize the unique and individual in cultural creation, but in the main only as a corrective to the predominant causal-mechanistic frame presented by the natural sciences. Moreover, history also developed its species of determinism. Natural science had developed the notion of an invariable uniform process, largely as a reaction against the interventionism presented in miracle and catastrophic happening. So history in the nineteenth century developed an anti-apocalyptic attitude in its predominantly counter-revolutionary frame, especially after the Romantic reaction against the French Revolution.

CONTINUITY AND IRREVERSIBILITY OF CHANGE

To Ranke and his successors the essence of historical development was continuity. Successive generations of his students viewed history more and more in terms of step-by-step development, each step being only a microscopic advance upon the other. An event such as the French Revolution might appear to be an abrupt change, but actually the basic institutional changes which came to the surface violently had been going on long before and would have come about anyway. All that revolutions did apparently was to accelerate changes, and many historians felt that all the sound and fury of revolutionary action was so much wasted energy.

Nowhere was the continuity of historical development portrayed more convincingly than in the external politics of modern states. Here the Clausewitz formula, that war was the continuance of policy by other means, completely expressed this continuity. Revolution might in an analogous fashion be interpreted as the carrying through of trends in institutional development by other means. The two most violent forms of change, war and revolution, were deprived of their specific creative and fortuitous character.

Another aspect of this historical point of view was its emphasis on inevitable, irreversible forward movement. Rebirth by return to another age was as fantastically romantic as the leap into a future ideal society was visionary and utopian. Progress took place by slow orderly procedures in the manner, one might say, in which legislative bodies worked. The historian abhorred breaks in the continuity of development as much as the natural scientists were said to abhor a break in the causal chain of physical happenings.

The three most influential thinkers of the nineteenth century, Hegel, Darwin, and Marx, were especially concerned with stressing the continuity and irreversibility of change. Each presented an objective development as taking place without breaks and apart from individual creative effort. Hegel made the whole of Western development the product of the gradual unfolding of the self-consciousness of the universal reason in which the torch of the reason is passed on from the hands of one people to another. Each people makes its appearance on the stage of history at the appropriate time and then moves to the background to make way for another. Likewise for Darwin, the various species develop out of original simple forms by a process of gradual adaptation to the environment. They come and go in response to changes in that environment, which is itself a process of development. Marx presented history as the rise and fall of classes, culminating in the proletarian society. Each exploiting and exploited class arises in response to a change in the methods of production, and, when these cease to support them, they make way for others.

In each instance, their disciples tended to minimize further the significance of the irrational factors such as the dialectical union of opposites, or the struggle for survival, or the revolutionary overthrow of exploiters by the exploited, in the interest of presenting an irreversible, continuous, forward movement. They did this largely under the influence of what appeared to be the inevitable progress of mankind toward higher and higher levels of enlightenment and toleration, material welfare, and control over nature. A fundamental change in attitude began in the early twentieth century with the questioning of this deterministic frame of nature and history.

The dissolution of the conception of a universal causal-nexus in the physical order is better known than the similar disintegration of the conception of an irreversible chain of causation in history. Just as it is no longer possible to represent the universe by a mechanical model, so history can no longer be portrayed simply as a succession of events tied together by calculable political, economic, social, and intellectual relationships. Both the physical and historical worlds acquired a depth dimension when the surface rational order was seen to be both a simplification and a distortion of the fundamental indeterminacy and discontinuity of life.

Until about 1900 the physical world was regarded as being composed of good hard stuff, like billiard balls, very large in the form of planets and very small in the form of atoms. The existence of the atom as the smallest particle was still viewed as hypothetical until Planck and others revealed its inner world. This inner world of protons, neutrons, and electrons revealed the physical world to be infinitely more complex than formerly surmised. Energy was shown to be in the microphysical world not subject to the continuous flow that the macrophysical order seemed to imply. Furthermore, relativity and subatomics revealed that such absolutes as causality, time and space, upon which science had been based, were not characteristic of the universe, but were derived from certain metaphysical assumptions made with regard to the universe. In short, it was recognized that while the methods of science may not change basically, the qualities attributed to the world do change. Science seeks increasingly to become aware of these presuppositions so as not to be controlled by them.

History, in dealing with human affairs and culture, went through a comparable mutation. In the Middle Ages and the Renaissance man viewed himself and the universe in relation to a transcendent world of heights and depths. In the Enlightenment and Romanticism he looked forward and backward in terms of striving for an ideal order or of recapturing an idealized one of the past. In the twentieth century both the vertical-transcendent and the horizontal-historical orientations are being abandoned in a world which is becoming increasingly disenchanted as it is deprived of magic and myth. Both the transcendent myth of heaven and hell and the immanent myth of moving toward a new order have lost most of their substantival reality, at least in the minds of the educated. Hence the closed universe of surface-depth or outside-inside with respect to rational and irrational forms of action and motive becomes the characteristic orientation of twentieth-century man.

The transition to this point of view in historical thought was reflected especially in Wilhelm Dilthey, Max Weber, and Oswald Spengler. They were not concerned with the rational as the reflection of eternal verities, nor as an instrument of progress in the creation of a new world order, but as a historical phenomenon which was molding the world about them. They were also concerned, in the face of the loss of religion, with the need for a *Weltanschauung* reflecting a total view of the universe and serving as a means of orientation in the world. Finally, all were influenced, at least implicitly, by the polarity of *Kultur* versus civilization, with *Kultur* reflecting spontaneity and creativity, and with civilization embodying technology and mass society.

THE LIFE-FORCE AND THE TYPOLOGY OF WORLD-VIEWS

Like so many of his academic predecessors, Wilhelm Dilthey (1833–1911), the son of a pastor, first studied theology and then abandoned it for the pursuit of philosophy. The point of departure in his thinking was the nineteenth-century world of positivistic rationalism. He sought, however, to arrive at a more creative expression of rationalism by going back to its sources in the Enlightenment and even in the Renaissance. He became a great admirer of Erasmus and Lessing, particularly of their proposal for a religion without dogma, whereby the manifold creativeness of life might be experienced directly without the intervention of doctrine or formula. Such a faith allowed for the tolerance of all forms of human expression and reflected a fundamental orientation toward the world as totality—that is, a *Weltanschauung*.

Dilthey's historical writings dealt primarily with the relationship between philosophical and religious ideas and the individual's experience of the world as it was reflected in the great thinkers from the Renaissance to Romanticism. Also characteristic was his objection to the contemporary emphasis upon the document as an objective historical yardstick. One must go beyond the criticism of the document to an intuitive perception of the thought-forms of the great thinker so as to plumb the fundamental ethical and religious dimensions of the creative life spirit.[5]

According to Dilthey, we derive a sense of reality in the outer world from our experience of resistance to the realization of our intentions. A perception of the boundaries and limits of knowledge is achieved. Also, the subject-object relationship acquires an experiential basis, rooted in feeling and will as well as in intellect.

This point of view was also the basis for Dilthey's emphasis on psychology. Psychology, he felt, should not devote itself to discovering the principles or laws of knowing, but to developing an intuitive understanding of how thought systems arise in the unique experiences of individual thinkers and how they come to rational self-consciousness. Understanding seems here to approach a form of divination. It becomes a faculty of knowledge superior to abstract discursive thought and comparable to the mystic spark.

According to Dilthey, man can be known only through probing the thought structures and forms in which the creative stream of life comes to expression in history. The creative life-force is revealed in its highest moments especially in the thought and art of great philosophers and men of letters. But to understand the great thinker it is necessary to trace his ideas back to those fundamental and total experiences of the universe of which the ideas are but a conscious reflection. Analysis of the thought structures reveals basic types of

Weltanschauung which recur in different garb again and again. They reveal that there is no one valid philosophic point of view, only that the plurality of views has a common source in the creative well-springs of life.

Emphasis on a creative life-force and its intuitive grasp by way of a typology of *Weltanschauung* suited the quest for dynamic actuality in the period between the two world wars. Only then were the scattered and fragmentary writings of Dilthey finally brought together and made easily available.

THE RATIONAL PURSUIT OF IRRATIONAL ENDS

Unlike Dilthey, the sociologist Max Weber (1864–1920) was primarily concerned with expanding the world of the rational at the expense of the irrational. The calculated adaptation of means to the realization of ends or goals represented, he argued, the distinguishing feature of Western rationalism, not shared by Eastern cultures. It has manifested itself especially in the de-mystification of the world (*Entzauberung der Welt*) for Westerners.

In a lecture given to university students, *Scholarship as a Vocation or Profession* (1919), Weber indicated that the life of reason involved a commitment—virtually an act of faith. Science, the supreme expression of Western rationalism, by its very nature is not concerned with ultimate goals but only with those common immediate ends for which appropriate means to realization can be provided. Science should eschew the pursuit of eternal verities. One must rely on empirical fact, have faith in the progressive cumulative character of scientific knowledge, and avoid attempting to answer questions not to be solved by its analytical methods.

But Weber also asked the question as to why the emergence of such rational structures as science, capitalism, and bureaucracy has been peculiar to Western culture. By a comparative study of the impact of religion on various cultures he sought to show how the irrational achieved expression by rational means. The Western faiths, especially Calvinism, developed a psychology within the rational frame of "the calling" which promoted an acquisitive activism along with rational calculation, both characteristic of capitalism. "Vocation" or "calling" constituted the chief rational frame through which Western man in modern times has achieved his greatest successes, particularly in the dominant fields of economics and science.

In Calvinism the achievement of God's glory became transformed into a rational dynamic in calling or vocation, particularly when secularized. Contrary to Marx's idea, religious irrational motives were antecedent to economic rational ones. Marxism insisted on the priority of the economic or material basis, and Marx thought of religion as mere ideological superstructure. To Weber socialism represented only bureaucracy carried to its extreme limit.

To understand Weber's general point of view, one should make the important distinction between a *substantival rationalism* and a *functional rationalism*. Substantival rationalism, characteristic of the Enlightenment and in the main also of the thought of the nineteenth century, accepted the notion of a rational order inherent in the universe which manifested itself in state and society—for example, in the conceptions of natural law and natural rights. Functional rationalism, on the other hand, is a distinct expression of a technological point of view. It is pragmatic and instrumental in its concern only with means-end relationships.

For Weber this functional point of view was realized especially in the employment of "ideal types" to master the world of empirical fact. These take the place of the conception of natural law with its assumption of inherent and invariable uniformity of operation. An ideal type presents a model of human action—that is, as it would occur if it followed a direct logical and functional road toward the achievement of a projected end and was not diverted by caprice.

We have already seen how such ideal types of science and capitalism were projected by Weber to arrive at their essential rational structure. On the basis of similar historical abstraction, Weber projected the three fundamental types of leadership based on different conceptions of legitimacy. The first was based on the traditional forms of aristocracy and monarchy which inspire reverence for the past. The second was based on the jurisdiction of office as defined by law, and the third on the charismatic leadership which assumes that the leader is the voice of God or of the people and requires unconditional obedience. Weber was inclined to ascribe an important role in history to the latter irrational and revolutionary type. He himself opposed the personal rule of William II and favored democracy, but largely because it provided a better system of recruiting a ruling elite.

Since Weber predicated on the one hand the irrational world of values and on the other the world of rational instruments, the unitary substantive, rational universe of the nineteenth century world was split asunder and the realm of the rational was reduced to the stature of the mere instrumental and functional. This notion harbored the dangerous implication that, in the last analysis, what counted most was the development of the most efficient means for the realization of ends, since there can be no rational choice of ends in terms of their intrinsic value. This was a position not unlike that taken by the Sophists at a very critical juncture in Greek development toward the end of the fifth century, B.C.

KULTUR VERSUS CIVILIZATION

Oswald Spengler gave a new significance to the dualism of irrational and rational; he transformed them into the polarity of *Kultur* and civilization. Both Dilthey and Weber saw the freeing of individual creativity as the peculiar role of the West. Dilthey viewed it from the side of the creative life-force manifested in the diversity of rational forms; conversely, Weber saw it from the side of rationalism as the peculiar Western achievement of the de-mystification of the world whereby man is enabled to gain increasing mastery over the means of realizing values. Spengler, in presenting the life-force as the creator of a plurality of cultures—eight of them thus far, each completely independent of the others—nullified the West's role as liberator of the individual from magic and myth. This rationalism represented to him only the end-phase of a particular culture, that of the West.

Oswald Spengler (1880–1936) was completely unknown to the world of scholarship until the appearance of the first volume of his *The Decline of the West* in 1918. The second volume appeared in 1922. He was a mathematics teacher in a secondary school in Hamburg from 1908 to 1911, after which he retired to Munich to become a free-lance writer. His doctoral dissertation was on the ancient philosopher of the flux, Heraclitus, who had also influenced Nietzsche, who, along with Herder, Goethe, and Bergson, exerted the greatest influence on him. The first volume of *The Decline of the West* appeared at a psychological moment which in part, at least, explains its astounding popularity. It made German defeat seem only part of a general failure of the West, involving both victors and defeated. He tells us that he began the work under the influence of the second Moroccan crisis (1911). He had the feeling that the West stood on the brink of a turning point which would usher in war and crisis, and eventually destroy the bourgeois individualistic society and culture, bringing to fruition a mass society with dictatorial rule.

Spengler's point of view ran counter to the prevailing linear conception of history as a unified development of mankind. The idea of the unity of mankind's history was presented in the Christian-theological, the liberal-progressive, and also the Marxian-socialist conceptions. Spengler in a sense returned to the ancient cyclical idea in which the recurrence in the life of nature, expressed in seasonal growth and decay and in the cyclical movement of the heavenly bodies, became the basis of the historical perspective. The linear conceptions beginning with the Christian-theological broke with the cycle of nature in assuming that man, either in his religious, cultural, or technological development, transcends nature in a movement toward a far-off goal of perfection. But Spengler went beyond the ancient cyclical idea and that of Goethe in presenting each culture as a closed entity, a windowless monad, with its own unique soul which gives individuality to all its forms.

Instead of the continuous development of mankind, Spengler confronts us with the rhythm of the rise and fall of cultures, each emerging like a plant in a definite landscape and going through the phases of spring, summer, autumn, and winter. The cycle may be very briefly summarized as follows: each culture goes through an early collectivistic myth-building phase; then the individual genius disassociates himself from the group; finally decline sets in with the appearance of the functionary who reflects the welfare interest of the masses of the great city.

In approaching the end of its creative cycle, each culture becomes increasingly rationalized—that is, intellectualized and technologized as it becomes detached from its creative springs in the life-force. It is closest to these sources in the springtime of myth-building and farthest removed in the winter of rationalism, called civilization. The modern West has reached the stage of civilization comparable to the Roman phase of antiquity, where creation, in the sense of myth, epic, and sage reflecting an ontological order, is no longer possible because of what might be called the hardening of the cultural arteries. All that man can do at this stage is to build bridges, machines, and empires. He can be creative only in a functional sense.

Finally, in Megalopolis with its mass society, man sinks back into the herd. The great Caesar who combines the qualities of both a demagog and a military chieftain will be the natural leader of this end-stage, where life loses all significance except that of the conflict for survival.

Spengler assumed that the spirit of Prussianism, descended from the Teutonic Order and embodied in the recent past in an efficient military-bureaucratic state, was the most appropriate expression of rationalism in the present stage of Western development. It was better adapted to that phase than Anglo-Saxon individualism, which was really an anachronism. Prussian state socialism was also better adapted to the new climate than Marxian socialism which, in its projection of a coming ideal order, merely provided an ersatz myth for the masses. Prussianism embodied no creative solution for the ills of a dying culture. It not only put the patient in a strait jacket; it also put discipline in his soul to meet his fate.

Spengler gave no consideration to causal factors in this pessimistic picture of inevitable decline. In fact, he argued that cause and effect relationships apply only to a spatial concept of movement, whereas only the conception of destiny, with its time dimension, is appropriate to history. Destiny has, however, no rational character; it merely signifies an inevitable and unavoidable specific course of development like that of a plant or animal. There is no freedom here except for the life-force which throws up out of its inexhaustible creative reservoir the cultural souls which are then launched on their respective destinies.

Human existence thus swings between the two great poles of creative culture and rationalized civilization, which appear also as intuition against reason, or as *Gestalt* against law, or most inclusively, as life against death. They are not only poles between which one oscillates in daily life, but they are the terminal points of each closed cultural existence. In this eternal recurrence there are no general verities of a religious or humanistic sort which stand above the cultures and give significance to human existence.

The German intellectual protest against civilization which began in the late nineteenth century reached a climax in Spengler's *The Decline of the West*. Evidences that Western society was definitely embarking on the last phase of its career were to be discerned in mass democracy, technology, the conception of progress, and proletarian socialism. But while Prussianism might offer to Spengler the most appropriate reaction to this end-phase in its stoical acceptance of the loss of creativity, to many others it was too sterile in emotional and vital content. These turned to the notion of an irrational breakthrough.

MAN'S SELF-ESTRANGEMENT

Three nineteenth-century thinkers, Marx, Kierkegaard, and Nietzsche, became in the postwar period the chief prophets of a new means of freedom from the dead weight of the past and the meaningless progress of the future. They have already been dealt with, in the context of their own time, as critics of the prevailing middle-class order of things. While they were largely viewed then as critics of a particular aspect of that order—religious, economic, or cultural—in the twentieth century they came to have a positive influence as protagonists of total repudiation.

Of the three, Kierkegaard was least known until World War I, when the translation of his works into German was begun. Marx's prestige was greatly enhanced by the Russian Revolution, and his thought was accorded a more profound interpretation. Nietzsche had heretofore exerted perhaps the greatest influence in the Latin countries as the philosopher of decadence before the war, but after the war he became almost a new revelation to the Germans. All three struck a responsive chord in their concern with man's alienation or estrangement from his true self, brought about by the process of a rationalization whose chief characteristic was that of externalization.

Marx asserted that under capitalism man becomes a mere commodity. He is no longer man but labor with a price tag attached to him. He is no longer a total being but is specialized as to skills in order that he may command the highest price in the mass production market.

Kierkegaard saw in German Idealistic philosophy, in Hegel particularly, the rationalistic inclination to bring religion down to the level of state and culture, thereby making religion just another sphere of human interest. In becoming largely an expression of middle-class humanitarianism, which made it indistinguishable from social welfare and individual philanthropy, religion lost the sense of an impassable gulf separating the transcendent from man and the world. This gulf was the basis of tension between God and the individual man, which makes man, through inwardness and subjectivity, a "concrete spiritual individual." [6]

Nietzsche argued that man's self-estrangement had begun with Socrates and Jesus. Socrates initiated it by emphasizing the theoretic and contemplative at the expense of the emotions and the will. Jesus definitely accelerated the process by the thwarting of the natural heroic instincts—by exalting meekness, humility, and penitence. By the late nineteenth century Western man had reached a point where the leveling of his natural instincts and values, through rationalism and humanitarianism, had left him without a real sense of a distinguishing quality and superiority, a condition which Nietzsche called nihilism. In the end, he argued, mass man will be led to resent all the values inherited from the past and will complete their destruction.

In all three thinkers a feeling of alienation from their fellowmen enabled them to view their society and culture both from the inside and from the outside. In the case of Marx, we have already noted the harsh poverty and sense of being misunderstood during the long period of exile in London. The resentment of the exile was to play an important role in the lives of many of his disciples, for example, Lenin and Trotsky.

In Kierkegaard the estrangement had a more deliberate character. A sense of alienation from God, derived from much introspection and the morbid sense of guilt which obsessed his father and which seems also to have enveloped the son, turned him from the prospects of a brilliant career to virtual isolation. The consequent turning inward was revealed in a series of autobiographical and confessional works which, distinguished especially by subtle psychological analysis, sought the way back to religious health.

Nietzsche's career followed a similar course. We have sketched it briefly from a professorship at Basel, acquaintanceship with and repudiation of Wagner, to *Kultur*-pessimism. In the last stages of increasing isolation, before mental darkness descended on him, he composed the greatest of his works, *Thus Spake Zarathustra* (1883–85) and *The Will to Power* (1895). He referred to himself as "dynamite" which would destroy the traditional values. But he also became to many not merely a nihilist force but the way back to an affirmation of real human values.

THE WAY TO SALVATION

Although the proposed ways to salvation of these three led to quite different goals, yet the ways have much in common. Above all, they assert that *the way is all-important*, for in following it the ends are realized.

The way for all three was a descent to the depths, whether in the form of the increasing distress of the proletariat, or the deepest despair of being alienated from God, or the leveling of all values leading to nihilistic destruction. But, most important, this moment of descent to the depths also marked the dawn of a new day.

For Marx, the proletarian must become conscious that he is at the bottom of a society which exploits and dehumanizes him and that he has nothing left to lose but his chains; the moment that he and his fellows arrive at this realization, a new era will begin.

For Kierkegaard, as for Luther, man must realize his own complete impotence in order that he may again be conscious of the impassable gulf between himself and God. He must consign himself to the depths of disillusionment and despair. To acquire this sense of impotence is particularly difficult for modern man, since, through science and humanitarianism, he has come to preen himself on his great powers and goodness. He seeks always to inch up on God and, through art or morality, to find a common ground with God. To be a Christian means more than being a member of a church—he must again become a disciple. To become a disciple he must actually strip himself of all pretensions in order that in his aloneness he may confront the transcendent absolute.

For Nietzsche, also, the way leads through denial to affirmation. The stages are: first, the Christian-Judaic command "Thou shalt," then the modern rational assertion "I will," leading to the realization that God is dead and that all values are gone. Finally, there will come for the superman the affirmative assertion "I am," in which he accepts both the heights and depths of life, both its heroic and tragic qualities.

For Kierkegaard and Nietzsche there was no end-state in which one comes to rest. They regarded this notion as a bourgeois illusion. Nietzsche thought of socialism as merely aiming at the extension to all people of the security and prosperity now confined to relatively few of the middle class. Even Marx made no attempt to lay down the blueprints of the coming collectivist society.

For Kierkegaard there is no resting with the sense of having attained the favor of God. The tension between man and the transcendent allows for no metaphysical or religious cushion on which to rest one's head. To argue so would be to again place man's achievement on a level with the divine.

Also, to Nietzsche the clear affirmation is only transient, for life is always dangerous to the coming superman. It involves an affirmation or acceptance of eternal recurrence rather than progress toward a goal.

Even some Marxists, among them Trotsky, began in the 1920's to talk of the necessity of "permanent revolution." There was always the danger that the proletarian, once in the saddle, would lapse into bourgeois habits of mind. In fact, the French theorist, Georges Sorel, who was both a pupil of Marx and a father of Fascist theory, argued that the worker must be continually imbued with a revolutionary *élan* by holding before him the prospect of the promised land which he will never actually enter. Sorel attempted a fusion of Marx and Nietzsche.

A most important characteristic of the intellectual climate of the twentieth century in Germany was its syncretistic character, the blending and harmonization of ideas and notions from very different sources. In this atmosphere ideas were cut loose from their old moorings and assumed a completely free-flowing character, which explains the pervasive character of the ideas of these iconoclasts.

Their kind of thinking was not really revolutionary in a rationalistic sense but radical in a completely iconoclastic sense. It projected no new order of things, at least not in the case of Nietzsche and Kierkegaard. There are no divine or ideal essences which can be embodied in concrete fixed forms, whether in nature or in history, thereby acquiring a permanent and sacrosanct character. There is but the sheer dynamism of mind, whose nihilistic and irrationalistic bent becomes apparent in the following tendencies:

First, Kierkegaard, Marx, and Nietzsche repudiated the humanistic and humanitarian values of liberalism. These values were ideal distillations derived from the ancient classical heritage, and given new personal vitality in Christianity and its offshoots, the Renaissance and Protestantism. They reflect the growing tolerance and enlightenment in modern society. The iconoclasts argued that they were ersatz, artificial substitutes for the traditional faiths. Hence, they lack the roots in the basic conditions of human existence which the ancient faiths had. Actually, they served largely as a decorative façade for the bourgeois pursuit of material gain and prestige. Kierkegaard and Nietzsche denied the possibility of an historical increment of values assumed by progressive liberalism.

Second, this unmasking of the pretensions of middle-class society and culture was the product of carrying rationalism to the point where one must take the leap off the top rung of the ladder into the irrationalism of revolution, of commitment, or of sheer affirmation. Rationalism reaches this point when it proceeds beyond its own basic presupposition that reason should free man from traditional bonds to where it raises the question whether it should not also free him from the bonds of rational order itself. In fact, one is led to doubt doubt itself, and to make the leap into faith, not however as a system of doctrine but as a faith in having faith. To many of the exponents of the new dynamism this meant the restoration of the ecstasy of the moment, whether in a mystical sense or as the heroic deed on the battlefield or on the barricades.

A third tendency, which follows from the others, was the insistence on the necessity for a total change, not in institutions but as the decisive act of revolt against the given order, or of commitment as a disciple, or, again, of affirmation of eternal recurrence. What was contemplated was a complete reversal, called by Nietzsche "the transvaluation of values." This did not really mean the transformation of values from within but the putting of a different set of values in place of existing ones—for example, the replacement of the existing values derived from Judaic-Christian sources by the ancient classical heroic and tragic ones or by the more primitive tribal ones revolving around friend and foe and the myth of the hero. This transvaluation involved a complete repudiation of the past as historical evolution and continuity as embodied in a tradition or heritage.

These ideas represented a fundamental reaction against the gradualistic conception of progress of the late nineteenth and early twentieth centuries. History was again to assume a dynamic and catastrophic character rather than to slowly evolve toward a goal of perfection. These notions were quite in harmony with the psychology of the turbulent times which followed World War I.

XIV

Reactions to Nihilism

*T*he German situation at the beginning of the twentieth century
was not unlike that in the days of Erasmus, Paracelsus, and
Luther at the beginning of the sixteenth century. We encounter
similar yearnings for the regeneration of man and society, the "taste"
for the apocalyptic reversal, and the vision of a Third Age or *Reich*.
Even the setting bears many resemblances: catastrophic war, the
threat of upheaval from below, and the violence of mercenary war-
bands.

It may also be contended that the three trends—the new humanism, life philosophy, and existentialism—endeavored, as did the
thinking of Erasmus, Paracelsus, and Luther, to overcome man's
alienation from cultural form, from the Antaean vital sources of life,
or from the consciousness of the precariousness of existence.

THE CULT OF FORM AND CHARACTER

Modern humanism arose in the Renaissance as a reaction against
the one-sided view of man presented in scholastic thought. It sought

to recover the true image of man from the writings of pagan and Christian antiquity. The neo-humanism of the eighteenth century, in its reaction against utilitarianism and rationalism, had again discovered an affinity between its *Geist* and the Greek genius. In the late nineteenth and twentieth centuries the threat of technological man made necessary a new appeal to the ancient humanist norms.

It has been said that Greece became the "cultural fatherland" of the Germans. Greece had been highly idealized in the past simply because the Germans felt no direct cultural continuity with it, as the Latins had with Rome. But the vast philological and historical study of Greek culture and of its Latin tradition in the nineteenth century emphasized the continuity of the classical heritage of the West. A great line of German scholars had pursued this study; their influence on education was especially reflected in the classical *Gymnasium* with its emphasis on cultural achievement.

There was also an aesthetic and philosophic line of approach which presented humanism as a way of life. This approach, inaugurated by the Romantics, culminated in Nietzsche, who had argued that the scholars misrepresented the Greeks. The norms of Greek culture were to be found not merely in Periclean Athens but also in the myth and orgiastic cults of archaic society. Greek life actually presented two poles: the Apollonian and Dionysian, in continuous tension with each other. The latter was amorphous and creative; the former clear-cut and plastically formative.

The philological-historical approach reluctantly took cognizance of this point of view, at least to the extent of probing deeper into the well-springs of Greek culture. The *polis* was now recognized to be something more than the frame within which Greek culture developed. To separate the culture from the *polis* was to convert the former into dead historical cargo. One obviously could not restore the totalitarian and aristocratic political and social forms of the *polis*, but one could promote the ideal of *paideia*, of which Plato was the great representative. One could therefore seek to unite aesthetics and ethics, to fuse beauty and goodness, and to unite the cultural and the political. In short, Greek culture must become a total commitment and not merely an intellectual ideal, as something admired from afar.

The most radical and influential exponent of this view was Stefan

George (1858–1933) and the circle of disciples which reverenced him as the great master. He was a poet who thought of himself as a prophet for mankind in general and for Germans in particular; he was a guide leading men back to a purely spiritual kingdom. Natural vitality and *Geist* were to be reconciled; the amorphous creative movement of the Dionysian was continually to seek expression in the plastic harmonious forms of the Apollonian, never coming to rest there, however. From these ideas followed his reaction against the current naturalism in art and the pursuit of comfort and security in the Wilhelmian *Reich*. Most of George's poetic achievement falls in that period, but his educative influence extended into the postwar period, through the circle of his disciples.

George was the leader of a cult brotherhood much like that of the ancient Pythagoreans. It had its local chapters in four or five cities. The master periodically visited these local groups and talked with the members about their thinking, writing, and reading. The attainment of perfection of form along with intimacy of friendship was the goal. These circles, embodying intellect and honor, were to constitute centers of radiation in the sea of chaos around them. This formless world, which had lost all the heroic qualities and sought nothing but peace and comfort, faced a cataclysm, which was necessary to redeem it. Out of the cataclysm would appear a savior, a man from the depths, who, like a Napoleon, would purge it of its dross and bring about a reversal of values.[1]

George was very harsh in his criticism of the Germans. More specifically, he castigated the north German disposition to romantic diffuseness as contrasted with the great clarity of form of the Rhineland, with its Roman tradition represented in Hohenstaufen and Renaissance cultures.

THE SEVERING OF THE UMBILICAL CORD

Not only was contemporary man being alienated from the humanistic cultural norms, but more important, many thought, was his growing isolation from the creative springs of the life-force. Science and technology were building an elaborate apparatus which stood between man and the life-giving stream. The French philosopher, Henri

Bergson (1859–1941), and Nietzsche were the chief intellectual influences in juxtaposing the rational order to the life-stream and the vitalistic natural forces. According to Bergson, the creative *élan* of the life-stream can be grasped only by instinct and intuition, through which one merges with it. Reason lifts one out of it, abstracting from the vital life-force only lifeless structures.

This philosophy of the life-stream no longer regarded *Geist* or mind as an extension or development of the creative life-force but as an aberration, perversion, or decadent phase of it. To Herder in the eighteenth century, and even to Dilthey, *Geist* represented the creative life-stream come to consciousness and the consummation of its development.

Now in the twentieth century the continuity was broken most radically in the new notions about the evolution of the primitive, prehistoric, and archaic mentality. Old notions of the noble savage, of the primitive as the unspoiled child of nature, and of a lost paradise had been largely sloughed off. Basic to the new view was the conception of the rational mask underneath which there persisted the primordial drives reflected in archaic myth and magic. The collective unconscious was thus projected, especially by Carl Gustav Jung (born 1875). In the magical symbolism of the alchemical writings of Paracelsus and his predecessors, Jung argued, the deep archaic consciousness becomes especially apparent. Pathological states of mind also bring to light recollections of the deep strata of the unconscious which underlie our behavior. These are not merely individual; they lie beneath the consciousness of the whole race.

Perhaps the most radical antithesis between reason and the life-force appeared in the thought of Ludwig Klages (1872–1956). He was a rather unusual instance of a leading philosopher without academic position. His very consistently developed philosophy-of-life mysticism was based on the study of character and how it is revealed in handwriting. In the prewar days he was an outstanding leader in the development of characterology and graphology. He argued that writing opens a door to the images of color, sound, and form which float before men's eyes and which provide the dynamic link between man and life. These images—not things—communicate the total actuality of life. Man is rooted in the life of the universe through both

400

body and soul, which in the prehistoric were directly united in reciprocal relationship with each other. The villain in the picture is *Geist*. It detached man from life by the process of intellectualization and mechanization. Mind, in other words, was the enemy of both soul and body, since it drove a wedge between them.

The consequent process of the estrangement and alienation of man from the creative force of life began, Klages believed, with the development of a culture based on writing. It made possible a collective memory and cumulative experience. It brought to an end matriarchy, with its close contact with the life-force expressed in the fertility cults. In its place there appeared the primacy of the father and the development of the state and history, resulting in the breaking of the "telluric bond." This was the real "fall of man." [2]

Klages also presented a new conception of time with his repudiation of history and state. To him these two created a Promethean type of man who projected a future which separated the present from a dead past. Each present had reality only in being a step in the movement toward the future. Real time was a backward-going stream into the past. This is the living past in which the mythical view of life is immersed.

Here was a much more radical repudiation of history than is found either in the Romantics or in Nietzsche. Klages regarded world history, which replaced myth, as merely an expression of the power drives of the state. He was therefore no nationalist. In fact, his pacifism and individualism made him suspect to the National Socialists, although they also placed myth above history.

EXISTENCE AS CONSCIOUSNESS OF FINITENESS

In the realm of theology there was a similar retreat from the historical point of view. The Protestant situation in the postwar period became critical because of the liquidation of the old historic ties of monarchy with the church and the drive toward the complete separation of church and state under the Weimar Republic. Liberal theologians were becoming disillusioned with the prospects of cultural enlightenment and social gospel. These no longer seemed adequate in the face of the precariousness of man's cultural situation as revealed by the depths to which he could sink in the crisis of war and revolution.

The yearning for a return to a fundamental religious point of view became apparent in the renewed interest in Luther's theological position and in the "discovery" of Kierkegaard. The latter now became the point of departure for a new religious outlook, called variously "dialectical" or "crisis" theology. The Swiss Protestant theologian, Karl Barth, became the leading exponent of this view.

Kierkegaard's influence and the return to Luther and Calvin were evident in the great emphasis placed on the chasm between man and God. Liberal theology had tended to equate religion with moral, social, and cultural improvement and to make God one with an emergent universe. In dialectical theology, the absolute transcendence of God and the complete nothingness of man were stressed.

God is the completely unknowable as far as man is concerned. He is revealed only in His incarnation in Jesus Christ, other than which there is no revelation. This must be accepted as a pure act of faith; its historical support or non-support in biblical tradition is of no real significance. Furthermore, there is to be no world end ushering in eternity. Time and eternity stand juxtaposed at every moment. No external bridges exist, therefore, between man and God—only a state of inner tension in which man is continually aware of his complete inadequacy. Luther's basic experience of the immediate confrontation of man and God was here carried to its utmost extreme by stripping it intellectually of all the intermediaries of dogma, myth, and history.

The purpose of this dialectical theology was to free religion from its entanglement with moral do-goodism and with salvation by intellectual enlightenment and cultural advance in order to arrive at a purely religious experience. Man must, as Kierkegaard indicated, by an act of absolute, unconditional commitment, become again a disciple of Christ. There was to be no gradualism, no inching up to God. Faith was not to be a gradual illumination and sense of assurance but a leap actuated by despair.

The counterpart of this theological position in philosophy was called "existentialism." Its chief sources were Kierkegaard and Nietzsche. It turned its back on the various neo-movements in philosophy stemming from Kant and Hegel, both of whom had been concerned with the perennial problem of truth. They had asked the question: How can man know the world and what certainty does he have with regard to what he knows? Kant gave the answer of the categories of the mind; Hegel gave the answer of the dialectic of the cosmic reason. The existentialist was primarily concerned with the limitations of human existence as a consequence of man's being thrust into the world. He sought not to overcome man's alienation from culture as quality or form, or from life as creative vitality, but rather to recognize in them his true existential position as confronted with an end.

Existential philosophy was developed in German universities by Martin Heidegger and Karl Jaspers. They approached the problem of human existence from the psychological point of view. The consciousness of existence manifests itself in man's increasing awareness of the world about him and his concern with it. His very expanding knowledge with regard to the world makes for an increasing sense of apartness from it, of being "thrown into the world." Because he has no common destiny with the world, he is increasingly aware of his own finiteness.

The essence of existence is therefore consciousness of time as limitation and determination. This is not just a consciousness of shortness of time as measured by the duration of the universe or a notion like eternity. It is rather the sense of having a passing character of "onceness." In this awareness of existence as finiteness, man, according to Heidegger, is lifted completely out of the conditioning natural, historical, and transcendent circumstances and is stripped of nonessentials. In affirming his finiteness, of being thrown into the world, the complete *Entzauberung der Welt* is realized.

Philosophy here became really descriptive of an underlying psychological state of mind, and, like the depth psychology of Freud and his circle, it has also been called "depth philosophy." It seeks to bring to consciousness the fundamental anxiety and even dread involved in man's sense of finiteness, which becomes intensified as modern technology creates a second nature as against the given nature. It is especially in the relation of life and death that this depth dimension comes to consciousness—in the feeling that life is irrevocable—that it is a matter of once and for all.

Philosophy and religion were thus again brought into closer relationship with each other. Philosophy was to be more than a mere academic discipline; it sought to become again a way of life—not, however, by arriving at precepts to be followed but by illuminating man's actual existence, its borderline character on the frontier of life and death, of existence and nothingness.

These proposals for overcoming man's alienation from cultural form or from the life-force or from actual existence all suggested again the necessity for an inner liberation, this time by the recovery of a point of reference to which a dynamic polar relationship was to be established. This point of reference might be symbolized by GREECE, LIFE, or GOD, each, however, stripped of the usual traditional philosophic or religious connotations.

THE NEGATIVE CHARACTER OF THE WEIMAR REPUBLIC

Both the Reformation and Romanticism had also proposed the necessity of inner liberation, but coupled with it, as we have seen, the demand for a communal solidarity based on the new inner experience. In the decade and a half after World War I the concern with communal solidarity became a drive of such compelling force as to sweep everything before it. The sense of dissolution of all the old bonds of *Reich,* civic community, and *Kultur* in the maelstrom of party conflicts, inflation, and crisis in *Weltanschauung* within the improvised frame of the Weimar Republic gave the chief impetus to this drive.

Two extreme alternatives of revolution had presented themselves in the face of the defeat that Germany had suffered in 1918. The first of these, revolution from above, was quite in harmony with the traditions of the continental state. Military defeat brought reorganization of the government. This had been the Prussian reaction to Napoleonic conquest. The state had been reorganized to bring it in closer touch with the people. The monarchy had lost little of its real prerogative. However, in the course of World War I the monarchy had receded so completely to the background that a vacuum in the leadership of the state was created. This vacuum had been filled by a quasi-military dictatorship under the necessity of total mobilization, but it had not achieved any considerable mass appeal, and the default of the military in 1918 made revolution from above very unlikely. In any case, the demands of the victorious Allies that a democracy be established virtually rendered it impossible.

The second alternative, revolution coming from below, was much more in harmony with the mass character of twentieth-century society. But it was also non-democratic in character. Its model was presented by the Bolshevik Revolution in Russia, where a general staff of revolutionary tacticians with mass support established what was called a "dictatorship of the proletariat." This was to be a provisional revolutionary regime for carrying through a total reorganization of society, particularly the liquidation of feudal-aristocratic domination over the rural areas and middle-class capitalistic control of industry. An abortive attempt at this type of revolution, made in the early part of 1919 in Germany, was suppressed by Friedrich Ebert, with the aid of the military. He, as the leader of the strongest party, the Social Democrats, had taken over the reins of government. Ebert and the majority Socialists stood for the establishment of a democratic government, like that of the Western countries, out of which they were convinced a socialist republic would eventually grow. They opposed any ties with Russian Communism. Ebert had grown up under the wings of the Prussian state, with its army and bureaucracy, and naturally looked to these as the buttresses of order in society.

But both the military defeat and fall of the monarchy in 1918 and the suppression of the Leftist revolution in 1919 created liabilities for the new regime. In the end, they contributed to the radicalization of the Right and of the Left. The Right, made up of those who had been annexationists during the war, ascribed defeat to the stab in the back delivered by the democratic and socialist middle groups. The Left was filled with resentment over the bloody suppression and murder of their leaders. They adopted an equally intransigent attitude in going over to a close relationship with Russian Communism in order to promote the dictatorship of the proletariat and world revolution. The history of the Weimar Republic became, in fact, the conflict of the middle against these two extremes.

That republic might have drawn strength from promoting the dominance of one social group, for example, the middle class. But the old cleavages in society continued in aggravated form. The Junkers still held their large estates—with some fear and trembling —but they could take solace from the fact that the army still was the bulwark of order and that the Leftist revolution had been suppressed. The upper middle class, who had been most strident in their call for a victorious peace with annexations, were perhaps the most frustrated of all politically; they turned to the opportunities offered by the growing speculative inflation to line their pockets. The lower middle class, comprising shopkeepers and peasants, were most conscious of the squeeze between big business above and trade unions below. Neither they nor the growing class of white collar workers could think in terms of a positive program; they merely harbored resentments. The workers found themselves in an ambiguous position in the face of leaders who suppressed revolution and preached order with the help of the military but who nevertheless held out the prospect of social security with better wages and hours.

None of these social groups, either by virtue of numbers or ideology, could play a leading political role. They were distributed among a number of political parties none of which clearly represented class interests.

THE BREAKDOWN OF THE SOCIAL ORDER

In the 1920's a mass society emerged among the Western peoples. Its crystallization was largely the product of new technological developments represented by radio, movies, and the automobile, which brought in their train a new mass culture and a dissolution of the traditional high and low cultures. These manifestations were most apparent in the great city, whose sprawling peripheries began to envelop the countryside.

In Germany social and cultural changes were perhaps less the product of technological development than of the aftermath of the war. The loosening of traditional bonds of class, family, and church led to new forms of association. Particularly important was the perpetuation of the comradeship of the trenches in the various veterans' organizations and secret societies. The literature of the time, such as Remarque's well-known *All Quiet on the Western Front,* emphasized this aspect of army experience in what was known as *Fronterlebnis* (front-line experience). The Youth Movement lost its earlier romantic nature worship and turned to an emphasis on communal solidarity and a struggle for a new order. Still other important influences were the new cults, especially the important ones represented by Count Keyserling and Rudolph Steiner, who saw the light as coming from the mystic East.

Nowhere was the new attitude of mind and mood more definitely manifest than in Expressionism, which had made its appearance sometime before the war and attained fullest expression in Germany. No longer was art to be concerned with the description of nature or man; its function was redefined to express man's innermost experiences. Art, the Expressionists thought, should project these experiences in forms appropriate to the inner drives and yearnings. The quest for a new symbolism and the attainment of a new intensity of expression was especially evident in Paul Klee (1879–1940) and Ernst Barlach (1870–1938).

The street also became a very important political and social factor. Men moved from the inner security and comfort of the home, destroyed by war and inflation, to the street, where crowds, demonstrations, and gangsterism revealed the ferment of the time. It was not merely the harangues of demagogs and the marching demonstrators but also political murder and assassination which reflected the descent of society into the maelstrom of violence and the irrational. Political terrorism and violence, coming especially from the extreme Right, reached its culmination in 1920–21 in the murders of Rathenau and Erzberger. They had been guilty of the great betrayal in urging the signing and fulfillment of the Versailles *Diktat*.

In the minds of most people, the Republic was distinguished from *Reich*, *Volk*, and *Staat*. It represented merely parliamentary party politics. Most Germans had little respect for it and referred to it as "the system," much as the Russians had used the expression "the mess" to refer to government and society under the old regime. It could command no real respect from the heads of departments nor from the bureaucracy in general. The courts passed out easy sentences to political malefactors whose actions threatened the very safety of the Republic.

Its survival until 1933 in the face of attempts to overthrow it may be ascribed to the fact that there was no group strong enough to take over. Perhaps equally important was the circumstance that, since the Republic was the result of a considerable number of contending forces and interests, many of these derived some benefit from its continuance. Also, the bureaucracy and the army command maintained a neutral attitude; that is, although individual officials and officers might even participate in counter-republican movements, yet when it came to the actual seizure of power, neither the army nor officialdom as such gave positive assistance.

The general prevalence of the word "crisis" in the years from 1929 to 1933 was indicative of the deep-felt anxiety about Western society, brought on by economic collapse and its political repercussions. Economic society had taken the place of church and state as the dominating influence in peoples' lives. Since work had become the basis of a man's role and his status in society, unemployment on a vast scale with no prospect of recovery produced demoralization.

In Germany, as distinct from the Western democracies, the economic crisis tremendously aggravated the political crisis which had existed since 1918. It began in 1930 with bank failures and produced over 6,000,000 unemployed by 1932. This economic catastrophe came not long after the crisis of 1923 when inflation wiped out the savings of middle-class groups who had never fully recovered during the period of prosperity from 1924 to 1929. The rural areas had been in a state of prolonged distress since World War I. To these groups the growing ranks of unemployed were now added, producing a real social and political ferment.

The new economic crisis brought about the demoralization of the middle parties and made the creation of a parliamentary majority on the basis of the middle groups impossible. Instead of being drawn together by the menace of extreme Left and extreme Right, the rank and file were now being pulled in the direction of those extremes. The two largest parties, the Social Democrats and the Center, were driven by inner contradictions. The former clung to a doctrinaire Marxist notion of the common cause of the world proletariat in spite of opposition to the Russian Communist regime. The latter continued to be dominated by its Roman Catholic complexion, derived from the *Kulturkampf,* in spite of the support of large numbers of Protestants who were disillusioned with secular liberalism. Both were

Weltanschauung groups with an internationalist orientation and hence unresponsive to the basic change in national mood.

All in all, the middle classes were moving toward the intransigent Right group of the National Socialists while labor was leaning toward its counterpart on the extreme Left, the Communists.

THE BREAKDOWN OF THE PARTY SYSTEM AND YEARNING FOR BREAKTHROUGH

The consequent breakdown of the parliamentary party system of government led to the virtual establishment of a presidential-plebiscitary republic which represented a logical constitutional change. It was implicit in the dualism of the Weimar Constitution, whereby the president was elected independently of the legislative body and granted special emergency powers. After Hindenburg's election in 1932, the president was regarded by the national opposition to the Weimar regime as representative of the state, as standing above the parties which represented merely the fractional interests of social groups. Since both bureaucracy and army naturally looked to the president as the symbol of state power, the presidency filled the void left by the monarchy. The political theory of the time also represented him as the guardian of the constitution, as the one who must take decisive action to cut through the impasse, created by party politics, and safeguard public order in a crisis.

The chief exponent of this point of view was the jurist and political theorist Carl Schmitt. Like Pareto in Italy, he sought to develop an objective, that is, a really Machiavellian conception of politics. In opposition to liberalism, with its emphasis on formalism in law and politics represented by constitutional and parliamentary guarantees and procedures, Schmitt asked the question, What is the fundamental basis of law? He answered that it is force that makes law effective; it comes to the surface in emergency situations when the depths of public order are plumbed. It appears with the loss of the fundamental consensus necessary to a parliamentary regime based on the collaboration of parties. When this consensus breaks down, dictatorship, as the naked embodiment of force, is inevitable.

With the breakdown of the parliamentary party regime, the

fundamental pluralistic interests of the social order, represented by classes, corporations, and associations, came to the surface, divested of their former ideological and party dress. The parties no longer embodied the individual ideologies and programs of the social groups; they merely sought the widest mass support. Parliaments were no longer necessary and a plebiscitary democracy with dictatorship became inevitable.

The German middle parties—liberal, socialist, and clerical—had retained much of the ideology and psychology which, in the time of Bismarck, had attended their origin in the conflict with the Prussian state. Enveloped in this original matrix of *Weltanschauung* attitudes, they lacked the flexibility necessary for the give and take of parliamentary politics, whose essential feature was response to day-to-day shifts in public opinion. It particularly explains the lack of rapport of the leaders, who still lived in the old psychological atmosphere, with the rank and file of the party, whose chief concern was with the immediate crisis.

The conservative nationalist opposition to the Republic suffered steadily from a process of crumbling and ideological splintering and the drift to the radical Right. The fragmentation into heterogeneous clubs and circles undermined positive ideological conviction. They had concentrated on a negative reaction against the Weimar Republic, and in common with the parliamentary middle groups, had suffered from the extreme mobility and fluidity of public opinion, with the result that they had virtually lost contact with their old roots in the Romantic, conservative *Weltanschauung*. This meant a loss of roots in a total world view and the turning to the mere notion of a seizure of power. But here they were being outbid by the extremists, the National Socialists, who, as the name of the party indicates, sought mass support by propaganda appeals both to Right and Left.

This transformation of politics at the depth level of world and life view was conditioned by the interaction of four forces whose impact has been alluded to previously:

(1) The process of secularization in Germany now attained its most nihilistic extreme—more so than in Russia, where the religious messianism became transformed into Communist utopianism. The crumbling of traditional religious and idealistic values now allowed

free rein to the demonic qualities of power politics, technical organization, and mass emotion. In the Western democracies their subversive effects were mitigated by the persistence of liberal humanitarianism and religious revivalism.

(2) Stress has been laid on the German inclination to think in terms of national insurgence, of encirclement and breakthrough. In the nineteenth century these were counterbalanced by the strong sense of historical continuity, but in the twentieth century they were given new impetus by the renewed taste for the apocalyptic expressed in the leap of faith and the reversal of values. After World War I there also appeared in the minds of many the image that defeat and humiliation could be erased only by decisive action, which would be followed by national regeneration.

(3) The Weimar regime, by virtue of its improvised character, gave no real sense of stability or mission. In it, life did not seem to flow in a definite frame but was merely the result of contending forces. Disillusionment with regard to progress and reduction of the past to unique ages contributed to the feeling of change as movement without direction. It may be compared with that feeling of standing on the keen knife-edge of actuality as sheer change which we noted in both the early Reformation and early Romanticism. Kierkegaard and Nietzsche had given a new significance to the sheer dynamic of the moment. Here the heights and depths of human existence became the chief concern rather than the movement toward a nebulous goal in which a mythical last man inherits the efforts of all previous generations.

(4) The hope for cultural and spiritual regeneration which began with the turn of the century was a general European phenomenon but assumed a special character in middle and eastern Europe because of the problem of the role to be played with regard to the West. In Russia it was manifest in a turning away from Western materialism and the dogmatic rigidity of local ecclesiastical statism toward the peculiar mystical and metaphysical sources of Greek orthodoxy. Dostoevski had prophesied the coming of a new Age of the Spirit in which Russia would play a leading role in the regeneration and salvation of mankind. Its secularized parallel was the movement for social salvation presented by Bolshevism, which also pointed toward a new order of things to be inaugurated by Russia. The victory of this

secularist movement with its activistic *élan* over the mystical religious tendency provides an instructive parallel to the triumph of National Socialism in Germany.

THE EXPECTATION OF A THIRD REICH

Rebirth and renewal in Germany obviously had fewer ecumenical and messianic implications than in Russia. But this orientation appeared in a number of German writers of the nineteenth century, from Fichte to Lagarde. It became most apparent in the 1920's, first in the writings of Arthur Moeller van den Bruck (1876–1925), especially in his very influential work, *Germany's Third Reich* (1923).

During his sojourn in Paris in voluntary exile from the Wilhelmian *Reich* with its disgusting materialism, Moeller had collaborated with the prominent Russian writer Merezhkovski in the publication of a German translation of Dostoevski. Merezhkovski sought to unite Joachim of Flora's vision of a third Age of the Spirit with Dostoevski's nationalistic and messianic interpretation of Moscow as the Third Rome.[3] The followers of Joachim had also looked to the coming of a messianic leader who would inaugurate the new age. The cult of Dostoevski which developed in Germany, particularly during the decade after World War I, is indicative both of German orientation eastward and of preoccupation with breakthrough to a new *ordo*.

Moeller's idea of a Third *Reich* was in its beginning associated with this sphere of spiritualist and sectarian speculation suspended between the established and orthodox ways of religious and political thinking and the new ruthless technological secularism which was coming to the fore. The word "*Reich*" had for him a messianic significance embodying the sense of mission or role of the German in history. He did not view it in terms of the restoration of historic greatness but as the projection of a Third Age. In this forward-looking orientation, it became disassociated from its historical past. *Reich*, *Staat*, and *Volk* each acquired a distinct individuality abstracted from their specific historic frames and hence, a new dynamic vitality.

During his sojourn of almost a decade in foreign lands, Moeller rediscovered the individuality and distinctive quality of German nationality. Two books written after his return to his native land and under the impression of the war against the West reflect this rediscovery.

In *The Prussian Style* (1915) stress was laid on the virile and hard qualities of Prussianism reflected not only in the style of buildings but in Frederick William I, in Kant, and in army and bureaucracy. These were all cut from the same severe and sober piece of cloth without the decorative embroidery of decadent bourgeois art. This Spartan Prussia was really a middle-class discovery. Its simplicity and hardihood were contrasted with Wilhelmian flamboyance and Neo-romantic decadence. Prussianism thus took the place of historic Prussia after World War I, with the disappearance of dynasty and aristocracy as political powers. It now became a formative principle, as we have already noted in Spengler.

In the second work, *The Rights of Young Nations* (1919), directed toward Woodrow Wilson, Moeller virtually repeated Fichte's nationalist idea, contrasting the youthful, vital Germans with the decadent Western peoples, especially the French. Since the young nations had not acquired a definite style or form, *Kultur* was for them a dynamic creative force.

Moeller took exception to Spengler's notion that all peoples of the West would be caught in the widening stream of mass society, Caesarism, and technical civilization, which reflect the general decline of creativity. He argued that each nation is a unique entity capable of projecting its own destiny. The West won out in the war only with the help of a youthful people, the Americans. Likewise, in the East, another youthful people, the Russians, had made the breakthrough to a new destiny. For Moeller the Bolshevik Revolution was actually an expression of the Russian national sense of mission directed against liberal and socialist internationalism. If the Germans would break with the past completely, they could also effect that breakthrough to the future for which as a young people they possessed the necessary vitality and sense of mastery, which are the essence of race.[4]

In his *Third Reich*, Moeller sought to present the way of salvation out of the national division and impotence under the Weimar

Republic. The breakthrough to the future he saw foreshadowed in the revolution coming from the Right as well as from the Left. The old ideologies were bankrupt; they stemmed from the revolutions of the Western nations, which were international in orientation. Now it was the turn of the Eastern peoples, particularly of the Germans, to effect a national revolution.

THE POSSIBILITY OF CONSERVATIVE REVOLUTION

Moeller arrived at the idea of national revolution by an analysis of contemporary ideological movements. Against liberalism, with its embodiment in a mere party system and its quest for a mere harmony of interests, he juxtaposed socialism and conservatism as the two fundamentally valid ideologies because they had a *Weltanschauung* character. But Socialism as an international movement had no real enduring vitality; he cited the emergence of national Marxist parties as evidence. The real weakness of Marxism lay in its materialistic bias and its consequent failure to recognize the ideal values embodied in state and nation.

The lineaments of the true conservative thus began to appear; he is to be distinguished from the reactionary in that the latter was essentially the advocate of a static idea, that is, of a return to a particular historical situation, say, the Bismarckian *Reich*. The true conservative, on the other hand, recognized the dynamic of the recurrence of the basic archetypical forms embodied in the national character.

Most interesting of his basic ideas, perhaps, was Moeller's consideration of proletariat, democracy, and revolution as forms of participation within the frame of the national *Gestalt*. The proletariat was viewed by Marxism as international in character and therefore as separated from the remainder of the nation. The process must be reversed by building nationalism, first of all, on the proletariat, and making it revolutionary. Democracy could provide the means since it is an expression of the will of a people rendered articulate through its leaders. Unity of will derives from the individual quality of the *Volk* and not from a presumed transcendent imperative such as the welfare of humanity. In a revolution a people assert their will decisively and thereby achieve political maturity.

Moeller argued that the Western nations had had their revolutions through which they attained maturity, but Germany had not. The so-called revolution of 1918 was really imposed from the outside by the victors; it did not emanate from the will of the German people themselves. He hoped for the coming of a revolution in which *Staat* and *Volk* would be fused in the unified national will to recreate the great *Reich* of the middle, which would again serve as the axis for European society.

One feels that by revolution Moeller did not mean mounting the barricades but a fundamental transformation in *Weltanschauung* which would transcend the parties. It would produce among Germans a new national consciousness directed toward the realization of the new *Reich*. All his writings were aimed at bringing about this transmutation. This was also the object of the founding of the *Juniklub* in 1919, of which Moeller became a leading spirit. Its meetings were attended and addressed altogether by people who opposed the Weimar Republic—a considerable number came from the eastern borderlands. Some of its leading lights later played an important role in the National Socialist movement, and Hitler on one occasion spoke at a meeting. Its headquarters at 22 Motzstrasse in Berlin housed various other associations which had affiliations with the many political offshoots representing the Right.[5]

Among the hundred or more isms listed as current during the 1920's which reflected anti-liberal bias, the repetition of the following groups of words is characteristic: those implying solidarity, such as *Bund* (union), *Deutsch, Volk, Reich,* and *national;* ideological words such as *socialism, conservatism, bolshevism, imperialism, realism,* and *nihilism;* and words stressing the dynamic of movement such as *revolution, renaissance, front, insurgence.*[6] The appearance of these political designations in various combinations is indicative of the syncretistic process already referred to. It tended to wipe out differences in principles so that the old ideologies such as conservatism, socialism, and bolshevism lost definite configuration. They became mere gradations and consequently lost real significance as compared with the nationalistic ones of the first category and the names suggesting dynamic movement in the third group. Since the extremes of Right and Left met in the notion of nationalist revolution and no longer served really as a basis of orientation for ideological positions, revolution could proceed from either Right or Left and thus lost its earlier rationalistic significance completely.

For Moeller, the new order still had a spiritual quality already projected in the very expectation of a Third *Reich* and in the yearning for ideal harmony. The manner of its actual realization was not touched on. For Ernst Jünger and Adolph Hitler, however, the dynamic of movement was not derived mainly from the expectation of a new age but from the technological transformation and from the national unity achieved in World War I. Their point of departure was, therefore, a concrete historical event and, more than that, a highly personal experience of that event.

TECHNOLOGICAL TOTALITARIANISM

In his youth Jünger (born 1895) ran away from home to join the Foreign Legion. Brought back to the monotonous routine of school and home, he was rescued by the outbreak of the war; he joined as a volunteer. He excelled in shock-troop tactics, was wounded seven times, and achieved the very rare distinction for a mere lieutenant of securing the highest military decoration, that of the *Ordre pour le Mérite*. After the war he remained in the *Reichswehr* until 1923. It was in this period that he published the much-read journals describing his war experiences which combined vivid reporting of impressions with profound reflection on them.

The war, according to him, marked the end of the bourgeois order based on security, leisure, and culture. The drab existence and the cynical realism of the twenties showed that most of these values had gone by the board. The conviction emerged that a clean sweep was necessary—that nothing was worth clinging to in the old values. In the war a man at least experienced an elemental force. Hence Jünger desired to recover its hard simplicity as against intellectual subtleties, and its Spartan discipline as against bourgeois luxury and comfort.

For Jünger the war was first of all a great nihilistic experience. There was absolutely nothing romantic about this new form of warfare. In it he felt called on not to indulge in heroic deeds but to maintain a kind of cold courage whereby he could merge, so to speak, with its mechanized character, becoming a functional unit in it, retaining merely a theoretical detachment. The war brought about a forced acceleration of the technical process. The result was that machines were no longer mere tools employed by the individual as a free personality, but actually became a way of thinking and a way of being.

Technological totalitarianism was the product of that long process of *Entzauberung der Welt,* which, as Nietzsche pointed out, would culminate in complete nihilism. Everything would then assume a mere tactical or functional value; ideas, institutions, and personalities would have only the value of position. There would be no looking backward or forward; all one could do would be to intensify the process in which all are drawn and in which the elemental creative force became manifest as eternal recurrence.

The social aspect of this transformation was already provided, according to Jünger, in what war and inflation contributed to the proletarianization of the bourgeoisie and to the bourgeoisization of the proletariat. At the moment this process meant the end of the old culturally conscious bourgeoisie and of a class-conscious proletariat as well as the triumph of petty bourgeois mediocrity. But this social leveling and its counterpart, the leveling of all values, were necessary to the decisive affirmation of the new order.

In the second phase of World War I, Jünger saw the outlines of the new order becoming singularly manifest. Later he tried to sketch its characteristics in the essays, *Total Mobilization* (1931) and *The Worker* (1932). In these he held that war in our age does not represent an exceptional situation but is the most intense expression of that total mobilization which the technological drive seeks to realize. Its dynamic character was revealed in such polarities as front-line ecstasy (*Fronterlebnis*) and mechanization, as shock-troop thrust and functional organization, and finally more graphically, on the analogy of the gas engine, as "explosion and precision." [7] These polarities show that the technological order was not conceived as dead, soulless mechanization but as a highly intense process involving complementary rational and irrational aspects.

The distinctions between peace and war, between front and rear, and between soldier and civilian disappear. All are fused in the gigantic effort of total mobilization because it and technology are also fused in the effort to secure the maximum release of energy. The freedom of the individual which presupposes a dualism of romantic subjectivism or moral imperatives on the one hand, and the compulsion of work and mobilization, on the other, is obliterated. Only heroic effort of the will to achieve plus precise functional operation will prevail. There will be no conception of progress but only acceptance of technology as perfection.

In this new order everybody becomes a worker. In the individualistic bourgeois society, work is not central; it is only one of man's concerns. One presumably works as a matter of necessity, the burden of work being compensated for by the wage and the leisure and comfort this will buy. The long years of work have as their goal the achievement of sufficient property to retire, or to pass on to succeeding generations. Work, like war, has thus an interim character; it is only a necessary evil. In the new order, work will have nothing to do with mere life-maintenance or acquisition of property. Where life exists, its sustenance will be taken for granted. Work will provide a total goal; in it a person will achieve complete fulfillment and give form to life.

The *Gestalt* of the worker is already becoming apparent alongside that of the bourgeois. It is the inevitable reflection of the drive of technological perfection and not a consequence of a dramatic seizure of power. To the worker the world is a workshop for the conquest of the greatest technological power. For the bourgeois it is a museum of accumulated values, ideals, and things to be enjoyed at leisure. To the worker history has no meaning as an evolutionary development toward a far-off goal of human happiness and perfection.

Naturally Jünger's circle was oriented more toward the Left than toward the Right, toward the soviets rather than toward the democracies. In fact, the dominant notions of his circle were often referred to as National Bolshevism. It was not the mystic Russia of Dostoevski to which it turned, but to the technological order which Lenin was seeking in the transforming influence of electricity with an elite of activists.

In Prussianism, which had an affinity with bolshevism, Germany had also achieved a distinctive expression of organizational will and drive. Prussianism, shorn of its conservative and monarchical sentimentalism, involved *Gleichschaltung*, the will to total mobilization by which individual work is transformed into collective work.

Jünger seemed to be carrying the Prussian tour de force to its most radical projection in thought, even to the point of appearing fantastic. It must be viewed, however, in the light of the ferment of ideas and values which enveloped the youth of the time, especially the generation whose adolescence had come during the war. They had never really experienced the order and security of the Bismarckian *Reich*. Everything seemed possible to them. In this they were not unlike the generation of early Romantics.

But Jünger's technological Prussianism suggested the hard, arid quality of Prussian barracks life. It would hardly appeal to the rank and file, for it was too dependent on the radicalism of thought rather than on the appeal to political and nationalistic passion.

THE EXPERIENCE OF THE DEPTHS OF DEGRADATION AND DECADENCE

The more common recollection of the war was of its initial phase when a united national insurgence had swept over the people, convinced of the righteousness of their cause in waging a war of defense against encirclement. But often juxtaposed to this recollection of solidarity was the bitter image of betrayal, of the stab in the back. In the face of the Allied propaganda with its "hypocritical" proposals for international justice and a new order, both socialists and liberals had been tricked into sabotaging the war effort and had brought about humiliating defeat and enslavement.

These ideas were most common in the circles of conservatives and nationalists, but they were also strong among the officers and soldiers, who found it difficult to settle down after four years of violence. To overcome the sense of aloneness and general meaninglessness of life prevalent in the turbulent society of the postwar era, they were naturally drawn together into associations by the nostalgic recollection of the comradeship of the trenches. The large literature dealing with front-line experience kept alive the recollection of heroic struggle; it was perpetuated also in the conflicts of Free Corps with Communists within and with Poles without. Consequently, the return to the war was a way of recapturing a sense of meaning in the face of the general drabness and lack of hope for a satisfying life career.

The war had seemed for a short time to herald a new solidarity and a new vision among men, but defeat brought disillusionment and cynicism. The sense of let-down was reinforced for a time by the disillusionment with the new government and society, with its party politics, and its parvenu rich. But the longing already evident in the Youth Movement for the cleansing wind which would purge society of corruption and materialism again gained new strength. It expressed itself in the vague dream of a new social and political order which would manifest a solidarity of spirit peculiar to the Germans.

Before the war the Youth Movement had stood for the idea of organic community as an outgrowth of a return to nature. After the war it turned to the notion of struggle as the means of achieving solidarity.[8] The repetition of the words "*Bund*" and "front" in the ideological movements reflected the desire for an elemental solidarity for which one could fight to take the place of the confusion of ideological appeals. The combination of disillusionment and cynicism with nebulous dreams of a new communal solidarity provided the soil in which National Socialism came to maturity.

It took one fanatically determined and totally ruthless will directed toward united action, however, to crystallize the dance of ideological nuances, the chaos of moral values, and the conflict of party interests in the concrete vision of a *Reich*, not as a historical restoration but as a dynamic totality.

One fact begins to stand out in the consideration of the circumstances and events which brought Adolph Hitler to the fore, and that was his peculiar demagogic genius. He was capable of playing on the feelings of the masses like a great musical impresario, and yet he was also capable of creating a highly cohesive and disciplined organization of fanatical followers.

It has been suggested that to understand him one must go back to the great sectarian leaders of the sixteenth century, to Anabaptists such as Thomas Müntzer and John of Leyden.[9] There is no doubt that Hitler was a product of the sectarian nationalism of the borderlands. In his personality were fused two great resentments; the one embodied in this sectarian nationalism, the other arising out of the German sense of humiliating defeat due to encirclement and the stab in the back.

The formative period of his political attitudes was, as we have seen, the Vienna of Schönerer and his irredentist nationalism of resentment against all forms of internationalism represented by Jews, Marxists, clerics, and liberals. The Hapsburgs, the Roman Catholic church, and the socialists were considered the chief enemies of Germanism. The dominant characteristics of this sectarian nationalism were its fanatical intransigence, which converted everybody into either friend or foe, and its vision of a great German *Reich* to include all Germans.

Born in Austria on the Bavarian border in 1889, Hitler, during the four years of his Vienna residence, was steadily drawn to the *Reich*. In 1912 he went to Munich. Vienna, with its shopworn baroque splendor, ferment of nationalities, and artistic and scientific fads and fashions, later seemed to him to reflect the depths of national degradation and decadence. It was also associated with his failure to realize a youthful aspiration to become an artist; he obtained at best a very precarious livelihood as a painter of greeting cards. Though he hit the bottom of virtual destitution during the four years there, his mind constantly teemed with eccentric projects for the cultural and political regeneration of the German nation.

The war came as a great release. It meant being lifted out of his frustrating existence to a real sense of oneness with the great German *Volk*—to a level of heroic national action no longer possible in the old bourgeois society with its parties, ideological divisions, and feverish quest for material gain.

His fellow soldiers found him odd; he never griped nor went on furloughs, and he seemed to live completely within himself. He had enlisted as a volunteer, and, although he never rose above the rank of corporal, he secured the Iron Cross First Class, rarely given to men in the ranks. The end of the war found him in a hospital, recovering from wounds and gas.

At the close of the war he returned to Munich, the chief center of ferment in the *Reich*. In this atmosphere, he acquired a new purpose in life, becoming in 1919 a political propagandist and investigator for the army. He naturally came in contact with the numerous veterans' associations; with political, literary, and artistic clubs and circles; and with new political parties which seemed to spring into existence over-night. In them were reflected the mélange of crackpot ideas, romantic and visionary aspirations, bohemian tastes and perversions, violent re-sentments, and fanatical social and political hatreds which character-ized the postwar scene. Here he joined that small group which called itself originally the German Workers' party, later simply the National Socialist party. Being very small—it had only a half-dozen members—it offered Hitler the opportunity to develop his peculiar talents, which might have remained submerged in a much larger group.

On his own, he felt frustrated, a hollow man, without substance. But as a participant in the war and then in the party, he was the embodiment of a movement and became a dynamic force. He be-came conscious of this when he rose to speak among his comrades in the beer hall and discovered the influence he could wield over his hearers. His mind was centered on one idea: the tactics to be fol-lowed to increase the party's numbers and influence rather than party doctrine or theory, which most of its members loved to debate.

A program of twenty-five points was adopted in 1920. In it nationalism and socialism were combined. The former expressed the resentment against the unequal treaties, hostility to foreign immi-grants and Jews, support of the German law as against the Roman, and of a national army as against a professional military force. The socialist line was represented in the call for the nationalization of trusts, the abolition of "interest slavery," and the participation of workers in the benefits of technological advances. Finally, there was the advocacy of a strong and unified central authority in the *Reich*.

These twenty-five points remained the National Socialist party's official program throughout its career. The socialist provisions re-garding nationalization and worker participation were later virtually jettisoned. But at this time socialism was still as important as national-ism. The fusion of nationalism and socialism as a means of drawing the socialist workers back to primary loyalty to the existing national state had been attempted by Naumann without success. Now, how-ever, the fusion was intended to suggest to the worker the establishment of a new national order in which he would be much more than a hewer of wood and a drawer of water.

In the turbulent period from 1920 to 1923 the party grew rapidly in numbers. At the third party reunion (January 29, 1923), it comprised some ten thousand members, of whom some six thousand on that occasion marched before Hitler, hailing him as the *Führer*.

THE PARTY AS MOVEMENT AND THE REICH AS RACIAL TOTALITY

The National Socialist party assumed most of its characteristic features while still largely a local Bavarian movement in favor of the restoration of the monarchy. Munich was the chief center of agitation against communism, socialism, and the Weimar Republic. Bavaria had always been restive under Protestant and militarist Prussia. The fact that in the middle 1920's the Prussian government was dominated by Social Democrats made Bavarian opposition even more intense. Both the mounting inflation, reaching its peak in 1923, and the French occupation of the Ruhr to enforce reparation payments promoted the anti-republican agitation and the celebrated National Socialist *Putsch* of 1923 in Munich.

The failure of the *Putsch* taught Hitler the invaluable lesson that seizure of power was not merely a matter of pushing aside the party government centering in the *Reichstag* or in local legislative bodies. It involved the much more difficult problem of dealing with the heads of the army and bureaucracy, who, though not supporters of the Republic as such, yet thought of themselves as representing the state and as standing above politics; they aimed to defend the Republic against illegal seizure of power by a faction or party. Above all, both army and officialdom would crack down on separatism, such as a movement stemming from Bavaria might appear to be. In order to achieve legal access to power, a leader would have to create a mass following on a national basis capable of securing a majority in the *Reichstag*, and hence control of the government.

During his brief sojourn in prison for his illegal action, Hitler arrived at this clarification of tactics. He then dictated the first volume of *Mein Kampf*, published in 1925. It presented no party program nor systematic discussion of political philosophy but rather an incoherent mixture of autobiographical impressions and ideas. Its main purpose seems to have been to show that his point of departure was a *Weltanschauung*, a world view. It sought to show how the movement developed out of the intense personal experiences and convictions of one man. Few people seemed to have read it, but it nevertheless became the great symbol of the movement.

When Hitler came out of prison toward the end of 1924, he found that, in addition to being legally dissolved, the party had broken up into fragments led by quarreling lieutenants. There were striking personalities among them who reflected the diverse accents of socialism, of peasant reform, of dreams of a great *Reich*, of political romanticism, of National Bolshevism, and of anti-Semitism. The most basic cleavage which ran through the whole party was that between Gregor Strasser, the advocate of socialism who made Berlin his headquarters, and Alfred Rosenberg, the romantic nationalist from the Baltic who, in Bavaria, had sought to assume the mantle of party leadership during Hitler's imprisonment. They were united, however, in their basic resentment against things as they were. The fact that romantically inclined intellectuals, declassed adventurers, gangster-minded advocates of violence, and respectable bureaucrats were willing to submerge their mutual differences of opinion constituted the measure not only of that common resentment but also of the power of Hitler's personality, which was its most complete embodiment.

In terms of intellectual and cultural attainments many of these men were by far Hitler's superiors, yet they stood in awe of him and became his compliant followers. Hitler never read anything that did not fit his specific purposes. He was never outside of his own country; therefore he knew nothing about the outside world. But it was this very narrowness combined with fanatical zeal which gave him a unity of purpose and sense of destiny directed toward a specific goal. His singleness of purpose stood out in contrast to the bewildering diversity of ideologies and values under the Weimar Republic. It won not only the party members but other men who had themselves attained to some degree of prominence in the world. The outstanding comparable influence in history was that of Ignatius Loyola, the founder of the Society of Jesus.

In the second volume of *Mein Kampf*, published in 1927, the sense of prophetic destiny became especially manifest in spite of its turgid incoherence and almost hysterical quality. It presented the basic notions of the *party as movement* and of the *people as a dynamic race* to which Hitler gave undeviating adherence throughout his career.

The supreme aim was the revival of Germany as a great *Reich*. This could be achieved only by a total mobilization of all the energies of the population, not principally through economic and technological development, but by an integration of all classes. The workers, especially, must be fused with the total nation and drawn away from the Marxist delusion. The inertia of the bourgeoisie, arising out of faith in property and culture, and their tendency toward party fragmentation, as evident in the parliamentary regime, must be overcome. A single party, National Socialism, must assume leadership of the total nation, not merely of the impersonal state. By their sheer neutrality and insistence on autonomy, such agencies as the army and bureaucracy had demonstrated their inability to assume such leadership. The leadership of the single party was not a matter of the mere predominance of one ideology or program but was embodied in the inflexible unity of will of that one who felt himself to be a man of destiny—Adolph Hitler.

The broad basis of unity was to be found in the German race purified of its alien elements. As a racial entity, it naturally turned to the assertion of basic survival values through the extension of its power and the achievement of living space. Not peace but war and conflict are the unifiers of races; no greater crime, Hitler argued, could be perpetrated than that a race allow itself to become supine and suffer dilution and disappearance from the stage of history by being submerged in the welter of alien groups. The great German race, being the embodiment of the heroic Nordic and Aryan qualities, must assert its own peculiar individuality.

There was nothing original here. These conceptions of the party as movement or as national revolution and of racial imperialism were to be found in the lumber-room of Italian fascism, of the Pan-

German movement, and of irredentist nationalism in Austria and the Sudeten.

THE RADICALIZATION OF SECTARIAN NATIONALISM

But the significance of the propaganda of the National Socialists lay not in originality or consistency of their ideas; they were complete ideological opportunists who borrowed from both Right and Left. They were a product of the ideological syncretism of the time, accepting and rejecting ideological positions to suit the tactics of the moment. Symbols were much more important than ideas. Words like "blood" and "soil" suggested group solidarity and rootedness in the earth. The hierarchical organization of the party with its uniforms, banners, and marching columns had the same significance. The two most basic appeals of National Socialism lay in the disciplined military organization of the party and in the attraction of the almost mystical sense of unity represented in the Romantic concept of *Volksgemeinschaft*.

But this combination of functional rationalism and irrational appeals had a special coloration derived from the fanatical zeal characteristic of Hitler, which was transferred to the party as a whole by the deliberate intransigence derived from the sectarian nationalism of the borderlands. This was to be transmitted to the whole nation. Since Germany had come to be labeled a pariah among nations, she must live the part. The party was to provide the model by raising a barrier between its members and the outside world so there would be no reconciliation and merging with that world. It would achieve one will—its members obeying blindly and having no personal sense of fate. The hatred of the world must be provoked by terrorism and brutality; therefore the continuous incitement of party membership against Jews, Marxists, liberals, and clericals.

The Nazis were the twentieth-century culmination of the sectarian drive, tremendously enhanced by the dynamic of secularism. As such they manifested the three chief sociological characteristics of sectarianism: first, in the intransigent resentment against the world about them; second, in the charismatic relationship of leader and following; and third, in the expectation of a breakthrough to a new age.

The opposition to a world order based on natural law, to legal-constitutional forms, except as camouflage, and to historical continuity reflected the sectarian opposition to incorporation of the dynamic of spirit in either rational or historic forms.

National Socialism did not present a systematic body of doctrine or theory, nor was it the ostensible instrument of the aspirations of a particular social class. It did not conceive of the nation in terms of a self-determination expressed in particular political institutions nor in historical and cultural organic forms, although it might give lip service on occasion to both.

It felt no necessity to justify itself before the bar of history. It was, after all, not the embodiment of a class mission nor of a national mission which conceives of itself as realizing the potentialities of humanitarian values. Even in national insurgency, it recognized only the means of breaking through the restrictions on power represented by the vested interests of all kinds, embodied in state, society, and religion.

Uninhibited by any of these restrictions, it hoped to effect a complete break with the immediate past. It was thus in harmony with the technological drive which also sought, as has been pointed out, to overcome the limitations of space, time, causality and substance. Permanent war was the inevitable consequence of this attempt at breakthrough on both the sectarian and technological levels.

Secularized sectarianism linked with the technological drive was a characteristic of both National Socialism and Russian Communism. Its prominence among Germans and Russians may be attributed to the consciousness of occupying a border situation between two cultural worlds and to the feeling of belonging to the dispossessed and underprivileged. Obviously these feelings differed as between Russian and German. With the Russian they were of long duration, a consequence of his ambiguous situation of being at once a participant and an outsider in the European family of nations and yet having an almost messianic sense of his own ecumenical destiny.

Some of this ambiguity was inherent in the German feeling of occupying a middle position between Byzantine East and Latin

West. Up to World War I, however, most Germans still thought of themselves as an eastward outpost of Western Christendom and civilization. However, German defeat in the war led to a reaction against the West; the Germans no longer felt themselves to be the borderland of Western Christendom, yet felt Slavdom and Bolshevism to be alien to them. Because France had ceased to be the creative axis of the West toward which German cultural life stood in polar tension, the middle position of the Germans became one of isolation from both West and East.

The German carried his notion of the *Volk* to a radical extreme where it was not merely regarded as unique of its kind but as the source of cultural superiority and dominion. This accentuation may be ascribed also to the fact that the West itself no longer had a sense of cultural mission. Its science and technology, on which it now prided itself in particular, were being expropriated by alien cultures. It seemed that these achievements were not a necessary outgrowth of its historic culture but merely the expression of the very decline of its cultural creativeness. In any case, science and technology were not necessarily expressions of humanism and humanitarianism but might in fact be regarded as antithetical to the unique expressions of Western culture.

XV

The War of Technologies

*T*he triumph of National Socialism is not to be regarded as a temporary aberration of the German people, a mere departure from the normal course of historical development, which has since been rectified. Russian Communism was once so regarded by many Westerners. Both inaugurate the twentieth-century transition from the ideological to the technological world which may produce similar responses elsewhere.

National Socialism went through two phases. First, there was the phase of internal consolidation or *Gleichschaltung*, made necessary by the fragmentation of classes and ideologies, so as to create a unity of national will centered in party and leader. Second, there was the drive to expand beyond the narrow limits of middle Europe into the eastern plains to create the broad basis necessary for a global power position. Again we encounter the irrational will to unity joined with the functional technological drive toward domination.

After Hitler's assumption of the chancellorship on January 30, 1933, the movement toward internal unity went through two phases. First, under the guise of a national insurgency and by ostensible legal-constitutional means, National Socialism consolidated its power and secured the support of ruling groups. Second, after purging its own ranks of those who would found a new social order on the basis of the national insurgence, the party proceeded to a systematic *Gleichschaltung* of the whole body politic to achieve a totalitarian mobility.

Both Fascism and National Socialism assumed that it was not basically a lack of material resources and misguided policy or even the wrong values that led to decadence and defeat but an inadequately heroic and unified will. Both were obsessed with the notion of a degeneration in national or racial quality.

UNITY OF WILL AND NATIONAL INSURGENCY

Hitler aimed not at the internal reorganization of Germany to effect a new redistribution of power among the social groups nor at a restoration of the old monarchical-hierarchical order but at the achievement of a new inner cohesion on the basis of the party as the embodiment of the leadership principle and the friend-foe relationship. His chief immediate goal was to overcome the four principal sources of division among Germans: the dualism between government and people characteristic of both the Bismarckian *Reich* and the Weimar Republic; the multiplicity of parties and ideologies especially peculiar to the latter; the local and regional divisions, a relic of the old Empire; and, finally, the pluralism of cultural values and interests which came with the dissolution of the old social order and the new technological revolution.

Both the old monarchical-aristocratic forms and the more recent liberal-democratic ones were viewed as static and obstructive to the expression of the unified will of the *Volk*. The National Socialists did not seek a fundamental change in the constitutional order but the unhampered expression of the national will through a party which was not a program but a movement. Hitler and his party lieutenants were not concerned with replacing the old political and social structure with a new one, but rather with replacing the powers and vested interests of state and community with the dynamic of the party movement. This was the fundamental meaning of the party as "permanent revolution." The passage of the Enabling Act on March 23, 1933 granted dictatorial powers to the government for the next four years. It made the *Reichstag* unnecessary and the parties superfluous. The final dissolution and prohibition of all parties came on July 14, 1933, and a single-party state was established in which the National Socialist party virtually served as the parliament. The electorate was no longer allowed to engage in public discussion and choice of parties. The main object was the achievement of a united front presented through the one party and, within it, through its monolithic leadership. Moreover, both *Volk* and state were fused in the united will of the party, which no longer served as a mere intermediary between them. Consequently, the duality of the state agencies—bureaucracy, army, and courts on the one hand, and the *Reichstag* and parties on the other—was transcended in the integral party.

The crescendo of movement did not derive its momentum from the party alone; it also derived from a popular insurgence not unlike that of the first stages of the revolution of 1848 and of that in the first phase of World War I. Popular opinion enthusiastically accepted the new unity of direction from above as the crystallization of the national will, but it did not necessarily accept the Nazis, who were still regarded by many as either crackpots or gangsters. There was a strong feeling that now at last Germany, after an interim of fifteen years, was being resurrected from the impotence induced by the conflict of parties and ideologies. Again there was a strong hand at the helm, giving Germans once more a sense of destiny, even though the goal was not known. The Nazis cleverly promoted this feeling and rode into complete power on the crest of the wave of national insurgency.

SUPPRESSION OF A NATIONAL AND SOCIALIST REVOLUTION

But this popular insurgency threatened to assume the proportions of a national revolution which might have engulfed the party and its leader. The consequent crisis within the party came to a head in the blood purge of June 30, 1934. It began with the question as to what the relation was to be between the S.A. (*Sturmabteilung*), the party military organization, and the army, the *Reichswehr*. In this context a bitter controversy arose as to the goals of the nationalist revolution. A wide fissure developed between the party leadership and the S.A.—a cleavage which had been in the making from the time of the latter's establishment.

The party leaders had assumed positions of power and secured the rich plums of office and wealth. Most of the "old fighters," who had stood by in the days of humiliation and tribulation, were pushed to the background, and they saw many newcomers reap the harvest of the ascent to power.

Apparently the leadership and many of the rank and file of the S.A. looked to the establishment of a new social order. They, like Gregor Strasser, who had been ousted from the party leadership, took socialism seriously and not merely as a propaganda instrument. It is argued that the influx of ex-Communists into the S.A. contributed especially toward the development of a radical wing, which in 1934 began talking of the necessity of a second revolution to realize the original ends of the movement from which it had departed, National Socialism. In the minds of the S.A., "nationalism" served merely to define the form of socialism which aimed at a corporatively organized society.

These ideas were all very nebulous. They reflected the lower middle-class resentment against interest slavery, big business, and bureaucracy. The original appeal of the party had been to these ideas. Now, after the party had come into power, they were being steadily by-passed by the party's swing toward rearmament and heavy industry. Some of the extremists aimed at National Bolshevism involving a fundamental social revolution comparable to that in Russia.

Initially, the most definite public opposition to the S.A. came from a conservative front comprising army generals, political leaders, and industrial magnates. They were concerned with bringing the revolutionary movement to a halt in order that stability and a sense of security might again be restored. Their hope was to absorb the movement into the state organization to bring about its containment. The conservative, military, and industrial element would then take over under Hitler, who could still be useful. After all, the Nazis had suppressed the party and trade union organizations of the liberal and socialist Left, and Hitler could still be of great service as the Pied

Piper of the masses. But the actual reins of power would be held by the conservative front.

Both the ideas of the Left and Right of the nationalist revolution ran contrary to the basic rationale of the party as revolution. They viewed the party as a mere means toward ends—either of socialism or nationalism—lying beyond the party and leading to the establishment of a so-called new order. In it the party was to be assimilated and lose its identity.

Three considerations particularly induced Hitler to action against the S.A. extremists. First and foremost, the extremists constituted a definite threat to his leadership by proposing to cut down the supremacy of the party. A second revolution might very well place the S.A., as the embodiment of popular forces, above the party.

Second, the S.A. in power would certainly step up the tempo of violence by a resort to direct revolutionary action. The step-by-step tactics of following legal and constitutional procedures which had proved so successful would be abandoned and the conservative and influential sectors of society would be frightened into active opposition.

Finally, Hitler needed a strong army in order to regain mobility for Germany in foreign affairs. After all, the great aim was to undo the Versailles settlement. It was pointed out by such generals as Blomberg and Reichenau, who were favorably disposed toward National Socialism, that the fusion of the *Reichswehr* with the political soldiery of S.A. would destroy the laboriously built-up technical efficiency of the military arm. The S.A. units had shown their military inadequacy in maneuvers.

After much hesitation, Hitler finally moved to rid the movement of its malcontents in the purge of June 30, 1934. Revolutionary violence was brought to an end with one supreme act of violence. According to Hitler's statement some time later to the *Reichstag*, only seventy-seven persons lost their lives. Actually, hundreds were murdered as the party leaders and their agents settled scores with those who, even though outside the party, had incurred their enmity.

As the National Socialist movement is being studied more and more today, this purge begins to loom as marking a decisive turning point within it.[1] The party was no longer bound by strings, either to the Right or to the Left, nor by the threat of being poured into the mold of either an authoritarian or a socialist regime. The Right lost out not only as a result of the fear instilled by the purge but by the loss of the Left as a counterpoise to the party leaders.

COLD REVOLUTION

Hitler could now achieve what may be called "revolution-in-depth." This aimed at a slow dissolution of the inner substance of institutions with the retention of surface legality and order, by working from underneath the atmosphere of latent terror to intimidate the opposition. This "cold revolution" would bring about a fundamental change in the character of people. It would cut them loose psychologically from their ancient moorings and transform them into a dynamic mass to be molded by the *Führer*.

After 1934 National Socialism lost much of its supporting momentum or drive, not only as a consequence of the liquidation of the social and political radicalism of the S.A. but also by virtue of the general exhaustion of popular insurgency. The latter had kept pace thus far and in fact at times had surged ahead of the movement. But the blood bath revealed the temper of the movement and threw a cold shower on popular enthusiasm. These losses in external impetus were compensated for, however, by the acceleration of the power drive of the party itself.

Since the national insurgency no longer carried the populace along with the party, it was necessary for the party to use systematic means to promote popular participation. The promotion of mass propaganda and latent terror came to dominate completely. The Nazi leaders sensed that faith and fear are closely allied in the mass mind.[2]

The system of latent terror replaced the sporadic gangsterism of the S.A. with a careful surveillance extending to the lowest cells of community life. Janitors in apartment houses and waiters in restaurants were entrained in its service. In the background there was always the mysterious terror of the concentration camp and the periodic and unexplained disappearance of this or that person. In the case of prominent persons, the charge was generally one of treason, which at least aroused doubt in people's minds, rendered susceptible to the friend-foe distinction by the very demoralization of political convictions. Naturally, the distinction between dissent and disloyalty virtually disappeared.

Systematized terror served to induce people to give, at most, passive assent to the regime. To secure active support it was necessary to bring about what has been aptly called "restoration of political beliefs." [3]

The disintegration of political ideologies had destroyed the feeling of participation in the national community as a going concern. The emerging mass society comprised only fragmented individuals filled with an all-pervading anxiety, augmented by inflation and depression. Yet, paradoxically, this pathological disorganization, according to the Nazis, could be overcome by a return to the basic forms of communal solidarity and its mythical roots. The consequent tension between the rational functionalism of the technics of terror and the irrational appeals of the racial myth provided the chief dynamic of the National Socialist regime.

THE COLLECTIVE SUBCONSCIOUS AND RACIAL MYTH

The solidarity of the *Volksgemeinschaft* was continually juxtaposed to the fragmentation of *Gesellschaft*. The former was presumably based on the intimate sense of unity growing out of basic ties of blood and soil, of the tribal sense of friend and foe plus rootedness in a particular landscape. In the latter, these ties had been displaced by calculated values and conventions resting upon individual self-interest. Both liberalism and socialism were based on this self-interest, liberalism emphasizing the competition of individual interests, and socialism the conflict of class interests as the means of achieving a harmony or equilibrium but not a real solidarity. The *Volksgemeinschaft* was a matter of *Erlebnis*—it was lived—and not an artificially contrived harmony of interests.

The propaganda of words with image-provoking implications was intended to produce a mythical consciousness, the necessary basis of a sense of communal solidarity. Myth pointed to that which is unchangeable and eternal and therefore recurrent in the depths of human relationships, such as leadership and inequality. These basic qualities of the racial community were juxtaposed to the leveling tendencies of liberal democracy and Marxian socialism which produced merely the amorphous mass of atomized individuals. Nothing was left to the latter but the calculation of interests.

Modern man, in de-mythologizing the world, tends to become paralyzed in the face of the multiplicity of conscious decisions and deliberate choices which the vast rationalized society requires of him. Therefore, he seeks to make the technological apparatus as all-inclusive as possible and thereby reduces all behavior to automatic processes. This becomes a flight from freedom, from the insecurity of making decisions into the social insect-heap of automatons. This insecurity, it was charged by National Socialists and others, was the drive behind the collectivism of Marxian socialism.

Racial mysticism must be viewed as one of the various forms of what has been called return to the Antaean sources, to the "earth as stability, as man's 'basic' security." [4] The Antaean tradition involved a reassertion of the vitalistic elements in human experience, whether as Dionysian creativity or, more commonly, as sex, blood, and soil. It sought to overcome man's sense of alienation from his roots in the earth brought about by the disenchantment of the world in nineteenth- and twentieth-century technical rationalization.

The underlying notion of Hitler's racial myth was the fundamental inequalities among peoples and individuals. It stood in direct opposition to liberal humanitarianism, democratic equalitarianism, and to Marxian collectivism. In the eastern borderlands, especially, of course, in the Soviet Union, great emphasis was placed upon class as a means of achieving national unity. Class and nationality had become closely associated in the past in that middle-class Slavs frequently had spoken the German language, had assumed German names, and had come to regard themselves virtually as Germans. The peasants and workers, however, clung to the native language. In the Soviet Union a leveling process took place whereby the community was purged of all those who presumably stood outside the proletarian class, and thereby national as well as class aliens were eliminated within each ethnic group.

But the German, with his traditional sense of hierarchical class order based on the persistence of the variegated social structure inherited from the later Middle Ages, was naturally disinclined to accept class solidarity as the basis of national unity. He sought a unifying principle in the notion of the racial community. Race could be juxtaposed to class as a term of wider classification and significance than the rather parochial notion of nation. Race was in fact the means of separating nation from class. This cleavage was already anticipated in sectarian nationalism from which, as we have seen, the racialism of middle Europe came to derive its chief impetus.

Another fundamental attribute of race was survival, that is, purity. Races always stood in danger of dilution, especially in the modern world of peace and security. In primitive and warlike times, they provided, so to speak, their own antidote in the heroic qualities bred by wars of resistance against amalgamation, by the tribal relationship of friend-foe, and by the example set by leader and elite. The Nazis held that a return must be made to these forms of racial purification.

LOWER MIDDLE-CLASS KULTUR

The Nazi intellectuals made much of what they called the "sickness of European culture." This malady, they argued, was reflected especially in the fluidity of artistic expressionism and philosophic relativism. The widespread influence of Max Weber, Stefan George, and Sigmund Freud, and of the circles of disciples around them, promoted the dissolution of all standards and definite configurations into a "dance of nuances" presenting mere empty possibilities. The prominence of a number of Jewish thinkers in these circles naturally led them to ascribe this *Kultur Bolshevismus*" to the spread of the "Semitic disease." There was no recognition of the fact that National Socialism itself was the very incarnation of the mobility and fluidity of power divorced from all traditional and constitutional restraints.

But in contrast to this political dynamism, National Socialism was also inclined toward traditional cultural and social forms. Here the lower middle-class complexion of the movement became definitely apparent. This group, situated between the cultured and well-to-do upper bourgeoisie above and the factory workers below, comprised shopkeepers, peasants, petty officials, and a large mass of white collar workers. The heterogeneous social mass was caught between the big business of heavy industry and commerce above and proletarian socialism and trade unionism below, both international in orientation. Consequently, the lower middle-class elements developed a nationalist xenophobia and turned to traditional corporative forms of economic life, to an authoritarian family ethos, and to late Romantic forms of culture. These constituted the means of counteracting the fluidity prevalent at the top and bottom levels of the social scale and safeguarding their middle position. Having no definite ideology of their own, as did the liberal bourgeoisie or the socialist workers, as compensation they naturally turned to the reassertion of traditional and provincial middle-class values to which they accorded an almost sacrosanct quality—values to be defended against the cosmopolitan and sophisticated influences coming from above and below.

The Nazis, like the *Biedermeier* of the first half of the century, were attracted to the homey forms of the late nineteenth-century Romanticism. In the decoration of their homes, many Nazi leaders indulged in the lower middle-class penchant for gingerbread and gimcrackery. Only in the public spectacle of the gymnastic field-day or of the great party assemblies with their marching columns, banners, and crowds, did they and the Communists and Fascists strike out in new directions in the revival of public forms of cultural expression suitable to the mass society of the twentieth century. While the great road system reflected the new technological age, the many new public buildings expressed a neo-classic arid monumentality which was supposed to be Prussian and imperial in spirit.

The underlying social conservativism was also exemplified in the lip service accorded the traditional family and its authoritarian complexion. Especially for economic reasons growing out of the conduct of small businesses, the family was more the center of lower middle-class life than it was for the upper or lower classes. The Nazis talked a great deal about the dignity of woman to be restored through *Kinder,* (children), *Kirche* (church), *Küche* (kitchen). This emphasis on sentimentalized traditional values alongside the brutality and tyranny of concentration camps and the garrison state illustrates the dualism characteristic of a movement which oscillated between romantic illusions and cold technical reality.

438

THE HEGEMONIC DRIVE OF SECTARIAN NATIONALISM

Even as the party broke through the constitutional restraints on power, the *Volk* would burst the state frontiers of old Europe so as to give itself freedom of movement. The external drive was only an extension of the inner dynamic—it recognized no limits such as those involved in maintaining a European order based on the balance of power.

In its external expansive drive, National Socialism manifested the same polarity of technical rationalism with romantic irrationalism. The first was determined by the enormous expansion of the state's power range by the new advances in military technology; the second by the accentuation of the hegemonic drive by sectarian nationalism.

The *Reich* as *Lebensraum* represented a dynamic conception of space; it involved more than the conquest of specific territories. As the geopoliticians pointed out, one should no longer think in terms of sacrosanct frontiers but of a field of economic, cultural, and political forces which transcend the old state boundaries. In contemporary architecture the house is no longer viewed as so many walls, floors, and ceilings providing shelter but as "formed space for living." So the state is no longer to be thought of in terms of sovereignty exercised over certain territories and their inhabitants, and limited by definitely marked boundaries, but as power radiating from a single source in all directions.

The drive to war which activated the Nazi leaders, and which they sought to communicate to the masses, did not spring from the sense of a world mission to extend German commerce and *Kultur* abroad, as had been a strong motif before World War I. It derived its basic intensity and force from the pent-up resentments embodied in a sectarian nationalism which professed to see not only the world arrayed against it but lesser racial breeds lording it over a superior people. These resentments were extended to the German people at large through the recurring refrain of the defeat and humiliation by the stab in the back within and of their encirclement by foes without.

Reared in the parochial nationalism of the eastern borderlands,

Hitler had little appreciation of the dimensions of outside forces and powers, especially of the United States and the Soviet Union. Hitler's contempt for other nationalities as racially decadent or inferior influenced his view of the world in general. He had some appreciation of the dynamics of the Communist movement, at least to the extent of taking over some of the tactics and technics of Bolshevik party warfare. But by many Germans, the Russian masses were regarded as basically Asiatic aliens who had in the past been held down by a Europeanized ruling class, which had been liquidated by what was virtually a *Jacquerie* led by Jewish "Reds." In their view, America lay on the periphery of things and was mainly absorbed in materialistic interests and pursuits, as were the English. As for the French, they were thought of as so decadent as to be inevitably doomed to defeat and even liquidation.

It was this perspective of seeing the world altogether from the inside that gave Hitler's National Socialism at once its tremendous propulsive power and its lack of psychological insight into the unique individual strength of the other peoples and states in the world arena.

The domination of the party as the dynamic movement of the state, the *Reich* and the *Volk*, it should be stressed, was the product not merely of the Nazi seizure of power but of the emasculation of old political and social forms and attitudes.

The Prussian state tradition had embodied the notion of politics as the pursuit of limited, that is, possible, ends. But *Prussianism* as a formative principle had assumed an increasing tour-de-force character in the thought of Moeller and Jünger, for example. The *Reich* had lost its old regional lineaments and had become transformed by means of the war imperialism from a civilizing mission among the peoples of the border into a drive for domination. Likewise, the conception of *Volk* had lost its implications of humanitarian mission and had become associated with indelible cultural or racial characteristics.

THE SOFTENING OF THE OPPOSITION

In the outward expansion of the Third *Reich* there were also two phases comparable to those which characterized the expansion of the power position of the National Socialist party within. In the first phase, from 1936 to 1939, the *Reich* was concerned with a step-by-step advancement of its claims to nationals and territories which it had lost as a consequence of defeat in World War I. This phase was comparable to that of national insurgency. The second phase, which began with the Polish War in 1939, was characterized by the sweeping aside of the frontiers of old Europe, which stood in the way of the achievement of living space. The ring of small states which immediately encircled Germany was dissolved so as to provide freedom of movement to make the breakthrough, particularly to the eastern plains.

It will be recalled that National Socialism expanded its power in a step-by-step occupation of individual constitutional positions. These positions were employed merely to camouflage the virtual emasculation of the legal-state order itself, leaving mere external husks. Externally, the same procedure was followed, to begin with, in bringing about the dissolution of the "Versailles Treaty system" by employing as a justification the basic principle underlying that framework—national self-determination.

The Western powers were kept continually off balance by the piece-by-piece disintegration of the bases of European order. From 1934 to 1939, this procedure and its nationalist justification, along with the prevailing war weariness, prevented the Western peoples from decisively intervening until at last driven to it by the sudden awareness of their own danger.

The reluctance to act decisively was the product also of the ideological demoralization, most evident, as in the case of the Germans, among the middle-class ruling groups of the Western democracies. They wavered between fear of revolution from the Right and from the Left. The distinction in the minds of many of them between Social Democrats and Communists came to be virtually effaced by the popular front collaboration. Generally speaking, they were most afraid of the menace from the Communist Left and saw in the march of the Nazi and Fascist dictators a fortunate counterpoise to the world revolution promoted from Moscow.

With the acquisition of Austria in 1938, Hitler inaugurated the breaking of the chain of encircling states to the east that the postwar treaties had forged. The annexation of Austria had a special significance. It meant the realization of the chief aspiration of the *Grossdeutsch* ideal. With the inclusion of his own homeland, Hitler himself could no longer be looked on as a foreigner, but as a native of an ancient province of the *Reich*, now restored. The Third *Reich* now was completed in the fusion of the two sources of its expansive dynamic, namely, Austrian sectarian nationalism and the technical-organizational ethos of Prussianism.

The invasion of Poland on September 1, 1939 marked the beginning of the great expansive drive. The German steamroller overran most of old Europe in a series of campaigns referred to as *Blitzkrieg*. The *Wehrmacht* took the wraps off the secret weapon with which Hitler had thus far been threatening the Western world. Actually, this involved no new weapons, as such, but the coordination of airplane, tank, motor truck, and motorized artillery—all employed in World War I—making possible the breakthrough which resulted in new mobility and war-in-depth. It was the development of the armored division with its combined thrust of tank, dive bomber, and mobile artillery that provided the means of overcoming the stalemate of trench warfare. The effectiveness of this weapon was first demonstrated in the Polish campaign, during which the German military machine demolished the Polish army, which still used cavalry, and took the chief fortified positions within the brief time of four weeks. Another new aspect of war, equally significant, was the inauguration of a systematic policy of liquidating the Polish intelligentsia and well-to-do middle classes and of deporting Poles from the border areas and colonizing these with Germans.

The large Jewish population in Poland was also given "special treatment"—extermination and incarceration in ghettos. The anti-Semitic movement had entered a new phase after 1938, when the assassination of a German official by a Jew furnished the trigger action for the already projected systematic extermination. Anti-Semitic propaganda and violence was increased to a fever pitch both within Germany and in the conquered areas. It was intended not only to serve as a means of whipping up German public opinion against the foe within and without, but to turn the seething mass of national hatreds and resentments in middle Europe away from the German toward the Jew, who had played such an important role in the economic and intellectual life of that area.

BLITZKRIEG AND LEBENSRAUM

The changed character of warfare was reflected also in the autonomous development of those various functions, such as intelligence, and especially the S.S. (*Schutzstaffel*), concerned with maintaining supervision over the loyalty of the leadership and with the rule of subject territories, which in the past had not existed or had been merely auxiliary to the army. The multiplication of services and Hitler's all-over direction combined to reduce the stature of both the military arm and of its brain trust, the General Staff. The old Prussian elements no longer dominated them. Calculated moves of a diplomatic and military character were of much less importance in a war of technics and terror. World War I had already demonstrated that the utilization of great firepower and the deployment of great masses of troops made rational direction very difficult. Moreover, the two-level character of World War II, the shock-troop tactics of a *Blitzkrieg*, and the underground struggle between partisans and S.S. made planning difficult and put a premium on the intuitive approach of Hitler. Consequently, World War II, under the driving force of Hitler's personality, developed by a kind of inner momentum, from breakthrough to breakthrough, to a crescendo on the vast spaces of the Russian steppes, and ended abruptly in complete collapse.

It is significant that, while the technics of war had changed fundamentally, the general strategical considerations had not yet responded to that change, at least as far as Hitler was concerned. He found himself in the same position that Napoleon had been in: he was conqueror of Europe, but he was confronted by a combination of geographical obstacles and psychological capacity for resistance in the peripheral peoples of the British Isles and Russia which proved insurmountable.

Hitler also decided that if England could not be dealt with directly, she must be attacked elsewhere—in northern Africa and in the Near East. But thereby the theatre of war began to widen greatly beyond Europe, and eventually beyond Hitler's comprehension and grasp. Hitler's thought apparently revolved mainly within the orbit

443

of Europe and did not envisage the position of Europe in the emerging global situation. The influence of the geopolitics of General Karl Haushofer extended only to the technics of conquest and not to the creation of a new world order. This became apparent, in the course of the war, in Hitler's failure to coordinate the strategical efforts of the Berlin-Rome-Tokyo axis.

The war entered its final and decisive military phase with the attacks upon the Soviet Union and the United States in 1941. In this phase of the war the positive goals of both the National Socialists and their Japanese allies were projected. For the Nazis, they were the conquest of the economic resources of the great Russian hinterland; and for the Japanese, those of the Pacific hinterland. The have-not nations, or, as they sometimes called themselves, the proletarian peoples, sought by conquest to acquire a global power position and outlets for their surplus population.

The plan was for densely populated Europe to find food and minerals in the great heartland of Eurasia, with its limitless resources, assumed to be under the inadequate exploitation of the inferior Slav. This aim was an extension of the continental ambitions of the annexationists, envisaged in the last phases of World War I, when for a short time the German high command had conquered Poland, the Ukraine, and Rumania as far as the Black Sea.

For both Japan and Germany, the striving for *Lebensraum* involved breaking out of the cramped situation of insularity and of a narrow continental position. It involved flowing out into the wide open spaces and releasing pent-up national energies.

But here they came face to face with those peoples represented by the Americans and the Russians, who had, in the conquest of wide continental areas, developed a similar expansive *élan*. Both of these peoples were definitely on the threshold of abandoning an isolationist attitude and policy for a global orientation. Neither the Japanese nor the Germans appreciated the strength of the new forces which confronted them in the global arena. Because of their initial rapid successes, they thought that a tough military spirit plus close-knit organization would carry all before it.

In contemporary warfare great technological acceleration brings about rapid shifts in relative military potential. The Allies overcame the initial technical superiority of the Germans when they developed a combination of amphibious technics along with mechanized shock-troop tactics. The Germans naturally tended to cling to the technics and tactics used so successfully in the early stages of the war. Toward the end of the conflict, when things began going badly, Hitler sought to bolster German morale by the promise of eventual victory to be brought about by new weapons such as guided and atomic missiles. At the time it seemed to many merely a different version of the old miracle notion whereby the Germans would be rescued at the last desperate moment if they would only hold out. This threat of a totally new weapon induced the United States to turn its attention to that vast and momentous enterprise, the production of an atomic bomb.

To the last, Hitler and some of his lieutenants were animated by the wholly irrational notion that if they resisted to the last ditch—that is, to use the phrase of Lloyd George, applied by him to German efforts in World War I, until "five minutes beyond twelve o'clock"—victory might yet be snatched from defeat. Perhaps nowhere was the irrational driving force of the National Socialist movement more manifest than this fatalism born of intransigence and resentment.

THE GERMANIES IN THE GLOBAL SITUATION

In the new global world, Europe finds itself to be one center alongside of a number of others, including the United States, the Soviet Union, the British Commonwealth, China, and India. It has ceased to be the radiating focus of an expanding world civilization. Lacking a controlling center, it cannot play a unified role in the global arena, as these others can. The individual national units comprising Europe tend to be increasingly dwarfed by the colossal global powers.

The National Socialist movement was, among other things, an attempt to re-establish the German *Reich* as the axis of a Europe which would again be able to assert itself among the other global powers, as it had in the time of Charlemagne and Otto the Great. But, now caught between the strong bi-polar attractions and repulsions of the U.S.A. and the U.S.S.R., it is unlikely that Europe will succeed for the time being in achieving unity under a hegemonic empire. The rhythm of hegemonic thrust and counteraction of coalition, which provided the basic pattern of European politics for about four centuries, seems likely to be in abeyance. Western Europe seems destined in the conflict of global powers to play the former role of central Europe as a power vacuum.

In this Europe, the Germans find themselves politically divided between West and East. Practically all the Germans occupying the old colonial area of the Middle Ages have been separated from the bulk of their compatriots in West Germany either by being included within the Soviet zone, as is old Prussia, or by being restored to independence, as is Austria. Most of this colonial area is again under Slav dominion. The retreat of the Germans from the eastern borderlands is perhaps most manifest in the ten million or so either expelled by Czechs, Poles, and Russians, or refugees from the Soviet zone. Austria and Prussia, which were politically the most dynamic regions of the modern *Reich,* now follow an independent course.

We thus encounter the Germanies again, now divided into three rather than thirty-nine or three hundred parts. West Germany has virtually lost the two chief capitals, Vienna and Berlin, in which German political and social life centered, at least in the century before World War I. It is actually the Third Germany lying along the Rhine, a main avenue of humanist and liberal currents, to be distinguished from the Prussian and Austrian Germanies. West Germany has become an extension of Christian Europe facing toward the schismatic and infidel East. The strongest unifying influence within this Christian and conservative Europe is the Roman papacy.

The way was prepared for the cultural re-integration of West Germany with the West by a diaspora of ideas and values coming from the exiled and borderland German spiritual and cultural leaders such as Einstein, Freud, and Schweitzer; Gropius and Mann; Tillich and Jaspers. Their ideas had reached fruition as early as the cultural ferment of the 1920's, and achieved a world-wide orientation in relativism, existentialism, psychoanalysis, and the *Bauhaus* during the 1930's and 1940's. They represent the attempt to achieve a new cultural orientation for the West, no longer to be dominated by the frames of rationalism and historicism. But along with the spiritual and cultural wave there is the impact of the German technicians, who have played a major role in the technological cold war between the East and West. These two groups re-enact, so to speak, the basic polarity of German thinking which has become symptomatic of the emerging technological world in general.

NATIONAL SOCIALISM AS A PHASE OF THE TECHNOLOGICAL REVOLUTION

Not only was the war of technologies inaugurated by National Socialism but it contributed decisively to the breakthrough of the Atomic Age. World War I was really a war of goods and men, with technology playing a major role only in the production of goods and ideologies still providing the spur to action. In World War II, however, the Nazis not only introduced technology as a tactical instrument, thus restoring mobility to war, but created the irrational dynamics necessary to technological warfare. The promotion of mass mobility by the tactics of intransigence and purges kept the populace in flux and prevented the crystallization of religious and ideological molds.

The tendency of historians to deal with National Socialism as a totally alien phenomenon has its sources largely in the impact of the surface aspects of terrorism and brutality of the regime plus its projection of apparently incredible and fantastic notions about race and *Reich*. All of these were essentially part of a propaganda of deed and word behind which the rationale of the technological breakthrough made itself apparent.

It is not to be assumed that the Nazi leaders themselves were fully aware of this mainspring of their actions. Their hegemonic drive, carried to extremes both within and without, led them to an emasculation of historic forms and attitudes while allowing the forms to appear largely intact on the surface. The illusion was created, characteristic of the technological breakthrough in general, that the changes affect only external instruments and not the psychological substrata of human existence. The ideological revolution sought to establish a new order in terms of institutions and appropriate attitudes. The technological transformations set the collective psyche in motion while retaining the old shells of constitutional, corporative, and social order.

The terroristic violence and ideological opportunism of National Socialism represented aspects of an accelerated transition in a country in which the traditional political and social shells had remained more completely intact than elsewhere in western Europe. The disassociation of the collective psyche from the historic shells was, however, more complete there than elsewhere. There was no tradition of revolutionary action—only of national insurgence—among the Germans to buttress the modern liberal and democratic institutions, which in themselves constituted, as evidences of modernity, a rejection of the persisting monarchical, aristocratic, and corporative forms. The German psyche was thus divided in its allegiance and very susceptible to being wrenched psychologically from its moorings.

National Socialism derived its positive content from the sectarian motif of the expectancy of a new *Reich*. This expectancy was secularized as transitional in Russian Communism but as the here and now of the dynamic intensity of the moment in National Socialism. The former was still oriented toward the future utopia, but to the latter the Thousand-Year *Reich* was neither a span of political history nor a vision of utopia, but "the deed of the moment," a total mobilization of all forces.

National Socialism was not oriented toward history as fulfillment of a purpose nor toward nature as a rational order nor toward individual search for meaning in nature and culture. Its significance lay not in the projection of new institutions or ideas but in the tremendous acceleration of the dynamics of technological development.

Notes

Introduction

1. Max Bense, *Technische Existenz* (Stuttgart, 1949), pp. 191–231; Friedrich Delekat, *Über den Begriff der Säkularisation* (Heidelberg, 1958), pp. 5–73; Alfred Stern, "The Irreversibility of History," *Diogenes*, No. 29 (Spring 1960), pp. 1–15.
2. Cf. Delekat, *op. cit.*, pp. 18–43.

Chapter I

1. The discussion of the religious ethos of Ottonian art is indebted to Arnold Hauser, *The Social History of Art* (New York, 1951) I, 174–197; Richard Hamann, *Geschichte der Kunst* (Berlin, 1933), pp. 231–249; Hans Weigert, *Geschichte der deutschen Kunst* (Berlin, 1942), pp. 120–138.

Chapter II

1. Friedrich Lütge, *Deutsche Sozial- und Wirtschaftsgeschichte* (Berlin, 1952), p. 89.
2. Fritz Gause, *Deutsch-slawische Schicksalsgemeinschaft* (Kitzingen/Main, 1952), p. 76.
3. Hauser, *op. cit.*, pp. 214ff.
4. Hamann, *op. cit.*, p. 37.

Chapter III

1. Lütge, *op. cit.*, pp. 142–151.
2. J. Huizinga, *The Waning of the Middle Ages* (London, 1948), *passim*.
3. Joseph Lortz, *Die Reformation in Deutschland* (Freiburg/B., 1939), I, 124ff.
4. Hauser, *op. cit.*, I, 273ff.

Chapter IV

1. Willy Andreas, *Deutschland vor der Reformation* (Stuttgart, Berlin, 1932), p. 555.
2. *Ibid.*, pp. 589–594.
3. Will Erich Peuchert, *Die grosse Wende* (Hamburg, 1948), p. 399.
4. Margaret Mann Phillips, *Erasmus and the Northern Renaissance* (London, 1949), pp. 76f.
5. Heinrich Boehmer, *Road to Reformation, Martin Luther to the Year 1521* (Philadelphia, 1946), p. 36.

Chapter V

1. Andrew L. Drummond, *German Protestantism since Luther* (London, 1951), p. 13.
2. Quoted in *ibid.*, p. 40.

Chapter VI

1. Cf. Mario Pensa, *Das deutsche Denken* (Erlenbach-Zürich, 1948), p. 65.
2. Jakob Taubes, *Abendländische Eschatologie* (Bern, 1947), p. 89.
3. Cf. Donald Brinkmann, *Mensch und Technik* (Bern, 1946), pp. 105–131.
4. *Ibid.*, pp. 120–129.
5. Cf. *ibid.*, pp. 141ff.
6. H. T. Pledge, *Science Since 1500* (New York, 1947), p. 62.
7. Otto Heckmann, "Galilei und Kepler," in *Gottfried Wilhelm Leibniz, Vorträge der aus Anlass seines drei hundert Geburtstages in Hamburg abgehaltenen wissenschaftlichen Tagung.* Hrsg. von der Redaktion der Hamburger Akademischen Rundschau (Hamburg, 1946), p. 236.
8. Cf. George H. Sabine, *A History of Political Theory* (New York, 1937), pp. 416–420.

Chapter VII

1. Friedrich Heer, *Europäische Geistesgeschichte* (Zürich, 1953), pp. 549ff.
2. *Ibid.*, pp. 487ff.
3. Weigert, *op. cit.*, p. 412.
4. Cf. Werner Hager, *Die Bauten des deutschen Barocks, 1690–1770* (Jena, 1942), pp. 43–69.
5. R. Alewyn and Karl Sälzle, *Das grosse Welttheater; Die Epoche der höfischen Feste in Dokument und Deutung* (Hamburg, 1959), pp. 44ff.
6. Hager, *op. cit.*, pp. 23ff.
7. Alewyn and Sälzle, *op. cit.*, pp. 48–70.
8. Lewis Mumford, *Technics and Civilization* (New York, 1934), pp. 107–167.
9. Emil Ermatinger, *Deutsche Kultur im Zeitalter der Aufklärung* (Potsdam, 1935), pp. 188–189.
10. Cf. Luis Diez del Corral, *The Rape of Europe* (London, 1959), p. 261.
11. Emanuel Hirsch, *Geschichte der neuern evangelischen Theologie* (Gütersloh, 1951), II, 156–179.
12. *Ibid.*, p. 401.
13. Hugo Leichtentritt, *Music, History, and Ideas* (Cambridge, Mass., 1938), Ch. 7.
14. Cf. Hans M. Wolff, *Die Weltanschauung der deutschen Aufklärung in geschichtlicher Entwicklung* (Bern, 1949), p. 15.
15. Cf. Ermatinger, *op. cit.*, pp. 21–25.
16. Cf. Rudolf Stadelmann, *Deutschland und Westeuropa* (Schloss Laupheim-Württemberg, 1948), pp. 22–25.

Chapter VIII

1. Ermatinger, *op. cit.*, p. 250.
2. Cf. Taubes, *op. cit.*, pp. 135f.
3. Thomas Mann, "Goethe's Career as a Man of Letters," *Essays of Three Decades* (New York, 1948), p. 49.
4. Cf. G. H. Streurman, "Goethe, De universale mens," in *Grote filosofieën en de huidige mens* (Amsterdam, 1959), pp. 46–53; Karl Jaspers, "Goethes Menschlichkeit," *Rechenschaft und Ausblick* (München, 1951), p. 50.
5. Streurman, *op. cit.*, p. 49; Ernst Lehrs, *Man or Matter* (New York, 1950), pp. 242–254.

Chapter IX

1. On the changing content of the conception of revolution and the German attitude toward the French Revolution, this discussion is indebted to Karl Griewank, *Der neuzeitliche Revolutionsbegriff* (Weimar, 1955), pp. 193–259; Eugen Rosenstock-Huessy, *Out of Revolution* (New York, 1938), pp. 126–136, 188–195; Kurt v. Raumer, "Deutschland um 1800," *Handbuch der deutschen Geschichte* (Konstanz, 1959), III, 10–69.
2. Raumer, *op. cit.*, pp. 21–23.
3. Rudolph Stadelmann, *op. cit.*, pp. 22f.
4. Friedrich Meinecke, *Die Entstehung des Historismus* (München und Berlin, 1936), II, 523–535, 618–627.
5. Friedrich C. Sell, *Die Tragödie des deutschen Liberalismus* (Stuttgart, 1953), p. 30f.
6. Jean-Edouard Spenlé, *Der deutsche Geist von Luther bis Nietzsche*, trans. by Ludwig Munzinger from the French (Meisenheim am Glan, 1949), p. 64.
7. Rudolf Stadelmann, "Die Romantik und die Geschichte," in *Romantik, ein Zyklus Tübinger Vorlesungen*, ed. by Theodor Steinbüchel (Tübingen und Stuttgart, 1948), p. 168.
8. Adolf Köberle, "Die Romantik als religiöse Bewegung," in *Romantik, ein Zyklus Tübinger Vorlesungen*, ed. by Theodor Steinbüchel (Tübingen und Stuttgart, 1948), p. 77.
9. Cf. Willy Bremi, *Der Weg des protestantischen Menschen* (Zürich, 1953), pp. 184–197.

Chapter X

1. Cf. Sell, *op. cit.*, pp. 89ff.
2. Lütge, *op. cit.*, p. 306f. and p. 337f.
3. Sell, *op. cit.*, p. 108.
4. Karl Löwith, *Von Hegel bis Nietzsche* (Zürich, 1941), pp. 42–98.
5. Taubes, *op. cit.*, p. 166.
6. Löwith, *op. cit.*, pp. 94ff.
7. L. B. Namier, *1848: The Revolution of the Intellectuals* (Oxford, 1944), p. 4.

Chapter XI

1. Translated from the second German edition by N. I. Stone (New York, 1904), pp. 11f.

Chapter XII

1. Cf. Louis Sauzin, "The Political Thought of Constantin Frantz," in *The Third Reich*, ed. by Maurice Baumont, John H. E. Fried, and Edmond Vermeil (New York, 1955), pp. 112–147.
2. Helmuth Plessner, *Das Schicksal deutschen Geistes, im Ausgang seiner bürgerlichen Epoche* (Zürich und Leipzig, 1935), pp. 60–104.
3. Cf. Hans Meyer, "Die Weltanschauung der Gegenwart," in *Geschichte der abendländischen Weltanschauung* (Würzburg, 1949), V, 484–489.

Chapter XIII

1. Ludwig Dehio, *Gleichgewicht oder Hegemonie* (Krefeld, 1948), pp. 196–214.
2. Cf. Sell, *op. cit.*, pp. 292f.
3. Cf. *ibid.*, p. 296.
4. Walter Goerlitz, *History of the German General Staff, 1657–1945*, trans. by Brian Battershaw (New York, 1953), p. 4.
5. Carlo Antoni, *Vom Historismus zur Soziologie*, trans. by Walter Goetz from the Italian (Stuttgart, n.d.), pp. 48–56.
6. F. H. Heinemann, *Existentialism and the Modern Predicament* (London, 1953), p. 33.

Chapter XIV

1. Claude David, "Stefan George: Aesthetes or Terrorists?" in *The Third Reich*, ed. by Baumont, Fried and Vermeil, pp. 287–317.
2. Cf. Helmuth Plessner, *Zwischen Philosophie und Gesellschaft* (Bern, 1953), p. 24.
3. Cf. Erich Frank, *Philosophical Understanding and Religious Truth* (London, 1945), pp. 170f.
4. Roy Pascal, "Revolutionary Conservatism: Moeller van den Bruck," in *The Third Reich*, ed. by Baumont, Fried and Vermeil, pp. 333–338.
5. *Ibid.*, pp. 331f; Armin Mohler, *Die konservative Revolution in Deutschland* (Stuttgart, 1950), pp. 92f.
6. Mohler, *op. cit.*, pp. 88f.
7. J. P. Stern, *Ernst Jünger* (New Haven, 1953), pp. 44f.
8. Theodor Litt, "The National-Socialist Use of Moral Tendencies in Germany," in *The Third Reich*, ed. by Baumont, Fried and Vermeil, p. 440.
9. J. J. Schokking, "Nazism's Way to Success," in *The Third Reich*, ed. by Baumont, Fried and Vermeil, pp. 479ff.; Heer, *op. cit.*, pp. 6of.

Chapter XV

1. Cf. Hermann Mau, "Die "Zweite Revolution"—der 30. Juni 1934," *Viertel-jahreshefte für Zeitgeschichte* (1953), I, 119–137.
2. Cf. Eric Hoffer, *The True Believer: Thoughts on the Nature of Mass Movements* (New York, 1951), pp. 57–125.
3. Sebastian De Grazia, *The Political Community: A Study of Anomie* (Chicago, 1948), p. 178.
4. Harry Slochower, *No Voice is Wholly Lost . . . Writers and Thinkers in War and Peace* (New York, 1945), p. 130.

Bibliography

General

Bense, Max. *Technische Existenz*. Stuttgart, 1949.
Dehio, Ludwig. *Gleichgewicht oder Hegemonie*. Krefeld, 1948.
Delekat, Friedrich. *Über den Begriff der Säkularisation*. Heidelberg, 1958.
Gollwitzer, Heinz. *Europabild und Europagedanke: Beiträge zur deutschen Geistesgeschichte des 18. und 19. Jahrhunderts*. München, 1951.
Heer, Friedrich. *Europäische Geistesgeschichte*. Zürich, 1953.
Heimpel, Hermann. *Der Mensch in seiner Gegenwart*. Göttingen, 1954.
Hofer, Walther. *Geschichte zwischen Philosophie und Politik: Studien zur Problematik des modernen Geschichtsdenkens*. Basel, 1956.
Joachimsen, Paul. "Zur historischen Psychologie des deutschen Staatsgedankens," *Die Dioskuren*, I (1922), 106–177.
Kohn, Hans. ed. *German History: Some New German Views*. Boston, 1954.
Pensa, Mario. *Das deutsche Denken*. trans. by Walter Meckauer from the Italian. Erlenbach-Zürich, 1948.
Plessner, Helmuth. *Das Schicksal deutschen Geistes im Ausgang seiner bürgerlichen Epoche*. Zürich und Leipzig, 1935.
Ritter, G. *Europa und die deutsche Frage*. München, 1948.
Sell, Friedrich C. *Die Tragödie des deutschen Liberalismus*. Stuttgart, 1953.
Schüssler, Wilhelm. *Um das Geschichtsbild*. Freizeiten, 1953.
Spenlé, J. E. *Der deutsche Geist von Luther bis Nietzsche*. trans. by Ludwig Munzinger from the French. Meisenheim am Glan, 1949.
Stadelmann, R. *Deutschland und Westeuropa*. Laupheim-Württemberg, 1948.
Taubes, Jakob. *Abendländische Eschatologie*. Bern, 1947.
Taylor, A. J. P. *The Course of German History: A Survey of the Development of Germany since 1815*. London, 1945.
Tillich, Paul. *The Interpretation of History*. trans. by N. A. Rasetzki and Elsa L. Talmey. New York, 1936.
———. *The Protestant Era*, trans. by James Luther Adams. Chicago, 1948.
Troeltsch, Ernst. *Deutscher Geist und Westeuropa*. Tübingen, 1925.
Vietsch, Eberhard. *Die Tradition der grossen Mächte*. Stuttgart, 1950.
Weber, Alfred. *Kulturgeschichte als Kultursoziologie*. Leyden, 1935.

Part 1: From a Sacred Ordo to the Freedom of Faith (800–1600)

Bechtel, Heinrich. *Wirtschaftssil des deutschen Spätmittelalters*. München und Leipzig, 1930.
Benz, Ernst. *Ecclesia Spiritualis*. Stuttgart, 1934.
Bremi, Willy. *Der Weg des protestantischen Menschen*. Zürich, 1953.
Burdach, K. "Die seelischen und geistigen Quellen der Renaissancebewegung," *Historische Zeitschrift*, CXLIX (1934), 477–521.

Bibliography

Dilthey, Wilhelm. "Weltanschauung und Analyse des Menschen seit Renaissance und Reformation," *Gesammelte Schriften*, II. Leipzig und Berlin, 1929.
Dvorak, Max. *Kunstgeschichte als Geistesgeschichte*. München, 1924.
Erdmann, C. *Die Entstehung des Kreuzzugsgedankens*. Stuttgart, 1935.
Fichtenau, H. *Das karolingische Imperium*. Zürich, 1949.
Hampe, K. "Das neueste Lebensbild Kaiser Friedrichs II," *Historische Zeitschrift*, CXLVI (1932), 441–475.
Heer, F. *Aufgang Europas*. Wien, 1949.
Holl, Karl. "Luther," *Gesammelte Aufsätze zur Kirchengeschichte*, I. Tübingen, 1932.
Joachimsen, P. *Die Reformation als Epoche der deutschen Geschichte*. München, 1951.
Kämpf, Hellmut. *Das Reich im Mittelalter*. Stuttgart, 1950.
Koehler, Walther. *Dogmengeschichte als Geschichte des christlichen Selbstbewusstseins*. 2 vols. Zürich und Leipzig, 1943.
Mayer, T. "Das Hochmittelalter in neuer Schau," *Historische Zeitschrift*, CLXXI (1951), 449–472.
Peuchert, Will-Erich. *Die grosse Wende*. Hamburg, 1948.
Schramm, P. E. *Kaiser, Rom und Renovatio*. 2 vols. Leipzig, 1929.
Stadelmann, R. "Das Zeitalter der Reformation," *Handbuch der deutschen Geschichte*, ed. by A. O. Meyer. Darmstadt, 1936. II, 1–125.
———. *Vom Geist des ausgehenden Mittelalters*. Halle/Saale, 1929.
Tellenbach, G. *Church, State and Christian Society at the Time of the Investiture Contest*. trans. by R. F. Bennett. Oxford, 1940.
Thompson, James W. *Feudal Germany*. Chicago, 1928.
Torsten, Oswald. *Riche: Eine geschichtliche Studie über die Entwicklung der Reichsidee*. München und Berlin, 1943.
Troeltsch, Ernst. *The Social Teaching of the Christian Churches*. 2 vols. New York, 1949.

Part 2: *From a Cosmic Order to the Creativity of Spirit* (1600–1850)

Antoni, Carlo. *Der Kampf wider die Vernunft*. Stuttgart, 1951.
Baeumler, Alfred. "Einleitung," *Der Mythus von Orient und Occident. Eine Metaphysik der alten Welt* (aus den Werken von J. J. Bachofen) ed. by Manfred Schroeter. München, 1926.
Balet, Leo. *Die Verbürgerlichung der deutschen Kunst, Literatur und Musik im 18. Jahrhundert*. Leyden, 1936.
Brunschwig, H. *La Crise de L'État Prussien*. Paris, 1947.
Bussmann, W. "Friedrich der Grosse im Wandel des europäischen Urteils," *Deutschland und Europa, Festschrift für H. Rothfels*. Düsseldorf, 1951, pp. 375–408.
Cassirer, Ernst. *Die Philosophie der Aufklärung*. Tübingen, 1932.
Fischer, F. "Der deutsche Protestantismus und die Politik im 19. Jahrhundert," *Historische Zeitschrift*, CLXXI (1951), 473–518.
Franz, Erich. *Deutsche Klassik und Reformation*. Halle/Saale, 1937.
Gode-von Aesch, Alexander. *Natural Science in German Romanticism*. New York, 1941.
Gottfried Wilhelm Leibniz, Vorträge der aus Anlass seines dreihundert

Geburtstages in Hamburg abgehaltenen wissenschaftlichen Tagung. Hrsg. von der Redaktion der Hamburger Akademischen Rundschau. Hamburg, 1946.

Hintze, Otto. *Die Hohenzollern und ihr Werk.* Berlin, 1915.

Köberle, Adolf. "Die Romantik als religiöse Bewegung," *Romantik, ein Zyklus Tübinger Vorlesungen,* ed. by Theodor Steinbüchel. Tübingen und Stuttgart, 1948.

Kohn-Bramstedt, Ernst. *Aristocracy and the Middle Classes in Germany.* London, 1937.

Meinecke, Friedrich. *Die Idee der Staatsräson in der neueren Geschichte.* 3 Aufl. München und Berlin, 1929.

———. *1848, Eine Säkularbetrachtung.* Berlin, 1948.

———. *Weltbürgertum und Nationalstaat.* 7 Aufl. München, 1928.

Meyer, R. W. *Leibniz and the Seventeenth-Century Revolution.* Chicago, 1952.

Mommsen, W. *Grösse und Versagen des deutschen Bürgertums, Ein Beitrag zur Geschichte der Jahre 1848–1849.* Stuttgart, 1949.

———. *Stein, Ranke, Bismarck, Ein Beitrag zur politischen und sozialen Bewegung des 19. Jahrhunderts.* München, 1954.

———. "Zur Beurteilung des Absolutismus," *Historische Zeitschrift,* CLVIII (1938), 52–76.

Pascal, Roy. *The German Sturm und Drang.* Manchester, 1953.

Rothfels, H. "1848—One Hundred Years After," *The Journal of Modern History,* XX (1948), 291–319.

Schieder, T. "Das Problem der Revolution im 19. Jahrhundert," *Historische Zeitschrift,* CLXX (1950), 233–271.

Schnabel, F. *Deutsche Geschichte im 19. Jahrhundert.* 3 Aufl., vols. I and II. Freiburg im Breisgau, 1947.

Stadelmann, Rudolf. "Die Romantik und die Geschichte," *Romantik, Ein Zyklus Tübinger Vorlesungen,* ed. by Theodor Steinbüchel. Tübingen und Stuttgart, 1948.

Valjavec, F. *Die Entstehung der politischen Strömungen in Deutschland, 1770–1815.* München, 1951.

Vossler, O. *Der Nationalgedanke von Rousseau bis Ranke.* München, 1937.

Wittram, R. *Das Nationale als europäisches Problem.* Göttingen, 1954.

Part 3: *From Historicism to Technical Existenz* (1850–1950)

Antoni, Carlo. *Vom Historismus zur Soziologie.* Trans. by Walter Goetz from the Italian. Stuttgart, n.d. English trans., *From History to Sociology: The Transition in German Historical Thinking,* by Hayden V. White from the Italian. Detroit, 1959.

Arendt, Hannah. *The Origins of Totalitarianism.* New York, 1951.

Baumont, Maurice, John H. E. Fried, and Edmond Vermeil, editors. *The Third Reich,* a study published under the auspices of the International Council for Philosophy and Humanistic Studies and with the assistance of UNESCO. New York, 1955.

Conze, W. "Die Krise des Parteienstaates in Deutschland 1929–30," *Historische Zeitschrift,* CLXXVIII (1954), 47–83.

Bibliography

Daluces, Jean. *Le Troisième Reich,* I. Paris, 1950.

Erdmann, K. D. "Die Geschichte der Weimarer Republik als Problem der Wissenschaft," *Vierteljahreshefte für Zeitgeschichte.* Stuttgart, 1955, III, 1–19.

Freyer, Hans. *Theorie des gegenwärtigen Zeitalters.* Stuttgart, 1955.

Goerlitz, Walter. *History of the German General Staff, 1657–1945.* New York, 1953.

Holborn, Hajo. "Der deutsche Idealismus in sozialgeschichtlicher Bedeutung," *Historische Zeitschrift,* CLXXIV (1952), 359–384.

Kassner, Rudolf. *Das neunzehnte Jahrhundert, Ausdruck und Grösse.* Erlenbach-Zürich, 1947.

Lilge, Frederic. *The Abuse of Learning, the Failure of the German University.* New York, 1948.

Lukács, Georg. *Die Zerstörung der Vernunft.* Berlin, 1954.

———. *Schicksalswende.* Berlin, 1948.

Martin, Alfred von. *Der heroische Nihilismus und seine Überwindung.* Krefeld, 1948.

Mau, Hermann. "Die Zweite Revolution—der 30. Juni 1934," *Vierteljahreshefte für Zeitgeschichte.* Stuttgart, 1953. I, 119–137.

Moras, Joachim und Hans Paeschke, editors. *Deutscher Geist zwischen Gestern und Morgen, Bilanz der kulturellen Entwicklung seit 1945.* Stuttgart, 1954.

Plessner, Helmuth. "Deutsches Philosophieren in der Epoche der Weltkriege," *Zwischen Philosophie und Gesellschaft, Ausgewählte Abhandlungen und Vorträge.* Bern, 1953. pp. 9–38.

Rauschning, Hermann. *The Revolution of Nihilism, Warning to the West.* New York, 1939.

Rosteutscher, J. H. W. *Die Wiederkunft des Dionysos.* Bern, 1947.

Slochower, Harry. *No Voice is Wholly Lost . . . Writers and Thinkers in War and Peace.* New York, 1945.

Veit, Otto. *Die Flucht vor der Freiheit.* Frankfurt/M., 1947.

Vossler, O. J. "Bismarcks Ethos," *Historische Zeitschrift,* CLXXI (1951), 263–292.

Westphal, Otto. *Feinde Bismarcks, Geistige Grundlagen der deutschen Opposition, 1848–1918.* München und Berlin, 1930.

Index

Index

Index

The manuscript was edited by Alexander Brede and Bernard Harris and the book was designed by Richard Kinney. The type face used for the text is Janson, cut by Merganthaler Linotype in 1932. Janson is based on the type face cut by Nicholas Kis in Amsterdam, 1690, but erroneously accredited to Anton Janson. The display face is Weiss Roman, designed by Professor E. R. Weiss and cut by Baur in 1926. The book is printed on Warren's Olde Style Antique Wove and is bound in Holliston Rex Linen over boards. Manufactured in the United States of America.

DATE DUE